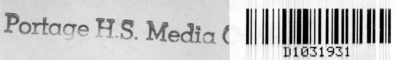

The Kentucky Derby

The First 100 Years

PETER CHEW

The Kentucky Derby

The First 100 Years

Houghton Mifflin Company Boston 1974

CHEW

Portions of this book have appeared in slightly different form in *Catholic Digest, National Observer,* and *Travel & Leisure.*

The charts appearing on pages 185–283 of this book are reprinted by special arrangement with Triangle Publications, Inc. (Daily Racing Form). Copyright 1906, 1907, 1908, 1909, 1910, 1911, 1912, 1913, 1914, 1915, 1916, 1917, 1918, 1919, 1920, 1921, 1922, 1923, 1924, 1925, 1926, 1927, 1928, 1929, 1930, 1931, 1932, 1933, 1934, 1935, 1936, 1937, 1938, 1939, 1940, 1941 1942, 1943, 1944, 1945, 1946, 1947, 1948, 1949, 1950, 1951, 1952, 1953, 1954, © 1955, 1956, 1957, 1958, 1959, 1960, 1961, 1962, 1963, 1964, 1965, 1966, 1967, 1968, 1969, 1970, 1971, 1972, 1973 by Triangle Publications, Inc. Reprinted with permission of copyright holder.

FIRST PRINTING H

Library of Congress Cataloging in Publication Data

Chew, Peter.
The Kentucky Derby, the first 100 years.

Includes bibliographical references.
1. Kentucky Derby — History. I. Title.
SF357.K4C38   798'.43'0976947   74-625
ISBN 0-395-18482-7

TO GINNY

Acknowledgments

Special thanks to Mrs. Ted Campbell, associate librarian, Keeneland Library, Lexington, Kentucky, my research assistant; and Mrs. Ellen Joseph, my editor at Houghton Mifflin Company.

Gratitude as well to Mrs. Amelia King Buckley, associate librarian, Keeneland Library; Ted Bassett, president of Keeneland Race Course; Miss Mary Jane Gallaher, Lexington writer; Lynn Stone, president of Churchill Downs; Mrs. Mary C. Lethbridge; Mrs. Jean Tucker and public information staff, the Library of Congress; Kent Hollingsworth and Edward L. Bowen of *The Blood-Horse*; Arnold Kirkpatrick and William H. P. Robertson, *The Thoroughbred Record*; Miss Susan Stephenson, librarian, Selima Room, Prince George's County Memorial Library, Bowie, Maryland, branch; Phillip E. Borries, Lexington newsman; Miss Elizabeth A. Chew; *Courier-Journal* and Louisville *Times*; Olin Gentry, manager, Darby Dan Farm; Mrs. Margaret Glass, Calumet Farm; Peter Fuller; photographer John C. Wyatt of Lexington; Whitney Tower, *Sports Illustrated*; Paul Mellon; H. A. "Jimmy" Jones; Henry Forrest; Loly "Boo" Gentry; John I. Day, Thoroughbred Racing Associations (TRA); Sam Kanchugar, New York Racing Association (N.Y.R.A.); Mrs. John B. "Penny" Tweedy, and the late Mrs. Marjorie Weber of Louisville.

Contents

Illustrations

The Kentucky Derby

The First 100 Years

Secretariat wins 1973 Kentucky Derby.

Chapter 1
The Most Important Race of All

GRANTLAND RICE ONCE MADE the mistake of asking Irvin S. Cobb, the homespun philosopher of Paducah, to explain what made the Kentucky Derby so special. Said Cobb:

If I could do that, I'd have a larynx of spun silver and the tongue of an angel. But if you can imagine a track that's like a bracelet of molten gold encircling a greensward that's like a patch of emerald velvet . . . All the pretty girls in the state turning the grandstand into a brocaded terrace of beauty and color such as the hanging gardens of Bablyon never equaled . . . All the assembled sports of the nation going crazy at once down in the paddock . . . The entire colored population of Louisville and environs with one voice begging for some entry to come on and win . . .

And just yonder in the yellow dust, the gallant kings and noble queens of the kingdom, the princesses royal, and their heirs apparent to the throne, fighting it out . . . Each a vision of courage and heart and speed . . . Each topped as though with some bobbing gay blossoms by a silken-clad jockey . . . But what's the use? Until you go to Kentucky and with your own eyes behold the Derby, you ain't never been nowheres and you ain't never seen nothin'![1]

Well, the Kentucky Derby hasn't been like that for some time. But Cobb was right. The Derby is America's greatest horse race. It ranks with the World Series, the Indianapolis 500, the Davis Cup, the Super Bowl. The Derby is "the most exciting two minutes in sports."

Joe H. Palmer, the most literate of turf writers, said: "To men who have never seen a horse race, and never will, the twin towers of Churchill Downs and the roaring lane to finish of the Kentucky Derby have symbolized racing."[2]

On the first Saturday in May, more than 100,000 persons — the ritual figure put out by Churchill Downs — crowd into the jerrybuilt grandstands in Louisville to watch the one-and-a-quarter-mile classic for three-year-olds. There are older stakes in America, such as the Preakness and the Belmont, and $100,000 races without number. But the Derby is the oldest *continuously run* classic. And no matter what horsemen say about the race's deficiencies as an intelligent test of the nation's best three-year-olds — and the deficiencies are serious, most agree — they *all* want to win this one.

Stardust, riches, and a measure of immortality attend the owners, breeders, trainers, jockeys, and grooms connected with a Derby winner. The instant the winning colt flashes under the wire (only one filly has ever won) he's usually worth at least $1,000,000 for stud purposes — and some have been syndicated for four and five times that amount. Secretariat was syndicated in early 1973 for $6,080,000; the syndicators figured the colt had the best chance to win the Derby. Secretariat won, and the members, who each paid $190,000 for the privilege of breeding one mare a year to Secretariat, were relieved. When Secretariat went on to take the Preakness and Belmont in awesome style, the value of the shares rose even higher.

"When I die, I'll be remembered as the owner of Dancer's Image," says Peter Fuller, a millionaire Cadillac dealer in Boston, of his disqualified 1968 Derby winner.

Some in Louisville are not enthusiastic about the Derby, however. On Derby Day 1973, the *Courier-Journal* said in an editorial entitled "Some thoughts in the home stretch":

"The nation's most prominent celebration of avarice has its 99th renewal at Churchill Downs today. You see, probably more money changes hands on this event than any other — to the delight of all but the

"The Kentucky Derby is a triumph of the business and promotional talents of the late Colonel Matt J. Winn (pointing), an attractive and popular figure." Shortly after the 1934 Derby, won by Cavalcade, Winn candidly told James J. Hart (pen name "Jim Henry") of the Louisville *Herald Post*: "My first love was the Kentucky Derby, and I saw to it that the owners of the three-year-olds with box office appeal flirted with no other stake but the Derby when Derbytime came around. And we played one society queen against another until we steamrollered Louisville into a one-day capital of celebrities."

Internal Revenue Service, which doesn't always get its fair share.

"Out at the track, everything will be in its place, with the patricians and the powerful safe in their boxes, and the rabble fenced into the infield. It's a scene rescued out of the distant past, when the king and his court hangers-on crowded into the royal box to watch the knights in tournament, with *les miserables* crowding around the sidelines in sackcloth . . ."

For years, the paper's investigative reporters have been peering under racing's blankets in Kentucky. They have reported on alleged shenanigans in other races on the Derby Day card — an ideal day for a betting coup — and have investigated the financial connections of racing commission members. *Courier-Journal* reporters have slipped past drowsing guards on the Churchill Downs backstretch to demonstrate how easily it can be done. Reporter William "Billy" Reed was allegedly knocked down by hard-punching Dr. Alex Harthill, the controversial veterinary who attended Dancer's Image in 1968. Dancer's Image had been disqualified after phenylbutazone or "bute"

— an analgesic — was found in his system after the race, and Reed had come to Harthill's barn to interview him. In the doctor's view, the paper has been engaged in a vendetta against him and racing in general. Reed and the *Courier-Journal* failed to file charges against Harthill.

The Kentucky Derby is a triumph of the business and promotional talents of the late Colonel Matt J. Winn, an attractive and popular figure. As a boy in 1875 standing on the seat of his father's flat-bed grocery wagon in the infield, Winn saw Aristides win the first Derby. He saw every single Derby thereafter — seventy-five in all — before his death in the fall of 1949.

Winn was a big, pink-faced man, the son of Irish immigrants who had made their way from New Orleans to Louisville. An interesting combination of Irish and southern charm, Winn had been a successful merchant tailor before involving himself in the management of Churchill Downs and other racetracks. He once ascribed his longevity to an insistence upon the best bourbon and visits to French Lick Springs, Indiana, to recover from the quantities of Estill County ham, roast turkey, beaten biscuits, and other Derby delicacies.

Winn first concerned himself with management of an ailing Churchill Downs in 1902. From the outset the Derby had been a race of more than local significance, but for a variety of reasons it had slipped badly by the turn of the century. Single-handedly, Winn transformed the event into a race of national significance.

Old Rosebud with Johnny McCabe up won the 1914 Kentucky Derby in a record time of 2:03 2/5 that stood until 1931 when Twenty Grand covered the course in 2:01 4/5. The first of five Derby winners bred by John E. Madden at Hamburg Place in Lexington, the game little gelding was plagued by lameness. Old Rosebud made numerous comebacks and ran until age eleven.

Corum, and Red Smith. For such men, Derby week was often on the house, as it was for such radio commentators as Ted Husing, Bryan Field, and gravel-voiced Clem McCarthy. The syndicated stars dubbed Winn's race "The Run for the Roses." The long homestretch at Churchill Downs became "Heartbreak Lane." They churned out wonderful stories, often with an admixture of schmaltz, and sent them across the land.

Many of the newsmen's stories were of Matt Winn, for he was the Derby. Of Winn, Joe Palmer had the last word:

"It is no longer possible to write anything new about Colonel Matt Winn. He came into Kentucky through Cumberland Gap (it is a baseless legend that he cut it himself) about 1770. After clearing the land of canebrakes and Indians, he gave his mind to further improvement and invented bourbon whiskey, the thoroughbred horse, hickory-cured ham, and Stephen Foster. It was not until 1875 that he risked the combination of all these elements and produced the first Kentucky Derby."[3]

From ancient times, horse racing and the festival spirit have been synonymous. So it's perhaps not surprising that the Derby Stakes at Epsom, the prototype of Winn's race in England, was conceived during a race-week carouse not unlike the goings-on in Louisville the first week in May.

The year was 1799; the scene was The Oaks, the country house that the twelfth Lord Derby rented

The center of American racing gravity, then as now, lay in New York. Winn courted the big eastern stables that raced there. A number of New York notables, including August Belmont II, were on hand for the 1914 race won by Old Rosebud, a first-class local horse. Winn's big break came the next year when Harry Payne Whitney agreed to run his superb filly, Regret, in the Derby. She led from wire to wire, the only thoroughbred of her sex ever to win the race. "I do not care if she never wins another race, or if she never starts in another race," said an exultant Whitney. "She has won the greatest race in America, and I am satisfied."

The Derby was made.

In the decades that followed, Winn wooed New York sportswriters such as Damon Runyon, Grantland Rice, Frank Graham, Dan Parker, Bob Considine, Bill

Only one filly has ever won the Kentucky Derby: Harry Payne Whitney's Regret, shown with jockey Joe Notter who led from wire to wire in 1915. "She has won the greatest race in America, and I am satisfied," said Whitney.

One of five Kentucky Derby winners bred by John E. Madden at Hamburg Place in Lexington, Commander J. K. L. Ross's Sir Barton also won the 1919 Preakness and Belmont Stakes. The colt was retroactively honored as the first of nine winners of the Triple Crown. The following year, Sir Barton lost to Man o' War by seven lengths in a match race at Kenilworth Park, Windsor, Canada, the last race of Big Red's career. Johnny Loftus, Sir Barton's scowling jockey, was a top rider but bore the cross of being aboard Man o' War during the colt's only defeat the previous year and received a good part of the blame. He left the turf an embittered man some years later and was last heard of working in a machine shop in New York. When elected to the Jockeys' Hall of Fame, he failed to appear at the ceremony.

John E. Madden (in straw hat) gives jockey instructions. Madden occupies a unique niche in Derby history. In 1897, he bought the two-year-old Plaudit from Ed Brown, a prominent black trainer of the day, and won the Derby with the colt the following year — on Plaudit's first outing as a three-year-old. The five Madden-bred Derby winners were all foaled in the same red-and-black-trimmed barn on Hamburg Place: Old Rosebud, winner in 1914 in 2:03 2/5, a record that would last nineteen years. Sir Barton, whose first winning race was the Derby of 1919; he went on to win the Preakness and Belmont, and when the concept of the Triple Crown fell out of columnist Charlie Hatton's typewriter in the 1930s, the colt was honored retroactively as the first winner of the Triple Crown. Paul Jones, long-shot winner of the 1920 Derby, a race best-remembered because Man o' War did not run. Zev, winner in 1923 and America's leading money-winner for a time with more than $300,000. Flying Ebony, far from an outstanding horse, but a good one in May 1925 when he won the Derby four years before Madden's death.

John E. Madden's purpose in life was to sell horses, and Kentuckians regard him as the greatest horse trader since David Harum and the greatest all-around horseman: breeder, trainer, owner. Madden's formula: Buy low, break and train the horse, win a few stakes, then sit back and wait for a buyer. And he did this time and time again. For this reason, Madden, whose life spanned the years 1856 to 1929, was known as "The Wizard of the Turf." The New York Times often referred to him simply as "The Wizard" without further identification. Born of Irish immigrant parents in Bethlehem, Pennsylvania, Madden left a $9,000,000 fortune at his death, most of it acquired in the racing game and traded on Wall Street. He started out trading draft horses, road horses, and trotters at county fairs. Eventually he drifted into the thoroughbred market.

Hamburg Place today: Tranquility, though a beltway and urban sprawl are near at hand. Hamburg is more than 2000 acres, and Madden's grandson, Preston Madden, and his wife live there, raising yearlings for the market. Preston Madden has inherited his grandfather's passion for horses and his penchant for selling them at a profit. He has also inherited some of his grandfather's candor. No longer, he concedes, is it possible to come into the Bluegrass as his penniless grandfather did and accumulate a fortune in the thoroughbred breeding business. "One of the toughest things is that a man who didn't grow up in Kentucky doesn't have a real 'in' when it comes to getting stallion services," he recently confessed to Lexington writer Mary Jane Gallaher. "This is one area where money doesn't particularly count. It's more who you know, who you grew up with, who you went to school with. If it is not a closed circle, it isn't far from it."

from General John Burgoyne, commander of the British army in America's War of Independence and an uncle by marriage.

The sporty Lord Derby was famed for his Epsom Week parties. He kept servants and chefs on duty around the clock so that fine food and spirits would be available at his houseguests' whim. There was dancing, gaming, cockfighting in the drawing room, and racing each afternoon.

Heat racing over distances of four to six miles per heat was the custom at that time with mature horses, though the trend toward shorter "dashes" had been gaining momentum. To dramatize the new trend, the youthful Lord Derby and his friend, Sir Charles Bunbury, hit upon the concept of a one-mile race for three-year-old colts and fillies to be run at Epsom Downs the following year. (The distance was extended to one and a half miles, its present length, in 1784.) The idea had suddenly come to the two men while celebrating the success of Lord Derby's Bridget in the inaugural running of The Oaks, a one-and-a-half-mile sweepstakes for three-year-old fillies, another of their brain children. Lord Derby and Sir Charles supposedly tossed a coin to decide whether the new race would be called the Derby Stakes or the Bunbury Stakes. Had Sir Charles won the toss, the Louisville classic would doubtless be "the Kentucky Bunbury" today.

Bunbury's contribution to the English turf, and indirectly to American racing and the Kentucky Derby

The 12th Earl of Derby for whom the Epsom and Kentucky classics are named, to say nothing of hundreds of other lesser derbies around the globe. The Derby race was conceived during a wild party at Lord Derby's estate, The Oaks. " 'Seldom has a carouse had a more permanent effect,' " said Lord Rosebery, 100 years later, according to Robert Mortimer in his *History of the Derby Stakes* (London: Cassell & Co. Lt., 1962).

Sir Charles Bunbury (1740–1821) was the foremost figure on the English turf in his day.

to come, were substantial. Racing was his life, his beautiful Lady Sarah having run off with a lord, complaining that Sir Charles cared more for his horses than for her. She must have had a case, for he never remarried and devoted himself wholeheartedly to racing thereafter.

Though still in his thirties in 1780, he was already a dominant figure on the English turf. As "perpetual president" of the Jockey Club he did much to civilize English racing, which was in a scandalous state in the late eighteenth and early nineteenth centuries.

Races were routinely fixed; horses often ran under false colors, false pedigrees, false names; blackleg gamblers bribed jockeys to pull favorites and grooms to feed them opium balls or to lame them. The racetracks were unruly places, swarming with pickpockets, cardsharps, touts, and freaks.

"Horse racing and cockfighting are carried on here to a pitch of absolute madness," wrote Mirabeau of Epsom. "There are neither lists nor barriers at these races. The horses run in the midst of the crowd who leave only a space sufficient for them to pass through, at the same time encouraging them with gestures and loud shouts. The victor, when he has arrived at the goal, finds it a difficult matter to disengage himself

from the crowd, who congratulate, caress, and embrace him with an effusion of heart which is not easy to form an idea of without having seen it."[4]

Sir Charles expanded the power of the Jockey Club to cope with the problem. He attained a measure of lasting fame when he told none other than the Prince of Wales, later King George IV, that "no gentleman would start against him" if he kept Sam Chifney as his jockey. Chifney had ridden two highly suspicious races aboard the prince's horse, Escape.[5] The Prince was furious. He defended his jockey, but pensioned him off and quit the turf for a time. Sir Charles set a style that would be emulated by other "dictators of the turf" as they were called, and by Americans who would take such men as their models.

This passion for the thoroughbred running horse has been with Kentuckians since frontier days. And if English racing was unruly in the late eighteenth century, so were the wild gallops through the streets of Lexington and later of Louisville and outlying towns. As early as 1780 when Diomed was winning the Epsom Derby, the settlers were racing horses down South Broadway in Lexington. Three years later, an Indian stepped from the canebrake and shot a race rider from the saddle as he was pulling up on a race path in the country not far from Boonesboro. That same year, Louisvillians were racing horses down Market Street.

"On May 4, 1780, Sir Charles' chestnut colt Diomed, Sam Arnull up, won the first running of the Epsom Derby over Budrow, Spitfire, and six other horses. This amazing horse was to have a powerful impact upon the American thoroughbred, and his descendants would win many Kentucky Derbies."

These races took their toll of unwary pedestrians, and sometimes of horses and riders as well. In one village, two impromptu races were started from opposite ends of the same street at approximately the same time, neither group of racers aware of the others' intentions until it was nearly too late. The horses raced head-on down the street, and only by frantic maneuvering of the jockeys were accidents avoided. Eventually, racing moved from the narrow, quarter-mile race paths in the country and from Main Street to informally organized racecourses within and without the towns.

On May 4, 1780, Sir Charles's chestnut colt Diomed, Sam Arnull up, won the first running of the Epsom Derby over Budrow, Spitfire, and six other horses. This amazing horse was to have a powerful impact upon the American thoroughbred, and his descendants would win many Kentucky Derbies.

Diomed was by Florizel a son of Herod. Diomed sired Young Giantess, the dam of Eleanor, with whom Sir Charles won The Oaks and his second Derby Stakes in 1801. Aside from a few winning offspring, Diomed failed to distinguish himself in the breeding shed. At the advanced age of twenty-one, he was dumped on the eager American breeding market. Diomed entered stud in Virginia amidst warnings from detractors in England that he was not much of a sire and was losing his virility.

It must have been the air.

"He quickly gave the lie to his critics. Far from lacking in virility, he was in the habit of coming out of his stable at a dashing gallop and serving mares with all the fire and impetuosity of a young horse; and he not only got his mares regularly in foal, but enabled them to produce one high-class course performer after another."[6]

Diomed founded a dynasty that forged ties of blood between the English Derby and its Kentucky namesake. Fifty-two of the first sixty-one winners of the Kentucky classic carried the blood of a Diomed descendant, Lexington — 1850 to 1875 — whom turf historian William H. P. Robertson of *The Thoroughbred Record* flatly calls "the most successful stallion in history."

"Lexington sired more than 600 colts and fillies, an amazing 260 of them were winners, most notably, Asteroid, Norfolk, and Kentucky."

In twenty years of stud duty at Robert Aitcheson Alexander's famed Woodburn Farm, Lexington led the sire list for sixteen years, fourteen years in succession, a record that no other American stallion has ever equaled. After Lexington lost his eyesight the stallion was known as "the blind hero of Woodburn." Lexington had been a phenomenal racehorse in his day, once running four miles against the clock in a world record 7:19 3/4.

Only one other thoroughbred, Man o' War, another Diomed descendant, ranks as high as Lexington in the affections of old-time Kentucky horsemen. When owner Samuel D. Riddle retired Big Red at the end of his three-year-old season in 1920, the Lexington Chamber of Commerce announced that schoolchildren would strew flowers in the colt's path during a parade through town. Riddle put a stop to it. "He's only a

horse," telegraphed Riddle. He never convinced Lexingtonians of that.

Sadly, America's greatest racehorse never ran in America's greatest horse race. Sam Riddle believed, as many horsemen still do, that the first Saturday in May is too early in a three-year-old's year to run a mile and one-quarter with 126 pounds aboard. (Nineteen twenty was the first year that all entrants carried 126 pounds; the weights in previous years varied down to a low of 97 pounds in some instances.) Years later, in 1937, Riddle either went against his better judgment or else changed his mind, for he entered War Admiral, one of Man o' War's sons. The game little colt won the Derby, the Preakness, and the Belmont Stakes, one of only nine thoroughbreds to win the Triple Crown. Another Man o' War progeny, little Clyde Van Dusen, had won the Derby in 1929 in the colors of H. P. Gardner.

When Big Red died on November 1, 1947, after a highly successful twenty-year stud career, during which time 1,000,000 tourists trooped through Faraway Farm to see him, 2,000 horse lovers turned out for his funeral, which was broadcast nationwide by radio. Sam Riddle notwithstanding, local merchants draped their storefronts in black. *The Blood-Horse* magazine ran a tribute:

> *. . . Some others will remember the day he came back to Kentucky and, under colors for the last time, was cantered along the sloppy stretch of the old Kentucky Association track, the faint light of winter gleaming on his golden coat.*
>
> *The horsemen who came from all over the world to see him in his prime at Faraway will remember him vividly — the massive body, the wide sweeps of muscle, the great chest and abnormally wide spacing between his forelegs, the die-cut perfection of his legs and feet, the slight dip of the back deepening with the years, the high head, the imperial air, the feel of power and mastery. They will not look to see another like him.*

There were many such sentimental tributes to Big Red. The most famous of all was uttered by Will Harbut, his stud groom: "He was de mostest hoss."

First-time Derby-goers from out of state are often surprised to discover that there are only a dozen or so thoroughbred breeding farms scattered around the countryside near Louisville. Instead, most of the state's nearly 350 horse farms are to be found seventy-five miles to the southeast in Fayette, Woodford, Scott, Bourbon, and two or three other counties of the inner Bluegrass surrounding Lexington.

Early on, horses raised in the Bluegrass began, as the saying goes, to outrun their pedigrees. No one is certain when *Poa pratensis*, the Kentucky strain of bluegrass, first appeared in the Lexington region, but nature's other ample endowments were in place when the settlers arrived.

"The soil, in the first place, was obviously fertile; it was this characteristic which made the section the magnet for pioneers," said Joe A. Estes, the late editor of *The Blood-Horse*. "And as it was a rare outcropping of the deep Ordovician limestone, at the apex of what geologists call the Cincinnati anticline, it was rich in calcium and phosphorous. This legacy of phosphatic limestone, inherited from millions of shells and skeletons deposited centuries earlier when Central Kentucky was an ocean bed, was now to be used to build the skeletons of horses. It was essential that the race horse have a framework strong enough to withstand the enormous strains put upon it by his prodigious musculature and his desperate courage.

"At the same time, the framework must be so light that it would require a minimum amount of energy for its locomotion. In accomplishing this ideal of maximum strength and minimum weight the phosphatic limestone which forms the basis of Central Kentucky's soil has proved its efficacy . . .

"Another advantage possessed by Central Kentucky as a breeding ground for horses was its rolling topog-

"Only one other thoroughbred, Man o' War, another Diomed descendant, ranks as high as Lexington in the affections of old-time Kentucky horsemen." Man o' War is walked by his famous groom, Will Harbut.

Samuel D. Riddle (right), proud owner of Man o' War.

Man o' War's greatest son, War Admiral, led from start to finish in the 1937 Kentucky Derby with Charlie Kurtsinger in the saddle. Pompoon was second, Reaping Reward third. War Admiral went on to win the Triple Crown. Another Man o' War offspring, the gelding Clyde Van Dusen, won the Derby in 1929.

raphy and the porous nature of its subsoil, assuring adequate drainage at all times — for hard feet and bone cannot be developed by horses raised on marshy, soggy, or ill-drained land."[7]

Estes mentioned one other vital factor that has led to the phenomenal success of the Bluegrass. "It was to be found neither in the nature of the country nor in the heritage of the thoroughbred blood, but in the character of the people who came to be called Kentuckians. Such was their heritage, from the colonies to the East and from their ancestral background in England, that they needed action, adventure, creation, conquest . . . When there were no Indians to be chased, there were arguments to be settled, and in Kentucky it usually takes a horse race to settle an argument."[8]

Many of Lexington's first settlers were land-hungry second sons from plantations in the Carolina low country and Virginia where the raising and racing of bloodhorses was endemic. They poured through the Cumberland Gap in the Alleghenies hard on the heels of Daniel Boone and other hunter-explorers. They followed the Wilderness Trail and camped beside the sparkling waters of Elkhorn Creek, which today meanders through the meadows of the horse farms. Boone called this region "the New Eden." The settlers of 1775 and thereafter agreed.

Lexington thus became an agricultural center. Only recently has an influx of light industry begun to change the character and tempo of the old town.

Louisville, located in an arm of the strategic Ohio River, was settled in the spring of 1778, three years later than Lexington. The town developed in the natural course of events into a center of commerce and industry.

Among the original settlers of Louisville were twenty families who accompanied General George Rogers Clark and his soldiers downstream from Pennsylvania to harass British forts. Clark was an ancestor of Colonel M. Lewis Clark, Jr., the Kentucky Bourbon who fathered the Louisville Jockey Club, Churchill Downs, and the Kentucky Derby. After a trip to the Derby Stakes at Epsom, Colonel Clark conceived the Derby in the early 1870s as a showcase for the output of Bluegrass breeding farms, racing then being in severe post–Civil War doldrums. The Derby proved to be a marvelous fillip.

From earliest days, there had been a touch of Old New Orleans about Louisville, a flair for strong wine, fast music, and blooded horses. Louisville is still the scene of extensive partying during Derby week, but many of the out-of-town guests are business connections of the local gentry. "There is still a residuum of quality folk to be seen at the River Valley Club party and at Derby breakfasts given by the Bonnies and others," says Arthur Krock, a distinguished ex-Kentuckian who remembers Louisville after the turn of the century. "There are a few strongholds of aristocracy in Louisville, but not many."

Sacrilege of sacrileges, many Louisvillians rent their coveted Churchill Downs' boxes out for Derby Day at scalpers' prices, the one-day rental covering the seasonal cost of the box. Then they watch the race in the comfort of their homes on television. Many of the boxes are rented to Lexington horse people, few of whom would consider for a moment missing the race, which they consider theirs.

"They watch the Derby with an almost hypnotic concentration because it is, to breeders of thoroughbreds, the most important race of all," concluded Joe Estes. "For it is racing which reveals good horses and good mares, first through their own performances; and second, through the performances of their produce. And the most important single race in America for this purpose is the Kentucky Derby because, with fewer exceptions than must be made for any other race, it brings together for a test of their racing class, and hence a test of their potential breeding class, the best horses from every crop of foals."[9]

In other words, owners and trainers can avoid competition in one $100,000 race in New York by shipping to New Jersey or some other state where the company is less keen. But they can't duck the Derby.

Churchill Downs.

Chapter 2
The Presiding Judge

Major Barak Thomas.

LIKE SO MANY Confederate veterans, Major Barak Thomas returned to the Bluegrass country with little more than his frayed uniform to his name. His experience reflected the many changes in racing wrought by the Civil War, in whose cold ashes the Kentucky Derby was born.

The only negotiable property that Thomas found upon his return was an untried filly of racing age by Lexington out of a mare that he had owned with his late brother. The filly's name was Hira, and Thomas wasted no time getting her in trim for a stakes race at the old Woodlawn course in Louisville.

Hira won.

With the winnings, Thomas made a down payment on a farm, which he named Dixiana, and transformed into a famous thoroughbred nursery. The farm was also celebrated for the sign at the front gate: "Nothing but good race horses wanted. Agents for the sale of books, patent medicines, sewing machines, wheat farms, and especially lightning rods, not admitted. Visitors who come by my home are always welcome."[1]

Hira kept winning. In time, Thomas would entertain rich Yankees with twenty-year-old bourbon served in the many gold and silver bowls won by his fleet mare.

Hira proved to be an outstanding broodmare, producing Himyar, who went to the post the overwhelming favorite for the fourth running of the Kentucky Derby in 1878. Fearing foul play, Thomas slept in Himyar's stall the night before the race. He was thus the first of a number of men who would take such precautions on Derby eve, including California trainer Mesach Tenney who bedded down with winner Swaps before the 1955 race.

Thomas's precautions were to no avail, for they got to his horse during the race. After being left at the post, Himyar started his big run heading into the turn for home, after which jockey after jockey was heard to yell: "Here he comes! Stop him." Bumped and battered, Himyar finished two lengths back of the winner Day Star.

Like his dam Hira, Himyar proved a success at stud. Himyar's get included Domino, "the black whirlwind" whom Thomas sold as a yearling. In the colors of Wall Street tycoon James R. Keene, and his son Foxhall, Domino raced to the two-year-old championship in 1893. At stud, Domino founded one of this country's most important bloodlines, one that includes untold Derby winners.

Before the Civil War, men such as Thomas bred and raced horses for sport. After the war, they bred horses for the market. The old way of life was gone.

The Bluegrass, said writer J. Soule Smith, "is a poem in itself and its men and women have the distinct outlines of figures in a Shakespearean drama."[2] Such a man was Robert Aitcheson Alexander of Woodburn Farm, who exemplified the old ways and foreshadowed the new. More than any other man, Alexander established the pattern for the vast modern-day breeding farms such as Claiborne and Spendthrift.

As early as 1860, Alexander had ceased breeding for his own racing stable and started breeding for the market. The yearling sales every June beneath the old trees at Woodburn were forerunners of today's sales at Keeneland Race Course, where yearlings are averaging nearly $57,000 and one yearling brought a price of $600,000 in 1973.

The Alexanders were an immensely wealthy shipping and banking family of Edinburgh, Scotland. Alexander's grandfather, William, who settled in Virginia in the 1780s, had been a close friend to Benjamin Franklin, whom he had come to know when Franklin was serving in Paris. The Alexander family in 1791 acquired the 2700-acre Woodburn tract on the banks of Elkhorn Creek in Woodford County, which Robert took over in 1849.

Under Robert, Woodburn grew to 4000 rolling, wooded acres where he also raised standardbred horses; Durham, Alderney, and Ayrshire cattle; and Southdown sheep. A lifelong bachelor, Alexander was educated at Cambridge University, then studied animal husbandry for two years in Europe.

Woodburn, still occupied by Alexanders, is a beautiful, white-columned mansion with lovely cherry and mahogany woodwork, fireplaces of carved marble, glittering candelabra, and a handsome double-library with time-mellowed, leather-bound volumes. On the walls hang oil paintings of Woodburn thoroughbreds and livestock by Edward Troye, the Swiss artist, whom Alexander commissioned during the Civil War.

Robert A. Alexander.

Woodburn Farm.

Alexander was a member, along with Henry Clay and John C. Breckinridge, of the Kentucky Association for the Improvement of the Breeds of Stock, which had opened the state's first permanent racetrack in Lexington in 1828. Racing continued unabated at the old Association track until it closed down in the Depression year 1933. Keeneland opened as a unique, nonprofit enterprise three years later and has held uninterrupted race meetings in the fall and spring since that time.

In 1856, Alexander entered the thoroughbred business in dramatic fashion: He paid Richard Ten Broeck $15,000 for Lexington, the highest price ever paid up to that time for an American stud horse. Not until Man o' War went to Sam Riddle for a mere $5000 at the Saratoga Yearling Sales in August 1918 was there a bargain to compare even remotely with Alexander's historic purchase.

Lexington sired more than 600 colts and fillies, an amazing 260 of them winners, most notably Asteroid, Norfolk, and Kentucky, all foaled in 1861. Today these three would be called "super horses." Woodburn horses dominated the turf from 1864 to 1880, and their descendants continued to make racing history long past the turn of the century.

Woodburn-breds won all the big stakes races of the day — the Travers, Belmont, Jerome, Dixie, and Saratoga Cup — and won them year after year. They won, as well, the Jersey Derby, which antedates the Kentucky classic by eleven years. Woodburn-bred winners of the Kentucky Derby were Baden Baden, in 1877; Fonso, 1880; Joe Cotton, 1885; Chant, 1894; and His Eminence, 1901.

Toward the end of the Civil War, and for a period thereafter, guerrilla bands in Federal uniforms raided farms such as Woodburn and made off with prize horses, though they didn't always succeed in getting the ones they had come for. "They asked for Asteroid, but in the dusk of the evening, the trainer gave them an inferior horse and so saved the best in my stable," wrote Alexander to a friend in 1865.[3] In the same letter, Alexander describes his hair-raising hand-to-hand combat with a raider whom he gamely succeeded in beating and disarming. But Alexander became so discouraged in 1866 that he advertised Lexington and his other stallions and bloodstock.

"In New York, scouting for a buyer, he met Harry Belland, who was on his way to Woodburn after a four-year stay in Canada. In 1862, Alexander had given Belland thirty-four Woodburn horses to race and sell there. For four years, Belland had operated without instructions from Alexander. He had raced over most of Canada, selling horses whenever he could get good prices. To his employer's tremendous surprise, Belland reported that the stable's earnings and sales amounted to over $300,000.

"Exclaimed Alexander: 'You have saved Woodburn!' "[4]

Alexander died in 1867, and his brother A. J. Alexander carried on the breeding operation until his death in 1902. Historian John Hervey said:

"While Kentucky had taken precedence of all the other states as a breeding region and the industry had assumed larger proportions there, it was pursued in a more or less instinctive, unsystematic manner, along the lines of pure personal adventure or avowed commercial expediency.

"This had been, in reality, the general horse-breeding system throughout the nation. From colonial times onward, there had been what were truly great breeders — but their operations remained, as a rule, side issues in which they engaged principally for their personal gratification.

"Robert Aitcheson Alexander was the first gentleman of great wealth and high social position who deliberately engaged in breeding as his life work with the avowed purpose of introducing the most intelligent and approved methods, the end in view being the 'improvement of the breed of horses.' "[5]

The war destroyed racing and breeding centers throughout the South. As a nonsecessionist slave state, Kentucky contributed its sons to both sides. Despite violent incidents such as those at Woodburn, however, the Bluegrass region fared better than most, racing continuing at the old Association course under both Blue and Gray occupation.

The war brought about another profound change. Before the war, especially in the South and West, gameness and stamina were considered the mark of a real racehorse.

"An animal which could not reel off three four-mile heats in less than eight minutes each had best be put to pulling a cart," observes Kent Hollingsworth, editor of The Blood-Horse. Boston, Lexington's fiery sire, won thirty such four-mile heat races, nine three-mile heat races, and one two-mile heat race. The war ended all that. The trend toward "dash racing" had begun before the conflict. Now speed was king. And soft-boned two-year-olds, raced sparingly heretofor and then only late in the season, were now raced early and hard, as had long been the practice in England. "Ante-bellum racing and the ante-bellum thoroughbred, when the four years of strife were over, had become not merely war-wrecked, they had become old-fashioned," said John Hervey.[6]

To this day, many horsemen lament the shift toward speed and precocity. In 1917, Man o' War's breeder, August Belmont II, said, "In olden days, there was something stout about the American thoroughbred that was superb . . . That we have not the same type today is not due to faults in breeding, but to the abandonment of the long-distance races which, in the early days of the turf, did so much to increase the stamina of our racers."[7]

When the war ended, New York became the heartland of big-time racing. Saratoga racetrack opened before the war's end in the upper part of the state. And in 1866, Jerome Park held its first meeting on Long Island not far from the spot where America's first formal horseraces were held in the 1660s. But there were only a few places to race — half-a-dozen tracks of any consequence between New York and New Orleans — and the meetings were brief and purses small. Woodlawn Race Course opened in Louisville in 1866, only to go under because of financial difficulties four years later as the Oakland course had done twenty-two years before.

Even though Kentucky-breds proved their superiority at northern tracks, the market for racehorses had all but dried up. The most royally bred Bluegrass yearling in the late 1860s was going for $150 tops.

Into this situation, with a possible solution, stepped Colonel M. Lewis Clark, Jr., a well-connected Louisvillian in his midtwenties. Clark was convinced the answer lay in the creation of yet another racetrack in Louisville, one that would offer rich classic races that would provide both a showcase and a testing ground for Kentucky-breds and attract the best horses nationally.

Considering the dismal fiscal history of Louisville racetracks, and the severely depressed condition of the state's economy in the late 1860s and early 1870s, Clark's plan was an ambitious one. Undaunted by negative arguments, he sailed for England in 1872 to study their racing practices.

In England, Clark was the guest of Admiral John Henry Rous, the last of the English Jockey Club's "dictators" in the mold of Sir Charles Bunbury, though far sterner. Admiral Rous was relentless in his prosecution of crooked racetrackers, and he obviously made a strong impression upon the young Louisvillian for Clark spent the rest of his life pursuing a similar course at Churchill Downs and at other tracks in the Midwest. Of Clark it would be said in later years that he could "smell a turf job as far as a buzzard scents carrion, and he has a faculty of nipping disreputable schemes in the bud."[8]

By the time of Clark's arrival in 1872, the Derby Stakes at Epsom had been firmly established for decades as the biggest turf event of the year — and often the most scandalous. Undeterred by the low state of English racing morals, Clark returned to Louisville

"M. Lewis Clark, Jr., was a promoter. Before groups of Louisville businessmen and Bluegrass breeders, he outlined his plan for formation of a jockey club, construction of his dream track, and a series of rich stakes races."

with plans for a series of races modeled upon the Epsom Derby and other great English classics such as the Oaks for fillies.

Clark was a promoter. Before groups of Louisville businessmen and Bluegrass breeders, he outlined his plan for formation of a jockey club, construction of his dream track, and a series of rich stakes races.

"He prophesied that the winner of the Kentucky Derby within 10 years would be worth, or sell for more money than, the farm on which he was bred and raised, and that one offspring of a Kentucky Derby winner would fetch more as a yearling than did his dam and the dam of his sire combined," according to *Turf, Field and Farm* in 1897, noting that Clark's prediction had already come true.[9]

Clark also appealed to Louisville's competitive instincts. He argued that Cincinnati, the town's bitter trade rival, had its music festival. New Orleans had its Mardi Gras. Louisville needed something of the sort to draw attention to itself.

Louisville in the 1870s was a bustling, cosmopolitan city of over 100,000 persons. The busy harbor rang with the bells of steamboats just in from or bound for New Orleans. The surrounding plantation country was in ruins, but Louisville's zest for trade had put her well along the road to recovery by 1874 when Clark was making his plea for a racetrack. One had only to walk down Main Street with its stately brick townhouses to realize there was plenty of money in Louisville, much of it made during the war. The Galt House, which Charles Dickens compared favorably to the best hotels in Paris, reflected Louisville's flair for elegance, as did the Pendennis Club, a haven for the town's aristocracy. "Marse Henry" Watterson's vigorous editorials had made the Louisville *Courier-Journal* a nationally known paper.

While money for stock in a racetrack was hard to come by, the town fathers heard Clark out and agreed to support him. Besides, Meriweather Lewis Clark, Jr., was a hard man to turn down.

"A typical Kentuckian of the 'colonel' type; tall, massive, magnificent, and majestic, he always made a picture as he stood in the judge's stand faultlessly attired, with a flower in his button-hole and field glasses to his eyes," recalled a Jockey Club friend after Clark's suicide in 1899.[10] Clark had a great bushy mustache, penetrating eyes, a high forehead, and hair slicked down in the fashion of the day. Interestingly, he never owned racehorses and never bet on them. The only horse anyone could remember him owning was a white mare named Rozinante who pulled him back and forth between Churchill Downs and Louisville in his buggy.

On June 22, 1874, a small group of Louisville businessmen met at the Galt House and adopted the articles of incorporation of the Louisville Jockey Club and Driving Park Association, M. Lewis Clark, Jr., president and presiding judge.

There were 320 original members of the association, including a number of prominent Lexington horsemen, each of whom subscribed $100, Clark having estimated that $32,000 would be sufficient to build the Louisville Jockey Club Course, as it was originally called. (In 1886, a Louisville newspaperman named Ben Ridgely was the first writer to refer to the Louisville Jockey Club course as Churchill Downs.)

Clark leased eighty acres of land three miles south of the town's southern limits in beautiful, rolling country from his uncles John and Henry Churchill in behalf of the association. Clark was a perfectionist, however, to whom cost was no issue and by the time the one-mile oval had been built and graded to his satisfaction, the $32,000 had been used up. A local merchant came to the club's rescue with a loan, enabling Clark to build a grandstand for 2000 persons and stables for 400 horses. Next to the grandstand, Clark built a small clubhouse where he would live during race meetings and entertain Jockey Club members and guests. When the weather was warm and sunny, these parties were held on the lawn overlooking the lovely course to the gay accompaniment of music, the laughter of the city's belles, and the popping of champagne corks.

"The course is the finest and safest in the country," according to an article in the *Daily Louisville Commercial*. "The turns and stretches are a quarter of a mile each, and are respectively 60 and 80 feet wide. The soil is light and the track is as near a water level as can be, so the time over it ought to be as good as that at Saratoga and Lexington."[11]

It was. The first trainers to work their horses over the new strip couldn't believe their stopwatches. That the track was fast would be borne out again during the inaugural meeting.

At Longchamp racecourse in Paris, Clark had first seen the primitive prototype of what we know today as the pari-mutuel machine. He brought four of the machines home with him in the expectation of introducing them at the inaugural meeting. To this end, he placed one of the machines on display in the lobby of the Galt House weeks before the meeting. The betting machines had been developed in 1865 by Pierre Oller, a Parisian, to rid racetracks of crooked bookmakers. Oller called it the "mutuel" method of betting, the word in French meaning "between ourselves." Under this system, people bet in a common pool overseen by the Jockey Club, which retained 5 percent for its services.

"In France, the creation was known only as 'mutuels.' When introduced in New York in 1877, the machines were referred to as 'Paris Mutuels.' For some unknown reason, the 's' in Paris was dropped and they since have become known rather generally as 'pari-mutuels' although the 'pari' is superfluous."[12]

There is some evidence that the machines were on the grounds opening day, but most of the customers apparently avoided them. They were used later in the six-day meeting on a limited scale but were not employed extensively until 1878 in Louisville.

The traditional Kentucky system of betting was auction pools, and these were held on Derby eve at the Galt House and the Louisville Hotel and on race day at the track itself. In this system of betting, the auctioneers chalk the names of the entries on a blackboard. "The persons assembled in the 'auction ring' were asked to start their bids. A player, who thought one horse, because of his past record, his workouts, or his condition, was outstanding, would make a bid on that horse. Someone else would 'up' the bid, and so it went until the bidding stopped. The last bidder handed his money to the auctioneer, and had that horse running for him in the race.

"Bidding would then start on the next horse, the next, and so on, until all horses were auctioned off. Very often, some horses in the race, regarded as outclassed, would not influence any separate bid, and were grouped as the 'field.' The man who bought the field had all those horses running for him.

"The total money bid into the pool, less 5 percent as the auctioneer's commission, was paid to the man who had bought the ultimate winner. The number of pools auctioned off was limited only by the number of pools the players demanded."[13]

Clark ordered a beautiful silver bowl, seventeen inches high and eight inches in diameter, designed for the winner of the first Kentucky Derby. For weeks before the race, the heavy bowl rested in its pink satin case at Kitts & Werne jewelers on Main Street.

Clark involved himself in the smallest details. He saw to it that each Jockey Club member was given a stylish silver horseshoe pin enabling him to gain access to the course and clubhouse. He organized a ladies' committee whose members vied with one another in sewing brightly colored silk purses for the prize money. The purses were hung at the finish line, where the winning jockeys grabbed them on their way back to the scales to weigh out. Clark even involved himself in the selection of the night watchmen and the men who drove the mule-powered watersprinkler wagons around the racecourse.

At his parties before the Derby, Clark liked to mix a mint julep, pour it into a huge loving cup, and present it with a flourish to his guest of honor, whereupon the guest would take a sip and pass it along. Clark's guest for the fourth running of the Derby in 1878 was Madame Helena Modjeska, the Polish actress, and her husband, a count. With a bow, Clark passed the loving cup to Madame Modjeska. She took a sip, sighed with pleasure over the mixture of bruised mint leaves, powdered sugar, crushed ice, and Kentucky bourbon, and sipped again — and again. "This one, I will keep," she said, turning to an astonished Clark. "You, please, will make another for the Count."[14]

Clark's Derby dinners at the Pendennis Club were the source of conversation for days thereafter. Prominent men and beautiful, elegantly gowned women were always present. The food was superb. The wines were impeccable. The decorations were imaginative.

At one memorable dinner, Clark's guests sat around the outer rim of tables drawn into a giant circle in the center of which was the reproduction of a country pond. A miniature fountain played over floating islands of moss and ferns. Newly hatched goslings, soft and fuzzy, paddled vigorously to and fro greedily devouring bread crumbs tossed to them by Clark's delighted guests. Another celebrated party took place the evening of May 9, 1889, after Spokane had beaten Proctor Knott by a nose in what was at the time one of the most exciting — and disputed — finishes in Derby history. This time, Clark had laid out in exquisite detail a miniature Churchill Downs with tiny wooden horses and jockeys arranged on the track in the order of their finish that afternoon.

The Kentuckian was in such demand as a presiding judge that to get him Garfield Park in Chicago asked him to write his own terms, which were readily accepted. Clark's contract called for $100 a day, a carriage to and from the racetrack, a personal servant in the judge's stand, plus his living expenses — which were considerable. Each evening of the race meeting, the imposing figure of M. Lewis Clark, Jr., occupied a private table in the center of his hotel's dining room in Chicago. There were pink shades over the candles set in antique candelabra at his special table.

But Clark was not in demand because of his conspicuous consumption. Racetracks liked him because he was a man of "remarkable courage, devoid of prejudice, and absolutely impartial; a man whom no rascal can outwit, and no bullying daunt."[15] A jockey whom he had suspended for some skullduggery paid him a compliment. Clark, he said, "was a holy terror to jobbers and crooked work on the track in general."[16]

Turf, Field and Farm agreed: "When he thought the betting looked suspicious, bets were declared off, jockeys were changed around, and 20 minutes allowed for the making of a new book. He has been known to protect the public from welching bookmakers, and has made many of the layers of odds pay a winning ticket, notwithstanding it had the wrong serial number, or a clerical error."[17] The magazine's editor spent a day with Clark in the judge's stand and left this vivid description of Clark's meticulous methods:

"The judge's box is 12 feet from the inner rail of the track and just high enough to permit a line on the heads of the horses. A tightly drawn cord between the two sighting rods helps in arriving at a correct decision when the finish is close.

"The main dependence, however, is in the quick sighting from rod to rod, and the eye must be trained to this just as it is trained in quickly sighting a rifle at the head of a squirrel. The object in placing the stand back from the inner rail is to guard against the possibility of overlooking a horse finishing on the rail.

"Colonel Clark takes his seat in a big chair in direct line with the rods, and before him is a table or little platform with all the instruments of administration under touch of his fingers. The clerk of the scales hands him a list of the jockeys, and one name selected at random is made the pivot of position allotment.

"The work is upward and downward alternately from this pivot, and as soon as it is complete, the sheet of paper is folded and handed to the assistant starter. Under this method it is impossible for an outsider to know in advance the position that a horse will have at the post. The knowledge is confined to the presiding judge and the assistant starter.

"Half an hour is given for the betting on each race, and two or three times during this interval the quotations from the [betting] ring are brought to the presiding judge, and he compares them with an estimate of chances carefully prepared in advance. If anything looks suspicious, a button is touched and a bell which rings in the betting pavilion is a signal for speculation to stop, and a single ring means saddle, and two rings means post. These signals are promptly obeyed, and there is neither confusion nor delay.

"As soon as the flag is flashed, the judge presses a button marked 'off' and the occupants of the ring know that the horses are in motion. When the horses finish, Colonel Clark has a pad before him with blank spaces for first, second, and third horses. He jots down the numbers as he sees them pass the rod, signs his name and hands the slip to his two associate judges. If they agree with him, each adds his initials and then the formal announcement is read, and simultaneously the board giving the starters and time for the next race is swung into position.

"When the horses return to the stand, the winner takes his place in a half-moon circle, and all the others are grouped around him, with heads facing the judge. Permission to dismount is then given, and saddles are quickly removed. There is no talk, no discussion, everything moving with clocklike precision. If a question should arise . . . the dispute is settled then and there.

"The presiding judge and his assistants do not leave the stand for any purpose until the last race has been run. Tea and light sandwiches are served at five o'clock . . . A record of every horse ridden with spur or whip is kept, and this is always ready for reference. If a horse that has been ridden with whip or spur is brought out minus persuaders, an explanation is asked, and if it is not satisfactory, a change is ordered.

"It is practically one man authority, but it works well, and prevents fraud. Punishment always swiftly follows crime and thus acts as a deterrent. There is no appeal from the decision of the presiding judge."[18]

Chapter 3
The Little Red Horse

Like M. Lewis Clark, H. Price McGrath also gave elaborate parties, and though guests undoubtedly whispered behind his back, whenever McGrath gave a party at McGrathiana, they all generally accepted: General John C. Breckinridge, A. Keene Richards, General Abe Buford, all of them.

The man who bred and raced Aristides, winner of the first Kentucky Derby in 1875, was the most expansive host in the Bluegrass, a region noted for its hospitality. McGrath had been a brawler, a high roller, and a thoroughly nasty piece of work when as a young man he left Kentucky to seek his fortune as a professional gambler. But this was conveniently overlooked when he came home to Lexington in 1867 and started buying costly blood horses.

McGrath bought the old Gilbert farm three miles north of Lexington on Newton Pike and assumed the role of an Irish laird. On a hill nestled in a lovely grove of locust trees, he built a mansion with a white-columned portico fashioned after the United States Hotel in Saratoga Springs, New York. He was fifty-three and a confirmed bachelor.

Each spring and fall on the Sunday before the opening of the race meetings at the old Association track in Lexington, McGrath hosted burgoo feasts that went on all afternoon, often with the public in attendance. In the east wing of the house, a bar was set up under the supervision of "Old Pete," a black man. From a huge kettle over a crackling wood fire in the back yard drifted the aroma of burgoo, Kentucky's celebrated beef stew. Farther out in the yard, servants barbecued the Southern mutton, Cashmere goat, and pig, raised at McGrathiana.

"Under the locust trees, on the rich blue grass carpet, the long tables were set, and at half past one o'clock the feast commenced. First came burgoo and burgundy as an appetizer, then came the roasts and side dishes with champagne, after which those indulged in pastry who had any room left . . . It was a magnificent feast and the wit came out as the wine frothed and bubbled."[1]

There were quiet times at McGrathiana, too, and according to a visitor in the fall of 1870, McGrath had

H. Price McGrath, gambler.

bought not only respectability but a glorious peace.

"When I formed my acquaintance with McGrathiana yesterday, the sun was but an hour high, and the tall trees cast long shadows far out on the lawn. The air was mild, a balmy breeze stirring from the South. The mansion, with its well-shaded galleries, looked fresh and inviting . . . The ladies in their white dresses, seated where they looked out upon the West, gave in reality a fairy tinge to the picture.

"Our carriage swept around the curve, and when we came to halt, a dozen pair of hands were outstretched to welcome us. And prominent among the welcoming group was the solid figure of the Lord of McGrathiana . . . learned in the school of gallantry. The compliments of the day passed and a toast was proposed . . . little mountains of ice in a large china bowl, green islands of fragrant mint, and a restless ocean of champagne.

"But to fully enjoy this glorious nectar, you must raise it to your lips at McGrathiana. Gather in a circle on the porch beneath the dome supported by lofty pillars, watch the lengthening shadows crowned with the rich tints of an Italian sunset, and turn now and then to gaze upon the dreamy herds and the high-bred horses, the pictures of contentment in the blue grass fields; and the wine cooled by the ice and flavored with the mint will enthuse you with a life that knows no cross of care, no threatening cloud."[2]

McGrath had come far and fast. He was born of humble Irish stock in the little town of Keene and was raised in Versailles, not far from Lexington. Early on, the boy was shifting for himself.

"In later years, he liked to recall that when he was eight he gave the first dime he ever earned to his employer, Col. E. M. Blackburn of Elmira Stock Farm in Woodford County, and asked that Colonel Blackburn purchase a primer on his next trip to Versailles.

"McGrath said he sat on a fence all day, anxiously awaiting the return of his employer. Finally he saw in the distance a horse and buggy clip-clopping up some dust on the homeward lane.

" 'Sir, did you get my book?' young McGrath inquired as Colonel Blackburn drew abreast of him.

" 'Nope,' came the reply. 'It cost 12 1/2 cents.'

" 'Thus, for 2 1/2 cents,' McGrath would say, 'I was deprived of an education.' "[3]

McGrath was trained to be a tailor and as late as the age of twenty-one was reported singing in a church choir. Suddenly, says Henry Chefetz in *Play the Devil*, McGrath kicked over the traces and put Versailles behind him.

"He started out assisting crooked dice artists that flourished in Lexington during the race meetings . . . A hearty eater, he could hold his liquor, sing the gay and ribald tavern songs of the day, bend the boys back

with laughter over a dirty joke, and also speak with authority on horses . . .

"With the soul of a racketeer, McGrath succeeded in frightening pusillanimous visiting gamblers who got up faro banks in Lexington, Frankfort, and Paris . . . He chiseled an interest out of them at no cost to himself, by strong arm methods. Those he could not persuade, he publicly accused of cheating, and the naive faro players believed in their popular friend and allowed themselves to be steered by the gamblers who supported McGrath."[4]

As *Blood-Horse* managing editor Edward L. Bowen has observed, Kentucky was too small a place to contain a man of McGrath's energy and talents. The Irishman started dealing his own faro games; he worked the riverboats on the Ohio and Mississippi; he joined the '49 Gold Rush to California and relieved prospectors of their gold in games of chance. He made his way to New Orleans where he joined two other men in the operation of a swank gambling den at Number 4 Carondolet Street, McGrath serving as the host and trouble-shooter.

"When the Civil War came, his partners poured much of their profits into supporting the Confederate Army and proffering charity upon widows, wives, mothers, and children of soldiers. McGrath poured his profits into his racing stable."[5]

When Union forces took over the town, General

Jay Gould.

John C. Breckinridge.

ner, and founder of Monmouth Park; and Morrissey . . . who eventually got elected to Congress and who, in 1863, established racing at Saratoga."[7]

McGrath cashed in his chips and headed home. Once established in Kentucky again, he devoted the rest of his life to racing, breeding, and betting on horses. Though he is remembered as the owner of Aristides, his best horse and his favorite was Tom Bowling, the fiery three-year-old champion of 1873. "The greatest racehorse, sir, that ever looked through a bridle," he used to say. McGrath considered Tom Bowling to be Lexington's greatest son, and many turfmen agreed with him. When financier Jay Gould asked him what he would take for the colt, McGrath replied that he wouldn't even take Gould's Narragansett Steamship Company, then valued in the millions. The steamship company would be forgotten, said McGrath: Tom Bowling's name would live forever. If you failed to agree, you had better duck, for McGrath had a quick temper.

One day in May 1873, McGrath had Tom Bowling at the Lexington track to run in a mile-heat sweepstakes. "He stripped back the blanket and waited for some glowing praise on the appearance of his colt from John C. Breckinridge, who had moved up or down, depending on one's sense of values, from his position as major general and Secretary of War for the Confederacy to president of the Lexington track.

" 'Well, he's grand looking and he is fast,' Breckinridge conceded. 'I like him very much for a quarter or half-mile, but he'll never stay a mile.'

"McGrath flushed. 'If that's the case, I'll change his name to Breckinridge! . . . You couldn't stay yourself. You beat Bob Letcher for Congress — that was one quarter; you beat Leslie Combs for the Senate — that was another quarter; and you won the Vice Presidency — that was three quarters; but when you ran for President, old Abe Lincoln beat you — 'cause you couldn't stay the route!' "[8]

McGrath was right about Tom Bowling, though the horse proved a bust as stud, and in 1892, he was bought for fifty dollars at an auction in Lexington.

McGrath knew horses, and he spared no expense to get the best bloodlines. So it's not surprising that he was able to come up with the favored entry of Chesapeake and Aristides for the first running of the Kentucky Derby at Colonel Clark's new racetrack in Louisville on May 17, 1875. Chesapeake was thought to be the best in the field. He was a big bay colt by Lexington out of Roxana and had been coming to the peak of his form at the Lexington track in the weeks before the Derby. The colt was a bad actor at the post who liked to finish with a tremendous rush from far back in the pack.

McGrath's Derby strategy was to employ Aristides

Ben Butler was installed as military governor, and he "looked askance at the way Southern sharps were fleecing his hard-spending soldiers with fixed horse races and the like."[6] The gamblers quickly discovered that if they made discreet payments to General Butler's brother, the heat abated. McGrath, says Bowen, drew the line at this and skipped town, returning only after General Butler had moved on. When McGrath tried to get things going again at Number 4 Carondolet, he somehow ran afoul of the authorities and was sent to federal prison for a year.

In greatly reduced circumstances after his release, McGrath joined forces with a St. Louis gambler named Johnny Chamberlain, who had $50,000 to invest. With Chamberlain's money and with McGrath's charm, muscle, and moxie, the pair hoped to open a gambling house in New York. Instead, they joined a syndicate headed by John Morrissey, the bareknuckle prize fighter and Tammany bully boy, and built a fancy gambling house at Number 5 West 24th Street. The gaming den was an instant success. Millions of dollars rolled in during the first few months.

"Here were three guys destined for fame and respectability in thoroughbred racing: McGrath, breeder and owner of the first Kentucky Derby winner; Chamberlain, owner of the first Preakness Stakes win-as a "rabbit" to go out winging on the front end and soften up the field for Chesapeake's winning rush. This strategy was to go awry.

Aristides, too, was royally bred. He was by Leamington, the fine imported English stallion, out of Sarong, she in turn by Lexington. Leamington would also sire Pierre Lorillard's Iroquois, the first American winner of the Derby Stakes at Epsom, in 1881. In 1872, a horseman by the name of Aristides Welch bought Leamington from his American importers for the Erdenheim Stud outside Philadelphia. McGrath and Welch hit it off together, and the Irishman named the offspring of Leamington-Sarong for his friend.

"Aristides was a compact little golden-red chestnut standing fifteen hands one and three-quarter inches with a white star on his forehead and white-stockinged hind legs."

Aristides was a compact little golden red chestnut standing fifteen hands, one and three-quarter inches with a white star on the forehead and white-stockinged hind legs. At age two, Aristides had won three of nine races; significantly, his wins had come toward the end of his campaign when he showed signs of being able to go a distance.

Another highly regarded Derby entry, though unraced at two, was Frank B. Harper's Ten Broeck, who would mature into one of America's greatest distance horses. Ten Broeck had gone to the post for the first time in the Phoenix Hotel Stakes at Lexington one week before the Derby and won easily, leaving Aristides, among others, up the track. (Aristides hadn't run well, for he had cut his legs during the running on the muddy track.) A few days later, Chesapeake whipped Ten Broeck badly in a two-mile race at Lex-

ington, establishing himself as the Derby favorite.

J. B. Rhodes's Searcher had run a mile in a sensational 1:41 3/5 not long before the Derby, attracting followers, and C. A. Lewis's Verdigris also had his backers.

The response to Colonel Clark's meeting on the part of racing men in Kentucky and Tennessee had been overwhelmingly enthusiastic. Forty-two horses had been entered in the Kentucky Derby by the March 1, 1875, deadline. The conditions were "$50 pay or play." This meant that the fifty dollars nominating fee would go toward the purse whether the horse started or not. To this sum, the Louisville Jockey Club and Driving Park Association added $1,000. Thus the winner's share would be $2,900 with $200 for the second horse.

By Derby eve, the field had been winnowed to thirteen colts and two fillies. They were listed in the original scales book:

A. Buford's b.c. Baywood 100 (J. Carter)
W. Cottrill's ch. f. Ascension 97 (W. Lakeland)
A. B. Lewis & Co.'s b.c. Vagabond 100 (Jas. Houston)
Robinson, Morgan & Co.'s br. c. Rob Wooley 100 (W. Walker)
S. J. Salyer's br. c. Bill Bruce 100 (M. Jones)
J. A. Grinstead's ch. f. Gold Mine 97 (Standford)
H. P. McGrath's b.c. Chesapeake 100 (Wm. Henry)
F. B. Harper's b.c. Ten Broeck 100 (M. Kelso)
Springfield & Clay's ch. c. Warsaw 100 (P. Masterson)
H. P. McGrath's ch. c. Aristides 100 (O. Lewis)
J. B. Rhodes' br. c. Searcher 100 (R. Colston)
Springfield & Clay's gr. c. Enlister 100 (Hollaway)
A. Buford's ch. c. McCreery 100 (D. Jones)
C. A. Lewis' Ch. c. Verdigris 100 (H. Chambers)
C. H. Rich's b.c. Volcano 100 (H. Williams)

Billy Lakeland on Ascension was the only white jockey in the Derby field.

The original Derby distance was that of the Epsom prototype, one and a half miles, but there the similarity in the two races ended. For the Epsom course, in the shape of an irregular horseshoe, is of grass, an up hill, down dale affair. The Kentucky Derby, which is still being run over the original course, is contested on a flat dirt track around two turns.

On Derby eve, McGrath checked into the Galt House and took part in the lively bidding in the auction pools. There is no record of how much he bet, but it can be assumed that it was in the tens of thousands of dollars, for such was his style.

There was interest in the Derby far beyond the borders of Kentucky. In New York, the *Spirit of the Times* felt the race would be closely watched for its influence upon the big races in the East such as the Belmont Stakes. For its part, Louisville hadn't been so excited about a horse race since Wagner, the pride of Louisiana, beat Kentucky's beloved Grey Eagle in four-mile heats at the old Oakland track nearly forty years before. The Derby was scheduled as the second race on May 17, 1875, opening day of the inaugural meeting. Because May 17 was a Monday, the *Courier-Journal* recommended that the city's employers observe a half-holiday.

By midmorning on race day, which dawned cloudless and sunny, festive race-goers were streaming toward the course south of town in victorias, spring wagons, hacks, fringe-topped buggies, and every conceivable form of conveyance. Coal wagons packed tight with Negroes who had been given the day off rattled down Third Street behind floppy-eared mules adorned with jingle bells. Tallyhos drawn by teams of high-stepping hackneys set off from the Pendennis Club with cargoes of society belles in frilled organdies and plumed hats clutching parasols to protect them from the rays of the warm spring sun. Other Louisvillians rode little mule-drawn trolley cars on tracks newly laid along Fourth Street to within walking distance of the racecourse gates. Still others climbed aboard either the Short-Line or Louisville & Nashville (L & N) railroads, which ran excursions to the track from downtown depots.

Early arrivals at the course found workmen still pounding nails into the support columns of a temporary fifty-cent-admission field stand. The one dollar main grandstand, with a special section for women, was filled before noon. Beneath the grandstand, black women in bandannas and long-aproned skirts prepared corn bread, fried fish, fried chicken, and burgoo.

Many people drove their carriages and wagons across the track into the center field, tethered their horses, and spread picnics. In the woodland near the track, sharpies set up games of chance — craps, shell games, "spindle," and chuck-a-luck — for those who couldn't wait for the action of the first race, a one-and-a-quarter-mile "dash" got under way at 2:30 P.M.

The clubhouse was an island of tranquillity. Some even watched the day's racing from rocking chairs on the wide verandah. As the women wandered about the greensward trailing their long gowns, twirling their parasols, and sipping lemonade, the strains of Strauss waltzes and an occasional polka drifted across from the grandstand, where Schneider's band was performing. Later, the band would re-establish itself on the clubhouse lawn and play for President Clark's post-Derby party.

Bewhiskered horsemen from the Bluegrass came by the score, sipping mint juleps and talking horses, members of what Colonel Clark liked to call "the old set": Colonel Jim Pepper, Brigadier General Abe Buford, Daniel Swigert, A. J. Alexander. Pepper was a wealthy distiller and thoroughbred breeder, a dandy of a man in a plaid suit with a nosegay in the button-hole, stylish yellow driving gloves, and field glasses slung jauntily over one shoulder. Abe Buford had been a dashing Confederate cavalry commander. He now served as starter at the Lexington races, where he was known to throw hard clods of turf at jockeys who didn't react fast enough to his instructions. Swigert had been the Woodburn farm manager and after Robert Alexander's death he branched out on his own and became a distinguished breeder in his own right. Swigert bought and developed Woodburn-bred Spendthrift, one of Kentucky's greatest sires. "In Biblical language, Spendthrift begat Hastings, and Hastings begat Fair Play, and Fair Play begat Man o' War."

In the whitewashed frame stables on the back-stretch, the high-mettled racers were getting hungry, their feed having been cut back in anticipation of the afternoon race. Many of them pawed the straw and wandered back and forth restlessly in their stalls.

Many of the trainers, like most of the jockeys, were black men, products of the plantation system. By 1875, jockeys and trainers were beginning to gain recognition, and the jockeys' last names were now included on the programs.

Riding Bonaventure, Billy Lakeland won the first race by a nose, beating Captain Hutchinson, with the ace black jockey Bobby Swim aboard.

Suddenly, it was Derby time. The fifteen thoroughbreds pranced onto the track before a throng of 10,000 persons, a huge crowd for those times.

Colonel W. H. Johnson, president of the Nashville Blood Horse Association, stood on a box at the half-mile pole across the field from the stands, his red starting flag at the ready. Contemporary accounts of the start are confusing, but it's to be assumed that Johnson, as was the custom at that time, had two assistants, one with a drum, another with a flag, posted up the track.

"The fall of the flag was the official gesture that started the race and also gave the timekeepers the signal to start clocking, while the drum was beaten so that jockeys, who might have been too busy with a fractious horse to see the flag fall, would hear a starting signal.

"In the early years, the starter would stand on his box and his chief assistant would take a position 125 yards up the track. The starting mark was a line drawn through the dirt from one side to the other,

the butt of a flag being used to cut the line. The jockeys took their horses well back of the line and walked up for a start.

"If the starter did not like the lineup, he would hold his flag aloft, and then the assistant, down the track, would wave his flag, to tell the riders to go back and line up again. This was known as the 're-call.'

"When the starter liked the lineup, he would slam his flag down, the man with the drum went into action, and the fellow down the track would lower his flag, and drag it along the ground as he ran for the outer rail to escape the oncoming horses."[9]

McGrath's jockeys, William Henry on Chesapeake, and Oscar Lewis on Aristides, wore his Irish green silks with orange sash. As the horses made their first walk-up approach, three of them whirled, the jockeys' silks flashing in the sun as they struggled to bring their mounts under control. This set Chesapeake rearing and plunging, trying to pitch Henry.

"Take him back, Henry!" shouted Colonel Johnson.

While Henry tried to get Chesapeake settled down, the colonel shouted: "Come on!"

Johnson flashed his red flag down, the drum rolled, and his flag assistant up the track scooted for the rail as the horses thundered toward him. Chesapeake, the favorite, was almost left flatfooted.

According to the Louisville *Courier-Journal,* "Aristides, McCreery, and Volcano got off in front, Chesapeake, who is a vicious starter, being one of the last away. McCreery got to the fore before rounding the turn and was first passing the grandstand, with Aristides second, and Volcano third. Before they reached the turn, McCreery retired, as his owner expected, for he had not recovered from a severe attack of distemper contracted while at Nashville. That McCreery, like all the Enquirers that have appeared, possesses great speed, the half mile he ran in :50 1/2 with a hundred pounds up, proves.

"Aristides went on with the lead after McCreery retired, with Ten Broeck, Volcano, and Verdigris, who had begun to close up, not far in his rear. The others seemed to be outpaced, for Aristides was cutting out the running at an awful speed, getting back to the finish of the mile in the neighborhood of 1:43.

"Here Volcano dropped back, his rider with good judgment taking a pull on him. Lewis, on Aristides, seemed, too, to take a pull on his horse, expecting Chesapeake, his stable companion, to come in and take up the running; but where, oh where, was Chesapeake? Away back in the ruck and not able to do anything for his stable.

"Fortunately for the favorite, Price McGrath was near the head of the stretch, and taking in the position of things at a glance, waved his hand for Lewis to go on with the good little red horse and win if he could all alone.

"Right gallantly did the game and speedy son of Leamington and Sarong answer the call on his forces, for he held his own all down the stretch, in spite of a most determined rush on the part of Volcano and Verdigris, and dashed under the wire winner of one of the fastest and hardest races ever seen on a track.

"Aristides forced the pace all the way for his stable companion, Chesapeake, and so had no respite at all, which makes his performance a very remarkable one. Volcano was a good horse indeed, and was dangerous up to the last instant, as was Verdigris, which had beat him at Nashville. Bob Wooley came in fourth and Ten Broeck fifth, well up. The speedy Searcher did not show in front in any part of the race. Ascension disappointed her backers somewhat. She looked overworked and did not have any speed. Wooley has greatly improved on his two-year-old form. Ten Broeck ran like a good horse."

The race was over. Aristides had run the one and a half miles in 2:37 3/4 — then the fastest one and a half miles ever run by a three-year-old in this country. Colonel Clark's dream race had proven to be just that. On the morning of the race, the *Courier-Journal* had said prophetically: "Today will be historic to Kentucky annals, as the first 'Derby Day' of what promises to be a long series of annual turf festivities which we confidently expect our grandchildren 100 years hence to celebrate in glorious continuous rejoicings . . ."

Chapter 4
"Who did Haggin think he was"

BETWEEN ARISTIDES in 1875 and Regret in 1915 — when the Kentucky Derby was re-established by the presence of a great eastern stable — Churchill Downs went through more ups and downs than Eliza on the ice.

Depression, reluctance to change with the racing times, local opposition to gambling, upheavals in management, all contributed to the track's instability. And in 1899, the following item appeared in *The Thoroughbred Record:*

"On Saturday, April 22, about nine o'clock, Colonel M. Lewis Clark ended his life with his own hand in his room at the Gaston Hotel, Memphis, Tennessee, by sending a pistol bullet into his brain. He had been in ill health and confined to his room.

"When his physician called to see him, he found Colonel Clark lying across his bed, dead, his right hand still clasping the pistol, and a bullet hole through his right temple. Many theories are advanced concerning the cause of the suicide of Colonel Clark, but the most probable is that it was the result of very bad health. It has also been said that financial embarrassment caused his self-destruction, but even if this is true, there has as yet been produced no evidence of it."[1] Clark's death marked the end of the ancien régime. In his last days, he often lamented the loss of old friends and the Derby's decline as a social event.

Joe Estes divided Derby history into three general periods: 1875 to 1898, 1899 to 1914, and 1915 onward.

During the first period, purses were not high, but the race attracted crack horses, both eastern and local, who were to leave their stamp on the breed and succeeding Derby winners: Hindoo, who included the 1881 Derby in a string of eighteen straight victories;

Ben Brush, winner in 1896 of the first Derby run at one and a quarter miles; and Plaudit in 1898.

From Manuel in 1899 through Donerail in 1913, mediocrity characterized the Derby fields. The race had become a local affair, getting by on its tradition, in Estes's view.

Signs of decline were apparent even earlier. The Kentucky Derby had begun to lose prestige after the 1897 race when Typhoon II upset the great Ornament, who was given a suspicious ride. Few eastern stables shipped to the Downs for the Derby, overshadowed as it was by the American Derby at Washington Park in Chicago.

When a homely animal named Elwood won the 1904 Derby, his trainer, C. E. "Boots" Durnell, didn't bother to show up for the race, having had a spat with his wife, who owned the horse. She had wanted to run the horse; he hadn't. She won the argument, of course, and had someone else saddle him. Elwood came home ahead of a horse named Ed Tierney, and Mrs. Durnell became the first woman to own a Derby winner.

Because Donerail in 1913 paid $184.90 — the longest-priced winner in the race's history — the colt brought beneficial publicity to the Derby. But it was not until the following year that Old Rosebud inaugurated the modern era when America's greatest racehorses, more often than not, have made up the Derby fields: Exterminator, Sir Barton, Zev, Black Gold, Bubbling Over, Gallant Fox, Twenty Grand, Cavalcade, Omaha, War Admiral, Whirlaway, Count Fleet, Assault, Citation, Swaps, Carry Back, Northern Dancer, Majestic Prince, Riva Ridge, Secretariat.

Eighteen eighty-six proved a bad year for Colonel Clark and his Kentucky Derby. First, the race starter won his threat to walk out with his crew unless Clark

"He is a lean greyhound of a horse," begins one contemporary description of the great Hindoo, 1881 Derby winner and important sire. "Full eye, sharp, thornlike little ears, legs fore and hind that seem made of hammered iron. His depth of chest dwarfs his neck and head. And with pardonable pride, his owners, the celebrated Dwyer Brothers, trace him back to the stables of purest Arabs . . ." According to another account: "He lived in an age of Turftitans. He battled with giants and more than held his own."

Ben Brush stumbled at the start of the 1896 Derby, nearly tossing his rider Willie Simms, but rallied to win by a nose over Ben Eder. His flanks were dripping blood from Simms's spurs by the time the colt was cantered back to be unsaddled, and the black jockey expressed regret that he had had to punish the horse. Twenty-five thousand people turned out for the race, including August Belmont, arriving in Louisville in his private railroad car.

Elwood, who got home first in 1904, will not be found on any list of great Derby winners. But his owner, Mrs. C. E. Durnell, had faith in him — which was more than her husband, the trainer had — and she attained a measure of fame by becoming the first woman to own a Derby winner.

Donerail, with Roscoe Goose in the saddle, was the longest priced winner in Derby history, paying $184.90 and bringing much-needed publicity to the 1913 race. Holding the reins is T. P. Hayes of Lexington, Donerail's owner, breeder, and trainer — who did not bet on his horse that day.

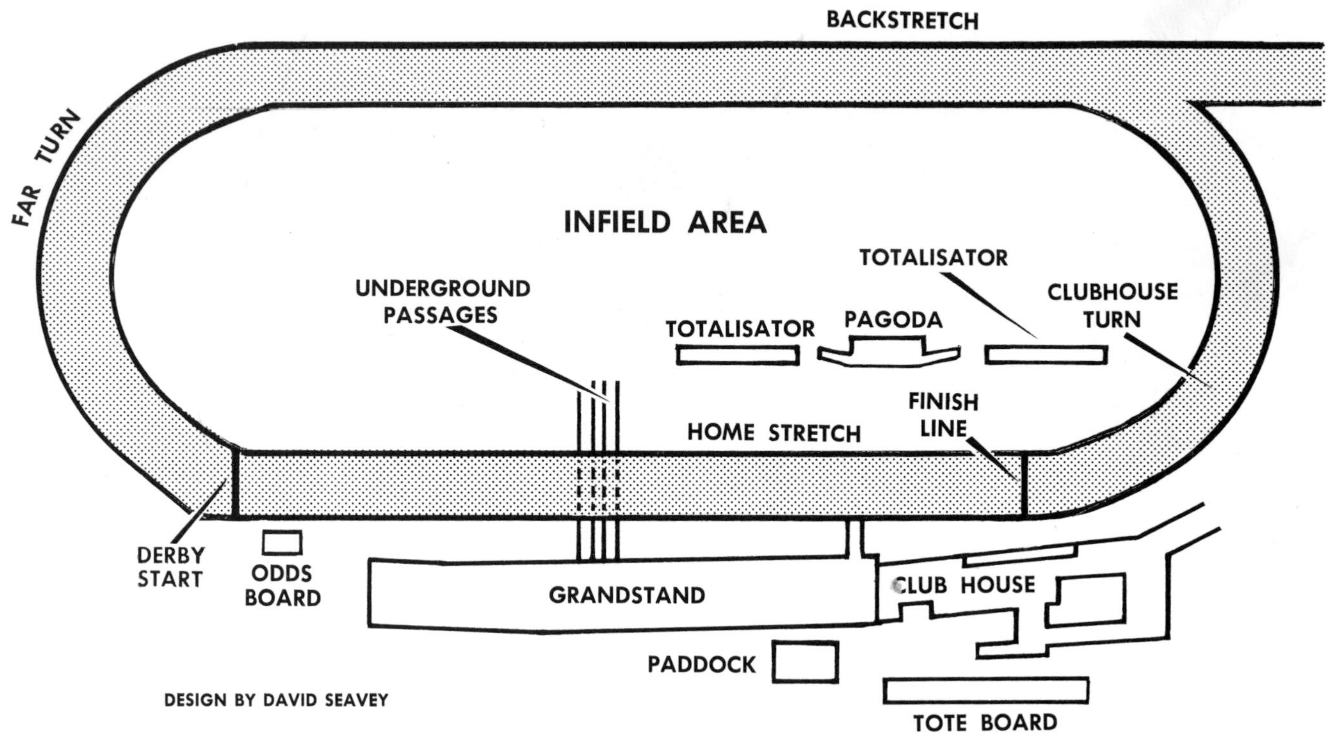

BACKSTRETCH

FAR TURN

INFIELD AREA

UNDERGROUND PASSAGES

TOTALISATOR

TOTALISATOR **PAGODA**

CLUBHOUSE TURN

FINISH LINE

HOME STRETCH

DERBY START

ODDS BOARD

GRANDSTAND

CLUB HOUSE

PADDOCK

TOTE BOARD

DESIGN BY DAVID SEAVEY

Layout of Churchill Downs.

Exterminator (left) works out at Belmont. With Willie Knapp aboard, he won the 1918 Derby and forty-nine more races in 100 starts through the age of nine. Colonel Matt J. Winn thought the gelding was the greatest all-around thoroughbred the country ever produced. Purchased ten days before the Derby as a workhorse to extend Willis Sharpe Kilmer's Sun Briar in prerace workouts, Exterminator went to the post in Sun Briar's stead when the horse failed to train well and won in the mud at thirty to one. Exterminator, a game animal, ran at all distances, under crushing weights. He reached his peak at seven, winning ten of seventeen starts, carrying 132 pounds in all but two races.

Because Exterminator was angular, the public called him "Old Slim," "Old Bones," and "The Animated Hatrack," and they kept making him the favorite long after he reached his prime at eight and nine and should have been retired. Exterminator became a folk hero.

upped his fee. Then one of Clark's officials insulted none other than James Ben Ali Haggin, a multimillionaire horse owner. Haggin, a Kentuckian, had gone west and made a fortune in gold, silver, and copper mining. In 1886, he arrived in Louisville with a big party of friends to watch his colt Ben Ali run in the Derby and a big string of horses to campaign at Churchill Downs for the balance of the meeting.

But there were no bookmakers on the grounds Derby Day, May 14, because they had gone on strike. Haggin, a notorious plunger, was furious.

Said the correspondent of the *Spirit of the Times:* "White & Company, who had leased the betting privileges from the club, demanded $100 per day from each bookmaker, for privilege to operate. The pencillers held a meeting, and agreed not to pay more than $2,000 in the aggregate, and on this difference, they split, there being no bookmaking on opening day . . . The trouble was intensified by the lack of necessary betting facilities. There were only four French mutuel machines, and such crowding and jostling I never saw before on a race course.

"The big speculators such as James B. Haggin, Ed Corrigan, and others were not slow to express their dissatisfaction at the strange state of affairs, Haggin going so far as to state that if a change was not made at once, he would remove his horses from the track.

"Haggin's great horse, Ben Ali, won the Derby that afternoon and Haggin, when asked that night about his threat, said:

" 'Yes, I did say that if bookmakers did not make some satisfactory arrangement, and commence operations on the track, I would take my stable away. I mean it, too. It is not because I care for the bookmakers, or for the man who has the betting privileges at the track, but for the reason that I desire to back my horses, and I can't do it unless there are bookmakers at the track. I have won the Derby, and will pack up and get out, unless the matter is arranged tomorrow . . .' "[2]

Next morning, a compromise was effected and twenty-three bookmakers showed up.

Then word got back to Haggin that one of the

29

Churchill Downs Club House, 1892. "The clubhouse stood apart in a grove of black gums, oaks, and maples," said James J. Hart in the Louisville *Herald Post* in 1934. "There was loveliness surrounding the old clubhouse, more mellowness and charm. Its wide verandas and spacious rooms were appointed like those of a private club, which indeed it was. Wonderful breakfasts were served. And in the cool shade of overspreading trees, you saw white-coated Negroes passing from the house to groups on the lawn, bearing trays of frosted silver goblets crowned with sprigs of mint. Coaching parasols twirled . . . Dear, dead days."

track officials, when apprised of Haggin's earlier threat, had asked "who did Haggin think he was" and "to hell with him anyway." Haggin was celebrating with his friends, and he exploded with fury when he heard of the official's remarks. Colonel Matt Winn later described what happened next:

"He called his trainer into a hurried conference, and before dawn, of the next day, every horse in Haggin's string was en route to New York.

"The treatment accorded Haggin brought about something equivalent to a boycott of Churchill Downs by eastern horse owners. Haggin was a powerful figure in New York racing, and a popular one. There was considerable ado at the time over the incident, and it is to be noted that no eastern owners of high class three-year-olds — except Mike Dwyer in 1896 — sent their horses to the Kentucky Derby post for over a quarter of a century."[3]

On the morning after the 1894 Kentucky Derby, won by Chant, the *Daily Louisville Commercial* asserted that the race had degenerated into "a bench show — a contest of dogs." The time was long past due, the paper continued, to cut the Derby distance from one and a half miles to one and a quarter miles

and face up to the fact that racing was no longer a sport. Racing was a business, and owners were no longer willing to run colts one and a half miles early in May for what the Louisville Jockey Club was willing to put up in the way of purse money.

"Above all other men of the West, for years M. Lewis Clark has stood for what is good and honorable in racing. He had held the Kentucky Derby to the standard of the extreme test of courage and endurance as well as speed; a noble contest, in which no penalties are imposed and no favors asked; a race in which victory brings to horse, owner, trainer, and jockey, victory above all money value. But when ideals, however admirable, become impossible, it is time to abandon them . . . The dollar is king, and the Derby of a mile and a half is dead."[4]

Too, the Jockey Club's finances were in bad shape. "Only one dividend of 10 percent had been declared since the inaugural meeting in 1875," said Mrs. Marjorie Weber, an authority on Derby history. Colonel Clark had turned all profits back into improvements of the track. This pecuniary instability came to a climax in the Derby of 1894 — thirty-five entries signed up and only five horses started the race.

Before the end of the year, the Clark regime had ended and a group calling themselves The New Louisville Jockey Club was formed. Its secretary was Charles F. Price, a former newspaperman, who later became presiding judge, a position he held for decades, carrying on Colonel Clark's tradition of swift punishment for wrongdoers on the turf. The new group spent $100,000 improving the grounds. They erected a grandstand on the west side of the track so the horseplayers would no longer have to squint into the late afternoon sun. The core of the stand, built primarily of brick, still stands today with the twin towers that are the Churchill Downs trademark. The grandstand was 285 feet long with a seating capacity of 1500 and room for another 500 to stand under cover. The stables and fencing were freshly whitewashed. Improvements notwithstanding, only four horses went to the post in the Derby of 1895, which Halma won.

The next year, the management finally cut two furlongs from the Derby distance, and the horsemen responded enthusiastically. One hundred and seventy-one horses were entered, and eight started. But in 1897 a depression hit the country and the Derby was afflicted again with small fields.

In 1897, eleven years after he had angrily shipped his horses out of Churchill Downs, Ben Ali Haggin moved back to his native Kentucky. He became master of Elmendorf Farm, built a twenty-five-room mansion christened Green Hills, and became the largest commercial breeder of thoroughbreds in America. At one point he owned 1,000 broodmares divided

between Elmendorf and a ranch in California. He had dealt the Derby a blow, but he was to buy, breed, and race horses on an enormous scale. When Haggin died in 1914, he left an estate of $20,000,000, one fourth of it in Kentucky property. According to the Lexington *Herald:* "As other men have established colleges and schools and libraries, James B. Haggin left as his monument the most magnificent breeding farm the world has ever seen."[5]

Haggin set a style that other millionaires have tried to emulate. With the exception of Claiborne, Spendthrift, and a few other big commercial breeding operations, most Bluegrass horse farms today operate at a staggering loss. In a few cases, such as the Alexander family, still occupying Woodburn but racing little, the money was made in pre-Revolutionary England. In other cases, such as Price McGrath and Ben Ali Haggin, the money was made by local men who left home to find Golconda and returned to Kentucky to spend it. In several cases, the money came from a variety of sources. "It comes from the family fortunes accumulated in some cases by the ones who are spending the incomes; in other cases by members of earlier generations," wrote Joe Jordan in the Lexington *Leader* a few years ago. "The founders of the fortunes . . . were individuals who prospected for gold and found it; drilled for oil and brought in gushers; got rich on war contracts; mixed politics with city, street,

This old woodcut shows Ben Ali being groomed after winning the 1886 Derby for his owner James Ben Ali Haggin.

James Ben Ali Haggin.

31

and sewer contracts, or with trolley franchises; fought desperate winner-take-all battles on Wall Street; invented useful machines, or invested in other men's brains; set up dime stores; ran textile mills, hotels, fleets of taxicabs, or steel mills; engaged in one phase or another of the gigantic automobile industry; sold patent medicine, machinery, dog food or soda crackers . . ."[6]

Standard Oil money has kept the Whitney horses in oats and hay; butcher shops and a horsecar line in Philadelphia started the Widener family; Singer sewing machines have kept the Clarks in thoroughbreds; taxicabs did it for the late John D. Hertz; gambling for Colonel E. R. Bradley; baking powder for Calumet. John W. Galbreath, the only man to own winners of the Kentucky Derby and the Epsom Derby, accumulated the wherewithal to operate Darby Dan Farm in real estate and construction.

In the late 1960s, fresh money from abroad began to enrich the Bluegrass, sending prices at the Keeneland Yearling Sales soaring to new highs every summer. Austrian Countess Margit Battyany feels that to win horse races, one must be prepared to spend money. So she acquired a horse farm outside Lexington to supplement her stud farms in Ireland and Normandy, a forty-five-stall training center at Chantilly, a ranch in Alberta, a hunting lodge in Austria, holdings in Uruguay, and a home in Switzerland where she masterminds her global racing and breeding operations via teleprinter circuits.

"You have to go on buying, you cannot sit," says the countess, whose fortune derives from chemical companies, barge companies, and other holdings in Europe.

Another recent arrival in the Bluegrass is Zenya Yoshida, Japan's leading thoroughbred breeder. In 1972, he bought more than $1,000,000 in American thoroughbred bloodstock and was a member of a syndicate that paid a record $600,000 for a Bold Ruler yearling at the 1973 Keeneland Sales. Yoshida's colors consist of a black-and-yellow-striped jacket with red sleeves and a black-and-yellow cap. He's forthright about his intentions: He wants to see his colors in the winner's circle at Churchill Downs on the first Saturday in May. He may succeed. He may never, no matter how much money he spends.

John E. Madden, the master of Hamburg Place, whom most Kentuckians look upon as the greatest all-around horseman in racing history, once said:

"It is this 'glorious uncertainty' which enables a poor man to get hold of a great horse, that makes racing the most fascinating and exhilarating sport in the world. It is this uncertainty that fills the grandstands . . . Our rich men derive little pleasure from the pecuniary profit they realize from winning races. They have all the money they want to make life comfortable. But it is the possibility of having their equine stars defeated by nags from a poor owner's stable that gives interest to the contests of the thoroughbred . . . A man must work hard if he hopes to win success, but on the turf, luck plays a more prominent part than it does in other lines of work."[7]

Distance poles on a standard one-mile racetrack.

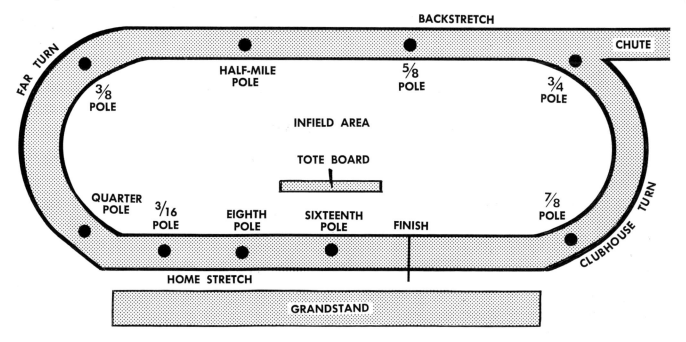

Chapter 5
Ike and Wink

THE JOCKEY with the best winning average in Kentucky Derby history — two victories, one second, and one third in four starts — lives today in a villa in Maisons-Laffitte, a few miles northwest of Paris. He's a black man in his nineties. And his name — Jimmy Winkfield — is all but unknown to the American public.

Had "Wink" not gone abroad in 1905 and spent the next twenty-five years winning races such as the Moscow Derby, Prix du Président de la République, and Grosser Prix von Baden, he might today share a fame comparable to that of Isaac Murphy, considered one of the greatest riders in American racing history. Murphy was the first man to ride three Derby winners, and according to his own records he rode 1412 races from 1875 to 1895, winning 628, or 44 percent. No rider has yet approached that mark.

Ike and Wink were quite different individuals. Wink was, by his own admission, something of a rascal as a young jockey, willing as the next man to do a little fouling if circumstances required. Ike was as celebrated for his clean riding as for his skill in the saddle.

Black jockeys won fifteen of the first twenty-eight runnings of the Derby, and only one of the fifteen riders in the 1875 inaugural was white. Jess Conley in 1911 was the last black jockey to ride in the Kentucky Derby. Besides Ike Murphy and Jimmy Winkfield there were many fine black riders including Oliver Lewis, William Walker, George Lewis, Babe Hurd, Erskine Henderson, Isaac Lewis, Alonzo Clayton, James "Soup" Perkins, Willie Simms, and Jimmie Lee.

Although Tod Sloan is credited with introducing the short stirrup to England, Willie Simms rode that

There were many prominent black trainers at the turn of the century, among them Ed "Brown Dick" Brown. He sold Plaudit to John E. Madden, who won the 1898 Derby with the colt.

way on Mike Dwyer's horses during a season in that country before Tod Sloan.

A number of black men trained Derby winners, including Raleigh Colston, who conditioned Leonatus in 1883. Colston had ridden Searcher to fifth place in the 1875 Derby. Dudley Allen trained Vagrant to win the 1876 Derby and Kingman the 1891 Derby.

Black jockeys have gone with the wind, and black horsemen themselves differ over the reasons. Winkfield believes black men were eased out of the sport once it became a profitable profession. Oscar Dishman, a successful trainer in Kentucky, disagrees: "There just aren't any small blacks any more. I would love to have a black boy if I could find one."

Why there are few black trainers anymore is more difficult to fathom. In August 1973, one black trainer emerged from obscurity in spectacular fashion, however. Harrison Johnson stunned Saratoga when his Gusty O'Shay won the rich Hopeful stakes, one of the most coveted of two-year-old classics, whipping Az Igazi. Gusty, a gelding, once ran in a $5000 claiming race and is by an unsung animal named Rose Argent out of a mare once claimed for $2500.

Winkfield was born in Chilesburg, not far from Lexington, on April 12, 1882. He went to work at Latonia racetrack for eight dollars a month when he was fifteen and made a spectacular debut as a jockey some time later in a race in Chicago. Breaking fourth from the rail, he cut straight across the path of the three inside horses as he drove for the rail and all four horses went down. The stewards put Winkfield down, too — for a year. When the suspension was up, Winkfield won his first race. He was on his way, a natural rider, brainy and tough.

The Thoroughbred Record, formerly *The Livestock Record*, shares the same birthday as the Derby, and its correspondent covering the 1901 race — won by Winkfield on His Eminence — was transported:

"Twenty thousand people saw the Derby run. The grandstand was a monster hillside of beautiful costumes and shining faces. From the field it looked like a huge waterfall of color, from which at intervals came a roar not unlike that which one hears at Niagara.

"The beauty and manhood of Kentucky and Tennessee were there, each waiting the result with bated breath and distended nostrils. Between the sand and the fence the space was black with men who prayed to all their paternosters that their choices might win. Beyond the stand and lawn, perched like blackbirds on everything which would give them a foothold and an uninterrupted vision, were men and boys, many thousands of them, stretching around the track almost as far as the eye could reach.

"To the left and right and in the field were gayly bedecked fashionable carriages and traps, their oc-

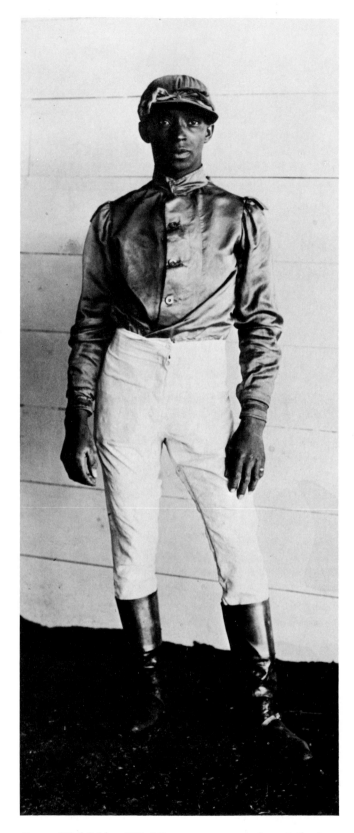

Jimmy Winkfield — "Wink" — as a young jockey at the turn of the century when he rode successive Derby winners His Eminence (1901), and Alan-a-Dale (1902). He has the best winning average in Kentucky Derby history — two victories, one second, and one third in four starts.

Winkfield on Alan-a-Dale.

cupants' gowns shimmering in the sunlight. It was one of the finest looking crowds ever seen on a race track.

"They were at the post only a short time — only four minutes. There was a little jockeying for positions, one false break; they were called back and lined up again. Then there was a flash of yellow and red, a long hoarse roar from the thousands packed in the stands and here they came, five good colts, closely bunched, with the black nose of Alard Scheck showing slightly in front.

"Before the colts had gone fifty yards, Winkfield had moved his charge up to first position, and as they passed the stand, His Eminence was a half-length in front of Scheck, while Driscoll had also moved up and was only a neck behind, with a length between him and Amur, Sannazarro bringing up the rear. They ran the first eighth in :13, and passed to the quarter in :25 1/2.

"His Eminence was beautifully rated by Jockey Winkfield, the colored boy . . ."[1]

Wink's first of two successive Derby wins was a cakewalk. His victory with Alan-a-Dale was another matter.

Alan-a-Dale was a "bad-legged" horse. So bad, that his owner dared not give the colt a pre-Derby race at age three for fear he would break down. Much of the colt's training took place in a sulky. A rider worked the horse out only when a speed drill was absolutely necessary. Alan-a-Dale had abundant speed, however.

A lot of Derby history is wrapped up in Alan-a-Dale. The colt was by Halma, winner of the 1895 Derby and the first Derby winner to sire a Derby winner. The colt's owner was Major Thomas C. McDowell, great-grandson of Henry Clay, and the animal was the third Derby winner to be foaled at "Ashland," Clay's ancestral home. The others were Day Star in 1878, and Riley in 1890.

A second McDowell horse, The Rival, was entered in the four-horse race. Alan-a-Dale was by far the faster of the two when his legs were functioning, and Winkfield used guile to obtain the mount. Major McDowell had contracted with Nash Turner, a prominent white jockey of the day, to ride one of his

35

entries, promising Turner he could have his choice. Winkfield was working both horses out in the mornings coming up to the Derby. He let The Rival run on, doing a mile and a quarter in about 2:09 most of the time. He held Alan-a-Dale back, never letting the horse go better than about 2:11. When Turner arrived in Louisville the morning of the race he chose The Rival. The favorite was a horse called Abe Frank; the fourth was Inventor, the long shot.

Nineteen-o-three was the first year an elastic web barrier was used to start the Derby. The first crude mechanical starting gates did not appear until 1930. The webbing was stretched across the track in front of the horses and attached to metal poles. Once the horses were in a reasonable alignment, the starter hit a button and the webbing flew up and out of the horses' way. They often plunged through the webbing before the break, tearing strands, and the assistant starter would have to tie the loose ends together.

"The Churchill Downs track in those days was covered by deep sand. Before a meeting the ground crew would push it to the outside, providing good running room along the rail but doubling the hazards outside. Winkfield made good use of the sand that day . . .

" 'Nash Turner led past the stands, but then I moved up on the turn and went into the lead by maybe three, four lengths goin' down the backstretch. Nash Turner was watchin' Coburn, the boy on Abe Frank, and Coburn was watchin' Nash, and nobody was payin' much attention to me. I guess I went those first two quarters in about 25 apiece, and then I got ahold of him; I worried about those legs.

" 'So I was coastin' in front there, goin' around the turn, and I felt him beginnin' to bobble, gettin' weak in the legs. I still had a length at the 3/8 pole, but I was really holdin' him now, tryin' to save him . . .

" 'So when the favorite come up on my shoulder I rode him out into that deep sand; it told on him, and he stopped. The other two horses tried to come inside me, but I ducked back on the rail; when they tried to come around I took them outside, too, both at once. Just a little, you know, enough to get 'em in that sand. And that's all that saved me. Alan-a-Dale got across the finish line by a nose, and he pulled up lame. Never raced again that year.'

"The time was 2:08 3/4 and Major McDowell gave Winkfield and Turner $1,000 apiece . . ."[2]

The following year, Winkfield missed a chance to become the only jockey in Derby history to win three *successive* Derbies and tie Murphy's record of three victories overall. He rode a bad race on a horse called Early, going to the front too soon, then relaxing, only to have a sore-heeled colt named Judge Himes slip past

him on the rail. When he finally saw Judge Himes coming, he tried to rouse his colt, but it was too late and he lost by three quarters of a length. His defeat upset him terribly, and recent visitors to Maisons-Laffitte say it still pops up in the conversation of the frail little old man with the slightly bowed legs and strong hands.

The *Courier-Journal* of May 3, 1903, carried this account:

"Jimmy Winkfield was heartbroken at his defeat, and blamed himself and not the horse. The little Negro had counted on winning the Derby . . .

" 'I made my run too soon,' he said, leaning wearily up against the railing in the jockeys' room while, as he talked, his voice broke and tears welled in his eyes. 'I wanted to win for the boss and had I followed instructions I would have won.

" 'We got off nicely and Early rated along just as I wanted him to, behind Woodlake and Bad News. I knew all the time that they would not stick, and Early was ready to go to the front whenever I called on him. Rounding the far turn, I made the fatal mistake and let out a rap. Early went right along, but Helgerson on Woodlake swung wide and left an opening on the rail for Judge Himes. Had I waited, I could have turned in there myself, and Judge Himes would have had to run around me. When I made my run I counted on Helgerson and Davis closing in behind me. When Judge Himes came alongside, Early simply did not have enough left to stall him off . . .' "

Winkfield lamented to a visitor in the early 1960s: "When that boy come to me at the 16th pole, I could have fouled him a little; I was a big favorite and they'd never disqualified me, not in that race . . ."[3]

Like Eddie Arcaro in his early days, Winkfield had a sharp eye for the main chance, and he went where the most money was, without thinking of the future. In the fall of 1903, he had promised to ride a horse for John E. Madden. When a bigger payment was offered him to ride the favorite in the race, he told Madden he'd forgotten and promised to ride for someone else. Winkfield finished up the track, the Madden horse came in third. After the race, Madden told Winkfield he didn't like to be double-crossed and that his name was going to be mud around the racetrack. When Winkfield got a chance to ride in Russia some months later, he went.

"I was tops in Russia," says Winkfield.[4]

He rode for noblemen and oil magnates in pre-Revolutionary times, winning a lot of races for them. Winkfield was good, the Russian jockeys were not, and owners quickly recognized the difference. Czar Nicholas had a small stable, horses of poor quality in Winkfield's view, and a reputation for paying poorly, so the black American never rode for the Czar, though legend has it that he did. Winkfield luxuriated in a suite in Moscow's National Hotel, developing and indulging a taste for caviar for breakfast. Weight was never a serious problem for him.

He was associated longest and most successfully with Michel Lazzareff, an oil man, first in Russia, and later in France after both owner and jockey had fled the Communists.

Winkfield was racing in Odessa on the Black Sea on April 4, 1919. When he heard the boom of artillery in the distance, indicating the Communists were on the move, he figured Odessa was no place for a boy from Chilesburg, Kentucky, to be. With a nobleman or two and other racing men and their families he left for Bucharest, bringing about two hundred thoroughbreds with him. After many adventures, Winkfield reached Warsaw on June 29 and promptly began riding races there. About one fourth of the racehorses he'd brought with him were either eaten en route or suffered other fates. He eventually made his way to France.

Winkfield quit riding in 1930 at forty-eight and became a successful trainer. Once again, he had to flee. When the Germans invaded France, he escaped to the United States, where he worked for Pete Bostwick in Aiken, South Carolina, for a while and then did some training. One day he gave a mount to a hungry young apprentice at Charles Town racetrack in West Virginia. His name was William Hartack, who is now tied with Eddie Arcaro for the most Derby winners — five.

Winkfield's son Robert is also a trainer. The two, and his son's family, live in the pleasant enclave in Maisons-Laffitte in the shade of chestnut trees. They have box stalls for nearly thirty horses, lush green lawns, and half-a-dozen racetracks are within easy driving distance. Wink is a happy man. When asked about his greatest racing thrill, he responds: the two Derby victories nearly seventy-five years ago when he was a cocky young kid from Chilesburg, Kentucky.

Isaac Murphy's life, on the other hand, was short, his last years sad ones. He was called "the colored Archer" for Fred Archer, the rider who dominated the English turf during the 1870s and 1880s. In some ways the comparison was apt, in others not. Archer was known as a "tin-scraper," meaning that money was an obsession with him, and when he rode, he punished his mounts severely with spur and whip. In this sense, he was quite unlike Murphy, who was as willing to ride for a poor owner as a rich one, and who was celebrated for sparing his horses, rarely using the whip. But Archer was a man who combined great sensitivity with a furious will to win, and in this respect the two men were similar.

The lives of both men ended early and tragically and for the same reasons: Their bodies were ravaged by the rigors of making weight at a time when scientific dieting methods were unknown. Archer took a physic that left him wasted and depressed. He shot himself in 1886 at age twenty-nine. Murphy's weight soared from around 100 pounds to 130 and 140 pounds in off season. When wasted from reducing, he would take champagne to perk himself up, and this led to a fondness that, combined with his weak physical condition, left him prey to illness. In 1896, at thirty-five, he died of pneumonia. Though he left his childless wife $30,000, most of the money was absorbed by debts, and she ended up in a pauper's grave.

Murphy's funeral was one of the biggest in Lexing-

Wink, seventy-nine, at his training center in Maisons-Laffitte, a few miles outside Paris. He is now in his nineties.

Jean Marquis for SPORTS ILLUSTRATED © Time Inc.

ton's history — white or "colored." Five hundred people of both races, including many prominent racing men, attended. He was buried in "Old No. 2" cemetery in Lexington. In time, the cemetery became neglected; vines crept over the crosses and headstones. For decades, Murphy's gravesite was lost, known only to a few old Negroes. After a three-year search, the gravesite was uncovered by the late Frank B. Borries, Jr., a Lexington writer, and six years later the jockey's remains were reburied in a Lexington park near the grave of Man o' War. Eddie Arcaro, whose lifetime winning average was a high 22 percent, presided at the ceremonies and said he doubted whether any jockey would ever come close to Murphy's 44 percent winning average. Arcaro said, too, that he would be proud to be buried beside Murphy one day.

Some purists argue that Murphy's percentage derives from his own records, and because of the sometimes haphazard record-keeping in that time, they cannot be verified. Others note that what records there are confirm Murphy's claims, and his most outstanding characteristic was honesty. The debate would appear irrelevant. Murphy was undoubtedly one of the great jockeys of American racing history.

Isaac Burns Murphy was born Isaac Burns on January 1, 1861, on the David Tanner Farm in Fayette County, Kentucky. His father James Burns was a freeman and a bricklayer who joined the Union forces and died as a prisoner of war. His mother was a laundress in the employ of Richard Owings, of Owings and Williams racing stable. In 1874, the seventy-pound Isaac started galloping horses for the Owings and Williams stable, then was trained by "Uncle Eli" Jordan, a black.

The first horse Isaac climbed aboard was appropriately named Volcano and tossed Isaac off. Isaac's mother changed his name to Murphy, in honor of her father with whom she lived after her husband's death. Isaac was riding races in 1875, the year of the Derby's inaugural. His first winning ride came aboard a mare named Glentina at the Crab Orchard track, where horses were raced in frontier days. His first big stakes victory came aboard a horse named Vera Cruz at Churchill Downs in 1877. He was on his way.

Murphy rode Buchanan to victory in the 1884 Derby, Riley in 1890, and Kingman in 1891, his last win a record in that it was the slowest Derby ever run at one and a half miles: 2:52 1/4. The time was seventeen seconds slower than Spokane's record and is the equivalent of running today's one-and-a-quarter-mile Derby in 2:17.

After the 1891 race, known as "the walking Derby," Kingman's black trainer and half-owner Dudley Allen explained what had happened: "I told Murphy to 'lay' for Balgowan. I told him if Balgowan walked, then he was to walk. And he came near doing it."[5]

The trainers of the other three horses were also giving their riders instructions to stay off the pace at all cost. Consequently, the four horses galloped around the course, sometimes four abreast like a cavalry troupe. A fourth of a mile from the finish, Balgowan's jockey broke ranks and drove for the finish, but Murphy was with him and went on to win.

Murphy's record of three Kentucky Derbies was not equaled until 1930 when Earle Sande came home with Gallant Fox and was not surpassed until 1948 when Eddie Arcaro won the fourth of his five Derbies, on Citation.

Though Murphy is remembered today for his Kentucky Derby record, he won other races that were more important at the time than the Louisville classic. He won five Latonia Derbies and four of the first five American Derbies in Chicago. He won the Swift, the Travers, Saratoga Cup, and celebrated match races in which he rode Salvator to victory over Tenny, with Ed "Snapper" Garrison, the great whip rider, aboard.

Murphy had a positively uncanny sense of pace. He rode with long stirrups and sat his saddle "like a black dart." He tried not to take more out of a horse than was needed to get the job done — and he frightened many owners, for this method led to hairbreadth finishes.

"A horse could jump straight up and down, yet Murphy never raised off his back," said one contemporary.[6] "He seemed part of the horse," was another description. "He would just lay down on his mount's neck and bring him home."[7]

Murphy's personality was pleasing, and he was said to be totally incorruptible. "Isaac could have made enough to buy a Bluegrass farm if he would have agreed to lose on Falsetto in the Kenner Stakes of 1879."[8]

Murphy once said to a jockey with an unsavory reputation: "You just ride to win. They get you to pull a horse in a selling race, and when it comes to a stake race, they get Isaac to ride. A jockey that'll sell out to one man will sell out to another. Just be honest and you'll have no trouble and plenty of money."[9]

On more than one occasion he reported to the stewards when he found himself on a "dead" one, a horse that had been drugged to slow down.

Murphy was both a smart and brave rider.

"Probably he never rode a more courageous finish than on Falsetto in the Phoenix Hotel Stakes at Lexington in the spring of 1879 when he drove his horse out of a pocket through a narrow opening between Ada Glenn and Scully, and won by a neck on the post."[10]

In a race at St. Louis on June 11, 1884, he went

Isaac "Ike" Murphy and friends at a clambake in the 1890s. The great black jockey rode Derby winners Buchanan (1884), Riley (1890), and Kingman (1891).

down with Bonnie Australian after a horse named Fishburn ran across in front of him. Revoke's jockey was badly injured, and Murphy succeeded in dragging him under the rail just in time.

Murphy probably never rode a smarter race than the American Derby of 1886 when he was aboard a horse named Silver Cloud who was given little chance. Murphy was running along in the ruck on the backstretch when he sensed the pace was slow and, as he put it later in an interview, "The notion struck me to send him to the front if that were possible. I struck him twice with my whip and before the other jockeys realized it, Silver Cloud was 10 lengths in the lead. The other riders set sail for us at once, but Silver Cloud was a race horse, that day, at least, and was drawing away at every stride, winning an easy race by a dozen lengths. The bookmakers cleaned up everything on that race. I don't think as much as $25 was bet on Silver Cloud."

No jockey in modern times has been held in the adulation that Murphy was. According to the *Courier-Journal* on May 15, 1891:

"Isaac Murphy, who piloted Riley to such a great victory, is a quiet, polite young man, who never made a bet in his life, never swore, and never was caught telling a lie. His integrity and honor are the pride of the turf, and many of the best horsemen pronounce him the greatest jockey that ever mounted a horse.

"His face, like a Sphinx carved out of ivory, is familiar on every racetrack in America . . . It is hardly an exaggeration to say that Murphy is the greatest judge of pace this country ever saw.

" 'I asked him to ride my horse Ban Fox at St. Louis,' said Jack Chinn to some friends when Murphy's name was mentioned. It was the time that Bankrupt was sweeping everything before him, and I asked Murphy if he thought he could beat Bankrupt in the race next day.

" ' "What can your horse do the distance in?" ' he asked me. 'I told him he could run the three-quarters — that was the distance — in 1:14 1/2.' ' "If he can do that I can win," ' said he, ' "because Bankrupt can't do it. I have watched the horse closely, and I believe if you head him off, he is a quitter." '

" 'The next day I took Murphy out and gave him instructions. He was to make the first quarter in :24 1/2, the half in :49, and the three-quarters in 1:14 1/2. Well, I put my trainer at the quarter with his watch and I stood at the half with my own. Bankrupt as usual shot out in the lead, and Ban Fox followed him two or three lengths behind.

" 'As Ban Fox passed the quarter my trainer looked at his watch. It was just 24 1/2. Coming by me, Bankrupt was still well in front and that black machine sitting on Ban Fox was sitting like a log. I glanced at my watch. It was just :49 to the dot. In the last quarter he closed up on Brankrupt, passed him, and came under the string an easy winner. I looked at the time when it was hung up. It was just 1:14 1/2.' "

Murphy had started downhill in 1890. In 1889, he had ridden 58 winners out of 195 mounts, but in 1890, he had only accepted 38 mounts, 13 of which were winners. The critical turning point came during a race at Monmouth Park on August 26, 1890, when he was charged with drunkenness while aboard a horse named Firenzi. Murphy's defense was that he was not drunk, he was weak from losing weight. Many turfmen came to his defense, and the theory was put forward that he had been drugged, a theory he came to believe as the years went by. But he never got over the incident, and he rode fewer and fewer mounts in his last years as his battle with the scales grew fiercer.

The *New York Times* of August 27, 1890, published this account:

"A popular idol was shattered at Monmouth Park yesterday. That Isaac Murphy, who has always been considered the most gentlemanly as well as the most honest of jockeys, should have made such an exhibition of himself as he did was past belief. He rode Firenzi in the Monmouth Handicap, and that he did so was alone the reason for the ridiculous way in which she was beaten, finishing last in a field of horses that she should have defeated with but little trouble.

"Murphy's trouble is probably due to the fact that on Sunday last he fell into the clutches of a gang of politicians who call themselves the Salvator Club. This crowd belongs in this city and includes a lot of the fixed stars of the political firmament. Loading a car and themselves up with liquor they went to Eatontown and at Chestnut Grove had a clambake with a liquid annex . . . These roysterers called themselves the Salvator Club because they had won a lot of money backing Salvator in his races this year . . . To Isaac Murphy who had ridden him, they gave a fine silver-mounted whip. There was drinking and toasting galore as usually accompanies such an affair . . ."

During the race, says the account, Murphy pulled the mare's head this way and that "and hauled her all over the track . . . Murphy's pitiful attempts to ride Firenzi culminated just after the mare passed the judges' stand last when she should have been first. He could not keep her straight, and she bolted over to the inner fence. Murphy had strength enough left to prevent a collision. That was all. As soon as he had practically stopped her, what strength he had was gone and he fell out of the saddle in a heap on the track . . ."

Eighteen ninety-five was his last year of racing. He won only two of twenty starts.

Trainer L. P. Tarlton, writing about Murphy in *The Thoroughbred Record* in the spring of 1896 after the jockey's death, said:

"In person, Isaac was about five feet in height, with short, straight legs, and long sinewy arms, and in full life would weigh about 130 pounds. He had a brown skin, with thin lips and straight nose. He countenance was open, with a happy, intelligent expression, almost childlike in its innocence, and in talking he looked you straight in the face with large, wide-open eyes, that seemed to say you can trust me and I will trust you . . .

"He went when a mere child to the race course with all its temptations and was there the recipient of most flattering and head-turning success. Yet with all its allurements he was truthful; did not bet or have others bet for him; or use oaths; or, until the last few years, intoxicant drinks, which was then begun to aid his strength against the exertions of 'reducing' necessary to his profession . . ."

Tarlton concluded: "One competent to judge said a few years ago: 'I have seen all the great jockeys of England and this country for years back, but, all in all, Isaac Murphy is the greatest of them all.' I believe the consensus . . . of racing men will confirm that conclusion."[11]

Chapter 6
Black Gold

THE FIFTIETH RUNNING of the Derby in 1924 was the most romanticized of them all. Black Gold, "the Indian horse," won it. Central to that Derby was a race between two cheap horses at a dusty fairgrounds in Chickasha, Oklahoma, in May 1909. Most of the crowd was Indian. Running were Black Gold's dam, Useeit, a green two-year-old, and Belle Thompson, a well-traveled old mare. Useeit was owned by a local man; Belle Thompson by Ben A. Jones, a Missourian who would go on to train six Kentucky Derby winners and whose son would train two more.

Useeit was little more than a pony; a "chunky little speedball" in the words of her jockey. Useeit could fly, but five furlongs was her absolute limit. Belle Thompson was a big, long-striding animal. When the flag dropped, Useeit sped away in front, churning up clouds of hot dust as the Chickasaw and Cherokees whooped and tossed their stovepipe hats in the air. At the quarter mile, Belle Thompson caught the mare and went on to win in a hard drive.

Standing quietly among the Indians was Al Hoots, a small-time rancher from Skiatook, north of Tulsa, a community that had been part of the Indian Territory until 1907, when it had been absorbed into the new state of Oklahoma. Hoots was a tall, dark Irishman who looked more Indian than his wife Rosa, an Osage. Like Rosa, he was shy and quiet. Hoots had raced quarter horses and a thoroughbred or two on the leaky roof circuit around Oklahoma. Despite Useeit's defeat, Hoots was smitten; he had seen his dream horse.

Hoots bought the mud-brown filly on the spot for eighty acres of cattle land. It was a costly, risky proposition, but one he would never regret. Moreover, two years later, a small oil field came in at Skiatook and Al and Rosa Hoots were among those to receive a comfortable income thereafter from oil

leases. The Indians had a phrase for the crude petroleum wealth bubbling up from the earth. They called it "black gold."

Bred in Oklahoma by wealthy rancher C. B. Campbell, Useeit was by Bonnie Joe out of Effie M by Bowling Green, a bloodline characterized by turf historian John Hervey as "almost the nadir of the unfashionable."[1] Unfashionable perhaps, but the Bonnie Joes could ever more run; they were prominent throughout the Southwest as sprinters. They were also durable. Useeit raced 122 times between 1909 and 1916, sometimes under lease to others. She ran in Calgary, Juarez, Louisville, New Orleans, and all over the Southwest. She won thirty-four races, finished in the money another thirty-eight times, and ran unplaced fifty times. Useeit took the track against Pan Zareta, a celebrated race mare from Sweetwater, Texas, but she wasn't in Pan Zareta's class. Few were.

Useeit attracted a large following because of her small size and big heart. She always gave her best. One day in New Orleans she caught the eye of Colonel Edward Riley Bradley. Bradley liked speedy broodmares, and he told Hoots to get in touch when he was ready to breed Useeit.

Useeit's career ended abruptly on February 22, 1916, when the mare ran fifth in the fifth at Juarez, an $800 claiming race. A man named Tobey Ramsey claimed Useeit and sent his groom around to Hoots's barn to fetch her. Hoots reportedly grabbed a rifle from his tack room and chased the groom away. Why Hoots had risked losing his beloved mare in a claiming race is unclear. There was probably a gentleman's agreement not to claim the mare, for Hoots was a respected man and his devotion to Useeit was common knowledge. In any event, Hoots refused to honor Ramsey's claim, an unheard-of action. Instead, he loaded Useeit aboard an Oklahoma-bound boxcar and climbed aboard with her. The Juarez stewards had no alternative but to rule Hoots and Useeit from the turf indefinitely.

Persistent Derby myth has it that as Hoots lay dying the next year in Skiatook, he had a vision: Useeit would go to the court of Black Toney, Colonel Bradley's great stallion in whose veins flowed the blood of Domino. The result of that union would win the Kentucky Derby.

Black Toney, in truth, was but one of several prominent stallions that Hoots had ambitiously selected for his mare before he died. Useeit was first bred to Ivan the Terrible, then standing in Tennessee. Rosa named the colt Tulsa. Then Useeit had a filly, Tuscola, by the Kentucky stallion Jack Atkin. Both won races for Rosa.

Not until 1920 did Rosa ship Useeit to Bradley's famous Idle Hour Stock Farm on the Old Frankfort Pike in Lexington. There Useeit was bred to Black Toney. On February 17, 1921, Useeit gave birth to a colt in an open meadow on the Horace N. Davis Farm across the pike from the Bradley acreage, now occupied by John W. Galbreath's Darby Dan Farm. From the outset, Bradley took a keen, fatherly interest in Rosa Hoots's colt. He must have influenced Rosa's choice of a name, for the Bradley horses were all given names beginning with the letter "B" and she named her colt Black Gold.

Hoots's trainer during Useeit's last racing years was Hanley Webb, and in the spring of 1922 Rosa sent Webb to Lexington to guide Black Gold's destiny. Webb's origins are obscure. He had been a lawman before joining Hoots to help with the Hereford cattle on the ranch and the horses at the track. When he took over as Black Gold's trainer, he was an old, lonely man, and a hard drinker; a stocky, bowlegged individual with a cigar invariably clamped between toothless gums.

In the early 1920s, the American turf was in a stage of transition. There had been a period of restrictive legislation, and racing was in the eve of a tremendous expansion. But it was still a primitive business, especially in the Southwest. Purses were small, the competition fierce. Hanley Webb was a caricature of the times. In his own way, he was fond of Black Gold. But he trained and raced his horses brutally hard. He'd sometimes send a horse to the post three or more times in one week. He ignored their ailments. Webb, it was said, trained thoroughbreds as though they were mustangs.

Olin Gentry, Colonel Bradley's farm manager for many years and now at Darby Dan, recalls that when Black Gold was a three-year-old in training at Churchill Downs he ran a nail into an already sore right forefoot. Bradley heard about it and as a courtesy sent his veterinary by to give the colt a tetanus shot. The old man wouldn't hear of it. Gentry is blunt. "Webb was the world's worst horseman."

In those days, jockeys thought little of grabbing one another's saddle cloths to throw horses off stride. Cal Shilling, a top jockey of the time, could ride three horses in one race according to legend: a horse in each hand, and his own. Shilling was eventually ruled off the turf for life. Jockeys rode each other into the rail. They "herded" the favorite. They pulled horses. When caught, they took their suspensions in silence. It was all part of the game.

Shortly after Black Gold was weaned, Webb showed up in Lexington. To everyone's surprise, he removed the colt from the Davis farm and installed him in a barn at the Kentucky Association racetrack in Lexington. Then Webb moved into an adjoining stall, and sawed a big hole through the wall so that he could keep his eye on Black Gold.

Webb started immediately exercising the weanling on a lunge line in a small lot where the colt was to spend the rest of his first year, a startling contrast to the flowing, white-fenced meadows of the great breeding farms surrounding Lexington where Black Gold's peers were gamboling. When the time came to break the colt, Webb sent for an Indian ranch hand of Rosa's named Chief Johnson. The Indian moved in with Webb, sleeping in a blanket on the dirt floor of the stall.

Black Gold always proved too much for Johnson to handle. Time and again the colt ran away with the Indian. On the theory that it would render the horse easier to handle, Webb had Johnson work Black Gold the wrong way around the track. Webb sent Black Gold on extraordinarily long gallops for a soft-boned yearling. Kentucky horsemen shook their heads. Yet Black Gold thrived.

On January 8, 1923, Black Gold ran for the first time at the Fair Grounds in New Orleans and won. Black Gold would meet his death at the same track five years hence, almost to the day. He kept winning. As the year wore on, however, the colt's record became uneven. He would win a race, then lose one he should have won. Black Gold's racing luck was consistently — some thought suspiciously — bad, his rider getting caught in jam-ups or failing to get away smartly at the start.

Watching Black Gold's erratic performance with gathering interest was John "J.D." Mooney, a New Orleans jockey whose brother Joe was also a rider. Mooney sensed that Black Gold was the greatest horse he had ever seen or was ever likely to see. He had ridden for Webb, but they had had a minor falling-out. Nevertheless, Mooney started angling for the mount

"Black Gold was on everyone's list of the top dozen or so two-year-olds."

on Black Gold, sending his agent Slim Stewart around to talk with Webb. The old man said he wasn't interested in changing jocks.

If Mooney had any doubts about Black Gold's class, they were erased by the colt's performance in the Bashford Manor Stakes at Churchill Downs on May 19, 1923, the day that Earle Sande won the Derby on Zev. Caught again in racing traffic, Black Gold fell to his knees, recovered, made up a prodigious amount of ground, and whipped a topflight field of two-year-olds.

On the next outing, Black Gold lost.

Mooney's father-in-law was Jim Heffering, a wealthy Canadian owner who raced in New Orleans every winter. Heffering had been nice to Webb and the old man liked him. When Heffering suggested that Mooney be given a chance to ride Black Gold, Webb finally acquiesced. He would remain loyal to Mooney thereafter, for Mooney and Black Gold were perfectly matched.

Like Al Hoots and Hanley Webb, Mooney stemmed from humble origins. He was the son of an Irish riverboat man on the Mississippi who had died when J.D. was a child. As a boy, J.D. had gone on the racetrack. And while he never became a name rider like Sande or Mack Garner or Albert Johnson, he could acquit himself well in their company. If they tried any rough stuff, he gave as good as he got.

In November, Mooney booted Black Gold home first in a race at Churchill Downs to wind up the colt's eleven-month, eighteen-race campaign. The Black Toney–Useeit colt had won nine races, placed second five times, and third twice. He had been out of the money twice. His earnings were a modest $19,163, the Bashford Manor being his only stakes victory.

Black Gold was on everyone's list of the top dozen or so two-year-olds. But 1923 was a vintage year, and at least three colts were ranked higher. They were Mrs. William K. Vanderbilt's Sarazen, winner of all ten of his races; George D. Widener's St. James, winner of the big juvenile stakes at Saratoga over the summer; and T. C. Bradley's Wise Counsellor, a late-bloomer hitting his peak in the fall. When the Kentucky Derby winter book was announced in February 1924, these three were favorites at ten to one. Black Gold was thirty to one. As fate would have it, Sarazen, St. James, and Wise Counsellor would all be scratched before Derby time, and Black Gold would go off the heavy favorite.

On March 6, 1924, Black Gold won the first of six straight races when he opened his three-year-old campaign at Jefferson Park in New Orleans. A week later, Black Gold cantered postward through a driving rain for the Louisiana Derby. All the jockeys wore mud pants except Mooney, who cockily wore his whites. When the webbing flew up, Mooney gunned the colt to the front from his outside post position. Once well clear of the thundering field, he slanted over to the rail, weaving back and forth to splatter slop on those in his wake. Then he clucked to Black Gold, felt the stallion's eager surge, and left the field far behind, his pants an impertinent white blur in the gathering murk. Webb shipped to Churchill Downs where Black Gold won another race.

Mooney was now devoting full-time to the colt. Lest a suspension find him grounded at Derby time, Mooney refused to accept any riding engagements. He was at the barn at first light to work the colt. Gradually, he won Webb around to more orthodox training methods. No longer was Black Gold rocketing the wrong way around the track with a frantic Indian on his back trying to hold him.

One day, Black Gold began to favor his left foreleg. Mooney anxiously examined the colt's hoof, then the leg for tenderness or swelling. He found none. Once running, the colt appeared to be all right. Mooney pleaded with Webb to call in a veterinary and a blacksmith. Webb refused. He felt, as usual, it was a mistake to coddle a horse. What Black Gold needed, he said, was more work not less. Mooney was worried sick.

Despite their differences and the strain of handling a Derby horse, the tough little Irishman and the stubborn Oklahoman remained friends. The jockey and his wife Marjorie had dinner with the old man whenever possible. Mrs. Mooney sensed a desperate loneliness beneath Webb's brusque manner.

On the backstretch, horsemen ridiculed Webb. They said that Black Gold simply proved the adage that "a good horse is dangerous in any man's hands." As for Mooney, some considered him "bush."

A Churchill Downs official called Webb into his office one day to inquire whether Black Gold, undoubtedly "the hot favorite" by post time, shouldn't have a name rider? "If Mooney don't ride him, the horse don't run," said Webb.

As Derby Day, May 17, approached, Black Gold's odds kept dropping, his soreness increasing. Even so,

he won the Derby Trial a few days before the big race. Trotting back to the stands, Black Gold limped slightly. A turf writer noted this in his account of the race next day. Few paid attention. Sarazen, St. James, and Wise Counsellor were all out of it now for various reasons. Black Gold was the favorite.

Many still refused to take the Indian horse seriously, for a big field of nineteen would go to the post, more than half of them from fashionable eastern stables. The high-flying Rancocas Stable of oil man Harry Sinclair and his trainer-partner Sam Hildreth had the second-choice entry of Mad Play, Laverne Fator up, and Bracadale, Earle Sande up. The famous light blue and Eton brown silks of Harry Payne Whitney would be worn by Ivan Parke on Klondyke and Pony McAtee on Transmute. Colonel Bradley believed that Black Gold was pounds the best but entered three thoroughbreds, Beau Butler, Baffling, and Bob Tail. Other good horses in the race were the bay Chilhowee, owned by the Gallaher brothers of Lexington, C. B. Head's Altawood, and H. C. Fisher's Mr. Mutt.

Black Gold drew the rail post position, then came Transmute, Klondyke, King Gorin, Revenue Agent, Thorndale, Altawood, Cannon Shot, Mad Play, Beau Butler, Wild Aster, Bracadale, Chilhowee, Bob Tail, Diogenes, Modest, Mr. Mutt, Baffling, and Nautical.

Rosa Hoots arrived in Louisville twenty-four hours before the Derby, a tall, motherly figure of great natural dignity. With Marjorie Mooney for company, she spent Derby eve in a tack room near Black Gold's stall.

Special trains from Chicago, Philadelphia, and New York rolled into town, transforming the railroad yards into a convivial colony of private cars alive with the clink of bourbon glasses. Others came by automobile, by boat down the Ohio River, and some even came by airplane.

Derby Day broke with somber, low-hanging clouds. A crowd that would swell to 80,000 started drifting into the rickety old stands, which had been expanded and refurbished for the Golden Jubilee Kentucky Derby.

In a sense, Bradley couldn't lose. If Black Gold won the Derby, it would reflect great credit upon his stallion Black Toney.

Later in the day, Hildreth and Harry Sinclair bet $10,000 in the pari-mutuels that Bracadale would finish third — a bet they never cashed, thanks to one of the more bizarre officiating mix-ups in Derby history.

The last race before the Derby was run and the blanketed Derby horses materialized on the backstretch across from the stands, filed around the clubhouse turn toward the paddock, grooms at their heads.

In the paddock, the time-honored pageant repeated itself, owners and trainers leaning down to talk with cocky little men in shimmering silks. Mooney stood silently with Webb and Chief Johnson. There was nothing to say. As the jockey aboard the eight to five favorite, he could expect to be the target of the other riders. In the Derby, then as now, the rule was anything goes, or as horsemen put it, "You take your best holt." Mooney would have to avoid trouble, especially in the stampede from the starting post.

The bugler blew "First Call" shortly after 4:30 P.M. Trainers gave riders a leg up. The little men adjusted their caps, knotted their reins, and tugged nervously at soft leather boots. Some stood up in their irons to test the stirrup lengths. Then they moved out of the paddock toward the alleyway between the grandstand and the clubhouse. Because Chilhowee had been plunging and rearing in the paddock, a pony man led him first, out of turn. Then came Black Gold, followed by the rest of the horses in their post-position order. The sun was now shining, only a few light clouds troubling the deep blue sky. A breeze played with the freshly planted flowers in the infield. The track was fast. The moment Chilhowee and the lead pony emerged into the sunlight from the alleyway and stepped into the open toward the track the crowd cheered and the band struck up "My Old Kentucky Home." The horses paraded to the right. At the clubhouse turn they wheeled slowly around. Most of the riders stood up in their irons and encouraged a canter or a brief run down through the corridor of sound between the grandstand and the thousands of persons lining the inside rail in the infield.

At the starting post near the turn into the home-stretch, the riders played the traditional game. "No chance, sir!" they shouted to starter Billy Snyder as they jockeyed for advantage. "No chance for *Chris-sakes!*" Diogenes suddenly broke through the webbing and had to be led back. Black Gold was jostled out of position by milling, keyed-up thoroughbreds. Black Gold, too, was led back to the rail by an assistant starter. The horses had been at the post just a few minutes when Snyder saw his chance: Nineteen noses were all pointed up track in a raggedy line. "Come on!" he shouted, springing the webbing.

The thoroughbreds bolted forward, their hoofbeats like distant thunder above the sound of the crowd. McAtee had Transmute away first, then came Sande who angled Bracadale over sharply to the inside, slamming Black Gold into the rail so hard that the crowd moaned. Mooney instantly steadied the favorite. But by now the jocks on Baffling, Chilhowee, and Green-tree Stable's Wild Aster had boxed him in; Mooney would have to bide his time as their prisoner for more than a quarter of a mile.

Sande had seized the lead going into the clubhouse turn with McAtee and Transmute tucked in behind him. Then came Black Gold and his unwanted escorts, followed by the rest of the field. Beau Butler, almost left at the post, was far back. The horse would never catch the leaders. As they streamed into the five-fur-long backstretch, Bracadale was running easily on the lead with the wind at his back. Mooney found a sudden opening and escaped from his box, but he was running a poor sixth at this stage and his partisans were losing heart. Bracadale passed the half-mile pole still in the lead. Baffling and Wild Aster were now falling back. Chilhowee was making his move, and far back, Black Gold was seen starting to thread his way forward. Flying into the far turn, Bracadale was on top, Chilhowee second, and Black Gold third. Altawood had started a strong move, and Transmute was right with him. Turning for home, Chilhowee was at Bracadale's throat, but Bracadale refused to quit. Black Gold was closing fast on the outside, Mooney riding like a demon. Altawood and Transmute were on Black Gold's heels.

A handful of photographers suddenly rushed out onto the track down near the finish line. Black Gold, frightened, lost stride. Mooney reached back and smacked him with his bat. Black Gold came on again. Less than 100 yards from the end, Black Gold thrust his nose, then his neck, then his withers ahead of Chilhowee. He flashed under the wire a half-length winner. Chilhowee led Bracadale by a neck. Another neck separated Altawood and Transmute.

A tremendous ovation greeted Black Gold and J. D. Mooney as the colt trotted back to the winner's circle, neck arched like a war-horse, ears sensitively pricked, his head swinging right and left as though to take everything in. Webb grabbed Black Gold's bridle and led him through the crowd. Two men came forward with the blanket of roses.

When Sande arrived back with Bracadale, he stared in disbelief at the results on the odds board in the infield. He thought he had finished second, yet he hadn't even been placed third, Beau Butler had. Beau Butler had finished back in the pack. Bracadale was placed fifth behind Altawood and ahead of Transmute. The placing judges had been confused by the similarity in the Bradley and Rancocas silks, both white trimmed with green in slightly different patterns. This was before the advent of the photo-finish camera, and although the Rancocas people complained bitterly for weeks, the official results were never corrected.

By evening, quiet had returned to the backstretch. Webb was alone in his tack room drinking heavily. He had announced that Black Gold came out of the race sound, but such was not the case. The colt was

Black Gold, "the Indian horse," stands calmly with trainer Hanley Webb at his head and John "J.D." Mooney in the saddle after winning the 1924 Derby.

Black Gold's Derby was the most romanticized in the race's history. Here, the principals — Hanley Webb, J. D. Mooney, and Rosa Hoots, the Osage Indian woman — awkwardly clutch their prizes on the winner's stand.

lame again, obviously in pain, his ears flat back. At one point, Webb walked into the colt's stall and braced himself unsteadily against the wall beside a wooden water cask. Like lightning, Black Gold let fly with his hind legs and his hoofs smashed the water cask to bits, spraying water over the old man.

That night in his hotel room, J. D.'s nerves finally caught up with him. He tossed and turned until dawn, rerunning in his mind the most narrowly won race of his lifetime.

Next day, Mooney urged Webb to give Black Gold a rest. Webb had invitations by the dozen to run the Derby winner. Webb was adamant: Black Gold would run.

The next Saturday at Maple Heights outside Cleveland, Black Gold ran in the $5000 Ohio State Derby and won. Then he lost two straight races at Latonia to horses he had beaten in the Derby. Then Mooney finally discovered what was causing the colt's lameness — a vertical, hairline split in his left forefoot, known as a quarter crack. The blacksmith recommended that Black Gold be turned out for a month without shoes, then have the simple operation prescribed in those days for quarter cracks. In time the hoof would grow back. Meanwhile, as a temporary measure, the smithy fitted the colt with a bar shoe, a horseshoe with the open end joined by a metal bar.

In mid-July, Webb shipped Black Gold to Hawthorne racetrack for the Chicago Derby. August Belmont II sent out his good three-year-old Ladkin to try to beat the Derby winner. Black Gold came from way back on a track deep with mud to win going away.

As the blacksmith had warned, the bar shoe was a temporary measure. Black Gold lost two more races then won the last race of his three-year-old year at Latonia on September 24, 1924. J. D. and Marjorie Mooney left for Canada. Before he went, J. D. said that he would not ride Black Gold the next year if the quarter crack wasn't fixed over the winter.

As the winning Derby jockey, J. D. Mooney was much sought after in Canada. The spring of 1925 found Mooney riding at Agua Caliente. Webb wrote him to come east, that Black Gold was in top shape. He mentioned nothing about the quarter crack. Marjorie and J. D. took the train from California to New Orleans, where they picked up their car and drove north to Lexington and a reunion with Webb and Black Gold. Mooney examined the hoof. Webb had not done anything about it. The Mooneys climbed back in their car and drove to Canada.

On December 5, 1925, a stud ad for Black Gold appeared in *The Thoroughbred Record*. He would stand at Jack Howard's Rockwood Farm outside Lexington. Black Gold had won eighteen races including four derbies and four derby trials. His total winnings were $110,503. Black Gold remained at Rockwood until late in 1927, proving sterile.

Then Webb wrote J. D. a letter. Black Gold was back in training. He was pointing the colt for the New Orleans Handicap at the Fair Grounds in February. He hoped J. D. would come back and ride him again. Before answering, J. D. checked with his brother Joe, who was still riding in New Orleans. Joe replied that the old man had the horse in training, and Black Gold was lame. In order not to hurt Webb's feelings, J. D. wrote that his Canadian owner would not release him to come south to ride. But he did suggest, "The best thing you can do is scratch him."

Webb ran Black Gold three times in December at Jefferson Park. Each time the horse came back defeated and lame. The old man's drinking habits and his treatment of Black Gold were now the talk of the backstretch. One story has it that he climbed aboard the horse one night and rode him to a saloon where he tied him, Oklahoma-cow-pony style, to a railing out front.

On January 18, 1928, Webb sent Black Gold to the post in the $1200 Salome purse at the Fair Grounds, where the horse had started his racing career five years earlier. Apprentice jockey Dave Emery was in the saddle. Black Gold showed a game burst of early speed. When the horses hit the homestretch, he was running fifth in the field of nine. A horse named Polygamia was on top. Down the stretch they pounded. Near the wire, Black Gold appeared to stumble. His right foreleg had snapped in two above the ankle; it was now held together, grotesquely, by his bandage.

Emery hopped off. The horse ambulance arrived and took Black Gold away to the dump in the stable area where they destroyed him. Next day he was buried in the center field next to the grave of Pan Zareta, another Fair Grounds favorite, who had died of pneumonia in 1918 while in training.

"I am responsible for his death," Webb told a reporter. "I never paid any attention to his lameness; he always seemed to work out of it. As God is my witness, I ran him in good faith."[2]

Chapter 7
"for money, marbles, or chalk"

BLACK GOLD belongs in a sense, to an even larger Derby legend, that of Colonel Edward Riley Bradley who won the race with Behave Yourself, 1921, Bubbling Over, 1926, Burgoo King, 1932, and Brokers Tip, 1933.

Tall, erect, and dignified, with the impassive face of the born gambler, Bradley lives today in faded photographs, striding across the clubhouse lawns at Saratoga, Hialeah, and Belmont in straw hat, stiff white collar, dark blue blazer, and white flannels. That he always carried a Derringer pistol in the left-

H. J. "Derby Dick" Thompson and Colonel E. R. Bradley.

hand pocket of that blazer would probably have come as a surprise to many of his racing friends.

The son of an Irish immigrant steelworker in Johnstown, Pennsylvania, he died on August 15, 1946, at eighty-seven in the study of his Idle Hour Stock Farm outside Lexington, Kentucky, leaving an estate of $10,000,000 including nearly 1500 acres of land and perhaps the finest band of broodmares ever assembled.

In his early teens, Bradley turned his back on the steel mills and went west with a school friend, George Turner. He worked in and eventually operated gambling joints in wild little West Texas and New Mexico towns and south of the border.

Bradley was an enigma. He never touched a drink, never used language stronger than "damn" or "hell," was an excellent shot, and could take a pistol apart and put it together again. He never went looking for a fight, but he never ducked one either. One day a friend scurried up to him in a hotel lobby to warn him that a big, tough Irishman of their acquaintance was in the bar telling everyone what he thought of Ed Bradley.

"Ed, he's drunk, he's mean, and he's got a gun, you better make yourself scarce."

Bradley headed for the bar.

"I understand you were looking for me," said Bradley to the Irishman.

The man paled. "Why, yes, Ed, I was. Have a drink."

Once one of Bradley's croupiers came to him in distress. He had come afoul of a gunslinger, a professional killer, and the man was gunning for him.

"Mr. Bradley, I don't want to run, but I don't want to get killed, either. I can't shoot worth a damn."

Bradley showed the man how to position himself on the stairs of his hotel, bracing his shooting hand in a crook of the banister. When the killer climbed the stairs, Bradley's man shot him to death.

In 1898, Bradley established — with the blessing of railroad-hotel magnate Henry Morrison Flagler — his famous Palm Beach Club. In this simple white frame house beside Lake Worth, the limits at the roulette, hazard, and chemin de fer tables exceeded those at Monte Carlo. Bradley became a man of power and behind-the-scenes political influence in the community. He bought the Palm Beach *Times* and Palm Beach *Post*. A preacher occasionally attacked him from the pulpit, and reform politicians made periodic, but futile stabs at shutting down "Bradley's Place," as it was affectionately known. Bradley gave generously to Palm Beach church charities and built a Catholic church near his gambling casino that grateful parishioners named "St. Edward's" in his honor. Bradley and his club drew money to Palm Beach. "The real reason for the popularity of Palm Beach is not its climate, or its hotels; it is Bradley's," said the New York *World*.[1]

The Beach Club never experienced a holdup. Bradley maintained his own Pinkerton force of eighteen. Sharpshooters watched the gambling action below from a latticed walkway above the octagonally shaped gambling salon decorated in Bradley's emerald green and white racing colors. He admitted women — a daring innovation. After dark, men had to wear dinner jackets. Drunks and poor losers were quickly ejected. The Beach Club closed down at Bradley's death, and Joseph P. Kennedy said, "When Bradley's went, this place lost its zipperoo."[2]

Bradley was a more astute horse trainer than the men he hired for the job, yet he never interfered with them. His passion was gambling and the only thing he cared to know about his horses was when they were ready to run. Often when a trainer fell ill, Bradley would take over the stable, improving its performance. He was, as well, a brilliant student of bloodlines and his influence on thoroughbred breeding was profound. He loved horses, and nothing was too good for his animals, which gave rise to the saying "living like a Bradley horse."

Of all his great horses, the filly Bit of White was his favorite. Bit of White was tiny, a mere 750 pounds, but she beat colts as easily as she beat fillies. Bradley likened her to "a piece of Dresden china." Yet Bradley proved dispassionate when a filly was born one year with a deformity that he feared would be passed along to the next generation. He ordered the filly destroyed lest, he told his farm manager, "she pollute the breed."

Bradley once said that "any man who reaches age seventy and thinks he has five friends is fooling himself." Yet Bradley was an intensely loyal friend and

Colonel Bradley's Beach Club in Palm Beach.

Rose and Joe Kennedy in Palm Beach, 1940.

49

The grandstand at Churchill Downs, 1922.

he inspired intense loyalty. He also said "there are no pockets in shrouds" and that he had no desire to be "the richest man in the graveyard," and he gave generously to public and private charities.

A complicated man.

"He was a combination of cold mathematics and groundless superstition, of gambling and godliness, inscrutable as night and plain as sunshine," according to an article in *The Blood-Horse*. "He was always coldly calculating and yet he earned the affections of people more completely than any man of the Turf of his time . . .

"He operated a gaming house from which he earned millions, in a state and country where gaming is definitely against the law. Yet the priest who delivered the eulogy at his funeral called him 'this saintly man' . . .

"A good loser himself, he quickly marked poor losers off his list. In racing he distinguished himself through the victories of the horses he bred and raced. But to an even greater degree, he was distinguished by his sportsmanship in defeat. He scrupulously avoided the practice of putting blame on somebody else. As far as he was concerned, the judges were always right.

"There was no duplicity in him. He was a gambler. He stood his ground."[3]

Bradley ran his first Derby horse, By Golly, in 1920, his last Derby horse, Burning Dream, in 1945. In the intervening years, Idle Hour Stock Farm dominated the Kentucky classic as no other stable had since its inception in 1875, and as no other stable would until 1941 when Whirlaway inaugurated the Calumet era.

Two of Bradley's Derbies were one-two affairs; Black Servant finishing second to Behave Yourself

in 1921; Bagenbaggage following Bubbling Over under the wire in 1926. His Bet Mosie finished second to Benjamin Block's Morvich in 1922, and Bimelech placed behind Milky Way Farms' Gallahadion in 1940.

Bradley horses raced in all but nine of the twenty-five Derbies between 1920 and 1945 — on a number of occasions he had as many as three entries in the race — and they were invariably a factor. "When in doubt, bet Bradley" was a popular saying of the period.

Bradley bought his first racehorse, a colt named Friar John, in the 1890s and won a number of cheap races with him. He was living in Chicago at the time where he owned a lake-front hotel and speculated in real estate. He had been feeling ill for some time, and his doctor suggested he lead a more active, outdoor life. Bradley took the doctor's advice and started a racing string that served to get him to bed every night by nine and up for six o'clock breakfast at the track so he could watch the workouts.

Bradley's next acquisition was a horse named Brigade with whom he pulled off a betting coup at Saratoga in the summer of 1899, betting $5500 on him at long odds. Brigade broke down near the finish line but managed to cross it first. With a portion of the winnings, Bradley bought a colt named Bad News from Kentuckian Hal Woodford.

"Why did you give a name like that to a race horse?" asked Bradley.

"Because, I've always heard it said that 'bad news travels fast,' and I hoped the horse would live up to his name," answered Woodford.[4]

Bad News traveled so fast for Bradley that he began nearly all his horses' names with the letter B. The sporting press dubbed them "Bradley's Busy Bs" and "Bradley's B-Brigade."

In 1906, Bradley decided to breed his own stock. He acquired from Miss Bessie Price a 336-acre tract five miles west of Lexington on the Old Frankfort Pike, land that had been in the Price family since Daniel Boone surveyed the original grant. Later, Bradley acquired another 1000 acres on either side of the pike beneath which he cut a tunnel so his horses could cross in safety. Mrs. Bradley named the place Idle Hour, which became their home, although they spent winters in Palm Beach and long stretches of spring, summer, and fall following their racing stable. The land is undulating, shaded by centuries-old trees and graced by a comfortable, if not stylish, white brick and frame house.

Today the property belongs to John W. Galbreath, who has renamed it Darby Dan Farm and retained a number of long-time Bradley employees, including farm manager Olin Gentry, who raised Bubbling Over, Burgoo King, Brokers Tip, and Galbreath's

Colonel Bradley's beloved Idle Hour as it is today. The Blue-grass farm has been renamed Darby Dan by its present owner, John Galbreath, who makes his home in Columbus, Ohio.

two Derby winners, Chateaugay, 1963, and Proud Clarion, 1967.

Gentry joined Bradley in 1922 and stayed with him as farm manager until the colonel's death nearly twenty-five years later. Their deep friendship was based on memories of hardscrabble days on the racetracks of the old Southwest where Bradley made book for a time and Gentry rode races.

Gentry came from the sun-baked country outside Dallas where his father had raised cattle and a few horses for racing. With his older brother Loyd, a top jockey in his day, Olin went on the racetrack before he reached his teens. The Texans rode at Juarez, across the border from El Paso; at Tijuana, Mexico; at the Fair Grounds in New Orleans; and as far west as California and Colorado until weight problems grounded them. Loyd became a trainer, and Olin turned to farm managing.

The Southwest was a rough league. Purses were skimpy, rodeo-riding was the rule, and trainers doctored their own horses, as there were few veterinaries on the racetrack. Missourian Ben Jones first made his mark as a trainer and a two-fisted fighter in the Southwest. Gentry remembers a day in El Paso when Jones pitched a cowboy through the plate-glass window of a bar after the man had insulted him. Matt Winn was part of this life, too, as he operated the racetrack at Juarez from 1909 to 1917, when Pancho Villa was riding high in the region.

The foundation of Bradley's Derby stock was laid, by lucky accident, in the summer of 1912 when he acquired for a mere $1600 a colt by Peter Pan, a son of Commando, out of Belgravia, she by Ben Brush, the 1896 Derby winner. Bradley named the colt Black Toney.

Black Toney was one of eighteen yearlings in the dispersal sale of the late James R. Keene, all of which were bought by William A. Prime, a heavy speculator on the New York Cotton Exchange and a friend of Bradley's. As Prime led his yearlings away the bottom fell out of the cotton market. Prime sent a telegram to Bradley:

"In urgent need of money. Make me an offer for the Keene yearlings."

Bradley made Prime an offer.

"Offer accepted," replied Prime. "Send money at once."[5]

Bradley didn't want all eighteen yearlings, so he put them up at auction on September 14, 1912. They brought $57,600, Bradley bidding in Black Toney and another colt.

"Bradley luck" was proverbial. But even Bradley's best-laid plans had a way of going awry in the Derby. Very often, his best horse lost, his lesser horse won.

Bradley had been breeding and racing thoroughbreds for fifteen years when, as his string went into winter quarters for the 1921 season, he first sensed that he might have a colt capable of winning the big race. Black Servant, by Black Toney, had raced seven times at age two, winning only two races. Even so, Bradley and his trainer, H. J. "Dick" Thompson, had a hunch that the colt had potential. Thompson — whose four Derby winners in twelve years would earn him the nickname "Derby Dick" — also believed that Behave Yourself was worth grooming for the race. Despite a pair of crooked hind legs, the horse had shown flashes of speed. Behave Yourself was by a

Olin Gentry.

51

Behave Yourself.

stallion named Marathon out of a Bradley mare named Miss Ringlets.

By 1921, there was keen national interest in the Derby. Although the Derby's prominence has been traced to the 1915 victory of Harry Payne Whitney's great filly Regret, Bradley always credited Emil Herz, who opened the first Derby winter book two years later. Other winter books opened in succeeding years, and in 1921, bookmakers in St. Louis, Chicago, Louisville, and New York quoted Derby odds.

Because entries in the winter books are not coupled in the betting, as they are in pari-mutuel wagering at the track on race day, it was possible to get 40 to 1 on Black Servant and 100 to 1 on Behave Yourself. Rancocas Stable's Grey Lag, Xalapa Farms' entry of Leonardo II and Bonhomme, and Harry Payne Whitney's entry of Prudery and Tryster were the favorites. Bradley's farm workers and stable help, many of his friends, and half the town of Lexington bet heavily on Black Servant in the winter books. Bradley did not, wagering heavily instead on his entry in the mutuels on Derby Day at odds of 9 to 1.

Bradley badly wanted Black Servant to win. The colt was by his stallion Black Toney and Black Servant was the better of the two horses. A week before the Derby, Black Servant had won the Blue Grass Stakes, beating Behave Yourself and three other Derby hopefuls. Also there was sentimental money riding on Black Servant in the winter books.

Bradley was particularly concerned that a close

friend from New York, J. Leonard Replogle, had bet $5000 on Black Servant and spurned Bradley's suggestion that he try to cover his bet by getting some money down on Behave Yourself at 100 to 1.

When Grey Lag was scratched at the eleventh hour, the Whitney entry of Prudery and Tryster was installed favorite, with the Xalapa entry of Leonardo II and Bonhomme second choice in the field of twelve.

Seventy thousand people attended the Derby, including most of President Warren G. Harding's cabinet. Thousands flowed into the infield and lined the inside rail along the homestretch within reaching distance of the horses, there being no fence in those days to keep them back.

When the webbing whirred up, jockey Lawrence Lyke broke Black Servant like lightning from postposition seven, cut over to the rail, and set the pace going into and around the clubhouse turn. Charles Thompson, breaking Behave Yourself from the pole position, took back shortly after the break and tucked in along the rail in the middle of the flying pack of three-year-olds. Down the backside, Black Servant gamely killed off one speed horse after another as they made runs at him. On the rail, Black Servant sailed on top around the far turn and into the homestretch as Colonel Bradley had planned. Running like the wind, Behave Yourself picked up one tiring horse after another until, at the eighth pole, he reached Black Servant's throatlatch.

The crowd along the inside rail went wild, jumping up and down and waving their hats in the air, as the two Bradley colorbearers ran for the wire. Suddenly a hat skimmed past Black Servant's head. He pricked his ears, momentarily losing stride, and Thompson seized the moment to spur Behave Yourself ahead, even though he was well aware that Colonel Bradley wanted Black Servant to win. When Lyke realized Thompson was trying to steal the race, he shouted, "Take back, you son of a bitch!" But Thompson wasn't about to take back, and Behave Yourself held on to beat Black Servant by a nose.

Colonel Bradley was furious, as were his stable help, who searched for Thompson after the race. Fortunately they couldn't find him. Bradley was particularly upset about the money Replogle had lost, but he needn't have been.

"After the race, he passed my box to say good-by, as he was hurrying to catch a train," wrote Bradley years later. "He carelessly tossed a batch of hundred-dollar mutuel tickets into Mrs. Bradley's lap, laughingly remarking that I could have them cashed and send him a check, as he had not time to wait and cash them.

"Thinking they were worthless, Mrs. Bradley was on the point of tossing them away, when she discovered they were winning tickets on the entry and worth $21,000."[6] Replogle had covered his winter book bet after all and wound up a winner.

Behave Yourself ran eight more times but couldn't win another race, and Bradley, again not wanting to "pollute the breed" by putting a crooked-legged horse to stud, gave the horse to his brother, who raised polo ponies in Colorado.

Black Servant went on to win several big stakes races, justifying the colonel's faith, and was highly successful at stud, siring Blue Larkspur, one of Bradley's greatest horses, and the stakes winners Barn Swallow, Baba Kenny, Black Mammy, Beezelbub, B'ar Hunter, and other Busy Bs.

After Idle Hour's one-two finish in 1921, Mrs. Bradley mentioned how much more fun it would be to finish one-two-three. So the next year, the colonel entered Busy American, Bet Mosie, and By Gosh.

Because he worked for an owner who liked to bet and bet heavily, Thompson was under more than usual pressure as a trainer. Whether for Bradley's betting or not, he earned criticism from other horsemen for drilling his horses too hard. In the 1922 Derby, he sent Busy American to the post with a sore, tightly bandaged leg and the assignment of running on the front end with Morvich, a great sprinter. Busy American ran gamely with Morvich to the clubhouse turn, where he bowed a tendon. Morvich hung on to beat Bet Mosie by one and a half lengths.

Even Bradley couldn't win 'em all: In 1922, Benjamin Block's sprinter Morvich from California held on to beat Bet Mosie and two other Bradley horses, By Gosh and Busy American. Albert Johnson is in the saddle.

Bubbling Over comes busting home for Colonel Bradley in 1926.

53

Two weeks before the 1926 Derby, set for May 15, Bradley received a phone call from his high-rolling friend, Leonard Replogle in New York. Replogle was calling from his club, where there was "a lot of Derby talk" and a number of men were anxious to bet on Pompey, the winter book favorite. Replogle knew he would get a vigorous response from the colonel, who was keen on his own colt Bubbling Over and the colt's stablemate, Bagenbaggage, from his second string.

"I told him that he could wager for me that Bubbling Over would beat Pompey," recalled Bradley years later. "When he asked me how much I wanted to bet, I told him that he could estimate how much I had, how much I could realize from the sale of Idle Hour Farm and all my horses, and to go ahead and bet it all if he could find takers.

"He phoned again, an hour or so later, and said that it seemed to have been mostly conversation and that he had been able to bet only $15,000. I told him to keep that for himself, and later I was able to place more than $100,000 through my betting commissioner, Johnnie Fay of Cincinnati, who had a connection with pool rooms throughout the country."[7]

Bubbling Over was by Bradley's imported stallion North Star III, a son of Sunstar, winner of the 1911 Epsom Derby, out of Beaming Beauty, a stakes winner. North Star III joined Idle Hour stud in 1918 and with Black Toney founded Bradley's Derby dynasty, accounting for many of his 127 stakes winners.

Idle Hour had not been impressed with Bubbling Over as a yearling, and the colt had not been made eligible for the big two-year-old stakes such as the Hopeful at Saratoga and the Futurity at Belmont, which Pompey ran away with. When Bubbling Over proved to be a runner, Bradley grew increasingly frustrated, for he knew that his colt was far better than Pompey. Bradley tried to arrange a $100,000 winner-take-all match race with Pompey's owner, W. R. Coe, but Coe emphasized that he was not a betting man.

"All right," said Bradley, "I'll run you horse for horse, and whichever wins can lead the other home."

Again Coe said no.

With $100,000 riding on Bubbling Over in the nation's pool halls, Bradley deemed it prudent to post a Pinkerton guard at his barn on the Churchill Downs backstretch. When Coe and his friends stopped by to look at the Derby colt, the Pinkertons held them at bay. Coe later chided Bradley about the private policemen, adding that Bubbling Over would get a good look at Pompey's tail as he chased Pompey around the Derby track. So Bradley bet one of Coe's friends $25,000 that Pompey would be viewing Bubbling Over's tail.

Despite Bradley's confidence and a mediocre field of horses, Bubbling Over was not a certainty. He was not a very sound horse and had poor vision. Unless Bubbling Over could take the lead immediately and hold it, as he had recently done in the Blue Grass Stakes, he became disoriented. The Bradley entry was made first choice by the crowd, with Pompey second choice in the field of thirteen, including Walter J. Salmon's Display, winner of the Preakness, which preceded the Derby in those days. Not until 1932 was the Derby regularly run on the first Saturday in May.

A few days before the race, Colonel Bradley summoned Albert Johnson, Bubbling Over's regular jockey, to Idle Hour.

"Albert, I'll give you $10,000 if you win," said the colonel. "I'll give you $5,000 no matter where you finish so long as you finish in front of Pompey."

"The field ran closely bunched for the first sixteenth and then Bubbling Over took command, closely followed by Pompey, Rock Man and Canter," according to a contemporary account of the fifty-second Kentucky Derby. "Bagenbaggage and Rhinock were among the last ones.

"Rounding the clubhouse turn, the son of North Star III was still in front by a length, while Pompey was in second place. Heads separated Rock Man, Canter, Champ de Mars, Light Carbine, and Bagenbaggage. There was no relative change in the running positions as the horses sped along the backstretch, but at the half-mile, Pompey began to show signs of weariness, and as they swung around the far turn, Rock Man had displaced the Eastern champion in second position.

"Pompey made a game attempt to come on again, but it was only too plain that he was beaten, and his backers gave up hope. In the meantime, Bubbling Over continued upon his triumphant way, and entering the home stretch Johnson clucked to him, with the result that he bounded ahead, and, drawing away from his rivals in the final furlong, came to the wire five lengths to the good . . .

"Bagenbaggage had moved up in the last quarter and, running with fine speed, gained steadily and finished a good second. Rock Man was tiring fast and just lasted to beat Rhinock a nose for third place . . .

"Pompey, the pride of the East, was thoroughly beaten."[8] It is believed Bradley left the Downs richer by $311,000, including first prize of $50,000, second prize of $6000, the $5000 gold Derby cup, and $250,000 in winning wagers.

Bubbling Over went wrong not long after the Derby and never ran again. In the stud, he produced many stakes winners, including Burgoo King, Bradley's 1932 Derby winner. Bubbling Over passed along poor vision to the mare Hildene, who went blind but produced many great runners for Christopher T.

Chenery's Meadow Stable, including Hill Prince, second in the 1950 Derby to Middleground, and First Landing, sire of Riva Ridge, winner of the 1972 Derby and stablemate of the great Secretariat, the 1973 Triple Crown winner.

Bradley's racing life encompassed many more interests than the big bet. In the mid-1920s he bought a controlling share in Fair Grounds racetrack in New Orleans, investing hundreds of thousands of dollars in improvements and innovations. Though his friend Joseph E. Widener was associated with the establishment of Hialeah racetrack in Miami in the mid-1920's, Bradley's behind-the-scenes political influence and business acumen made the track a success. During the Depression, when the track nearly went under, he removed $400,000 in bonds from Security Trust Company in Lexington, cashed them, and gave the money to Hialeah. He was a financial backer of one of the early mechanical starting gates, and he is credited with introducing from Australia the fiber skullcap, forerunner of today's skullcaps mandatory for all jockeys. He introduced barns with cross ventilation, showers for cleaning mud-spattered horses, and a solarium in which horses were exposed to measured amounts of ultraviolet rays. To teach apprentice jockeys to ride with their hands and heels, he established a rule forbidding them to use whips. Like Jack Price, owner and trainer of Carry Back, the 1961 Derby winner, Bradley was always open to new ideas, no matter how bizarre. Sometimes they didn't pan out.

Bradley supplemented the feed of Burgoo King, his 1932 Derby winner, with cod liver oil and dried fish and in a special stall treated the horse with ultraviolet rays. His most spectacular failure involved an attempt to fit eyeglasses on a nearsighted racehorse. When the eyeglass-blinkers were fitted over the colt's head, he panicked, tossed his rider, and ran off. Bradley accumulated a lot of equipment such as germicidal lamps and ultraviolet ray machines. One day he asked Gentry:

"Olin, is this stuff doing any good?"

"Mr. Bradley," replied Gentry, "it isn't worth a damn."

"O.K., give it to Saint Joseph's Hospital."

Like so many men of genius and near-genius, Bradley found the intriguing game of breeding racehorses with all its glorious uncertainties, heartbreaks, and unexpected rewards totally consuming. In contrast to the bedlam of the racetrack and the controlled tension of his Beach Club gaming rooms, Bradley enjoyed the peaceful rhythm of life at Idle Hour guided by the seasons and the eleven-month breeding cycle of the thoroughbred horse. Each fall, Bradley and Gentry spent many weeks studying breeding charts, planning matings, and selecting European bloodstock. Though Bradley was a wealthy man, he could not afford to buy winners of the Epsom Derby and Oaks or the French classic races for breeding purposes. Instead, he and Gentry searched the bloodstock volumes for brothers and sisters of such winners.

In this fashion in 1931 they bought a mare named La Troienne, by Teddy out of Helene de Troie. Though a failure as a runner, La Troienne came from a famous family of thoroughbreds in France. At Idle Hour, she became one of the most important foundation mares of the century. La Troienne produced Bimelech, Black Helen, and other progeny that earned nearly $450,000. Before La Troienne died in 1954, her daughters had produced winners of nearly $1,700,000.

In the latter part of February, the breeding season began at Idle Hour. Because it takes a mare eleven months to produce a foal, and because the universal birth date of thoroughbreds has been arbitrarily set on January 1, the trick is to have foals "drop" as close to that date as possible so they will be that much more mature when they run at two and three.

Halters were put on the foals almost immediately after birth and during their first few months they were gentled and accustomed to handling. For five to seven months, the foals ran and played beside their dams in the rolling meadows, then they were weaned. At fifteen months, boys were put on their backs for the first time. At two, the horses were sent to the track.

La Troienne.

55

Members of the Whitney family have run horses in the Derby fifty-nine times, for a total of four winners: Harry Payne Whitney's filly Regret in 1915; his Whiskery (above) in 1927; Mrs. Payne Whitney's Twenty Grand in 1931; Shut Out in 1942.

At most American farms, the horses are taken from their stalls, worked out, and returned to their stalls. In England, trainers work at a more leisurely pace — the horses are taken for long walks before and after workouts. Bradley adopted the English practice. Each morning the horses in training walked down the long, rolling meadows beneath the trees and crossed under the Old Frankfort Pike via the tunnel, making their way to the one-mile training track. After the workout, they walked back, and by the time they reached the barn, they were cooled out.

Though Bradley's horses won purses totaling more than $3,000,000 through 1945, Idle Hour operated at a loss year after year because Bradley spared no expense in caring for his horses or his employees. No employee who died in Bradley's service was removed from the payroll as long as one of his dependents lived. Too, Bradley sent monthly checks to a number of down-and-out companions from his gambling den days in the West. Every spring Bradley held his celebrated charity race meetings at the training track. The proceeds bought Thanksgiving and Christmas turkeys

and presents for the state's orphans in whom Bradley took a lifelong interest.

The Bradleys never had children. Mrs. Bradley died in 1926 while on a cruise to the Orient, and the colonel didn't remarry. He once outlined four principles on which the son he hoped to have would be educated, and they provide a clue to the Bradley enigma:

(1) That his mother teach him a sound religion at her knees from the age of 2 to 12 so that the fear of God would be instilled in his heart.

(2) That he learn the manly art of self defense, not to develop into a bully but to prove that he can take care of himself with his hands, and not have to be afraid of anyone hurting him physically.

(3) That he be taught never to lie under any circumstances. One who will not lie or steal or do anything to injure any other person.

(4) That he learn arithmetic. Then, when others are talking, he can be thinking in terms of figures and percentages. This will insure him financial success.

In addition to the stock market crash, 1929 was a bad year for Bradley. He suffered a coronary occlusion and had to sharply limit his activities. He watched one of the best horses he ever bred or raced get beaten in the Kentucky Derby. The horse, Blue Larkspur by Black Servant, was the overwhelming winter book and post-time favorite, along with running mate Bay Beauty.

A day or so before the Derby on May 18, trainer Dick Thompson was hospitalized with appendicitis and the horses were turned over to Chappie Hastings, the stable foreman.

It rained hard the morning of the Derby, continuing intermittently until noon. At 4:00 P.M., about an hour before Derby post time, the heavens opened with tropical fury, lightning flashed, and great stretches of the track were flooded from rail to rail. On the backstretch, blacksmiths busily applied mud caulks or "stickers" to the Derby horses. But Idle Hour's blacksmith insisted that stickers weren't necessary. He drove back to Lexington before the horses left for the paddock. Chappie Hastings, distraught, sought Olin Gentry's permission to have another man shoe his horses for the mud. Gentry told Hastings that he had no authority to make such a decision and suggested he see Bradley.

"I've *seen* Mr. Bradley," exclaimed Hastings. "He says the horse shoer ought to know what he's doing."

The big field of twenty-one that went postward included a pony-sized Man o' War gelding named Clyde Van Dusen, beaten handily by Blue Larkspur in a Derby prep race. The colt was named for his trainer, a fine little horseman. Van Dusen had obtained the riding services of Linus "Pony" McAtee, who had never seen or ridden the colt. The trainer made a point of visiting the jockey room before the paddock call to warn McAtee he would probably be shocked by the colt's small size and weedy appearance and to assure him that the colt could run. Even so, McAtee's jaw dropped when he saw Clyde Van Dusen in the paddock, and he admitted later that he had been "kind of scared," though somewhat reassured by the fact that he was on the second choice in the betting.

The crowd of nearly 80,000 persons took the rain good-naturedly. Interest in the race was high around the country and press and radio coverage was heavy. Many in the crowd watched "a score or so of cameramen trifle with disaster by juggling their heavy movie machines along the roof of the towering grandstand. These men jockeyed and aimed and pointed their machines until all were in excellent position to get pic-

tures of the stretch run, the turns, and the charge for the finish line."[9] The race was to be broadcast to England and the continent. The event probably had the biggest radio hookup of any sports event up to that time.

Blue Larkspur was the heavy favorite. The first bet of the day at the $100 window was $3000 on the Bradley entry. Bradley himself bet $125,000.

"At the post, there was a thirteen minute delay as the field was lined up. Blue Larkspur and Clyde Van Dusen were side by side, the former on the extreme outside. They broke almost abreast, with Blue Larkspur having a little the better of it. But immediately Clyde Van Dusen went to the front for the lead he was never to relinquish . . .

"Folking was second as they went by the grandstand, and Blue Larkspur was third, running out from the rail . . . In the backstretch run the spurt that was expected from Blue Larkspur did not develop and Clyde Van Dusen opened up more of a lead . . ."[10]

Time after time, Blue Larkspur made runs at Clyde Van Dusen but couldn't get his legs under him, shod as he was for a fast track. The little Man o' War colt won in buggy-horse time of 2:10 4/5. In a rare lapse of sportsmanship, Bradley later referred to Clyde

Mrs. Payne Whitney — "The First Lady of the Turf" — leads Twenty Grand in after his victory in the 1931 Belmont Stakes. The man in the left background wearing straw hat is John Hay Whitney.

When Greentree's Twenty Grand and the 1931 Derby field came busting around this turn, fans were still allowed to crowd up to the rail. Twenty Grand set a record of 2:01 4/5 in this running, coming from behind to win. Mrs. Payne Whitney's watermelon pink silks with black stripes on sleeves became famous. Greentree Stable is carried on today by her children, Mrs. Charles Shipman Payson and John Hay Whitney.

Van Dusen as the worst horse to win the Derby in twenty years. Blue Larkspur, with mud caulks, went on to win the Belmont Stakes in the slop and the first Arlington Classic in deep mud, beating Clyde Van Dusen. Unable to win another race all year, Clyde Van Dusen dropped from sight. Bradley and Gentry later learned there had been ill feeling between trainer Thompson and the blacksmith. Whether the blacksmith's decision about the caulks was based on malice or bad judgment was never determined.

Bradley regularly culled his broodmare band, which he maintained at thirty head. So Gentry was not surprised when the colonel nodded toward a mare named Minawand and said: "Olin, get rid of that old mare."

"We had bred her and bred her and bred her, and she couldn't produce anything that could get up a good trot," recalls Gentry. Gentry offered the mare free of charge to Bradley's friend, Horace N. Davis, owner of neighboring Bluegrass Heights Farm.

"I won't take her unless Bradley gives me a season to Bubbling Over and we go shares on the foal," growled Davis, looking his gift horse in the mouth.

When the Bubbling Over–Minawand colt was being weaned, Bradley looked him over, liked him, and bought out Horace Davis's interest. He named the colt Burgoo King in honor of James T. Looney, a man who used to travel around Kentucky preparing burgoo for parties. Burgoo King failed to win a single stakes race at two but breezed home in the 1932 Derby by five lengths over J. H. Loucheim's Economic, with Mrs. John Hay Whitney's Stepenfetchit third in a big field of twenty. A week later Burgoo King beat Tick On by a head in the Preakness. Burgoo King broke down before the Belmont Stakes.

Bradley had become the first man to breed and own

Burgoo King, winner of the 1932 Derby. Trainer Derby Dick Thompson is wearing binoculars around his neck.

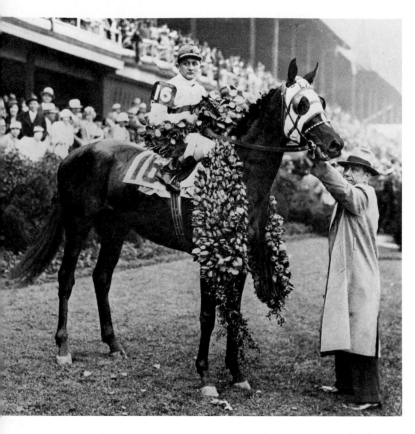

Brokers Tip, 1933 winner, Don Meade up. Derby Dick Thompson is holding the reins. Meade's face shows the strain of his fight with Herb Fisher. The fight would resume a few minutes later in the jockeys' room.

three Derby winners. He didn't have to wait long for his fourth. The following year he won the race with a bad-legged colt named Brokers Tip that had never won a race before the Derby and never won one after. The 1932 Derby is often referred to as "the rodeo Derby": It was the roughest of them all, marked by a whip-swinging, leg-locking battle between two jockeys lasting the final three sixteenths of a mile in full view of the crowd.

Brokers Tip was by Black Toney out of Forteresse, she by Sardanapale, winner of the French Derby and other European classics despite bad leg problems. Black Toney, however, had legs of iron and Bradley had earlier gotten a great mare, Black Maria, by breeding a Sardanapale mare to his stallion. He tried to repeat his success.

"Unfortunately, Brokers Tip went back to Sardanapale instead of Black Toney," recalls Gentry. "He had a half-deformed foot and he didn't have enough calcium in him to stand up as a weanling; his leg would just flop around. So I got old Dr. Ed Hagyard, the dean of the vets in those days, to come out and he had me put Brokers Tip on calcium. And instead of putting him in a plaster of Paris cast like they do

nowadays, he had some leather, like shoe leather, that was long enough to cover from below his knee to his ankle. He soaked the leather in water and he put it on wet — with cotton underneath it so it wouldn't rub him raw — and then bandaged it tight. When the leather dried it was just as hard as plaster of Paris.

"We left the colt in the stall for about two weeks, I think it was, and then we took the brace off. We didn't turn him out for a while, just walked him around each day until he got back to normal.

"There was a man named Kirswell who was a great horse shoer — trotting horse shoer — and Dr. Hagyard told me to get ahold of him and have a special shoe made for this horse. Dr. Hagyard said we'd build up one side of his shoe with leather and that this old man was such a fine mechanic that he could put a shoe over it and it would stay.

"So we got Brokers Tip to the races as a two-year-old, but he couldn't win.

"We sent him to Latonia as a three-year-old before the Derby. At that time there was a race called the Cincinnati Trophy. Head Play, who was one of the favorites for the 1933 Derby, won the Cincinnati Trophy that day. Brokers Tip got left at the post — but he made up 15 lengths on Head Play through the stretch to be beaten by a length.

"Brokers Tip came out of the race lame. He'd been shod by racetrack shoers in the meantime and they didn't know what they were doing.

"After the race, Mr. Bradley said: 'Olin, put that old man on the job again and shoe him and don't ever let anybody touch his feet until after he runs in the Derby.'

"I bet $40 on him in the winter books at 40 to 1. Nobody gave him a chance in the world.

"Before the Derby, the horse started going sore in the knees. Anything that Sardanapale ever had, Brokers Tip had. He couldn't run in the mud, because that hurt him; he couldn't run on a fast track, because a fast track hurt him. He had to have a track that was deep and soft, but not muddy."

Such a track materialized at Churchill Downs on the first Saturday in May 1933.

Head Play was by Mad Play, a brother to Man o' War. Head Play was owned by Willie Crump, an old-time retired jockey who had picked him up as a yearling for $500 and had developed him into one of the nation's top two-year-olds of 1932. Not long before the Derby, Mrs. Silas B. Mason offered Crump $30,000 and 15 percent of any part of the Derby purse that Head Play won. Crump was torn. He knew the chances of his ever finding another Derby colt were slim. On the other hand, the Depression was hurting the racing industry, which was going through what the British call a "bad patch." By Derby eve, Crump

The horseback fight to the finish of the 1933 Derby between Herb Fisher on Head Play (left) and Don Meade on Brokers Tip (right) resulted in one of the most dramatic racing photographs ever. Wallace Lowry, a *Courier-Journal* photographer, had been lying under the inside rail at the finish line with up-tilted camera and caught Fisher grabbing for Meade's saddle-cloth and Meade trying to shove him away.

still hadn't made up his mind. Finally he asked horseman Tobe Trotter for advice.

"Bill, even if he does look like a cinch for the Kentucky Derby, I'd sell him. Thirty thousand dollars won't bow a tendon or spring an osselet."[11]

Trotter must have struck a chord, for Head Play went to the post next day with Herb Fisher, wearing Mrs. Mason's bright orange silks, in the saddle.

W. R. Coe, hoping to avenge the defeat of Pompey by Bubbling Over in 1926, entered two Pompey offspring, Ladysman and Pomponius, whom the crowd made the favorites in the field of thirteen.

On the night before the Derby, light showers drifted across Churchill Downs, ending in a cloudy dawn. A cool wind played across the racing strip all day, and the sun appeared periodically. By Derby time, the track was rated "good," that is, somewhere between "fast and slow."

Though Head Play had been rambunctious at the post, Fisher got him away smartly with his field, dropping in behind the leaders, a pair of outsiders named Good Advice and Isaiah, as they rounded the first turn. Don Meade allowed Brokers Tip to settle into his stride among the tail-enders. Fisher took Head Play to the front at the half-mile pole, while Charlie Corbett began to move up through the pack with Charley O. At the far turn, Head Play was on top by a length over Charley O, who had skimmed along the rail. Coming into the homestretch, Fisher swung Head Play wide, carrying Charlie O out with him, and Meade came flying along the rail on Brokers Tip. For a moment or two, the crowd went wild at the prospect of a three-horse finish, but Charlie O suddenly tired and fell back, and Fisher slanted Head Play toward the

The starting gate used in the 1936 Derby.

Cavalcade, winner of the 1934 Derby, with his trainer F. A. Smith. Mrs. Sloan bought Cavalcade for a mere $1200 as a yearling. At two, he won only two of eleven races, but at three came into his own and started breaking track records early in the season. Besides beating Alfred Gwynne Vanderbilt's Discovery in the Kentucky Derby, giving veteran jockey Mack Garner a longed-for win, Cavalcade also won the Chesapeake Stakes, American Derby, Detroit Derby, and Classic Stakes before injuries sidelined the great horse.

rail until he was running flat out beside Brokers Tip.

Suddenly Fisher leaned down, grabbing at Meade's saddlecloth with his left hand. Meade shoved Fisher's hand away. Again Fisher grabbed for the saddlecloth, his right leg out of the stirrups, his right knee high in the air. Head Play's head jerked to the right as Fisher tried to keep his balance on the thundering animal. The horses flashed across the finish line so close together that the crowd couldn't tell which horse had won. As the two riders stood in their stirrups, Fisher slashed Meade with his whip.

Within a few seconds, number sixteen was dropped into the winner's slot on the "unofficial" board and the crowd let out a whoop: Colonel Bradley had won his fourth Kentucky Derby.

"When Fisher brought Head Play back to the finish, and dismounted, he immediately ran, with little short, jiggly steps in his riding boots, across the lawn to the stewards' stand to lodge a claim of foul against Meade," wrote Damon Runyon.

"Fisher broke down and cried as he talked to the stewards. Meantime, however, they had already drooped the neck of Brokers Tip with a rose blanket, and had handed Meade a big bunch of American beauties, and the photographers were busy taking pictures of the horse.

"The crowd waited anxiously while the stewards heard Fisher's case. Hundreds were out on the track, scurrying under the feet of the horses of the mounted policemen . . . Presently the red 'official' board went up and the result passed into history."[12]

When Fisher emerged from the stewards' stand, he dropped down on the steps and cried again. Then he ran to the jockey room to wait for Meade. When Meade entered, Fisher jumped him and the two men traded blows before newspapermen and valets pulled them apart.

The horseback fight to the finish resulted in one of the most dramatic racing photographs ever taken. Wallace Lowry, a Louisville *Courier-Journal* photographer, had been lying under the inside rail at the finish line. When the hypo dried and the development of the plate was complete, he had two thoroughbreds charging toward the line, Fisher's left hand locked around the front of Meade's saddle, Meade's whip hand clawing at Fisher's shoulder. The picture served to implicate Fisher. Though Meade, too, was a rough, foul rider at times, he was apparently innocent, if only because he rode a green horse that needed his complete attention. Turf writer G. F. T. Ryall said, "There is a certain finesse to foul riding, but the younger generation of jockeys seems to lack this as much as it lacks other touches and tricks of horsemanship."[13]

On the Monday after the race, the stewards — Charles F. Price, Thomas C. Bradley, C. Bruce Head, and Elijah Hogg — met and released this statement:

"The stewards, after careful investigation, including a hearing of jockeys H. W. Fisher and D. Meade, have suspended each of the latter for 30 calendar days for rough riding during the stretch running of the Kentucky Derby. Each boy, according to the evidence and observation, was guilty of grasping the equipment of the other. Jockey Fisher was given an additional five days for assaulting jockey Meade while in the jockeys' quarters after the race."[14]

The minor punishment was rendered all but meaningless when the stewards ruled that the suspensions would not prevent the jockeys from riding in stakes races. This decision further encouraged the belief among horsemen and jockeys that anything goes in the Derby.

By 1939, the years and recurrent heart trouble had slowed Bradley's pace but had not diminished his spirit. He was eighty. He still appeared at trackside at dawn to watch his horses work and to entertain guests at luncheons prepared by his chef. But he now sat in his car or in a special box at the races, and he could no longer make the trek to the receiving stand when his horses won: The trophies were brought to him or accepted for him by friends.

In 1939, Bradley produced his best runner since Bubbling Over and Blue Larkspur. The colt, Bimelech, came from the same mating — Black Toney and La Troienne — that had resulted in the great little race mare, Black Helen, and the top stakes horse, Big Hurry. At two, Bimelech ran six races, winning them all, including the Futurity at Belmont and the Pimlico Futurity in Maryland. After Bimelech's Pimlico win, Bradley issued one of his celebrated challenges. He offered to race his two-year-old star, at weight-for-

age, against Kayak II, the California three-year-old champion and/or Challedon, the Maryland three-year-old. The race would be one and one-sixteenths miles, and he was willing to run "for money, marbles, or chalk." There were no takers.

"Bimmie" was made the shortest-priced winter book favorite in the history of the Derby at the time, despite the fact that no winner of the Futurity at Belmont had ever gone on to win the Kentucky classic.

Derby Dick Thompson died during Bimelech's two-year-old campaign. Aging Bill Hurley, who had always handled Bradley's second string, replaced Thompson. If Thompson drilled his horses too hard, Hurley didn't drill or race them often enough to please the colonel, who wanted action above all else so he could bet. Hurley was reluctant to commit himself even when he thought a horse had a real chance. He used Bradley's bookmaker in Chicago, so Bradley would call the bookie to ask: "Has Bill bet on this

In 1934, Mrs. Isabel Dodge Sloan, mistress of Brookmeade Stable, became the first woman to head the list of winning owners. Her Cavalcade won the Derby the same year. Mrs. Sloan, born Isabel Cleves Dodge, inherited a $7,000,000 fortune in 1920 upon the death of her father, John F. Dodge, co-founder of the Dodge Motor Company. With this money she went a'racing, starting out with steeplechasers, then drifting into flat racing. Cavalcade, her best horse, was conceived in England by the mare Hastily, who was bred to the English stallion Lancegaye. Hastily dropped the foal in this country, however, and Mrs. Sloan bought Cavalcade at the Saratoga Yearling Sales.

On the left, Colonel E. R. Bradley: gambler.

one?" If the bookie said yes, Bradley would also bet.

During the winter of 1940, Hurley took a string of Bradley horses to Florida, leaving Bimelech at Idle Hour to fill out and mature. The winter and early spring, however, were particularly severe, Hurley's orders for Bimelech's work were somewhat ambiguous, and the result was that Bimelech grew fat and soft. When Hurley returned from Florida he threw Bimelech into a sudden, stiff regimen, working him hard every other day to get him ready for the Blue Grass at Keeneland on April 25. So awesome was Bimelech's reputation that only one horse, the sprinter, Roman, ran against him and his stablemate, Bashful Duck. With apparent ease Bimelech beat Roman by two and one-half lengths, and Bimelech's Derby odds plunged further.

Bimelech, however, was not a sturdy colt, and the race took a lot out of him. After the race, he "corded up," that is, a little ridge tightened down his spine. Gentry's friend Ben Jones noted the sign of strain in the colt and said: "Well, Olin, your horse is fat. But

if the old man doesn't run him again until the Derby, he'll win it." Gentry and Jones were dumfounded the next day when Hurley announced that after only two days of rest, Bimelech would go forth in the Derby Trial at Churchill Downs. Deciding to abandon his policy of never interfering with the trainer, Gentry asked Hurley if he didn't think it was a mistake to run Bimmie again before the big one.

"It would be with any other horse," conceded Hurley, "but Bimelech is an iron horse."

Again, Bimelech won, this time beating Gallahadion and other Derby hopefuls. As so often happens when a top three-year-old comes along, people compared Bimelech to Man o' War. It looked as though Bradley was a shooin for his fifth Kentucky Derby.

But several experienced Kentucky turf writers said that Bimelech looked "flat" after the race and expressed doubt about Hurley's training methods.

The sixty-sixth Kentucky Derby, on May 4, 1940, proved one of Bradley's worst failures. A dead-tired Bimelech managed to hang on gamely for second place behind Gallahadion, a mediocre, thirty-five to one shot owned by Mrs. Ethel V. Mars's Milky Way Farm.

"At no time able to clear his field, taking the lead only with difficulty at the home turn, holding it under pressure for but a furlong, and then surrendering and barely lasting to save the place by a nose, with the time unaccountably slow (2:05 on a fast track) his performance was one of the most bitter disappointments in Derby history."[15]

Bimelech, the horse his groom said "nobody could beat, leastwise if he was a horse!" had been beaten for the first time in nine starts.

"Bimelech came to the Derby unprepared, on the one hand, and overdone, on the other. His preparation was hasty and by no means the kind that such a test required. Nevertheless, he was asked to race three times within the space of but 10 days — something that would have been a tough assignment for a thoroughly seasoned colt. Had the two first races been soft spots, they might have not taxed him. But, in both he was called upon for extreme speed, nor was either just a sprint . . ."[16]

With more time between races, Bimelech came back to win the Preakness and the Belmont. When he failed to extend himself in the Arlington Classic, it was discovered that he had broken a bone in his foot.

Bradley tried once more. In 1945, he ran Burning Dream, but the horse finished in the ruck behind F. W. Hooper's Hoop Jr., the winner. Shortly before his death in 1946, Bradley wrote Colonel Matt Winn that he had a good horse in the barn for the 1947 running, though he didn't name him.

The Bradley era had really ended in 1940 with Bimelech.

In the early morning of August 15, 1946, Colonel Bradley was reading in his comfortable study lined with oil paintings of North Star III, Black Toney, and Blue Larkspur, the big Louisville cup that Bit of White had brought home from Churchill Downs when she set a track record for two miles, the four Kentucky Derby cups, photographs of Busy Bs, and other memorabilia. He suddenly became dizzy, and his sister, Mrs. Catherine Bailey, who had lived with him during his last years, summoned his physician Dr. Fred Rankin.

By 1:00 A.M. Bradley was dead.

Bradley had written his own epitaph in 1934 when Senator Huey Long of Louisiana, irked that Bradley had had dealings with anti-Long politicians in New Orleans in connection with Fair Grounds Racetrack, summoned him before a Senate investigating committee in Washington. The Kingfish asked Bradley what his occupation was.

"I'm a speculator, racehorse breeder, and gambler," replied the dignified Kentucky colonel.

"What do you gamble in?" asked Long.

"Almost anything," Bradley answered quietly.[17]

Chapter 8
"Devil's red, blue collar, blue hoops on sleeves"

EVEN BEFORE Colonel Bradley's death in 1946, Calumet Farm, starting with Whirlaway, had begun to dominate the Kentucky Derby.

Whirlaway sailed down the long Derby stretch on May 3, 1941 — blinkered head slung low, long tail flying in the breeze, Eddie Arcaro in the saddle — and went under the wire eight lengths ahead of his field. The tote board blinked the time: 2:01 2/5, a Derby record. Calumet Farm's little chestnut colt had shaved two fifths of a second from the record set by Greentree Stable's Twenty Grand a decade earlier. The new time would survive until 1962 when Decidedly lowered it one full second. Whirlaway covered the last quarter mile in 23 3/5, rocketing from fourth place on the turn for home to triumph over long-shot Staretor, Market Wise, and eight other colts. Not until 1973, when Secretariat set a Derby record of 1:59 2/5, was Whirlaway's last quarter mile eclipsed, Secretariat shading 23 1/5 for the last 440 yards.

Warren Wright's Calumet Farm had had a number of good horses before Whirlaway, and better ones thereafter, most notably Citation, but "Mr. Long Tail" won the first of the stable's eight Kentucky Derbies — and the first of its two Triple Crowns — setting the style for a stable that became the most powerful in American racing history.

Trainer Ben Jones always said that the temperamental Whirlaway had been his favorite Derby horse, though the colt had caused him the most sleepless nights. Arcaro felt that while Citation was the best horse he had ever ridden, Whirlaway was the most exciting.

From Whirlaway onward through the 1940s and 1950s, as Red Smith put it, "Calumet laid it over the competition like ice cream over spinach."[1]

To the public, Whirlaway was "Mr. Long Tail." In winning the first of Calumet's eight Kentucky Derbies, the colt set the style for what became the most powerful stable in racing history.

Iron Liege was the first of Bill Hartack's five Derby winners, and it shows in his face. Iron Liege was the first of two Derby winners to list H. A. "Jimmy" Jones (right) as trainer. Jimmy's father, Ben (left), totes the jockey's bouquet. The 1957 Derby was known as "The Bad Dream Derby" because Ralph G. Lowe, owner of Gallant Man, dreamed a few nights before the race that his jockey, Willie Shoemaker, would misjudge the finish and lose the race. Lowe told his trainer, Johnny Nerud. Nerud told Shoemaker. At the sixteenth pole, when Gallant Man was running head-to-head with Iron Liege, Shoemaker misjudged the finish line, stood up for a moment — and lost the Derby by a nose to Hartack and Iron Liege.

Ben Jones and his son Jimmy, a pair of shrewd country boys from northwest Missouri, had the Calumet horses in the glory days. Ben was probably the greatest horse trainer this country ever produced. Keeping up with the Jones boys was an impossible task. At times they divided the Calumet string into two divisions and cleaned up the big races on both coasts as well as the midwestern heartland in between.

Campaigning one division in the East in 1952, Ben Jones entered Hill Gail, Real Delight, Bubbley, and Mark-Ye-Well in fifteen stakes races and won them all. Son Jimmy, racing the other division in California, also won fifteen, though with less economy of effort. One afternoon at Hollywood Park, though, Jimmy entered horses in the fifth, sixth, and seventh races. He won all three and finished second and third in the seventh race to boot. If one Calumet star fell ill or lame on the eve of a big race, Ben Jones always seemed to have another one lurking in the barn to take his place. When Jimmy Jones was forced to scratch the 1957 Derby favorite, General Duke, because of lameness, he sent in Iron Liege to whip one of the finest fields in Derby history, including Gallant Man, Round Table, and Bold Ruler.

No other stable comes close to Calumet's Derby record of eight wins, three seconds, one third, and two fourths in seventeen starts. Colonel E. R. Bradley, with four winners, is the nearest contender. Besides Triple Crown winners Whirlaway in 1941 and Citation in 1948, the list includes: Pensive, 1944; Ponder, 1949; Hill Gail, 1952; Iron Liege, 1957; Tim Tam, 1958; and Forward Pass, 1968.

Like Whirlaway, Hill Gail inherited a crazy streak from Blenheim II, the sire of his dam Jane Gail, "a well-authenticated bitch" in the words of Jimmy Jones. And like Whirly, the son of Bull Lea could run, winning the 1952 Derby in 2:01 3/5 — just one fifth of a second off Whirlaway's record time eleven years before. When Hill Gail was acting up in the paddock before the race, Ben Jones asked his groom to straighten the horse's head and Jones punched Hill Gail in the nose. That calmed the colt momentarily. When the field was flying around the first turn into the backstretch, Eddie Arcaro sensed that Hill Gail was going to try to duck for the gap into the stable area. He reached back and slapped the colt with the whip, and Hill Gail nearly ran off with him, opening up a six-length lead down the backside and lasting to win from Sub Fleet in a driving finish.

Ponder, with Jimmy Jones holding the reins.

Pensive.

One morning in the fall of 1948 at Belmont Park, when the Jones boys had Citation, Armed, Faultless, Wistful, Bewitch, Fervent, Two Lea, Ponder, and Coal Town out on the track at one time, a clocker exclaimed: "Here comes Notre Dame folks!" Others on the backstretch and in the sporting press likened the Calumet record smashers to the New York Yankees' famed "Murderers Row" batting order.

For years, the Kentucky Derby was a Calumet family affair. The farm's great stallion Bull Lea, who ran unplaced in the 1938 Derby, sired Citation, Hill Gail, and Iron Liege, as well as Coal Town, second to Citation in the 1948 Derby, and Faultless, third in the 1947 Derby. Tim Tam was out of Two Lea, a Bull Lea mare. Pensive begat Ponder, who begat Needles, who won the 1956 race in the colors of the D & H Stable. Calumet has earned nearly $1,000,000 in the Kentucky Derby alone — $798,200 in prizes, and eight gold winners' cups valued at $50,000 or more. Finally, in the forty-one racing years 1932 through 1972, Calumet horses won 2199 races, 456 of them stakes, with total earnings of $21,135,825.21. Calumet topped the Leading Money-Winning Owners List twelve times during this period.

Calumet last headed the list in 1961, then went into a decline for a variety of reasons, including the demise of Bull Lea and the death of Ben Jones, the departure in 1964 of Jimmy Jones, and a failure to find replacements of the same caliber. In recent years, Calumet has been making a comeback. By 1971, the farm was fourth on the list with earnings just short of $1,000,-000. By mid-1973, there were further signs of a Calumet resurgence. In Raise a Cup, a bay son of Raise

a Native out of Spring Sunshine by Nashua, Calumet had one of the top two-year-olds of the season, a colt whom trainer Reggie Cornell considers one of the finest Calumet prospects in years. Raise a Cup was scheduled to carry the "Devil's red, blue collar, blue hoops on sleeves" of Calumet into the one-hundredth running of the Kentucky Derby in 1974.

In the old-time Calumet tradition, a stand-in was being groomed in the wings in the form of a colt carrying Bull Lea blood in his veins — Lothario by Nashua out of Mon Ange. Farm manager Melvin Cinnamon believes Lothario may be even better than Raise a Cup at the one mile and one quarter of the Derby.

Calumet Farm lies five miles west of Lexington on busy Versailles Pike leading to Louisville. Though the manor house, built in 1937, is not old, Calumet is the archetypal Bluegrass showplace: 850 acres of land; mile upon mile of white panel fences intersecting the meadows; white barns with quaint dormer windows trimmed in devil's red — a Chinese red with a hint of orange — and cool interiors paneled in pine, shiny chrome fittings on the stall doors; a three quarters of a mile training track; a lovely horse graveyard dominated by a statue of Bull Lea with flowering shrubs in the stable colors; towering elms and oaks and scented boxwood. And horses: proud stallions such as Tim Tam and Forward Pass, running a little to girth now that their racing days are behind them; phlegmatic broodmares and their playful foals grazing on a distant rise as in a painting by Troye or Stubbs. Parked beside the yearling barn is a big red-and-blue horse van with a little sign on the back: "Calumet Farm: Home of Citation." Yearlings are walked in and out

Seven of Calumet's eight Kentucky Derby cups line the third shelf in the trophy room at the farm outside Lexington, Kentucky. The eighth cup, for Forward Pass's victory in the 1968 race, was awarded on July 19, 1973, five years and seventy-five days after the event. Peter Fuller, owner of the disqualified winner Dancer's Image, fought the awarding of first place to Forward Pass in the courts. When Lynn Stone, president of Churchill Downs, presented the cup to Mrs. Margaret Glass, Calumet office manager, she said, "We'll just have to squeeze it in" among the 480 silver and gold pieces. "But I couldn't think of a nicer arrangement to have to make."

"Calumet is the archetypcal Bluegrass showplace: 890 acres of land; mile upon mile of white panel fences intersecting the meadows; white barns, with quaint dormer windows, trimmed in Devil's red."

of this van as part of their training. When they are loaded into commercial vans for the trip to Florida in the fall — bound for the racing wars — the procedure will be old hat to them.

Long before Calumet became famous as a running-horse farm, it was prominent as a nursery for standardbreds — trotting horses, having been bought for that purpose in 1924 by William Monroe Wright, founder of the Calumet Baking Power Company in Chicago. Calumet derives from *Chalumeau*, a French word meaning "reed." The word was used by the French in Canada to describe the ceremonial peace pipe of the American Indians, a long stem festooned with feathers, leading into a bowl of bright red clay, hence the red on the baking-powder can and in the racing silks.

William Wright, who rose from a baking-powder salesman to founder of a multimillion-dollar company, bred his first trotting horses on a farm in Illinois. His most famous product Peter Manning set a record of 1:56 3/4 for the mile in 1922. The record lasted until

1937 when Greyhound tied it and in the following year lowered it to 1:55 1/4.

Wright's stallion Guy Abbey sired Greyhound, one of the greatest standardbreds of all time, but Wright never saw Greyhound race because the gelding was not foaled until the year after Wright's death in August 1931. Nor did Wright see his horse Calumet Butler win the Hambeltonian, fulfilling Wright's life-long ambition. While Calumet Butler was winning his heats, Wright lay in a coma from which he never recovered.

At the urging of his only son Warren, Wright had sold his baking-powder company to General Foods in 1928 for $29,200,000 — one year before the Great Depression hit.

Warren Wright was not interested in standardbreds, but he and his wife were tremendously interested in thoroughbreds, so he wasted little time selling off his father's stock and converting Calumet, into which his father had poured millions of dollars, into a thoroughbred breeding farm.

Mrs. Wright, now Mrs. Gene Markey, was born Lucille Parker in the town of Maysville, Kentucky. She was fiery and beautiful, and Wright met her while she was working in Chicago. They were married in 1919. Two years after Wright's death in 1950, she married Gene Markey, a novelist and reserve rear admiral.

For the more than four decades of Calumet's existence as a racing farm, Lucille Markey has provided the continuity and competitive drive characterizing its operation. When Ben Jones started work in September 1939 as Calumet's trainer, she told him that winning the Kentucky Derby meant more to her than any other race, and his job was to win derbies. To this day she considers the Kentucky Derby the greatest horse race of them all.

Warren Wright, a thoroughgoing businessman, had much to do with the success of his father's company in the later years. Wright was a sportsman, too, but he was pained by his father's heavy investment in har-

Warren and Lucille Wright of Calumet.

Mrs. Gene Markey, shown with her husband, considers the Kentucky Derby the greatest horse race in the world. Since this picture was taken, the names of Iron Liege (1957), Tim Tam (1958), and Forward Pass (1968) have been added to this Kentucky Derby monument in her horse graveyard on the farm.

LEFT:

Tim Tam today. On stud duty at Calumet, along with Forward Pass, Tim Tam still reflects what one writer termed the "serpentine grace" that enabled the colt to win the 1958 Derby and Preakness. Tim Tam is notable on two counts: winning the Derby that was supposed to go to Silky Sullivan, the spectacular stretch runner from California — Silky finished up the track — and exhibiting tremendous courage in finishing second to Cavan in the Belmont Stakes after fracturing a sesamoid bone in his right front leg near the quarter pole. When the accident happened, the colt appeared to be on his way to Calumet's third Triple Crown. Tim Tam is by the Greentree horse Tom Fool out of Two Lea, a hard-running daughter of Bull Lea.

Bull Lea.

Wright didn't hesitate to put money in.

Although he had several quick successes, Wright discovered that money and business principles were not necessarily enough to get to the top on the racetrack, an arena where rationality does not always prevail. In the 1930s, Calumet was not winning as many races as he felt it should win.

When Ben Jones appeared, Wright was perceptive enough to sense that he possessed a talent verging upon genius, hired him and went along with Jones's methods, which were often far from businesslike. Earlier, Wright spotted a similar talent in a wild young Italian boy named Eddie Arcaro.

With former jockey William Knapp as the first of several trainers he would try before settling upon Ben Jones in 1939, Wright wound up his first racing year in 1932 with modest total earnings of $1150.

When Wright started buying thoroughbreds, he turned for guidance to his friend John D. Hertz, the Chicago taxicab and rental car entrepreneur. Hertz had bought Reigh Count for $12,000 and had won the 1928 Derby and more than $100,000 with him. Reigh Count's son Count Fleet would win the 1943

ness racing, a sport from which there was little or no monetary return in those days.

Warren was a small, formal man with white hair and a pink-and-white complexion. A perfectionist to the point of fussiness at times, he required reports in quadruplicate from Paul "Dutch" Ebelhardt, his long-time farm manager, and other key men in the Calumet operation — except Ben Jones. The trainer insisted that his time was better spent with the horses, and Wright left him alone. Little escaped Wright's attention as he tooled around his manicured farm on a blue motor scooter given to him by his wife. Wright had a quick, hot temper that cooled as fast as it flared, and he did not brood or hold grudges. According to his employees, he was businesslike but fair.

Wright was convinced that he could run a racing and breeding operation along business lines, and he succeeded remarkably. Few were the years when his horses didn't earn their own hay and oats. Sentiment rarely intruded: If an animal failed to perform, he was dispensed with.

"Once a visitor to the farm was carrying on at length about the quality and gameness of one of Wright's mares which had won races despite serious unsoundness. Wright listened a while, then announced: 'The best mare on this farm is Twilight Tear. If you don't believe me, look at the record. She's got the most money in the bank!'"

Wright stated his philosophy baldly: "The person who puts in the most money deserves to win the most races."[2]

William Woodward's Omaha, with Willie "Smokey" Saunders aboard, was a courageous, weight-carrying stayer. The rangy son of Gallant Fox, the 1930 Triple Crown winner, duplicated his sire's performance in 1935. In connection with Omaha's victories Charlie Hatton, the *Daily Racing Form* columnist, first used the term "Triple Crown." "The races are kind of like a road show," recalls Hatton. "'Triple Crown' was a journalistic device. It kind of fell out of my typewriter." Omaha wound up his career as a four-year-old in England, where the colt lost the two-and-a-half mile Ascot Gold Cup to the filly Quashed by a nose. Like so many great horses, Omaha proved a failure at stud.

Derby, Preakness, and Belmont Stakes for the Hertz stable. Among the broodmares bought at Hertz's suggestion was Nellie Morse, a Preakness winner, for whom Wright paid a Depression-days price of $6100. The mare was in foal to American Flag, a stakes-winning son of Man o' War. Nellie Morse proved a tenstrike. Her foal was Nellie Flag, champion two-year-old filly of 1934, the first year that Calumet-breds reached the racetracks. Nellie Flag was made winter book favorite for the Kentucky Derby, a signal honor since only one filly — Regret in 1915 — had ever been able to win the race. Wright was excited at the prospect of winning the first Derby he had entered.

He would lose.

Nineteen thirty-four was also the year Wright bought the contract of George Edward Arcaro. "The Master" was not under contract to Wright, however, when he won three Derbies for Calumet. When Arcaro went to work as Calumet's contract rider, he was only eighteen years old and had his first winner just two years before. He was a superbly gifted jockey, cocky and hot-tempered with a gathering reputation as a rough rider.

Born in Cincinnati — he weighed only three pounds at birth — and raised across the Ohio River in Southgate, Kentucky, Arcaro had been a sickly child. But he toughened up quickly, riding for "gypsy" trainers at such places as Agua Caliente where few holds were barred.

"I came into racing setting traps, grabbing saddlecloths, and leg-locking," recalls Arcaro.

Joseph A. Murphy, a prominent racing steward of the day, said of him: "Arcaro rode most of his apprentice years under me in Chicago. He was the roughest kid with whom I have ever had to deal."[3] After a sobering one-year suspension in the early 1940s Arcaro gave up such tactics.

The 1935 Derby was Arcaro's first, and the week before the race it looked as though he was a cinch to win it. On the Tuesday before the race, set for May 4, he won the Derby Trial with Nellie Flag, and trainer Bert Williams was even more confident than the Wrights that Nellie would turn the trick. Two days later, mother nature stepped in. "Fillies at all times are a cantankerous lot, but in the spring they are likely to be more cantankerous than ever," wrote Arcaro years later. "So it was with Nellie. After I had breezed her a mile in 1:41 on Thursday — the Derby was to be run Saturday — she entered that mood or physiological state inelegantly termed 'horsing,' and all our hopes . . . were dashed to the ground. It's unfortunate that mares are in season about the first of May."[4] The decision was made to run her anyway, and she finished a creditable fourth in the big field of eighteen, after twice suffering interference. Whether

she would have won in any event is questionable, for William Woodward's sturdy Omaha, trained by James "Sunny Jim" Fitzsimmons, was a tough horse to beat. Omaha won the Derby and went on to take the Preakness and Belmont Stakes, as had his sire, Woodward's Gallant Fox.

Wright bought his fair share of bad horses in the early days, but in 1936 he made two investments that secured the future of Calumet as a great racing stable. He paid $14,000 for Bull Lea, a yearling colt by Bull Dog, a top stallion, out of Rose Leaves, a beautifully bred mare. And he bought for $62,000 a quarter interest in Blenheim II, an English Derby winner, whom

William Woodward talking to Earl Sande convinces the jockey to make a comeback. Sande does — on Gallant Fox. Sande had been critically injured in 1924 in a spill at Saratoga. His thigh bone was broken close to the hip. Though he did ride again and retired to train and race his own horses, the speculation at the time was that he was washed up as a jockey. Woodward coaxed Sande out of retirement and put him aboard Gallant Fox in the 1930 Derby. As the horse came rolling home, Damon Runyon slipped a fresh sheet of paper into his typewriter and wrote these celebrated lines, which can be found in Frank G. Menke's *Down the Stretch:*

> Say, have you turned the pages
> Back to the past once more?
> Back to the racin' ages
> An' a Derby out of the yore?
> Say, don't tell me I'm daffy,
> Ain't that the same ol' grin?
> Why it's that handy
> Guy named Sande
> Bootin' a winner in!

Gallant Fox and Earle Sande, 1930 Derby winners. The 1930 win opened a Derby decade belonging almost exclusively to William Woodward, his venerable trainer James Edward "Sunny Jim" Fitzsimmons, and Belair Stud. Gallant Fox's son, Omaha, won the Triple Crown in 1935. Another Gallant Fox offspring, Johnstown, wound up the decade in 1939 with a ten-length Derby win and a victory in the Belmont Stakes.

Despite the stock market crash of October 29, 1929, "mere momentum carried on the sports world in a flush of opulence," noted *The Thoroughbred Record* of April 9, 1960. Gallant Fox — "The Fox of Belair" — ended the year with $308,278 in earnings, and Babe Ruth signed a two-year $100,000 contract with the New York Yankees.

Arthur B. Hancock imported to stand at Claiborne Stud in Paris, Kentucky. Bull Lea would win more than $90,000 for Wright on the racetrack and sire winners of more than $14,000,000 by the time of his death at Calumet in 1964. "Breed everything to Bull Lea," Ben Jones would say in later years when he was racing the great stallion's offspring. "They're sound, they're not crazy, and they can run like hell."[5] The Blenheims *were* crazy, but they could run like hell, too, and Wright discovered that Bull Lea and Blenheim mares went together like sugar and cream, for Bull Lea had a quiet temperament. "He damped down that hot Blenheim blood," says Jimmy Jones.

In 1938, the year before Ben Jones went to work for Wright, he and Eddie Arcaro teamed up to win their first Kentucky Derby with Lawrin, a brown colt owned and bred by Herbert M. Woolf, a Kansas City clothier. Among the horses who finished up the track was Bull Lea.

In 1956, only two years after he had gone to work for Wright, Arcaro left for Mrs. Payne Whitney's Greentree Stable. The reason was straightforward: Mrs. Whitney offered him $1000 a month, plus the usual 10 percent of purses won, against the $750 he was getting from Calumet. Greentree allowed him to ride for others in stakes races if the stable had not entered the races. Hence Arcaro was free to accept Ben Jones's offer of a mount on Lawrin.

Colonel Maxwell Howard's Stagehand, trained by Earle Sande, was the heavy favorite for the 1938 Derby, having won the Santa Anita Derby and the Santa Anita Handicap in California during the winter. Racing with Stagehand was his stablemate, The Chief, a top horse in his own right. When Stagehand suddenly ran a fever two days before the Derby and was scratched, William Woodward's Fighting Fox was made the favorite. Calumet's Bull Lea also had support.

Young Arcaro was not thrilled at the prospect of riding Lawrin. The colt had a spotty record: six wins in a heavy schedule of twenty-three races in eleven months, culminating in a victory in the Flamingo Stakes at Hialeah in late February 1938. Lawrin also had a crack in his left forefoot that required bar plates, which were heavier than regulation shoes and something of a handicap. Also, Lawrin had peaked too early. Knowing that the colt would tail off before the Derby many months hence, Jones had given him a long rest then started all over again with the colt, a difficult business at best with a young animal.

Lawrin came out for the first time in late April, finishing a dismal third in a prep race at Churchill Downs. In the Derby Trial, Lawrin finished a head back of The Chief, who won the race in track record time. Lawrin had spotted The Chief one pound in the weights, and, of course, Lawrin was wearing those heavy shoes. Jones decided to run the colt in the Derby with regulation lightweight shoes and risk lameness, knowing that the new footwear would feel light after the bar plates.

"Eddie, I'm going to tell you one thing that you must remember," Jones informed the skeptical jockey when he arrived in Louisville. "Any time you decide to make a move on Lawrin in the Derby, he'll give you an eighth of a mile in 11 seconds. Remember that."[6]

Whether or not Arcaro took Jones's optimism seriously, he decided to go out on the town the night before the Derby.

"I had brought along a little money of my own," Arcaro later recalled. "Went across the river, a little place called Greyhound, had a good time, drank a lot of whisky, lost all my money, and about dawn I figured it was time to get to bed. No sooner had I got back to my hotel and collapsed in bed than Ben Jones came banging on the door, said, 'Get dressed, Eddie, we got some work to do out at the track.'

"Well, he got me out there to go over the track. 'B.A.' was up on that big pony of his but he had me on foot, and we went all around it. He'd say, 'See how bad that is there on the rail? There's a hole there, I think; go stomp on it.' I'd stomp on it, and I thought my head would fall off."[7]

Arcaro and Jones covered every foot of the track. Then Jones took Arcaro back to the barn to go over race strategy for the umpteenth time, warning the jockey repeatedly to *keep Lawrin off the rail*.

"The race come up, and I went down to the paddock and B.A. says: 'You remember about staying off that rail now,' and I told him, 'Yeah, yeah,' I knew about the holes on the rail.

"Well, I had the inside post position, got knocked around coming out of the gate, and never did get away from that rail. I had horses outside of me nearly all the way, and I even went to the inside of the leader, Menow."[8]

Lawrin held on to win by one length over a fast-closing Dauber owned by Foxcatcher Farms, with Myron Selznick's Can't Wait third, Menow fourth, The Chief fifth, and Fighting Fox sixth in the ten-horse field. Lawrin's bad foot survived the strain.

When Arcaro wheeled the colt into the winner's circle, Jones was beside himself with excitement.

"That's my boy! Rode a perfect race!"[9]

Bull Lea finished eighth. Wright was impressed by the job Jones had done with Woolf's unsound colt. Indeed, he had been beaten before by Jones-trained horses of lower caliber than his own entries. So Jones went to work for Calumet in September 1939, beginning an association that would last until his death of a heart attack at seventy-eight in 1961. During this period, Ben Jones would saddle five Derby winners for the Devil's red and blue, and his son Jimmy would handle another two.

When Benjamin Allyn Jones — "Plain Ben" or "B.A." — and his son Horace Allyn Jones — "Jimmy" — joined Calumet, Ben had been training horses for twenty-five years, and Jimmy had been helping him intermittently since the age of nine. For nearly twenty years before joining Herbert Woolf, Jones had bred and raced his own horses for purses as low as $100 in the early days on the bush tracks.

"What I learned about training, I learned pretty much by myself," Ben often said. "If you didn't learn, you didn't eat."[10]

Ben Jones had an uncanny eye for a good horse. Hard-eyed under his white Jesse James hat, back ramrod straight, he would sit his white stable pony during the dawn workouts, ignoring scores of other men's horses as they went by. But the instant a horse with class came busting down the track, he instinctively turned for a better look. He could never explain how he knew the horse had quality, he just knew.

Jones had an uncanny eye for a bad horse, as well. "Trade 'em away for a dog — and then shoot the dog" was a favorite Jonesism.

Unlike most trainers with big strings of horses to keep track of, Jones never kept workout records in a notebook or even on a blackboard. He kept them in his head. Nor did he participate in the spit-and-polish Wright required at the farm. Jones's barn at

Nineteen thirty-nine, the year Ben and Jimmy Jones joined Calumet, Woodward and Sunny Jim Fitzsimmons (extreme left) won the Derby with Johnstown, Jimmy Stout up.

Woodward and Fitzsimmons were a remarkable pair. Traditionalists who wanted to win the classic distance races, they decried the commercialization that had crept into the sport.

Fitzsimmons, as reported in Horace Wade's "Tales of the Turf" in *Turf & Sport Digest* (June 1958), lamented: "Owners were sportsmen in the old days, interested in his horse for himself and not as a betting tool. Today the tote board shines so brightly it sometimes gets into people's eyes." Sunny Jim was as beloved a trainer as ever trod the backstretch at Churchill Downs. He began his career on March 4, 1885, at the Sheepshead Bay track on Long Island for four dollars a month and a free meal at midday. In his later years, he was brutally crippled with arthritis, yet he did not retire until 1963 when he was eighty-nine. Like any racetracker, he knew stinging defeats — Swaps beating Nashua in 1955, Bold Ruler finishing fourth in the 1957 Derby — and was quick to assume the blame if he thought he deserved it.

the track was shipshape in the important essentials, but he did not go in for fancy tack rooms and other frills. He was the first to arrive in the morning and the last to leave at night. "And he'd often slip back later to check the water buckets and things," recalls his old friend, Olin Gentry, manager of Darby Dan Farm.

There were times when Jones had as many as fifty to sixty men under his charge. He made a point of asking their opinions of the horses and how they were doing, and they were made to feel an important part of the operation. Men stayed with Ben Jones. Pinky Brown, his English-born exercise boy, was still galloping horses for Ben into his early seventies. He had broken many bones in Calumet service, for he was particularly good with rogue horses. "We were kind of like a traveling circus," recalls Jimmy Jones. "Always on the move with the horses."

Exercise boys and grooms gave one another wonderful nicknames at Calumet. Charles "Slow and Easy" Martin, a groom, was the stable jester. There were Lewis "Dogwagon" Wilson, Freddie "the Freeloader" Randolph, and others. When Calumet won a Derby, they pranced and waved their hats to the crowd as they led the horse back down the track from the winner's circle; their pictures were flashed around the country.

Both Jones and his son were tremendously popular with newsmen whom they would invite to the tack room for coffee around a little potbellied stove when at Churchill Downs.

"The folklore of sports is filled with the exploits of underdogs who sandbagged a champion, but the world loves a consistent winner for all that, and the Man in the White Hat always gave the citizenry something to anchor to," wrote Alex Bower.[11] In his sessions with the press, Jones always downplayed his horses' chances, but they learned to disregard his protestations. Bill Corum, who was to succeed Matt Winn as head of Churchill Downs, had heard Ben say that Ponder had no more chance of winning the 1949 Derby than a "Shetland pony." Whereupon Corum began his column: "I'm going to bet on Ponder if only because I don't believe a trainer Ben Jones entry should be held at 15 to 1 if Ben were running an old brown billy goat off a garbage heap."[12]

In his time with Calumet, Jones's year focused upon late afternoon of the first Saturday in May, the time of year when he is best remembered.

"With his galoshes buckled, that ratty-looking knitted muffler knotted about his throat, overcoat tails blowing in the wind, Jones would be standing outside the Calumet barn, holding his prospective best horse of the moment by a shank, watching the fellow munch grass, an hour at a time, while the trainer studied and studied the least little thing that would tell him something more about this horse.

"Nothing too much trouble, nor too trivial — where a horse was concerned — to engage Plain Ben's fullest attention. And therein lay much of his success."[13]

The Derbies provided him his greatest thrills, he said, but he was well aware of the Derby's perils. "I don't want to run any horse in the Kentucky Derby and take second money. It isn't worth it. This is a tough horse race, one of the toughest in the world. These horses are only three-year-olds and this is early in the year at a mile and a quarter. You can ruin a good colt running in the Derby and unless you win it, it really isn't worth it. There are too many other rich races ahead. When I run a horse in the Derby, I expect to win it."[14]

Ben Jones was of Welsh-Irish descent. He came from Nodaway County in the northwestern corner of Missouri, hard by the Iowa border, the son of Horace Jones, a cattleman. Horace Jones, as a boy, had driven ox-drawn wagon trains from Omaha to Denver. He later became a cattle agent in Ottumwa, Iowa, saved his money, and struck out for Texas in the late 1860s to buy cattle land. He never reached Texas. When he rode into the Nodaway Valley, he knew that he was home: Before him billowed thousands of acres of thick bluegrass.

Horace Jones was the man in Nodaway who made the market for hogs, farmland, or whatever happened to be for sale at the time. He founded the little town of Parnell — early photographs look like a prop for a Wyatt Earp movie — and the Nodaway Valley Bank, which is still doing business in the original building after more than a hundred years. He owned as well the hotel and the brickyard, and he gave the park to the town. "Parnell was pretty much his town," says Jimmy Jones of the grandfather for whom he was named. "He had a lot of civic pride."

Horace's son must have been a trial to him. Ben Jones rode his first pony when he was four years old, and thereafter, horses were his life. As a boy, he organized match races on a track at the farm and rode at local fairgrounds. Young Ben developed into a wild 'un. He had a hot temper and loved to brawl.

"Quick as a cat, and strong as a bull, he could lick any young buck in the county, and frequently did; and he would bet on anything."[15]

Ben and another boy had the town buzzing one day after they held an impromptu horse race smack down the center of Parnell's Main Street.

When Ben returned from State Agricultural College of Colorado, Horace hoped his son would settle down and either go to work on the farm or in the bank. The young man had other ideas: He was going to breed and race horses, a career that Horace viewed with a notable lack of enthusiasm. Ben's mother, however, stood behind him, and later Horace, realizing his son would not be swayed, built him a barn on the farm for his horses.

"Once I put three horses in a box car for Oklahoma City and had about $8 in my pocket," said Jones. "My mother asked me if I had enough money and I told her I would manage, but she went to the bank and drew out $100 and gave it to me. But I would have gone regardless of how much money I had. I just had to race those horses."[16]

Jones campaigned at one- and two-day county fairs in Oklahoma and Idaho for purses of $100, promoted match races, and even ventured into Indian country to race against their quarter horses. "I remember winning my first race at Juarez. The pot was $225 and I put my horses in a car right then and shipped them home. I knew that if I stuck around, I might not have the money to leave. I used to bet heavy in those days."[17]

Mrs. Jones did not take to the racetrack. She usually stayed home on the farm in Missouri when Ben set out on the circuit with his Jones Stock Farm, as the stable was called. Jimmy was born on November 24, 1906, and six years later, Ben took him along to Juarez for the winter racing. Mexico was in political turmoil in those days, and Jimmy can remember Francisco "Pancho" Villa watching the races at Juarez. Villa also quietly shook down the racetrack management, including Colonel Matt Winn, for equipment for his men and horses. One day, Villa's men started through the stable area, and the word went out that they were making off with black horses, possibly for use as an honor guard of some sort. Ben Jones had a black colt named Lemon Joe and when he heard Villa's men were coming down the shed row, he filled a burlap bag with soft mud and tied it to one of the colt's legs with bandages and tape. When Villa's men peered into Lemon Joe's stall, the colt was hobbling around, the perfect picture of a racehorse with bad legs. The men took Ben's saddle and bridle and passed on down the row.

Jones ranged ever farther and wider with his growing stable that eventually numbered twenty horses. Jones Stock Farm came to be known as a "busy stable" — one that was always hustling, always dangerous, always alert for an opening where one of its horses, no matter how bad, could win a race. If this meant journeying to some bush track outside Omaha, Ben Jones journeyed.

Jimmy Jones can remember being cooped up for two weeks in a boxcar with eight horses crossing the country to California and a winter's racing across the border in Agua Caliente. Other years, the Jones horses went aboard ship at Key West for the journey to Havana. Jones also raced his horses at the Fair Grounds and Old Jefferson Park in New Orleans.

"We did pretty well at the Fair Grounds, but many was the time we went dead broke at Jefferson Park and literally walked out of New Orleans," says Jimmy.

In the spring, they raced at Havre de Grace in Maryland and Churchill Downs; in the summer they raced at Mount Royal, Blue Bonnets, Kenilworth, and a dozen other tracks in Canada.

During the 1920s, the Jones Stock Farm was particularly successful thanks in large measure to a stallion named Seth, a cleverly named animal by Adam out of Purity by Deceiver.

"Back when we were racing at Juarez in Mexico, I think it was Cal Schilling, the great jock, who bought Seth and gave him to his brother Jim . . . I leased Seth one season and bred him and he got six colts but they were kind of small and puny, so I let the lease run out and sent Seth back . . .

"Jim died some time later, and Mrs. Schilling took Seth to Kentucky. Meanwhile those six colts I had by Seth turned out to be pretty fine runners. I happened to be in Louisville and met Mrs. Schilling and asked her where Seth was. She told me he was at Murphy's farm and eating his fool head off; that she'd like to sell him.

"I offered her $800 and after she cleared the sale with the courts she agreed to sell him to me. Old Circus Taylor went out to the Murphy farm and rode Seth back to Louisville. We put him in a boxcar and took him to Parnell."[18]

Seth was a beautifully bred horse. In his veins flowed the blood of Flying Fox and Teddy, forebears of Sir Gallahad III, who would found a distinguished line including Gallant Fox, winner of the 1930 Triple Crown. Though Jones could afford to breed Seth only to cheap mares, the animal proved an immensely successful sire. Seth was among the top twenty American sires between 1925 and 1929, and Jones was listed among the top ten breeders between 1923 and 1931. Tender Seth, Dolly Seth, Seth's Hope, and other Seths made Jones Stock Farm one of the leading race-winning stables in the nation in the 1920s, though not in purses won, for Jones steered clear of New York and competition from the big, rich stables.

In those days, even when the Jones stable was on a winning streak, Jimmy rarely knew the meaning of security, for his father still liked to bet, often on other men's horses.

One day at the Hawthorne track outside Chicago in the early 1920s, Jones lost $9000 in markers in the betting ring, which meant that he had bet the money on credit but was expected to show up next day and pay off.

"You look worried," said August "Sarge" Swenke, a friend who would later gain fame as Alsab's trainer. "What's the matter?"

"I'm going down to Missouri to sell off my cattle," replied Jones. "I went broke in the ring. I need nine thousand dollars."

"I've got some money over to the hotel," said Swenke. "Meet me over there at noon."

Swenke had $40,000 in cash in his lockbox due to a lucky streak in the ring.

"Here's ten thousand; no, eleven thousand," said Swenke.

"No," said Jones, "all I need is nine thousand to square myself with the bookmakers. I've got a good stable."

"Take it," insisted Swenke. "Old Yellowhand is running this afternoon. Yellowhand will win it by a country mile. Bet the two thousand on my horse."

"Sarge, I can't afford to lose another two thousand."

"Take it! And bet it on Yellowhand — he'll win as far as you can throw a baseball."

Jones bet the money on Yellowhand — and watched the horse hang on to win by the barest of noses. Jones was back in business. A few weeks later, Swenke was in hock to the bookmakers and Jones had a chance to reciprocate.

One day at the height of the Depression, Seth slipped and fell while galloping in his paddock, broke his neck and had to be destroyed. Jones never succeeded in finding another good stallion. "We started going downhill," says Jimmy. "We were producing a bunch of soft-boned horses."

In 1932, when Herbert Woolf offered Jones the job of training for Woolford Farm, he jumped at the chance and sold off most of his own stock. Once again, Jones's great ability combined with the output of a top stallion to produce a hard-hitting succession of winners. Ben and Jimmy Jones were with Woolf in Lexington when a fine racehorse named Insco, by Sir Gallahad III, went under the hammer, Insco having gone lame and been retired from racing. The sales in those days were held out under the trees, and just before the bidding started on Insco, whom Woolf had been advised to buy, the skies darkened ominously. When Insco was led out, Woolf opened the bidding at $500, and the heavens opened, hailstones raining down upon the horsemen, who scurried for cover. In the confusion, the auctioneer knocked down the horse to Woolf for his $500 bid. Insco was to sire Lawrin, Jones's first Derby winner, and many other good horses.

On July 14, 1939, Wright announced that Ben Jones with Jimmy serving as his assistant, would replace the late Frank Kearns as trainer of Warren Wright's Calumet Farm, effective September 1.

When Jones headed for Florida, the Calumet string included the four-year-old Bull Lea and a batch of yearlings, among them Whirlaway. Bull Lea had gone lame before Jones took over the stable, and he never did get a chance to race the colt. The first time Jones gave him a hard workout, Bull Lea pulled up lame again. At Wright's orders, Jones put the colt on a boxcar for Calumet Farm and stud duty.

"In his first crop, Bull Lea gave us four stakes winners — Armed, Twilight Tear, Duranza, and Harriet Sue — and we knew we had a real stud," said Jones.

Jones knew, as well, that he had an excellent runner in Whirlaway. The colt showed blazing speed in his workouts in Florida and later in Chicago. Whirlaway was also slightly mad, a characteristic of the Blenheims.

"That's why the British let Blenheim come over here," says Jimmy Jones. "He got so many crazy colts, those English trainers didn't want to fool with them."

Whirlaway, as Ben used to say, was "nervous as a cat in a room full of rocking chairs." Jimmy called him, simply, "a nut." There was nothing mean about the colt, he was simply nervous. In the paddock before his races, "he shook like an aspen." Whirlaway left the gate slowly, but his finishing kick was nothing short of miraculous — if he didn't duck for the outside rail just when $50,000 or more was in Ben Jones's grasp. This habit would cause Jones many sleepless nights.

Like most mortal thoroughbreds, Whirlaway was a "one run" horse. But once his run began, early, middle, or late in the race, it was almost impossible for the average jockey to hold him. Wendell Eads, the Calumet contract jockey during this time, was never able to control Whirly when the colt bolted for the outside rail, though he sometimes rallied the horse for a last dash to the wire after many lengths had been forfeited.

Whirlaway was a golden chestnut with a magnificent thick tail that nearly touched the ground, a beautifully balanced fifteen hands two inches with sturdy legs and an iron constitution inherited from his sire. Jones wouldn't let any of the grooms cut Whirly's tail or even thin it with a comb. "The Lord hung it there," said Jones. "He must have had a purpose."

Jones, too, had a purpose. He reasoned that horses with long tails flying in the breeze were less likely to have other horses run up on their heels during a race than horses with short tails.

With Eads in the saddle, Whirlaway went postward for the first time on June 3, 1940, at Lincoln Fields, Chicago, and won.

"I kind of knew Whirlaway was a runner when I got him," said Jones. "I remember his first race at Lincoln Fields. He broke and went to the outside fence and followed it around the entire five eighths of a mile, and still won. I didn't know how good he was but I knew he was something out of the ordinary and I kept close to him until he won the Derby. That is one thing I've learned. When you decide on your Derby horse, you have to stick with him."[19]

From his first race onward, Whirly ran erratically, sometimes bearing out, sometimes not. "A zigzag pattern had begun to form that was to mark Whirlaway's entire racing career with an unpredictable series of ups and downs, brilliant victories alternating with more or less glorious defeats."[20]

The crowds loved him, and Whirlaway wound up his juvenile year with seven wins in sixteen starts between June and mid-November 1940, his victories including the important Hopeful stakes at Saratoga. He was listed among the nation's top two-year-olds along with Woodvale Farms' Our Boots, Mrs. V. S. Bragg's Blue Pair, and C. S. Howard's Porter's Cap, all of whom he would beat in the Derby.

After Whirlaway had had a three-month rest, Jones announced in Florida that the colt would make his three-year-old debut February 8, 1941, at Hialeah in a six-furlong race. Horsemen and turf writers shook their heads: Only a horse made of iron could survive such a long, hard, two-year-old campaign and then embark upon an equally wearing schedule leading to the Derby. Whirlaway won the race by a head, but lost his second start ten days later after granting weight concessions. Criticism mounted again, and Jones did not start the colt for another five weeks — until Tropical Park where Whirlaway tired and finished up the track again.

Jones knew his horse and stuck by his guns, announcing that he would run Whirlaway in a five and one-half furlong dash at Tropical Park a few days later. By this time, Warren Wright was getting understandably nervous about his trainer. When he picked up the racing papers and read that Whirly was entered in the dash, he phoned Jones and suggested the horse be scratched, that Whirly was a distance horse, and the race at Tropical was not long enough to allow the colt to stretch out. Jones said the horse should run; he was the trainer and knew what he was doing. Wright backed down. Whirlaway won the race. He went north to Keeneland with a record of two wins and two thirds in four Florida races, and on April 10 the colt beat a field of Derby hopefuls at the Kentucky track. Ahead lay the Blue Grass Stakes and the Derby on May 4, for which Whirlaway had been the favorite all winter long despite uneven performances.

Jones had been working patiently with his wild-eyed colt all winter and spring in an effort to ease the colt's nervousness. The trainer would graze him in the infield while other horses were working out on the track, walk him around the paddock, and let him sniff the starting gate. Whirly did settle down to some extent, and it appeared as though the colt had dropped the habit of running out.

For Jones and Calumet, the Blue Grass was a disaster. Whirlaway bore out again, tired, and fell back, beaten six and one-half lengths by Our Boots. Jones ran him in the Derby Trial at Churchill Downs the Tuesday before the big race. Again Whirlaway bore out. This time, jockey Eads managed to straighten the colt out, and Whirly made a gallant effort to catch up but lost by part of a length to Blue Pair.

"A strange thing then happened. In its way, one of the strangest not alone in Kentucky Derby but all American turf history. Though he had just sustained two stinging defeats, and in each had reverted to the same bad habit that had cost him so much, Whirlaway remained the Derby favorite; notwithstanding that both the colts which had just beaten him, along with eight others, were down to start."[21] The public's extraordinary confidence in Whirlaway was neatly expressed by an old black cleaning woman at Calumet Farm when a houseguest asked her why Whirlaway had been beaten by Our Boots in the Blue Grass. "I don't know why he *wouldn't* run, mistuh. All I know is that he *kin* run."[22]

After the Florida season, Jones had asked Arcaro to ride Whirly in the Derby, and Arcaro replied that he would have to see whether or not Greentree was going to have an entry.

"I couldn't give an immediate answer even if I were so disposed, and at the time, I didn't want any part of this Whirlaway," said Eddie Arcaro. "I thought the horse was just plain crazy, likely to jump over the outside fence any time he felt like it."[23]

Though Whirlaway's chances looked hopeless, Jones remained confident that Whirlaway would win it. Jones sent a telegram to Arcaro:

"Don't fail to be here. I think we have the best chance of any horse in the race. Don't pay any attention to race today. He should have won by 10 lengths. I have room for you. Wire me when to meet you. Ben A. Jones."[24]

Arcaro was amazed to find Jones fairly bursting with enthusiasm when he arrived at the airport. "Eddie, this is the fastest horse in America right now, and with you riding him, I know he can't miss winning this Derby."[25] Warren Wright was equally confident.

Jones told Arcaro that in order to get a feel for the horse he should breeze Whirlaway a half mile in about fifty seconds on Friday morning.

"B.A. took me out to the track to work the horse, and he said he would sit on his pony at the head of the stretch and I was to take Whirlaway between him

"Whirlaway sailed down the long Derby stretch on May 3, 1941 — blinkered head slung low, long tail flying in the breeze — and went under the wire eight lengths ahead of the field, Eddie Arcaro in the saddle. The tote board blinked the time: 2:01 2/5, a Derby record."

and the rail. When I came around the turn I saw B.A. and that pony right there on the rail, and I just said to myself, 'If the old man is game enough to stand right there, I guess I'm game enough to run him down.' "[26] Arcaro buried his head in Whirly's mane, and Whirly flew through the opening on the rail. Now Arcaro shared Jones's confidence. And he was optimistic about controlling the horse.

"In that brief introduction, I discovered that he was not a horse that could be managed — that you had to take a long hold on him and freeze with it. You just couldn't reach up and take a fresh hold when he wanted to turn in a run. Although I might look like a coachman, I found out pretty quickly that it was the only way to handle him."[27]

On the day of the race, Jones had Whirlaway led across from his stable long after the other ten horses had reached the paddock. Accompanied by his celebrated exercise boy Pinky Brown on a stable pony, Whirlaway was jogged down the track to get accustomed to the huge crowd. Whirlaway finally appeared in the paddock. Arcaro was thunderstruck when Jones took a knife from his pocket and sliced the left cup from the red blinkers the colt was to wear. Whirlaway would be able to see the inside rail now. Jones had successfully used a one-eyed blinker on one of his own horses years earlier. But the Derby, as Arcaro said at the time, was a hell of a time to start experimenting.

There were no last-minute instructions. Early that morning, Jones had told Eddie: "I absolutely don't want you to get off with this horse. Actually, it would suit me better if you were left at the post on him. If you can get away badly, that will help.

"At some part of this race you are going to be in front. If it's at the sixteenth pole, that's okay, but don't take the lead at the quarter pole, or move up to the front on this horse on the turn. Just sit back there. When you call on him, he's going to give it to you."[28]

The skies were bright, the track lightning fast and

The following labels appear on the composite photograph:

OMAR KHAYYAM (1917) 2:04 3/5
PENSIVE (1944) 2:04 1/5
MORVICH (1922) 2:04 3/5
SHUT OUT (1942) 2:04 2/5
GEORGE SMITH (1916) 2:04
BUBBLING OVER (1926) 2:03 4/5
OLD ROSEBUD (1914) 2:03 2/5
BEHAVE YOURSELF (1921) 2:04 1/5
BOLD VENTURE (1936) 2:03 3/5
PONDER (1949) 2:04 1/5
CAVALCADE (1934) 2:04
COUNT FLEET (1943) 2:04
JOHNSTOWN (1939) 2:03 2/5
COUNT TURF (1951) 2:02 3/5
WAR ADMIRAL (1937) 2:03 1/5
DETERMINE (1954) 2:03
DARK STAR (1953) 2:02
MIDDLEGROUND (1950) 2:01 3/5
TWENTY GRAND (1931) 2:01 4/5
HILL GAIL (1952) 2:01 3/5
WHIRLAWAY (1941) 2:01 2/5
FINISH

A composite photograph prepared at the time of Whirlaway's spectacular victory in 1941 shows where earlier winners would have finished had they been in the race.

hard. The horses reached the post at 5:53 P.M. and were off a minute and a half later.

"Almost immediately, Dispose rushed to the front, with Porter's Cap in near pursuit and Blue Pair right with him. The son of Discovery spun off the quarter in 23 2/5 and half in 46 3/5, at which point he was an open length before Porter's Cap and Blue Pair, who were upon almost even terms.

"Five lengths behind came Our Boots . . . Dispose made the three-quarter pole in 1:11 3/5, retaining his advantage, with Blue Pair and Porter's Cap see-sawing behind him, sometimes one and sometimes the other showing slightly in advance as they contended for place.

"At this point, the other Californian, Staretor, long shot in the field at 36 to 1, had moved up to fourth . . . Our Boots was by now being looked in the eye by Whirlaway, sixth, he having gradually threaded his way through the tail-enders after getting away slowly and being inside to save ground.

"They were now rushing for the far turn, and as they did so, Arcaro loosed his hold upon the favorite and began his drive.

"As they rounded the upper oval, Dispose short-

ened stride and Porter's Cap closed upon him. Blue Pair, at the end of his tether, was dropping back, and Whirlaway came to him. The mile was completed in 1:37 2/5, and as they passed the post, Dispose was trying hard to hold on, but Porter's Cap had him by the throat and he was staggering, while Whirlaway, coming fast, was giving Blue Pair the go-by.

"A few strides more, and they had turned for home . . . The favorite, under Arcaro's strong handling forgetful of his bad habit, running straight and true and at terrific speed, shot through between the others, and took the lead. Close behind him came Staretor and Market Wise . . ."[29]

Eddie Arcaro said later that he had "never seen such power exhibited as when we hit the three-eighths pole, and I called on him for his speed. He literally took off, nearly catapulting me out of the saddle. As he

81

Ben Jones used to say Whirlaway was "nervous as a cat in a room full of rocking chairs." But the colt was calm on May 3, 1941, when posing for this winner's circle photo at Churchill Downs with Ben at his head. Standing on the platform behind Jones is Colonel Matt J. Winn, dapper in straw hat and boutonniere.

stretched his legs, I felt as if I were flying through the air. That final rush he showed me was stunning."[30]

Whirlaway's eight-length victory in record time made headlines across the United States and stirred up gossip on the backstretch. The trainer of one of the losing horses, recalls Jimmy Jones, believed that Whirly had been given cocaine; no saliva test had been taken of the Derby horses. Sportswriter Dan Parker of the New York *Mirror* took up the refrain, saying that "the whole purpose of the saliva test is being defeated when it is administered only in unimportant races."[31]

When Whirlaway won the Preakness and Belmont Stakes, Parker graciously apologized in his column.

Jones's preparation of Whirlaway, and earlier of Lawrin, set a trend that lasted, with some exceptions, until 1972, when Lucien Laurin announced that Riva Ridge would get only three prep races before the Derby.

The Blood-Horse's Edward L. Bowen said that Jones's successful methods "lent considerable reinforcement to the idea that the way to fit a three-year-old for 10 first-Saturday-in-May furlongs is to run him in Florida or California during the winter, and run him hard.

"When Ben A.'s son Jimmy took over officially for Calumet Farm, he trained like his father had. Jimmy ran Iron Liege nine times at three, and Tim Tam 10 times at three before their Derbies, and won back-to-back renewals."

The measure of Ben Jones's greatness lay in his ability to wage such a campaign with a young horse, bring him to his peak shortly after 5:30 P.M. on the first Saturday in May and then race him on, in many cases, for years thereafter. Few trainers were his match.

Chapter 9
"He ran so fast he scared me"

"Citation came to symbolize Calumet at the height of its powers: businesslike, professional, all but invincible."

EVER SINCE Man o' War was retired to stud after his three-year-old campaign in 1920, he has been the standard against which American racehorses have been measured. They called him Big Red, and those who saw him run could never forget him. Man o' War's great jack-rabbit-like strides measured nearly thirty feet. In two of his twenty-one races, Man o' War set five records at distances from one mile to one mile and five-eighths. The *Daily Racing Form* charts of his races more than fifty years ago invariably read "won easily," "won cantering," or "won eased up."

Like Secretariat, Man o' War was a golden chestnut with the look of a champion.

Man o' War died in November 1947 at thirty. One year later a colt who many horsemen believe was even greater than Man o' War blazed through his three-year-old year, winning the Kentucky Derby with ears pricked cheerfully. The colt easily won the Preakness and the Belmont as well to become the eighth winner of the Triple Crown. Twenty-five years would pass before another super-horse, Secretariat, accomplished that feat. Man o' War's successor was, of course, Citation.

In looks and temperament, Citation was totally different from Big Red. A well-molded dark bay, Citation stood just over sixteen hands, yet there was nothing eye-catching about his appearance. The colt's most distinctive feature was a finely shaped head and intelligent, expressive eyes. At the post Man o' War would rear and plunge. Citation was always calm, a typical Bull Lea. Big Red ran with reckless abandon, head high, mane flying. Citation ran smoothly — sportswriters referred to his "frictionless stride" — and sometimes glanced at the scenery when running in front.

Citation had no idiosyncracies to speak of, no stable

nicknames except "Cy." The colt was easy to handle. "A Chinaman could train him," Ben Jones used to say.

Citation came to symbolize Calumet at the height of its powers; professional, practically invincible, Calumet was once called a factory that turned out Derby winners.

Citation's greatness lay in his versatility. The colt won on tracks rated fast, good, heavy, muddy or sloppy in more than a dozen states. Citation won at four and a half furlongs and at two miles and ran equally well for seven different jockeys, including Eddie Arcaro, who considers him the best and most intelligent racehorse he ever rode.

On the turn for home in the 1948 Belmont Stakes, Arcaro decided to let Citation stretch out a bit, so he let out a notch or two — and quickly took hold again. "He ran so fast he scared me," said the jockey.[1]

Citation raced through the age of six. Of forty-five races, he won thirty-two, finished second twice, and unplaced once. Past his prime at five and plagued by tendon trouble, Citation set a world record of 1:33 3/5 for the mile.

Ears pricked cheerfully, Citation breezes home three and a half lengths ahead of stablemate Coal Town in the 1948 Derby.

Though an outstanding two-year-old champion, Citation's first two races at age three stamped his greatness. In the first race, a six-furlong sprint at Hialeah in early February 1948, Citation easily whipped a field of crack older horses, including stablemate Armed, Horse of the Year in 1947. Nine days later, Citation waltzed away from yet another field of seasoned horses.

Having trained two Triple Crown winners in Gallant Fox and Gallant Fox's son Omaha, Sunny Jim Fitzsimmons was asked at the time what he thought of Citation. "Up to this point, Citation has done more than any other horse I ever saw," said Fitzsimmons. "And I saw Man o' War."[2]

Early in that same month of February, the Jones boys unleashed a second sensational three-year-old in Coal Town, another Bull Lea and a half-brother of Citation. Because of illness, Coal Town had not raced at age two. At Hialeah Coal Town won his maiden race with style, and his second race by twelve lengths, equaling the track record for six furlongs. By spring, many horsemen thought Coal Town might be even better than Citation, whom Arcaro was scheduled to ride in the Derby. Arcaro began to wonder whether he was on the right horse.

In 1942, Arcaro had lost face when, against the ad-

vice of Greentree trainer John Gaver, he chose to ride Devil Diver rather than Shut Out. Shut Out won the Derby with jockey Wayne Wright aboard, while Arcaro finished back in the pack with Devil Diver.

When Arcaro asked Jones about Coal Town and Citation, Jones replied: "Eddie, if I thought Coal Town would win this Derby, you'd be on him."[3] Arcaro dropped the subject but continued to wonder, especially after Coal Town broke a ten-year-old record at Keeneland in winning the Blue Grass Stakes at one mile and one-eighth. Then Citation won the Derby Trial with ease.

"Calumet had a winning hand with two aces showing — Citation and Coal Town — and everybody knew it," wrote Kent Hollingsworth. "Four horses were sent out in the hope that the Calumet pair would bump into each other 10 yards from the finish and fall down. These were Ben Whitaker's My Request, Robert McIlvain's Billings, Mrs. J. P. Adams' Grandpere, and W. L. Brann's Escadru."[4]

During the dawn hours of May 1, 1948, rain fell on Churchill Downs, turning the track sloppy for the Derby.

Jockey N. L. Pierson was up on Coal Town with instructions to blast into the lead, keep going, and win it if he thought he could. Arcaro would bide his time for a while, then come on with Citation. "I think Citation will win because, in my opinion, he can catch and beat any horse he can see — and there is nothing wrong with his eyesight,"[5] said Jones. Jones did not say what he sensed to be the case — that Coal Town's courage did not match his blazing speed.

At the break, Coal Town shot away into the lead ahead of Billings, Escadru, and Grandpere, with Citation out away from the rail and My Request trailing. The horses sped around the clubhouse turn, and as they started down the backside, Arcaro grew uneasy: Coal Town was skimming along over the slop more than six lengths ahead and running strongly. Arcaro clucked to Citation and quickly left the others behind. At the far turn, Citation reached Coal Town's flanks and passed him at the quarter pole, Arcaro hand-riding to an easy three-and-a-half length victory, with Coal Town another three lengths ahead of My Request.

Citation breezed to easy wins in the Preakness and Belmont and went on to win nineteen of twenty races his three-year-old year, with total lifetime earnings of $865,150.

Had Citation been retired at that point, his reputation would be even brighter today than it is. But because no horse had ever won $1,000,000 Warren Wright chose to keep racing him. Late in 1948, Citation had developed an osselet, a bony growth on the ankle resulting from either a bruise or a strain. After

Ben A. Jones poses stiffly with Citation in the winner's circle after the 1948 Kentucky Derby. Owner Warren Wright and his wife, now Mrs. Gene Markey, are to his right with exercise boy Pinky Brown. In the saddle — Eddie Arcaro.

treatment, Citation was out of action for a year. He was never the same horse again.

At ages five and six, Citation ran on gamely though dogged by tendon trouble, sometimes losing races to horses that wouldn't have been on the track with him at three. Citation finally passed the $1,000,000 mark while racing in California in 1951, one year after Warren Wright's death, and Jimmy Jones shipped the colt home to Calumet.

Citation was the first equine millionaire. But it had been a hard road.

Chapter 10
"McCreary has lost his nerve"

A FEW YEARS after his victory with Citation, Eddie Arcaro tried for another Derby. On Derby eve, May 4, 1951, Arcaro was carving into a steak in Louisville's Old House restaurant; he would be aboard the favorite, Cain Hoy Stable's Battle Morn, next day.

Jack Amiel, owner of Count Turf, a member of the five-horse mutuel field, paused at Arcaro's table with his jockey, Conn McCreary.

"Who do you like?" asked Arcaro.

"Are you kidding? I like my horse," said Amiel. "I'm going to win it."

"You're *nuts*," said Arcaro.

"He's right, Eddie," said McCreary. "We're going to win it."

"You're *both* nuts," said Arcaro, turning back to his dinner.

When Arcaro left the restaurant later, he sent a parting shot across Amiel's bow: "Jack, Count Turf just isn't the kind of horse you bring to the Kentucky Derby."[1]

Few horsemen in Louisville would have disagreed with Arcaro's rude assessment. Sol Rutchick, the colt's trainer, had tried to talk Amiel out of running Count Turf, and when Amiel proved adamant, Rutchick refused to accompany the colt to Churchill Downs.

"This horse isn't a Derby colt," Rutchick had said a few weeks earlier at Jamaica racetrack in New York. "Keep him here and we'll make some money running him in sprints. Don't be foolish and put him in where he doesn't belong."[2]

At age two, Count Turf had won only one stakes race. Running a heavy ten-race schedule since turning three, Count Turf had won only one race of any kind, a six-furlong sprint in Florida. Count Turf was by

Big Jack Amiel leads Count Turf into the winner's circle. Jockey Conn McCreary started a comeback with this victory. Though Count Turf produced a number of good horses the colt was not a great success at stud. Amiel blames Count Turf's breeding failure on the fact that he was considered "an outsider" by clannish Kentucky horsemen who control much of the thoroughbred breeding industry. "They invite you to breakfast and give you biscuits — while they're figuring out how to take you," says Amiel. The Kentuckians did not send their best mares to Count Turf's court, he says, "and without mares, you have no stallion."

Reigh Count, Chick Lang up, won the 1928 Derby.

Count Fleet, the 1943 Triple Crown winner, and a grandson of Reigh Count, the 1928 Kentucky Derby winner. But until 1951, when he began to come into his own, Count Fleet had been a disappointment at stud. Count Turf's dam, a mare named Delmarie, by Pompey, had won three times in thirty-seven starts. Nevertheless, Count Fleet came from a family of game horses. As a two-year-old, Reigh Count was owned by Willis Sharp Kilmer. On August 24, 1927, the colt caught John D. Hertz's eye during a race at Saratoga.

"He was virtually left at the post but in that brief five-and-a-half furlongs, he picked up horse after horse," said Hertz. "He didn't finish in the money and when it developed that he couldn't pass the horse he was lapped with in the final yards, he reached over and tried to bite him."[3]

Hertz thought such a horse worth having and bought him from Kilmer for something under $15,000. With Chick Lang up, Reigh Count beat twenty-one other horses in the 1928 Derby, the biggest field in the race's history.

Jack Amiel did not have much in the way of owner's credentials. Smack from the pages of Damon Runyon, he had only been in the game a short time, studying bloodlines in his spare time while running his Turf Restaurant at Broadway and 49th Street.

Conn McCreary had been a topflight jockey, a come-from-behind rider who brought the crowds to their feet time and time again. In 1944, he had won the Derby aboard Calumet Farm's Pensive. With style and verve, he had threaded his horse forward; when the leaders swung wide coming into the homestretch, he ducked for the rail and drove all-out for the wire.

Somewhere along the line, McCreary had lost his magic. The late rushes began to die in midstretch. The favorites he rode began to lose. Since January 1951, he had ridden only four winners and was eking out a living galloping horses in the mornings. He had galloped Count Turf, and Amiel had observed that the colt seemed to respond to McCreary more than to the other boys.

Jack Amiel was a shrewd, observant individual who, as racing writer Herb Goldstein observed, had gotten

Johnny Longden takes Count Fleet for an early morning gallop. Son of Reigh Count and sire of Count Turf, Count Fleet was a Triple Crown winner in 1943.

Count Fleet on the way to winning the 1943 Derby. The colt went on to win the Preakness and ran away with the Belmont Stakes — twenty-five lengths ahead of the field — with Johnny Longden in the saddle. Count Fleet injured his right front ankle during the Belmont and was retired to stud.

ahead through "guts and guile." He had gone to work at age nine selling candy bars outside a motion picture house in Harlem, where he lived. "Amiel got smart early. After a few cold afternoons on that street corner in Harlem, he realized he could do better inside the theater. Five years later, he was running the concessions at half a dozen movie houses. In the summers, he hawked beer and peanuts at the Polo Grounds and Yankee Stadium."[4]

During the 1939–1940 World's Fair in New York City, Amiel operated three restaurants on the grounds. With the profits from this enterprise, he opened The Turf Restaurant on Broadway. He later became Jack Dempsey's partner in his steakhouse up the block. Amiel now manages Dempsey's restaurant; The Turf closed down in 1955.

Amiel applied his native intelligence to the racing business. At the Saratoga Yearling Sales, he bid in Count Turf for $3700. The yearling had been bred by Frank P. Miller, a Riverside, California, physician who owned the mare Delmarie. Hertz was horrified at the sight of Delmarie when the mare arrived at his Stoner Creek Stud farm in Paris, Kentucky, for her breeding date. Though well bred — her bloodlines were more impressive than those of Count Fleet — she was "a big common mare with sloping rump and nothing behind the saddle; ridged like a barn roof from withers to crupper."[5] Dr. Miller brought Delmarie and her foal back to California, then shipped the colt back across the country again to the Saratoga Yearling Sales where Count Turf's price proved a tremendous

disappointment. The yearling had one fault: He toed-out a little in front when he walked, causing many horsemen to shy away from him.

Jack Amiel and his trainer were cut from the same cloth, though they were to disagree violently about Count Turf. Rutchick, a Russian immigrant who had also gotten his start peddling candy in movie houses, had drifted into racing. A slick dresser, he looked like George Raft and was considered a good trainer. But with Count Turf, he managed to do most things wrong.

Rutchick headquartered his public stable of twenty horses at the old Jamaica racetrack where the gap leading from the track to the barn area was located at the three-eighths pole on the far turn. Accustomed to turning off here after his workouts, Count Turf started bearing out at the same spot during his races, a common enough occurrence with young horses. To prevent this, Rutchick equipped Count Turf with blinkers, a heavy chain bit and assorted straps and gadgetry. The equipment enabled jockeys to control the colt, but it took the animal's mind off the business of running. Rutchick also got it into his mind that Count Turf was a front runner. Amiel and the colt's riders thought that the colt would do better coming from behind. In the Dover Stakes at Delaware Park his two-year-old year, Count Turf's jockey deliberately held him back at the start — with Amiel's connivance — and came from behind to win.

By Wood Memorial time, some weeks before the Derby, Count Turf was rock hard and ready to run to the Rocky Mountains, though the colt had not been winning. Count Turf's performance in that race, though he finished out of the money again, convinced Amiel the colt could win the Derby and caused his split with Rutchick.

"He was stopped dead in the stretch," Amiel recalls. "Another horse come over on him. Still he made another run." Count Turf had closed gamely and fast, as he had in his last three races. Amiel was convinced that with the right rider, coming from behind, Count Turf would eat up the mile and a quarter of the Derby.

"Right then and there, I said: 'He's going down.'"

"'Take me to the jocks' room,'" Amiel said to Rutchick as the horses were cantering back from the race, won by Repetoire, with Battle Morn second, and Intent, third.

"What for?" asked Rutchick.

"I want to talk to Connie McCreary. I want him to ride Count Turf in the Kentucky Derby."

Count Turf, Rutchick still felt, had no place in the Derby. "And McCreary — everyone knows he's finished."

"If you won't go, I'll ask McCreary myself," said Amiel, flushing with anger.[6]

McCreary, now, couldn't believe his ears. He had been riding since he was fifteen when he left his home in St. Louis and showed up at Churchill Downs. With a wife and four children to support and bills that he could not pay, he was near despair.

"Are you going to send this horse to the Derby?" asked McCreary.

"Only if you'll ride him," said Amiel.

"I'm poison," said the jockey. "You know that."

"No," said Amiel. "I hear that, but I don't believe it."[7]

Rutchick made it clear that he wanted no part of Amiel's Derby expedition. He sent in his stead George

Count Fleet before his death at age thirty-three in December 1973. Count Fleet was a proud animal, says Charles Kenney, farm manager of Stoner Creek Stud in Paris, Kentucky, where the 1943 Triple Crown winner lived as a pensioner. "He wouldn't come trotting over for sugar, or to be patted. He knew he was royalty!" "The Count of Stoner Creek," as the old horse was known at the farm, did have one shameful secret: He was afraid of the dark. Stoner Creek Stud has passed into the hands of a trotting horse stable but as part of the sale agreement, Count Fleet lived out his days there.

"He just galloped," recalls Jack Amiel, owner of Count Turf, the surprise winner of the 1951 classic. Amiel stands just beyond stand-in trainer George "Slim" Sulley, hands on the bridle. Grinning from the saddle is Conn McCreary, whose life was radically changed by this victory.

"Slim" Sulley, a seventy-year-old horseman who had handled some good horses in his time. About two weeks before the Derby, Count Turf arrived by air at Louisville airport, the first Derby hopeful ever to arrive in this fashion.

"We practically trained him ourselves," says Amiel. On more than one morning, when Sulley wasn't on hand, Amiel took his workout cue from other Derby trainers. He stationed himself near the gap on the Churchill Downs backside and eavesdropped on his friend Max Hirsch and other top trainers such as John Gaver, Sylvester Vietch, and Ben Jones. If Hirsch ordered his boy to take King Ranch's Sonic on a five-furlong whirl in a certain time, Amiel told McCreary to do likewise with Count Turf.

Amiel recalls that McCreary probably won the Derby the first morning that Count Turf stepped onto the Churchill Downs strip for a gallop. Sulley had brought the horse out equipped with his heavy chain bit and restraining straps. "That's all got to go," said McCreary. "That horse isn't going to win the Derby with that stuff. If I can't control him with my hands,

forget the whole thing." Amiel asked about the colt's tendency to bear out.

"Put a simple 'D' bit on him," answered McCreary.[8]

Amiel agreed. McCreary took off down the track with Count Turf.

"He didn't go wide or nothing," says Amiel. "He went like a hoop around a barrel. I said: 'Jeez, the horse don't need a chain; if anything this horse shouldn't have a chain because his mind is not on running.' He was a different horse without that chain, a better horse."

One morning Count Turf ran a mile in an impressive 1:38 4/5.

Rutchick heard about the work and telephoned from New York:

"You know, Jack, you might have a chance if you had a good rider. McCreary has lost his nerve. Let me get you a good boy and bring him down."[9] Amiel ignored the suggestion.

On the day before the Derby, the Count worked a half mile in what the clockers listed as 45-4/5, fast time indeed. Amiel caught the colt in even faster time and he believes that some of the clockers did too.

Rutchick phoned again, offering to fly down Derby morning with a top jockey. Amiel remained adamant. "He's your horse," exclaimed Rutchick.[10]

After their Derby eve dinner, Amiel and McCreary went over their race strategy for the last time. The

Derby was a wide-open race without a standout horse, Battle Morn having been made favorite largely because Arcaro had chosen to ride him. The big field of twenty horses included Snuzzle, Sir Bee Bum, and Anyoldtime, all of whom belonged at Hagerstown running for $700.

Both men had agreed that Count Turf should come from behind. But before retiring, Amiel assured McCreary he had total faith in his judgment, and if conditions warranted, he could adjust the race plan accordingly once the running began.

On Derby Day, McCreary sat quietly in the jockeys' room. He heard one rider say, "I know my instructions are going to be to lay back and wait." Other riders chimed in with the same plan. McCreary realized immediately that with so many horses laying back, there would be a big traffic jam. Better, he reasoned, to fall in behind the first five or six horses and make his run late in the race from that position than to risk getting cut off.

The paddock was so crowded that two horses had to be saddled in the aisleway. Count Turf and his handlers were ignored by the people pressing against the fence to see the horses being saddled. Only one field horse in Derby history — Flying Ebony in 1925 — had ever won the race. Of the seventy-six sportswriters polled by Associated Press, not one had named Count Turf among the possible first three finishers.

The track was fast and very dusty. Because rain had appeared imminent, the track had not been sprinkled.

McCreary got away from his number nine stall with the first flight. By the time the field thundered past the stands, he was running eighth, behind Phil D and Hall of Fame running head to head on the lead.

"On the backstretch, Repetoire went to Phil D as Hall of Fame began to drop back, and Fanfare, which had everyone scared because he wore the devil red of Calumet, started up. McCreary took Count Turf up with him on the inside.

"Around the final turn, Repetoire was in front, but Count Turf, having got away from Fanfare, and with Phil D and Hall of Fame falling away, was moving to him on the outside."[11]

For McCreary, this was the 1944 Derby all over again. Count Turf was moving with tremendous power, responding nimbly as McCreary, weaving his mount between tiring horses gained on the leaders.

"He sounded like a can opener cutting through the field," said one of the other jockeys of McCreary later. "I'd hear him clucking and hollering as he picked up holes and shifted his horse back and forth."[12]

Count Turf circled a fast-fading Repetoire on the turn into the homestretch and set sail. Royal Mustang carried wide on the turn, rallied gamely, and made a

Timely Reward at Jamaica racetrack. Timely Reward finished up the track in the 1951 Derby won by Count Turf. The colt won $64,688 in his career. Timely just missed being in the first flight of the thoroughbreds of his time. Derby winners usually live out their days on stud duty at a beautiful horse farm. ("Yeah, he's happy, says groom Clem Brooks of Majestic Prince, the 1969 winner. "All he do is eat, sleep, and make love.") When the horses die, the grateful owner erects a statue or at least a gravestone over the grave. But the losers, such as Timely Reward — who was nearly destroyed because of leg problems — are another story. His owners, Mr. and Mrs. Wallace Gilroy, sold Timely. The colt began to drop down into cheaper races at cheaper racetracks — a familiar story. By the fall of 1954, when Timely was six, his leg troubles were so severe his owner considered having the colt put down. Danny Marzani, a former steeplechase rider, heard about the owner's plans and bought the horse for one dollar. Marzani vanned Timely to the Cornell School of Veterinary Medicine in Ithaca, New York, where an old veterinary friend removed part of the bone from Timely's left foreleg. After six months' rest, Marzani entered the colt in a race as a conditioner before training Timely to run over jumps. He came back lame. Marzani shipped Timely to George Ohrstrom, for whom he trained steeplechasers.

One day in 1963, a U.S. Park Policeman, Private Dennis R. Ayres, Jr., moonlighting as a blacksmith, was doing some work on the Ohrstrom farm when Timely — towering seventeen hands, the color of burnished mahogany — caught his eye. Marzani sold the horse to Ayres for one dollar, and Ayres called his superiors at Park Police headquarters in Washington. Now a sergeant decorated for bravery in the line of duty, Ayres credits Timely with his great arrest record: "I've just been a passenger aboard a good horse." Timely is now a pensioner on a Virginia farm.

run at Count Turf but couldn't catch him. Count Turf won by four lengths over Royal Mustang and Ruhe. Caked with dust, Arcaro came in a well-beaten sixth aboard Battle Morn.

"He just galloped," recalls Amiel, savoring the words he must have uttered a thousand times in the last twenty-odd years. "He win it all by himself."

Count Turf won it, as well, on three shoes, having thrown one when accelerating from the starting gate. The shoe was found and sent to Amiel.

In New York, a chagrined Sol Rutchick put out the story that he had missed his plane to Louisville, but few reporters believed him.

Amiel left Slim Sulley and a groom behind to ship North with Count Turf next day — the colt hadn't been nominated for the Preakness, but later beat the Preakness winner, Bold, in a race in New York — and he and McCreary took the night train to Manhattan. When the beefy restaurateur and his jockey reached their double compartment on the train, Amiel pressed a one-hundred-dollar bill into the palm of the dining car steward, asked that two thick steaks and a bottle of champagne be delivered to the compartment and ordered him not to tell anyone they were on the train. Amiel had brought the big gold Derby cup with him, refusing to leave it with a Downs official to have it engraved. He'd get it engraved himself. Neither Amiel nor McCreary had eaten since breakfast. They were hungry and exhausted. They loosened their ties and shoes and started to relax, admiring the cup that rested on the table between them. The steaks and champagne arrived. The beaming steward departed. Seconds later, the door burst open. In walked Red Smith, Frank Graham, Jr., and half-a-dozen other convivial souls from the sporting press. The party continued for hours as the train raced northward through the night and gray dawn. In New York, Conn McCreary — richer by his $10,000 riding fee and four $1,000 bonds Amiel had given him for his children — would find owners and trainers who had recently spurned him eagerly bidding for his riding services again.

Amiel, a widower, now lives alone in an apartment house on the upper West Side. Late each afternoon, he drives his big car down to a parking lot near Jack Dempsey's restaurant and takes his favorite table overlooking the tinselly bar, occupied mostly by tourists. His eyes miss nothing as he sits sipping a cup of coffee and going over the accounts. Gone are Damon Runyon, and Frank Graham, and Granny Rice, and the other writers who used to frequent The Turf, and later, Dempsey's.

Amiel still runs a few horses, and when he thinks they have a shot, he puts down a good bet. He's said to be an easy touch; a number of his waiters are bettors or horsemen temporarily down on their luck.

A handsome mantelpiece and mirror dominate the living room of his apartment. On the mantelpiece sits the big gold Derby cup. It's the first thing that catches one's eye when Jack Amiel loosens the safety chain on his door and welcomes guests inside.

Chapter 11
The Longest Derby

EVEN FOR an athletic young man fresh from veterinary school, it had been an exhausting, bloody business. Dawn was approaching, and all Alex Harthill could think about was getting back to Louisville, having a hot shower, and going to bed. For the past five hours on a spring night in 1948, Dr. Harthill had been dismembering and extracting a dead foal from a pain-wracked broodmare named Isolde at Warner L. Jones's Hermitage Farm outside Louisville. The foal was twisted around upside-down and backward in the mare's womb. Harthill and an assistant worked with a contraption called a Bennsch Saw, consisting of a wire running through a tube with a wire loop at the end. With his arms inside the mare's womb, Harthill first maneuvered the wire loop over the foal's head. Then his assistant pulled the loop tight, and the head was severed. Next came a leg, part of the trunk, another leg. Harthill's arms ached from the strain, and his legs cramped from crouching for long periods in a confined corner of the stall. "The mare was fighting me, and her muscles were fighting me," Harthill recalls. An assistant squirted oil into the already slippery region so the jagged bones of the foal wouldn't tear the mare's uterus during extraction and cause peritonitis to set in.

The mare was by imported Bull Dog, a son of the great Teddy, and Warner Jones had wanted to save Isolde at all costs. But Isolde's pain was intense, and two or three times he came close to asking Harthill to put her down humanely. Earlier in the evening, two other veterinarians had worked on the mare and, exhausted, had given up. Harthill was young and strong, self-confident, and amazingly skillful. Jones held on. Then suddenly it was over. Harthill had done his job well. The mare got back in foal the same season, and a few years later Isolde produced Dark Star, winner of the 1953 Kentucky Derby.

The young veterinary stripped down to his undershorts, tossed his blood-soaked overalls on the floorboards of his car, and headed down Brownsboro Road for Louisville at a fast clip. A state policeman flagged him down.

"I had some fast explaining to do," says Harthill. "I was covered with blood and my bloody clothes were on the floor of the car. He thought sure he'd caught a murderer."

In the twenty years that intervened between that

Dr. Alex Harthill.

"The horse that beat Native Dancer": That's how Harry Guggenheim's colt Dark Star was known after handing Alfred Gwynne Vanderbilt's gray Native Dancer the only defeat of his career in the 1953 Derby, one of the greatest upsets in the race's history.

spring night at Hermitage Farm and the first week in May 1968 when Harthill became a central figure in the Dancer's Image Derby scandal, he has combined a brilliant veterinary career — "He's the Ben Casey of the backstretch," says Lexington writer Mary Jane Gallaher — with a lot of explaining to racing commissions and other legal authorities about his extracurricular activities on and off the racetrack.

Quick to anger, Harthill has had a number of fistfights, including a well-publicized dustup with a college basketball coach. He has been charged, and acquitted, in New Orleans, of attempting to fix a horse race; charged, and acquitted, in Chicago, of illegally stimulating a racehorse. His bloodstock agent's and trainer's licenses in Kentucky were once temporarily revoked because of a technical infraction. A man of considerable charm and a self-styled "legendary figure," Harthill blames his problems on the jealousy of other veterinaries and horsemen and on investigative reporters of the *Courier-Journal* and Louisville *Times* who have shown a keen interest in his activities for a number of years.

Harthill's great-grandfather was a veterinary in Scotland, his father and grandfather were veterinaries in Louisville, and Alex was born into the profession. His father Henry Harthill had been a close friend of Ben Jones's of Calumet, and upon graduation from Ohio State's school of veterinary medicine, the Calumet horses were among Alex Harthill's first patients.

In 1948, when Calumet's Citation was winning the Derby, Harthill was treating the two-year-old Ponder for a serious wound inflicted when a groom accidentally stabbed the colt with a pitchfork. In time, Harthill became known as "the Derby vet." He obtained squatter's rights to an office in Barn 24 on the Churchill Downs backstretch — the only veterinary to have such an office — and the structure became known as "Harthill's barn." As the years went by, Derby horses with problems inevitably wound up in Harthill's barn in the weeks before the big race, horses such as Jack Price's Carry Back, whose shoe boil Harthill cured in time for the 1961 Derby. On September 6, 1972, the *Courier-Journal* ran an editorial calling for Harthill's removal from the barn. "The faith of bettors shouldn't be abused by allowing a veterinarian who has been under suspicion in case after case, here and elsewhere, to enjoy unique accommodations in a key security area of the Downs . . ." Harthill was asked to vacate his office sometime after this editorial.

Harthill became one of the first racetrack veterinaries — men who follow the horses from track to track, rather than simply serve a local track while it's in operation, then go back to routine farm cases. Harthill loved the backstretch. When the horses moved from Kentucky to Chicago, or Arkansas, or California, Harthill went along and of course knew the animals' histories.

Alfred Gwynne Vanderbilt's Native Dancer and rider Eric Guerin became racing's first television stars. The colt's 1952–1954 campaigns coincided with the early growth of the medium. The steel gray colt lost the 1953 Derby to outsider Dark Star and joined the long list of great horses that failed at Churchill Downs on the first Saturday in May.

In what appears to be suspiciously like a posed photograph of grooms celebrating Derby victory, Dark Star's handlers walk toward camera while the colt tags along behind.

Harthill numbers many owners, trainers, racing commissioners, and jockeys among his friends, including Willie Shoemaker and Eddie Arcaro. Eddie consulted him often about the quality of Derby mounts he had been offered. Many of Harthill's friends make light of his brushes with the authorities, and it's a source of some frustration to *Courier-Journal* reporters on his trail that their probes often founder for lack of cooperation from horsemen.

Peter Fuller, owner of Dancer's Image, second choice for the 1968 Kentucky Derby, knew nothing about Harthill when he asked for a good veterinary to take care of his colt during the ten days before the race. The Dancer had inherited the weak ankles of his sire, Native Dancer. Harthill was recommended, and Fuller accepted. Thus begins one of the most bizarre stories in racing history: "The Longest Derby," as it has been called.

At 4:40 P.M. on May 4, 1968, fourteen horses sprang from the starting gate in the ninety-fourth running of the Kentucky Derby. Two minutes, two and one-fifth seconds later, Fuller's steel gray colt flew across the finish line one and a-half lengths ahead of Calumet Farm's Forward Pass, the favorite. Three days later, however, on the following Tuesday, Churchill Downs stewards stunned the racing world with the announcement that Dancer's Image's postrace urinalysis had revealed that the colt won the race

The field pounds into the first turn in the 1968 Derby.

Lou Cavalaris and Peter Fuller (hand on bridle) lead Dancer's Image, Bobby Ussery up, into the winner's circle.

with traces of phenylbutazone, an illegal anti-inflammatory agent, in his system.

Angered and hurt by the charge, and protesting the innocence of his trainer Lou Cavalaris, Fuller defied custom that "the stewards' decision shall be final." He fought the case through the courts of Kentucky. Not until April 28, 1972 — nearly four years after the race — did the Kentucky Court of Appeals overturn a lower court ruling in Fuller's favor and decree that second-place-finisher Forward Pass was the winner and should receive the purse. The stubborn Fuller went back into court to obtain the $5000 gold Derby cup but lost that round, too. On July 20, 1973 — five years and seventy-five days after the running of the ninety-fourth Derby — Lynn Stone, Churchill Downs' president, drove from Louisville to Calumet Farm outside Lexington to present the cup with Forward Pass's name inscribed as winner.

Mrs. Gene Markey, Calumet's owner, was ill at her summer home in Saratoga Springs, New York, and did not attend the awkward little ceremony. There were no bands, of course; no crowds, no cheers — just Mrs. Margaret Glass, Calumet's office manager of more than three decades, farm manager Melvin Cinnamon,

two photographers, and a reporter from the Lexington *Leader*. Calumet had its eighth Kentucky Derby cup. Outside the paneled office where the presentation was made, Forward Pass grazed in his stallion paddock, switching at flies in the hot July sun. The longest Derby had finally ended. Most horsemen agree the Dancer's Image case was not Kentucky racing's finest hour.

Dancer's Image was foaled on April 10, 1965, in Maryland, and from the beginning, Bostonian Peter Fuller had high hopes for the colt. The colt's dam was a high-class stakes winner named Noor's Image, whose sire Noor had beaten Citation a number of times. Fuller had paid $20,000 to breed Noor's Image to Alfred Gwynne Vanderbilt's Native Dancer, the most he had ever invested in a breeding operation.

Fuller at one point considered naming his colt "A.T.'s Image" after his late father Alvan T. Fuller, Republican governor of Massachusetts from 1924 through 1928. A self-made man who opened his own bicycle shop at age fifteen, Alvan Fuller later obtained the Packard automobile agency in Boston and became wealthy. Governor Fuller was excoriated by liberals and radicals around the world when he refused to commute the death sentence of famed anarchists Sacco and Vanzetti, a decision that probably cost him the Republican vice-presidential nominations in 1928 and 1932.

"He simply believed in their guilt and stood

adamant against pressures under which others would have cringed," the Boston *Herald* defended him.[1]

Fuller was an independent, unorthodox, and popular governor, and his son inherited many of his qualities. As a child, Peter had been sickly but later became an outstanding athlete at Harvard University where he boxed and wrestled. Soft-spoken and gentlemanly, Fuller won fifty of fifty-five amateur boxing fights and was once described as "one of the nicest young men ever to beat somebody's brains out."

In 1949, he hung up his gloves and went to work in his father's Cadillac Automobile Company of Boston, the largest Cadillac-Oldsmobile retail dealership in the country, of which he is now president and owner. When Dancer's Image was foaled, Fuller had been racing on a modest scale for fifteen years. As a yearling, Dancer's Image ran in the meadows of Fuller's Runnymede Farm in North Hampton, New Hampshire, then was shipped to Ocala, Florida, for training, winding up at William McNight's Tartan Farm.

Fuller's trainer, Lou Cavalaris, convinced him that the colt's suspicious ankles were going to cause nothing but trouble and that Dancer's Image should be sold. So over the objections of Fuller's wife Joan, the gray colt went into Fasig-Tipton Company's Horses-in-Training Sale at Hialeah in February 1967.

Darby Dan's Proud Clarion convalescing from catarrh problems in the summer of 1967 at Belmont Park. A few months before, Proud Clarion had won the Kentucky Derby for trainer Loyd "Boo" Gentry. Bobby Ussery rode the horse to victory and had he won on Dancer's Image, he would have been the first jockey since Jimmy Winkfield to win successive Derbies.

A thorn from the rose blanket apparently found its way into Chateaugay's sleek hide, and the colt responded. Faintly amused at Chateaugay's antics, Braulio Baeza sits coolly aboard the 1963 Derby winner. Owner John Galbreath stands at right.

Reminiscent of a painting by Stubbs, a broodmare grazes peacefully at Darby Dan.

Olin Gentry (right) at Darby Dan.

"Pete, why do you want to sell him, he's so beautiful!" Joan Fuller kept repeating during the bidding.

Fuller had hoped to realize at least $35,000 but when the bidding stalled at $25,000, he bid the colt in himself for another $1000, paid the 10 percent sales commission, and had Dancer's Image back on his hands again.

"I told Lou the colt was his baby now, and that the rest was up to him."

Cavalaris won eight of fifteen races with Dancer's Image as a two-year-old, six of the victories in Canada where the colt was named the outstanding two-year-old of the year. However, not until the spring of 1968 did Fuller and Cavalaris sense that Dancer's Image might be able to go on to the classic distances of the Triple Crown races. After the colt had run a few poor races, a new jockey, Bobby Ussery, was tried, and the decision was also made to run the colt without blinkers. In his first race after these changes, Dancer's Image whipped Verbatim, a Derby hopeful. Fuller and Cavalaris began to make plans.

Fuller and Cavalaris decided to run the Dancer in the $100,000 Governor's Cup at Bowie on April 6. Two days before the race, the Reverend Martin Luther King, Jr., was assassinated as he stood on a motel balcony in Memphis. Rioting broke out in Baltimore, Washington, and other cities. Dr. King's funeral was set for the Monday following the Bowie race, and thought was given to canceling the Governor's Cup.

Flying down from Boston for the race, Fuller mulled over the death of Dr. King. As a trustee of Boston University, which Dr. King had attended and where Coretta King had studied at the conservatory of music,

Fuller had met Dr. and Mrs. King when the black civil rights leader had received an honorary degree. And while, as Fuller puts it, he hadn't studied Dr. King's position on every political subject, he did have the feeling that the black leader was trying to help his people through nonviolent means. As an amateur fighter Fuller had boxed and made friends with a number of blacks over the years. As a boy, his hero was Joe Louis, whom his father had taken him to see fight on more than one occasion. He felt that his relationships with blacks were natural ones, and that the civil rights movement had, ironically, put a strain upon them.

"I couldn't move about in their neighborhoods as freely as I was used to," says Fuller.

Fuller decided to donate the $62,500 winner's share of the Governor's Cup purse to Coretta King, to do with what she pleased, if the Dancer came home. Furthermore, he would publicize the gift in the hope that once the word got out in the black communities of the cities, some of the tension might be relieved for his gift would show that some members of the so-called Establishment cared, and cared deeply about Dr. King's murder.

Dancer's Image kept his part of the bargain. The gray streak came from back in the field — "God, you shoulda seen that sucker run!" exclaims Fuller — to win the Governor's Cup. Fuller reasoned that the time to get his message out, particularly in the Baltimore-Washington area, was during the televised presentation of the cup. Time and again he tugged the announcer's arm and whispered: "I've got something very important to say." But before anyone had realized it, the commercials and other trivia had eaten up the time. Next day, Fuller announced his gift with a press release, which was buried by most newspapers.

Meanwhile, Dancer's Image's big race in the Governor's Cup hadn't gone unnoticed. "About 10 days before the Wood," said Fuller, "the Tatum Bloodstock Agency in Kentucky came to me in behalf of a client, a Californian who wanted to give me $1 million for Dancer's Image. In $1000 bills. Cash. It was a fantastic offer, and I accepted it with one proviso. I'd promised to take my wife and seven children to the Kentucky Derby to see Dancer's Image run because the horse was raised on our farm in New Hampshire and is really a family pet. So I told the man from Tatum's I'd have to get my family's approval before I'd sell."[2]

Fuller called a family meeting. After the children had been heard, Joan Fuller said: "It's your horse and it's your decision. But if you sell I wouldn't be interested in going to the Derby."

Fuller protested.

"If you sell," said Joan, "I don't go to the Derby."

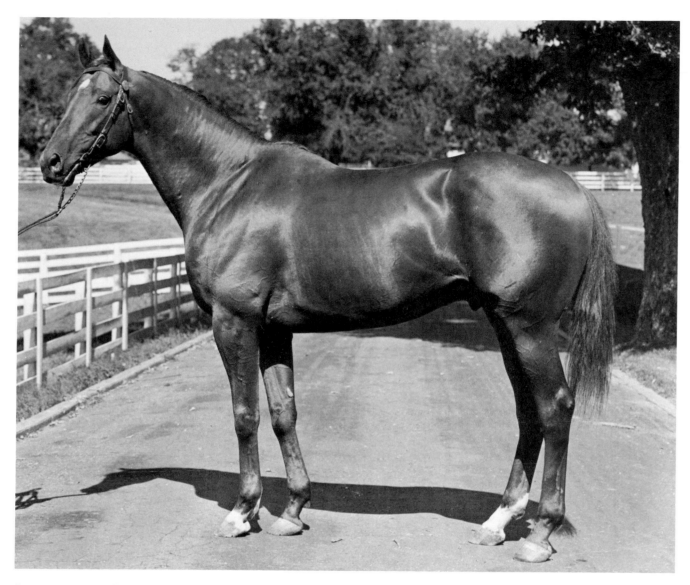

Swaps was originally owned by the Ellsworth brothers, Arizona cowpokes. In 1933, Rex and Reed Ellsworth, nondrinking, nonsmoking Mormons, rented an old truck and with $850 in savings from their fifty-dollar-a-month salaries drove across the country to Lexington, Kentucky. For $600 at the Fasig-Tipton Sales Company, they bought six mares and two weanlings and headed home. Rex became a power in California racing some years later, establishing a ranch near Chino. In 1946 he borrowed $160,000, sailed for Europe, and bought the stallion Khaled, a son of Hyperion, from Aly Khan. Khaled sired more than a dozen stakes winners, including Swaps, who won the 1955 Derby for Rex and his partner Mesach Tenney over Nashua and Summer Tan. Tenney rode to Louisville in the boxcar with Swaps and bedded down in an adjoining stall at Churchill Downs. Ellsworth and Tenney unsettled veteran Kentucky horsemen with their Spartan treatment of racehorses. "All horses need is good food, good care, and a good clean bed," Tenney said. "And they shouldn't be pestered by trainers and doting owners."

John Galbreath paid Ellsworth $1,000,000 for a half interest in Swaps when the colt finished racing. One year later, Mrs. Galbreath, the former Mrs. Russell A. Firestone, put up another $1,000,000 to buy Swaps outright.

FOLLOWING PAGE:
These foals gamboling at Darby Dan are potentially worth millions of dollars.

Forward Pass at stud, Calumet Farm.

"You can't sell the horse," added Peter Fuller, Jr., age eleven. "You just can't."[3]

When Peter Fuller told the Tatum Agency of his decision, the response was: "You must be kidding!"

"I am not kidding," said Peter, "but I am not about to explain, either."[4]

Fuller had some nervous moments during the running of the Wood Memorial, for Dancer's Image was running dead last down the backstretch at Aqueduct. Fuller turned his back on his family and squinted into his field glasses trying to will his gray colt on.

"All I could see were dollar bills flying away." Then Dancer's Image put on a powerful stretch run to beat Iron Ruler and Verbatim. During the winner's circle ceremony a television commentator announced Fuller's gift to Dr. King's widow.

The reaction in the black community was immediate.

"This Peter Fuller?" said a voice on the phone the next day. "Hey, we got a Nigger horse going for us, man. He's *dark* gray. Christ, he might win the Derby!" Letters came in from blacks, and before long, says Fuller, "The horse became a symbol of sorts; it was a delicate kind of thing."

The story got twisted around in the press, and word went out that Kentuckians had labeled Dancer's Image "a Nigger horse," which was not true. Fuller had received some nasty letters from Kentucky, but he says his reception in Louisville was friendly. The

year before, Dr. King had taken part in an open-housing demonstration in Louisville in the weeks preceding the Derby. Some of the open-housing advocates threatened to disrupt the big race to publicize their cause.

And a few days before the Derby, in what appeared to be a test run, several black teen-agers ran across the racetrack in front of a field of horses, nearly causing an accident. One jockey was quoted as saying he would have liked to run over them if he could. Dr. King argued against any demonstration at the Derby, and none was made. But National Guardsmen were everywhere to be seen, and the atmosphere had been dampened.

Dancer's Image was now a prime contender for the 1968 Derby. Fuller had the colt insured for $1,500,-000 and turned down a post–Wood Memorial offer of $2,000,000 for him. By this time, Kentucky breeders were telling Fuller that if the colt should go on and win the Triple Crown — won for the last time twenty years earlier by Citation — the animal would possibly be worth a $7,500,000 syndication price.

The colt was sent to Louisville ten days before the Derby and was met at the plane by Dr. Harthill and put in a stall in "Harthill's barn." Fuller was worried about security and asked Churchill Downs about the matter. They assured him that security was fine, that they had been protecting high-priced thoroughbreds for years. Even so, Fuller considered bringing his own security men. Finally he abandoned the idea because he thought it would draw that much more attention to his horse.

Had Fuller provided his own security, he would hardly have been setting a Derby precedent. From the race's inception, some trainers and grooms have slept with or near their horses. Ben A. Jones took elaborate precautions with Calumet horses at Churchill Downs, even constructing chicken-wire barricades around their stall doors. Groom Ed Sweat established himself in a tack room near Secretariat's stall in 1973, checking in on his horse every half-hour or so all night long.

From the time Dancer's Image arrived at the Downs on April 25, his right fore ankle was the subject of backstretch and press speculation. Visitors to his shed row found Dancer's Image standing with his front legs in a big tub of ice water every day. The colt's training schedule, too, was that of a bad-legged horse: gallops of three to four miles each day rather than tendon-straining speed drills. One reporter observed wryly that it looked as though Cavalaris was preparing Dancer's Image for the *Epsom* Derby. Cavalaris and his assistant Robert Barnard insisted that the colt's ankle problem was a minor one, that Dancer's Image had never taken a lame step, and that his ankles *im-*

Trainer Horatio Luro. The urbane Argentinian pulled off a neat Derby double when his gray colt Decidedly set a Derby record in 1962, then his little Northern Dancer came along in 1964 and broke Decidedly's record. Bill Hartack was in the saddle for both victories.

Born into a wealthy ranching and racing family that fell upon relatively hard times during the Depression, Luro came to America to make his way on the racetrack. A self-styled playboy in his early days, he once admonished a turf writer for asking him questions about horses on a Sunday. Sunday should be for *amour*. Luro became a disciple of Calumet's Ben A. Jones. Like Jones, Luro has an intuitive feeling for a good horse and is a stickler for detail. He carefully matches jockey with mount and pays close attention to his horses' moods.

Luro doesn't believe in rushing horses — or himself. "I like sunlight," he told reporters at Churchill Downs in 1962. "I do not get up at 4 o'clock. I get up at 6," *The Blood-Horse* reported. Consequently, his colt Decidedly did not show up for his work until eight-thirty or nine, long after most horsemen had put their charges back in the barns.

Luro and Decidedly, 1962 Derby winner. Though marred by the accident that caused Chris Chenery's Sir Gaylord to be scratched, the 1962 Derby was a good horse race. *The Blood-Horse* reported: "It was not only the fastest Derby in the race's 88-year history, it was one of the most exciting. The time of 2:00 2/5 was a full second better than Whirlaway's record which had stood since 1941. During the hectic mile and a quarter, the lead changed from the outsider Lee Town to Sunrise County to Admiral's Voyage to Roman Line before the gray Decidedly found an opening to the outside at the eighth pole. From that point on, with Bill Hartack riding hard, the gray moved away to be 2-1/4 lengths clear of the surprising Roman Line . . ." Ridan, the favorite, came in third behind Roman Line. Decidedly was by Determine, the 1954 winner, and was bred by George A. Pope, Jr., master of the 15,000-acre El Peco Ranch in Madera, California.

Bill Hartack, aboard Northern Dancer after his 1964 victory, is the Bobby Fischer of racing; blunt, irascible, independent — and the jockey with the best Derby record by far. "A lot of jocks get excited and rattled in the Derby; Hartack is just like always: like ice," says one trainer.

Hartack is tied with Eddie Arcaro with five Derby wins: Iron Liege (1957), Venetian Way (1960), Decidedly (1962), Northern Dancer (1964), and Majestic Prince (1969). However, Arcaro needed twenty-one attempts to win five times, while Hartack won his five in nine starts, a .555 batting average, which has been diluted somewhat by his finishing up the track in two more Derbies. Bill Shoemaker has won three Derbies.

For years Hartack has feuded with the racing press and has offended owners and trainers by telling them what he thought of their horses. Racing columnist Jim Murray once said Hartack had two drawbacks: "The first is his blunt honesty; the second is a disposition borrowed from the German general staff."

Born in poverty, the son of a Pennsylvania coal miner, Hartack has had to claw his way up. "Hatred is necessary for my work," he explained to Russ Harris of *The Thoroughbred Record* in May 1970. "I get mad when I ride. The madder I get the better I ride."

When Hartack goes postward in the Derby, he's furious.

proved after his gallops, which totaled eleven miles in the last three days before the Derby.

Lou Cavalaris is a big, cheerful man, the son of a Greek restaurant owner in Miami. Cavalaris's father had raced a few horses, and the boy had become interested in the sport. By the time Lou Cavalaris and Peter Fuller joined forces, Lou was running a busy public stable, Fuller being only one of a dozen owners for whom he worked.

"This past season . . . it was nothing for him to have horses in New York, Chicago, Detroit, and Toronto, simultaneously," according to *Turf and Sport Digest* in November 1968.

Cavalaris's busyness led him to the top of the North American trainers' list in 1966. He was enthusiastically recommended to Fuller by trainer Horatio Luro, the Argentinian who had won the 1962 Derby with Decidedly and the 1964 Derby with Northern Dancer.

Cavalaris was not on the job with Dancer's Image during Derby week, however, and partly for this reason, he and Fuller were to part company later. The trainer was off racing in Canada and Detroit, leaving the horse in the care of Barnard and groom Russell Parchen much of the time.

Seven days before the Derby, Dancer's Image had reared up and plunged about on the end of his shank while out grazing between the barns. He was an aggressive colt, and his hell-raising was in character. He must have wrenched his right fore ankle, for the next day, Sunday, it was swollen and hot. Cavalaris was in town and when Harthill recommended a dosage of four grams of phenylbutazone, the trainer agreed. Cavalaris had hitherto relied upon alcohol, liniments, ice tubs, and Azium, an analgesic less potent than phenylbutazone. The next day, the colt's ankle had lost its swelling and its inflammation, but the animal had developed a case of colic — diarrhea and stomach cramps — apparently from the bute. The trainer would later describe the attack as mild; Fuller remembers it as violent and serious, and he would argue that if Dancer's Image *had* had bute in his system during the Derby, the colt would have had a similar reaction the following day, which was not the case.

Phenylbutazone, trade name Butazolidin, or "bute," is neither a stimulant nor a depressant; it is an anti-inflammatory agent approved by the Food and Drug Administration and is used by many rheumatism sufferers. Ironically, Kentucky was one of the last states to outlaw Butazolidin, doing so most reluctantly in 1962 in the interest of uniform racing laws and under great pressure from other state racing commissions. Red Smith has noted that Kentucky has never been in the forefront of racing reforms and was "slower than most states to adopt the saliva test

Luro-trained Northern Dancer, Bill Hartack up, outlasts Hill Rise in a stirring finish to take the 1964 Derby and shave two fifths of a second from the record set in 1962 by Luro-trained Decidedly. Northern Dancer's record would stand until broken by Secretariat in 1973. According to *The Blood-Horse*, the race was probably won when Hartack "moved decisively with Northern Dancer at the five-furlong pole, taking Shoemaker and Hill Rise by surprise. The two horses had been running side by side behind a wall of three horses. Hartack eased his horse away from the rail and Northern Dancer spurted in front of Hill Rise and to the outside . . . Shoemaker said later that he . . . could not get his bigger horse moving in time to prevent Northern Dancer's nimble escape." Northern Dancer won by a long neck, running the last quarter in twenty-four seconds. In the process of making up ground, Hill Rise ran the last quarter in 23 3/5 seconds, equaling Whirlaway's famous final quarter.

and urinalysis, to put in film patrol cameras.

"Almost surely, horses have been doped for the Derby. Sir Barton, America's first triple crown winner who took the Derby in 1919, is celebrated as one of the great hopheads of history, supposed to have been coked to the eyes whenever he ran.

"In those days, 'touching up' was not uncommon:

Ethics only forbade double-crossing form players by running an animal 'hot' one day and 'cold' the next. Then the Federal Bureau of Narcotics got stuffy about illegal possession of drugs and horsemen with a parochial prejudice against Leavenworth stashed their hypodermics.

"However, the old school never accepted the notion that it was wrong to help a horse out. Old-timers still tell gleefully of seeing Derby horses enter the paddock 'with all their lights turned on' long after Sir Barton's day.

"Nor did Churchill Downs stewards ever win a reputation as hanging judges. They saw horses sloughed, impeded, and shut off in the Derby, and didn't lift an eyebrow for 93 years."[5]

The argument for outlawing Butazolodin is that a trainer can manipulate a horse's form by running him one week with bute, then withdrawing the analgesic when running the horse the next week. Yet Kentucky allows a trainer to condition a horse on bute but decrees that it must not show up in the horse's postrace urinalysis. Manipulation is thus still possible. Generally, bute leaves a horse's system in thirty to seventy-two hours, so Harthill had an ade-

Henry Forrest, trainer of Forward Pass.

quate margin of safety when he gave the colt a dosage six days before the race.

On Thursday, two days before the Derby, Dancer's ankle had filled with fluid again. Cavalaris was out of town, and Barnard was in charge. Harthill says that he told Barnard before witnesses — including Joe Hirsch of the *Daily Racing Form* — that the colt was in such bad shape he should not be galloped that day and should be scratched from the Derby. Also standing by, says Harthill, was a famous trainer, who reportedly said he wouldn't run a $1500 claimer in Dancer's condition. Hirsch refuses to confirm or deny the incident.

Harthill says Barnard told him the colt would have to gallop even if his leg fell off, for those were Cavalaris's orders. Harthill then gave the colt a heavy dose of Azium. The colt galloped.

Mrs. Jack Price reaches for the bridle of Carry Back, the 1961 Derby winner, with twenty-three-year-old Johnny Sellers aboard. (Mrs. Price's husband is the shorter of the two men at her left.) In a stirring finish Carry Back made up thirteen lengths in the last quarter to win. What Carry Back lacked in conformation and breeding the colt made up for in courage and speed. Carry Back was foaled at Ocala Stud Farm in Ocala, Florida, and now stands at Price's Dorchester Farm. He raced through the age of five, winning $1,226,665. Like his colt, Price has spirit. He started out as a "candy butcher" on railroad trains in the Cleveland station and went on to found a successful machine tool company that he sold to his brothers. With the proceeds, he went into horse racing. Price personifies the spirit of Ocala, the central Florida thoroughbred breeding center, and the self-made men who first came into the sport there in the mid-1940s to challenge the old, wealthy racing families who once dominated the sport. He's a forthright, irrepressible man.

108

Harthill subsequently told a number of people that he was so disgusted with the way Dancer's Image was being handled that he walked away from the colt that Thursday. He later gave a deposition in which he stated that he had never seen a colt so "butchered." Yet the next morning, Harthill was standing outside the colt's stall in Barn 24 at 7:30 A.M. when a group of newsmen appeared.

"Nothing wrong with the ankle that I can see," said Harthill. "Fact is, it looks better today than any time since he arrived here."[6]

Fuller was present, as was Cavalaris.

"O.K., Doc, but I've been away from this horse for a couple of days and want to be dead sure," said Cavalaris. "We'll send him three-eighths," he said to exercise boy Ernie Warme. "Break him off at the eighth pole."[7]

In the crowd that followed the gray colt to the track was Jack Price, owner-trainer of Carry Back, the story

"The biggest day of my life!" exclaimed groom James L. Stevenson, better known as "Popeye," after Kauai King came home in front in the 1966 Derby. A son of Native Dancer, Kauai King avenged the defeat of his sire thirteen years before, running the one and a quarter mile in 2:02 — the exact time that Dark Star ran when defeating the Dancer. Though a leading trainer at Churchill Downs, Henry Forrest had never had a Derby starter before Kauai King. Jockey Don Brumfield from Nicholasville, Kentucky, had been the leading rider at Churchill many times, yet he, too, had never started in the big race. Though a quiet, churchgoing bachelor, Brumfield couldn't contain his excitement after the Derby win. "I'm just the happiest hillbilly hardboot you've ever seen!" he yelled (Louisville Courier-Journal).

book winner of the 1961 Derby. Price caught Dancer's Image in :37 for his brief spin. The colt had run smoothly and returned to his barn in fine fettle. His twenty-four-hour recovery had been truly remarkable.

During the protracted hearings that followed the 1968 Derby, a number of veterinarians would testify that such a recovery was "consistent" with a dosage of phenylbutazone, that Azium could not have effected it. Others would testify that horses sometimes make remarkable recoveries without the aid of any drug.

Inconsistency marks Harthill's statements about Dancer's Image. Nine days before the Derby, and again two days after the Derby, he certified Dancer's Image sound for insurance purposes. Yet when asked during the hearings if he had bet on Dancer's Image he said no, that he would never bet on a horse with such bad legs. Yet the day after the Derby, he asked Peter Fuller if he might one day breed a mare to Dancer's Image when the colt went to stud, and Fuller had said yes.

Other strange happenings attended the 1968 Derby. Before the Blue Grass Stakes, Forward Pass's regular jockey Don Brumfield, a local boy from Nicholasville, Kentucky, had suddenly taken ill with food poisoning. Two years before, Brumfield had won the Derby on Kauai King, a Native Dancer colt trained by Henry Forrest, who was now conditioning Forward Pass for Calumet Farm. For the Blue Grass, Forrest secured the services of Milo Valenzuela, who had ridden Calumet's last Derby winner, Tim Tam, a decade earlier. As fate would have it, this was the second time that Valenzuela was to profit by another jockey's pre-Derby misfortune. In 1958, Bill Hartack was Tim Tam's regular rider, but Valenzuela won the mount in the Derby after Hartack suffered a fractured leg in a starting gate accident. (Interestingly, Henry Forrest had served a sixty-day suspension the year before when bute was found in a postrace test of one of his Calumet horses.) Forward Pass, a big bay standing sixteen hands two inches, won the Blue Grass by five lengths over T.V. Commercial, further confirming the colt as the Derby favorite.

After the Blue Grass, Forrest says he received an urgent phone call from Admiral Gene Markey, husband of Calumet's owner, instructing him to immediately sign up Valenzuela for the Derby.

Forrest had already discussed the possibility of the Derby ride with Valenzuela, and he knew there would be no problem getting him as jock. Nevertheless, he got on the phone right away from his Lexington motel. Eventually, he tracked the jockey down in a roadhouse between Lexington and Louisville where he was having dinner with Harthill, with whom he was spending Derby week. Valenzuela said he would be de-

lighted to ride Forward Pass. Brumfield was instructed to announce that he had taken himself off Forward Pass because he was still feeling ill and could not give the colt a ride that would do him justice. Brumfield would eventually receive a check from Calumet in the same amount as that given Valenzuela.

Fuller, meanwhile, was having a glorious time. In his early days in racing, he had been criticized in the sporting press for trying to mastermind his trainers, whom he fired with some rapidity. By now, he was consciously staying out of his trainer's affairs, and he says the talk of Butazolodin meant little or nothing to him. Fuller had brought sixty-five friends and relatives with him to the Derby he was totally confident of winning. They all stayed at the Brown Suburban Motel, journeying together to Churchill Downs in a bus.

"It was one of those once-in-a-lifetime things," says Fuller. "It was great fun, *really great* fun!"

Though a teetotaler, Fuller was the life of the big party from Boston. At one point, he jumped onto a chair to announce that he'd had a dream — "more of a vision, really" — in which Dancer's Image had trailed the field in the early running, then had come with a great rush to run down Forward Pass in the stretch. Fuller's partisans cheered. Fuller was so confident of victory that he made a dry run from his box in the stands to the winner's circle so that on race day he'd be sure to be in the circle in time to meet the Dancer, whom he referred to as his "pal."

On Derby Day, May 4, Harthill and Cavalaris felt the colt was fit to run, and the Churchill Downs veterinarian also gave Dancer's Image the green light. They decided against giving the colt any more medication, though Dancer's Image wore cold water bandages from the backstretch to the paddock, his handlers stopping every now and then to pour fresh ice water on them. Some observers said later that Dancer's Image favored his right front leg while cantering postward.

The ninety-fourth Kentucky Derby was to go off as Fuller had seen it in his "vision."

In the first run past the stands, Kentucky Sherry was in the lead, followed by Captain's Gig and Forward Pass. Dancer's Image was dead last, and Fuller says he could feel his friends' eyes on his back and knew they were saying to themselves: "You brought us all the way down here for this? *This* is your great horse?"

Henry Forrest was furious at this point. Valenzuela had come whipping out of the gate, then had taken Forward Pass back, then had gone to whipping again as the field rocketed into the first turn.

"Jesus Christ, he's a horse, not a Rhodes Scholar," exclaimed Forrest.

Lewis Finley, Jr., a Churchill Downs steward, represented the racing commission.

Leo O'Donnell, a steward.

"As Kentucky Sherry neared the three-eighths pole, Forward Pass hurried past a tiring Captain's Gig and took aim on the leader. Dancer's Image was ten lengths back in tenth place. The field swung wide on the final turn, Kentucky Sherry still maintaining a slight lead passing the quarter pole, with Forward Pass under strong urging and without a straw in his path. As the field swung wide, Bobby Ussery, who had been outside two horses on the turn with Dancer's Image, cut the corner sharply and dropped in on the rail. Suddenly, Dancer's Image was out of the pack and right at the leaders. Near the three-sixteenths pole, Ussery dropped his whip but Dancer's Image surged past the leaders and the running of the race was almost over. Dancer's Image drew away."[8]

Dancer's Image won by one and one-half lengths, Forward Pass led Francie's Hat by a neck, with T.V. Commercial fourth, and Kentucky Sherry fifth. Joan and Peter Fuller, followed by spiffed-up little Fullers clutching "Dancer's Image" signs, sprinted for the winner's circle. It was, said Peter Fuller later, "the most fantastic thrill of my life." Bobby Ussery had won the Derby the year before on Darby Dan Farm's Proud Clarion, and this victory made him the first jockey since Jimmy Winkfield — in 1901 and 1902 with His Eminence and Alan-a-Dale — to win consecutive Derbies.

At 7:30 P.M., Churchill Downs President Wathen Knebelkamp was still entertaining Joan and Peter Fuller and about one hundred guests in the track's private dining room. "Man, I'm telling you," Knebelkamp said, "when the 'official' sign goes up, I'm one happy fellah."[9]

Events were meanwhile transpiring in the Kentucky State Racing Commission's mobile laboratory on the backstretch that would make Knebelkamp a most *unhappy* fellah and transform Fuller's fantastic thrill into the keenest disappointment of his life. In this laboratory, commission chemists test the saliva and urine of the winner of the Derby and one other runner chosen at random, in this case, Kentucky Sherry.

Immediately after leaving the winner's circle, Dancer's Image was led to a detention barn where the saliva sample was taken. Then the Dancer was cooled out for half an hour. One hour later, a urine sample was obtained and sent to the laboratory.

"Each specimen is labeled and numbered — a white tag with a number, followed by the letter S for the saliva samples, and a yellow tag with a number and the letter U for bottles of urine," wrote *Sports Illustrated*'s Whitney Tower. "The labels are actually double tags. One half, with the horse's name and number on it, goes to the office of the track's three officiating stewards. The other half, with only the number on it, remains with the specimen. When the stewards receive all the tags representing specimens from the horses tested on any racing day, they put the whole batch in a small brown envelope which is then sealed, stamped across the fold in three places with red wax and locked up, generally overnight.

"Meanwhile, back at the trailer, lab technicians have taken each specimen, tested it in several chemical processes that take roughly three hours, and then marked each tag with a notice that reads 'negative' or very occasionally, 'positive.' Inasmuch as these tags have nothing but serial numbers on them, the chemists in the trailer are not aware of the names of the horses whose specimens they are testing."[10]

The specimen of Dancer's Image was labeled 3956 U and turned over for testing to Jimmy Chinn, a commission technician, in the trailer. All that Chinn knew was that the specimen came from one of the horses running in one of the ten Derby Day races. During the course of Chinn's tests, the specimen began to change color, and he knew he had a "positive." He immediately phoned his superior, Maurice Cusick, who in turn phoned Kenneth Smith, president of Louisville Testing Laboratory, Inc., under contract to the racing commission to test horses for illegal drugs or medication. Smith hurried to the laboratory and conducted tests of his own. At 11:30 P.M. he phoned Lewis Finley, Jr., the Churchill Downs steward representing the racing commission, and informed him that he had a "positive" on the Derby Day card. Finley

Trainer Doug Davis at Keeneland.

112

told Smith to submit his written report on Monday, the next racing day, which was the usual procedure.

On Sunday, Peter Fuller and his family were the guests of Warner L. Jones at his Hermitage Farm outside Louisville. Jones was talking in terms of syndicating Dancer's Image for $3,000,000, and Fuller was delighted. "I've spent $2 1/4 million on my racing operation in 15 years and syndication of this horse could get me out," Fuller told Gene Ward of the New York *Daily News* that morning.

Also on Sunday, chemist Smith must have had second thoughts, for he returned to his downtown Louisville laboratory, put some of the 3956 U sample in a mailing carton, and sent it air mail special delivery to Lewis Harris, a chemist in Lincoln, Nebraska, after first telephoning Harris and asking him to run routine checks on the sample and let him know what he found.

In a copyrighted story by Billy Reed, the *Courier-Journal* would later report that on that Sunday "on Finley's personal phone, calls of one minute each were placed to the residence of trainer Doug Davis, Jr., near Lexington, and to the residence of Dr. Alex Harthill in Louisville."[11]

Finley later told the *Courier-Journal*, "Offhand, I don't recall making the calls. Both Doug and Alec are good friends of mine, you know. Why Doug's dad was the one who helped me get started in racing."[12]

On Monday morning, May 6, Finley and stewards Leo O'Donnell and John G. Goode opened the brown envelope that matched up the tag number 3956 U with the name of the horse: Dancer's Image. When Finley discovered that the tainted specimen belonged to the winner of the Derby, he started to swear. He cursed some more when Smith failed to turn in his "positive." Smith said he had mailed a sample of the urine to Lewis Harris in Nebraska, and he thought the sample needed "further testing." The stewards informed Smith they were not interested in the findings of a chemist in Nebraska, that they were paying *him* to test horse urine. Smith said he would stake his life on the fact that he had a positive. The stewards told him, "Write up your report."

Cavalaris was in Lexington visiting horse farms, so the stewards summoned Robert Barnard and had security men search Dancer's Image's stall for signs of Butazolodin. None was found.

Doug Davis, whose horses were stabled near Barn 24, and who is a close friend of Harthill's, noticed the security men and found out what had happened. He left a message at the Brown Suburban Motel for Cavalaris to phone him as soon as he came in from

Peter Fuller's lawyers at Dancer's Image hearing.

The Dancer's Image hearing. Peter Fuller is stunned by ruling that his colt was drugged. From left to right: J. S. Friedberg, John A. Bell III, Chairman George Egger, Laban Jackson, and Stanley Lambert.

Johnny Longden warms up Majestic Prince for the 1969 Belmont Stakes. Majestic Prince had won the Derby and the Preakness and was exhausted. Trainer Longden urged owner Frank McMahon not to run the horse in the Belmont, arguing that the colt had lost a lot of weight and needed at least six weeks of rest. At first McMahon agreed. He had bought Majestic Prince for the then record price of $250,000 at the Keeneland Yearling Sales on Longden's advice. Longden brought the colt along slowly in California, realized he had an unusual horse, and waited patiently until the end of the year before racing him. With Bill Hartack aboard, the colt won the Kentucky Derby in a driving, head-to-head duel with Paul Mellon's Arts and Letters. The Derby and the Preakness took a lot out of Majestic Prince. At Pimlico the Prince stretched out in his stall and slept for hours. "Poverty creases" appeared in his rump for the first time, and his flanks tucked up. Leslie Combs II, the colt's breeder, had examined Majestic Prince and urged McMahon to take Longden's advice.

Lexington, then he got in touch with Harthill. That evening Harthill, Davis, Barnard, and Cavalaris met in Davis's room at the Standiford Motel. Davis later testified that Cavalaris was highly emotional, pacing back and forth protesting his innocence, pounding on the walls with his fists. After Harthill left, said Davis, Cavalaris asked him if he thought *Harthill* had given the colt the Butazolidin. Davis assured Cavalaris that Harthill would never do such a thing. But now Davis

says he suspected Cavalaris was going to try to pin the blame on Harthill.

Davis informed Harthill of his fears, whereupon Harthill conceived a bizarre scheme to "test" Cavalaris's honesty. He would grind up some Butazolidin and put it in the Dancer's feed, letting Cavalaris think he was doing it to help him, as this would lead investigators to think that outsiders had thrown the bute into the feed. Harthill reasoned that if Cavalaris were honest, he would refuse to go along with the scheme. Davis said bute was too hot to handle, so the two men decided to grind up aspirin, letting Cavalaris *think* it was bute. The distraught Cavalaris confused an already confusing situation by tossing half the contaminated grain onto a manure pile and saving one bag of the doctored grain.

Next morning, when Arthur S. Grafton and Edward S. "Ned" Bonnie, attorneys for Fuller and Cavalaris, heard about all this, they were horrified. Grafton disposed of the bag of grain in bushes near his home. That same morning — Tuesday, May 7 — the stewards announced that phenylbutazone had been found in Dancer's Image's system, and that purse money would be redistributed.

Pandemonium ensued. "Derby Winner Doped," read headlines across the United States. Cavalaris and Barnard were automatically suspended for thirty days. Fuller was dumfounded. That evening, Joan and Peter Fuller flew home to Boston. In the seat ahead of them, a man was reading an afternoon paper with news of the Dancer's Image case.

"They'll do anything to win the Derby," said the man to his neighbor.

"Who are they talking about?" asked Joan.

"They are talking about thee and me," answered Fuller.

The Fullers were met at Logan Airport by Governor John A. Volpe and a hundred people, including some of their children whom they had not taken to the Derby.

Fuller told newsmen at the emotional homecoming that security at Churchill Downs was laughable, that anyone could have gotten to his horse.

"Everything was such a marvelous dream . . .," he said. "And now this is all such a nightmare."[13]

In the dawn hours of Wednesday, the day Dancer's Image was scheduled to leave Louisville for Baltimore and the Preakness, *Courier-Journal* reporters Billy Reed and Jim Bolus sneaked into the Churchill Downs backstretch, made their way to Barn 24, and found the seventy-two-year-old guard sound asleep.

In the lengthy hearings that followed, Fuller's lawyers produced expert chemists from universities and elsewhere who testified that Kenneth Smith's tests of Dancer's Image's urine were sloppily conducted and inconclusive. Attorney General John Bayne Breckinridge, a descendant of John C. Breckinridge, and his assistant George Rabe produced witnesses who upheld Smith and his findings. For their post-Derby doctoring of the colt's feed, Davis and Harthill received minor punishment in the form of $500 fines.

Bad luck plagued Dancer's Image again in the Preakness when the colt ran third behind winner Forward Pass: Dancer's Image was disqualified for interfering with horses. Though veterinaries at Belmont Park said the colt was sound enough to run in the Belmont Stakes, Fuller did not want to run any more risk of injuring his horse and retired him. (The following year, Frank McMahon, owner of undefeated Majestic Prince, faced a similar, if slightly less dramatic decision. His horse was bone tired, and his trainer did not think the colt should run in the Belmont. Under pressure from racing officials, and some turf writers, McMahon ran the colt. Majestic Prince met his one and only defeat, developed leg problems, and never raced again.) Because, as Fuller puts it, "Warner Jones disappeared with the morning sun," after the Butazolodin scandal had cast a cloud over Dancer's Image, Fuller syndicated his colt himself, retaining many of the shares.

Through the remainder of 1968 after the Derby

Longden did not want to run the exhausted Majestic Prince in the 1969 Belmont Stakes. He told reporters he couldn't remember a horse that had been "worth a damn" after winning the Belmont. While some angry sportswriters hurried to their record books to come up with names of numerous Belmont winners, such as Native Dancer, who were indeed worth a damn after the Belmont, McMahon changed his mind. He ordered Longden to get ready to run the colt in the mile-and-a-half test. "Something has been said about my being a quitter," McMahon explained. Although many trainers criticized Longden for "putting the knock on the Belmont," they agreed that he was the best judge of whether the colt should run, especially in view of the fact that he exercised the horse himself and had done such a magnificent job bringing him through an undefeated career. They agreed as well with his thesis that "the way you can hurt a good horse is to drive him when he's tired."

Longden weighs Majestic Prince at Belmont. The colt weighed only 1080 pounds, forty pounds off the normal weight. Majestic Prince ran a game race in the Belmont to finish second behind Arts and Letters. Then he developed leg trouble and never ran again.

until early April 1969, Dancer's Image remained on the record books as the official Derby winner, even though the Kentucky Racing Commission had voted to award the purse to Mrs. Markey's Calumet Farm and Forward Pass.

In what some Kentucky racing writers considered an uncharacteristic fit of anger and poor sportsmanship, Mrs. Markey announced that she would not race her horses in Kentucky. "I can't see the point of racing where I can't win," she told Jim Bolus. "When a horse is disqualified, he's disqualified."

On April 10, 1969, the commission finally changed its rule concerning horses found with illegal medications in their systems, decreeing that they be placed last in addition to forfeiting the purse.

On December 11, 1970, it appeared as though Fuller's long, costly court battles had paid off; Franklin Circuit Court Judge Henry Meigs ruled that chemist Smith's tests were inconclusive and that Dancer's Image had, indeed, won the 1968 Derby. Fuller was ecstatic — but his ecstasy was shortlived. The racing commission took the case to the Court of Appeals, which upheld the original findings of the Churchill Downs' stewards.

Peter Fuller's dogged fight to clear his horse's name had cost him $250,000.

Chapter 12
A Divine Victory

CATHOLIC HORSEPLAYERS tell of a member of their faith who overheard a priest blessing a thoroughbred in the paddock before a race. Whereupon that horse won going away.

The horseplayer again spotted the priest in the paddock before the next race. This time the cleric was mumbling incantations before a droopy-eyed animal who turned out to be a long shot. Certain of a betting coup, the observant bettor hurried to the mutuel windows and bet a bundle on the blessed horse to win. Whereupon the animal in question finished dead last.

"Father, whatever happened?" asked the distraught horseplayer when he caught up with the priest after the race. "I'm a good Catholic, full of faith. I saw you bless one horse and he came in. I saw you bless the other horse and he finished nowhere."

"Son," replied the priest. "You can't be *that* good a Catholic. You obviously can't tell the difference between a blessing — and the last rites of the church."

After Dust Commander's stunning upset in the 1970 Derby, Catholic horseplayers had an even better story to tell. Furthermore, it was true. For Dust Commander received a blessing from Archbishop Emanuel Milingo of Zambia, and thereby hangs a delightful Derby tale.

The blessing took place in the leafy paddock of Keeneland Race Course before the running of the Blue Grass Stakes. The archbishop was in Dust Commander's paddock entourage that day as the houseguest of Mrs. Robert E. Lehmann, wife of the colt's owner. The late Mr. Lehmann, then a forty-nine-year-old retired building contractor from Ohio, had underwritten the African's education for the priesthood through the Society for the Propagation of the Faith.

In his own way, Mr. Lehmann liked to say, Emanuel Milingo had proven to be as good an investment as Dust Commander, whom the Ohioan had picked up at the Keeneland Yearling Sales for a scant $6500 in 1968. Emanuel Milingo became an exceptionally brilliant student, moving swiftly upward in the church hierarchy to the position of archbishop, which he had attained in 1969 at the age of thirty-nine. He had come to this country to raise money for the Zambia Helpers' Society, which provides trade school education for native Zambians, and he had stopped over to visit the Lehmanns at their Golden Chance Farms near Paris, Kentucky. Archbishop Milingo fell in love with the Bluegrass country and the thoroughbred horse.

Black African archbishops are uncommon visitors in the Keeneland paddock. Even so, the horseplayers paid little heed to the cleric or to Dust Commander, whose odds were thirty-five to one. Not that there was anything in Dust Commander's appearance or record to warrant special attention. The chestnut colt stood just over fifteen hands and weighed barely 900 pounds, the size of many stable ponies. By Bold Commander, a son of Bold Ruler, out of Dust Storm, Dust Commander was what trainers call "a useful kind of horse." The colt was durable, game, and liked to run a distance, despite the Bold Ruler blood in his veins. In twenty-two races at two and three, Dust Commander had earned over $50,000.

Mike Manganello was a "useful" kind of jockey, though not well known outside the Middle West, and he had never ridden the winner of a $100,000-plus race. He had one advantage over eastern jockeys with bigger names, however: He had ridden the Keeneland and Churchill Downs tracks thousands of times and in all weather.

Trainer Don Combs of Lexington had, since childhood, been torn by two ambitions — to be a lawyer

The seventeen-horse field in the 1970 Derby leaps away from the starting gate and heads down the long Churchill Downs homestretch, dubbed "Heartbreak Lane" by sportswriters. Dust Commander, the surprise winner, is second from left near the rail.

and to be a horse trainer. Three years before, he had finally resolved his dilemma by quitting law school at the University of Kentucky with but one semester to go. Now he had a small public stable, but to make ends meet, he managed an apartment house in Lexington in his spare time. He was handsome, poised, and a stylish dresser.

Just before the Keeneland bugler blew "First Call" for jockeys up, Archbishop Milingo stepped in front of Dust Commander and with utmost seriousness de-

livered the church's traditional blessing for domestic animals.

It didn't take the archbishop's quick mind very long to figure out how the pari-mutuel system works, though before his Kentucky visit he had never been to a racetrack. Once the horses had started postward, he bought a six-dollar combination ticket on Dust Commander and confidently assured Mrs. Lehmann that her colt would whip the ears off Naskra, Corn Off The Cob, Hard Work, and the other more highly regarded entries.

At the bell, Manganello drove Dust Commander straight toward the rail where he ran, saving ground around the sloppy track. Then he maneuvered his nimble little colt between horses and drove to a three-

fourths-of-a-length win over Corn Off The Cob, a star of the winter season in Florida, and Naskra, another respected Derby hopeful.

Racing and breeding horses runs a close second to Robert Lehmann's passion for big-game hunting, a priority that Kentuckians find difficult to fathom. Twice a year he disappears for weeks at a time to remote parts of the globe to try his luck. Thus it was not surprising that at the very moment his colt was winning the Blue Grass, Lehmann was on the border of India and Nepal, crouching in a treetop shooting stand where he had been stationed for eleven days. He had already shot one leopard and a tiger, but he was hoping for a record kill. That night, his wish came true: He shot a magnificent tiger, a ten-foot-long

beast weighing nearly 700 pounds, just 200 pounds less than Dust Commander.

When Lehmann phoned his wife from Calcutta, she told him of Dust Commander's win in the Blue Grass. He authorized her to go ahead with plans for the Kentucky Derby, an opportunity he had not foreseen when he left Kentucky for the roof of the world. Then he started home, arriving just twenty-four hours before the race.

Nineteen seventy was not a vintage year for three-year-olds. The Derby hopefuls had spent the winter and spring taking turns beating one another. Dust Commander had won a stakes race in Florida but then had hurt a leg and spent more than a month recuperating while a colt named My Dad George won the

Flamingo and the Florida Derby, with Corn Off The Cob second on both occasions. The smart money was going on these two. There was support, as well, for Silent Screen, the 1969 two-year-old champion and John Jacobs's entry of Personality and High Echelon.

Dust Commander's victory in the Blue Grass was considered accidental. He would be just one of seventeen thoroughbreds going postward in what Whitney Tower termed the most wide-open Derby in two decades.

It had been raining on and off for a week in Louisville, but on Derby morn the sun came out and the track started to dry. By post time the track was listed as "good," a synonym for "tiring." Jim Bolus of the Louisville *Courier-Journal* wrote: "Dust Commander is a forgotten colt. For some reason, most people don't want to believe that he's as good as he looked in winning the Blue Grass.

"It should be noted that the trim little colt, after pulling away to his Blue Grass score, worked out an additional furlong in the sparkling time of 12 seconds

to complete the Derby distance in 2:03 1/5 — on a sloppy track."[1]

The morning of the race, Archbishop Milingo had to leave for a church meeting in Covington, Kentucky, and Mrs. Lehmann asked him whether he shouldn't bless Dust Commander again.

The African replied that once an animal is blessed, he is blessed. He assured her, however, that he planned to watch the race on television and would try to give the colt an extra, spiritual "shove." Then he handed Mrs. Lehmann his $103 Blue Grass winnings from the six-dollar ticket and asked her to bet them on Dust Commander's nose.

Mrs. Lehmann recalls vividly that a worried look shadowed the African's features at this point. He said "a dark cloud hangs over the Derby" and while it would not involve Dust Commander, it was nevertheless upsetting him. He couldn't explain his feeling, but "the number four horse" would be affected.

Mrs. Lehmann and her husband drove to the Church of Annunciation in Paris before heading for Louisville. She wore a medal of the Immaculate Conception. Lehmann, still weary from his seventy-two-hour journey home, carried a rosary in his left pocket and four little "lucky bones" from the necks of the leopard and the record tiger he had killed.

Around his neck Manganello wore a Saint Christopher's medal that a horse owner had asked the Pope to bless for the jockey.

At the break, Dust Commander took a bouncing in the big field, but Manganello managed to tuck into a good position on the rail, as he had done in the Blue Grass. Feeling his horse full of run at the half-mile pole, he urged Dust Commander forward and as he said later, "let him start to pick up horses by himself." As the closely packed field surged around the far turn, a gasp suddenly went up from the crowd — a horse had gone down and his jockey now lay inert in the damp dirt. Several following horses jumped over him. The horse was Holy Land, number four; the jockey, Hector Pilar, who sustained a back injury that would ground him for nearly a year.

"As the closely packed field surged around the far turn, a gasp suddenly went up from the crowd — a horse had gone down and his jockey lay inert in the damp dirt, a number of following horses having jumped over him. It was the number four horse, Holy Land; the jockey, Hector Pilar, sustained a back injury that would keep him grounded for nearly a year."

In the crowded field of horses, Manganello realized that he would have to go to the outside. He swung Dust Commander wide into the homestretch, leaving most of the field behind. At the eighth pole, Dust Commander took the lead, beating My Dad George by five lengths, High Echelon third.

In her excitement, Mrs. Lehmann remembered the archbishop's winning mutuel ticket: The Zambia Helper's Society was richer by $1662.60, the result of his sensational parlay from the original six-dollar bet on the blessed little horse at Keeneland.

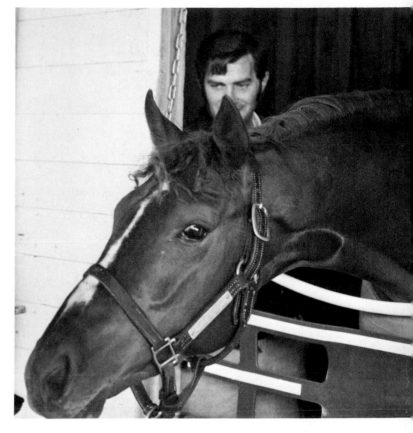

Dust Commander cadges a lump of sugar the morning after his 1970 Derby victory. In the stall with the colt is his young trainer, Don Combs.

Tough little Mike Manganello arranges his roses after his 1970 winning ride. In the background, a jockeys' room attendant sniffs an American Beauty from the jockey's bouquet.

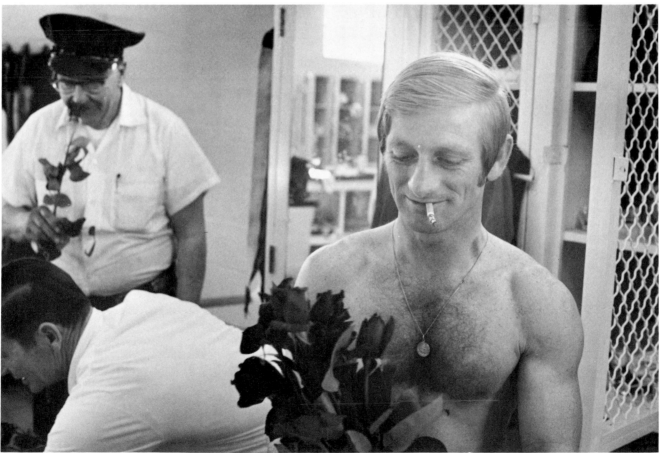

Chapter 13
Dr. Jenny's Masterpiece

TRAINER SIDNEY WATTERS, JR., had no premonition of tragedy on March 31 when he led his 1971 Kentucky Derby favorite toward the Belmont Park training track for a routine workout. Watters had waited a lifetime for a colt like Hoist the Flag and he had left nothing to chance. This morning was no exception.

Watters had run Flag sparingly at age two — only four races, all of them at Belmont in the space of four weeks in the early fall of 1970. The colt had won them all with impressive ease, although his number was taken down after the Champagne Stakes in the costliest disqualification in racing history: The $145,-025 purse and traditional jeroboam of champagne were awarded the owners of the second horse, Limit to Reason.

While the other Derby hopefuls were racing hard over the winter in Florida and California, Flag was legged up in the sandy soil and pine-scented air of Camden, South Carolina. Now the other Derby colts were showing signs of wear, and Hoist the Flag was blooming and raring to run.

To bring Flag to his peak on the first Saturday in May, Watters had laid out a progression of races at six, seven, eight, and nine furlongs. En route from Camden, Watters dropped Flag into a six-furlong allowance race at Bowie, Maryland, on March 12, which the colt won by fifteen lengths in 1:10 3/5, the fastest time of the meeting. On March 20, Flag had won the seven-furlong Bay Shore Stakes at Aqueduct in 1:21, the fastest seven eighths of a mile ever run by a three-year-old at that track. The time was just four fifths of a second off the track record set by Dr. Fager, one of the fastest thoroughbreds of the last decade. A few days hence lay the Gotham at one mile, to be followed by the Wood Memorial at one mile and one-eighth, then Churchill Downs.

Early one morning a few days after the Bay Shore, the phone rang in the bedroom of Boxwood Farm, the Middleburg, Virginia, estate of Flag's owner, Mrs. Stephen C. Clark, Jr., and her husband. Clark took the call from the head of a racing-breeding syndicate offering Jane Clark $4,000,000 for her high-flying Flag. Clark didn't bother to wake his wife up. He knew she wouldn't sell.

Since the Bay Shore, Watters had been putting Flag through long gallops at Belmont with Colum O'Brien, an Irish steeplechase jockey aboard. The Gotham in offing, Watters called for Jean Cruguet, Flag's regular jockey, to breeze the colt five furlongs in 1:02. With characteristic caution, Watters waited until 9 A.M. before heading for the track with his valuable charge on March 31. Two thousand thoroughbreds are in residence on Belmont's lovely tree-lined backstretch in the early spring, and equine traffic on both the main track and training track is freeway heavy in the hours just before dawn. By 9:00 A.M., Watters knew, the maintenance crews would have just finished harrowing and sprinkling the loamy strip. Flag should have a clear track. The procession set out from Barn 38, the trainer leading the way on his stable pony; Rob Cook, the colt's serious, devoted groom at his head; and Cruguet perched high on Flag's back. A camera crew from CBS Television tagged along to shoot footage of the Derby favorite's workout.

Watters asked Cruguet to break Flag at the mile pole and breeze him around to the three-eighths pole, then gallop out to the finish line. The French-born rider carried out his instructions, hitting the five-eighths point in 1:01 4/5, just a tick faster than ordered. A split second later, Cruguet felt Flag's right hindquarter give way. Cruguet took a fierce hold, but the colt's tremendous momentum carried

Forty-eight hours before his accident on March 31, 1971, Hoist the Flag gallops at Belmont Park with exercise boy up.

him fully another sixteenth of a mile — like a speeding automobile with a flat tire bumping sickeningly along on its rim. Cruguet hopped off to find Flag's right hind leg dangling helplessly.

Watters and Cook, followed by the track horse ambulance, ran toward the stricken animal. With Cook at his head, Flag hobbled into the low-slung trailer on three good legs. The door slammed shut. The driver headed for Watters's barn. Within minutes the backstretch hummed with the news: The Derby favorite had broken his leg.

Veterinary Mark Gerard hurried to Barn 38, Stall 14. He found that Flag's cannon or shinbone had been badly fractured. More serious, the long pastern bone had been brutally shattered. To the young veterinary, Flag's pastern felt "like a bag of loose rocks the size of marbles." Dr. Gerard had never seen a worse combination of fractures. Flag would never race again. It was even doubtful that he would ever walk on four legs. "I'm afraid it's an obvious destruction case, Mr. Watters, but let's get the x-rays," said Gerard.

Thomas Gorman, a veterinary representing Lloyd's of London, through whom Flag had been insured for

$500,000, agreed with Dr. Gerard's preliminary diagnosis and granted permission for the colt's destruction. Jane Clark could collect the insurance if she wished.

At first a horse senses only numbness when he breaks a leg while running. Then the pain floods through him. Flag broke into a clammy sweat when the pain came, and, as Rob Cook tried to soothe him and fight back tears, Flag bobbed his head up and down, lifting his broken leg gingerly. Dr. Gerard moved fast. First he administered phenylbutazone and Demerol to kill the pain. Then he x-rayed the leg with a portable machine and applied a temporary plaster cast lest the colt compound his fractures.

Watters went to the phone to break the news to the Clarks in Middleburg and ask what they wanted done with their dream colt. Mrs. Clark didn't hesitate. "Save him at all costs — as long as he doesn't have to suffer. There's an eleven o'clock from Dulles. See if someone can meet us at JFK with a car. We're on our way."

The x-rays magnified Dr. Gerard's fears. The cannon bone had suffered a five-inch longitudinal fracture, nearly half its length. The base of the cannon bone at the ankle had been split by a sharp shaft of bone like a twig cleaved by a hatchet. The long pastern had been pulverized. "It looks like a hammer

123

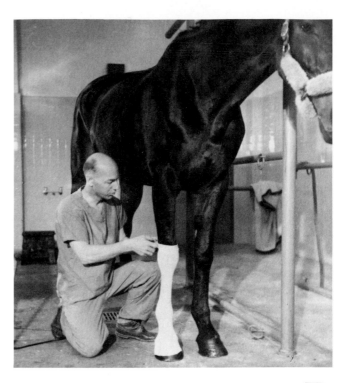

Trainer Sidney Watters, Jr., tries to fight back tears at the door of Hoist the Flag's stall at Belmont Park after the colt broke his leg. Groom Rob Cook tries to comfort the colt, whose head is bobbing up and down with pain.

The late Dr. Jacques Jenny shown at work on a less-celebrated patient than Hoist the Flag.

had shattered an ice cube," exclaimed Alfred Gwynn Vanderbilt, Jr., chairman of the New York Racing Association after viewing the x-ray pictures in Dr. Gerard's trailer near the main Pinkerton checkpoint on the backstretch.[1] The coffin bone inside the hoof, and the sesamoid bone, part of the ankle or fetlock, had also been fractured.

An 1100-pound thoroughbred such as Hoist the Flag, skimming along at forty miles per hour, exerts tremendous, piston-like force upon leg bones smaller in diameter than those of a human. The cannon is a scant one and a half inches in diameter at midpoint in its twelve-inch length, flaring to two inches at the ankle. The long pastern is three and a half inches long and one and a half inches in diameter. For a fraction of a second in the thoroughbred's stride, each leg in its turn must support the entire weight of the animal and the man on his back. Flag had somehow driven his foot down at a bad angle at the critical instant, plunging the cannon bone downward. In the second and third strides he had smashed the rest of his shock-absorbing apparatus.

The situation appeared hopeless. Dr. Gerard knew of only one man who could save Flag — Dr. Jacques Jenny, professor of orthopedic surgery at the University of Pennsylvania's school of veterinary medicine. Dr. Jenny had pioneered the adaptation of orthopedic

surgery techniques for thoroughbreds, and he had saved a goodly number of name horses, including Swaps, the 1955 Derby winner, Tim Tam, the 1958 Derby winner, the stakes horse Crème de la Crème, and Your Host, sire of the great Kelso. Dr. Jenny was considered one of the best veterinary surgeons in the world.

Jenny was fifty-four, a Swiss who had served in that country's cavalry. In this country, he had ridden as an amateur or "gentleman" rider in bone-cracking steeplechases. He was an aggressive man, an extrovert possessed of a driving energy that was the wonder of his colleagues. He kept himself fit.

Gerard knew that if he told Jenny the Hoist the Flag case looked hopeless, Jenny would be unable to resist the challenge. But Gerard also knew that Jenny had been undergoing chemotherapy treatments for cancer and had been in and out of the hospital in recent months. He was not aware that Jenny was now in severe pain most of the time. Jenny accepted the invitation to head a surgical team to try and save Flag. With his wife Eleanore, also a veterinary, he flew by private plane to Long Island and raced to Belmont Park by private car, arriving shortly before 4:00 P.M. By 4:30 P.M. the team had assembled to study the x-rays. Besides Dr. Gerard and Dr. Jenny, the team included Dr. Donald Delehanty of the New York

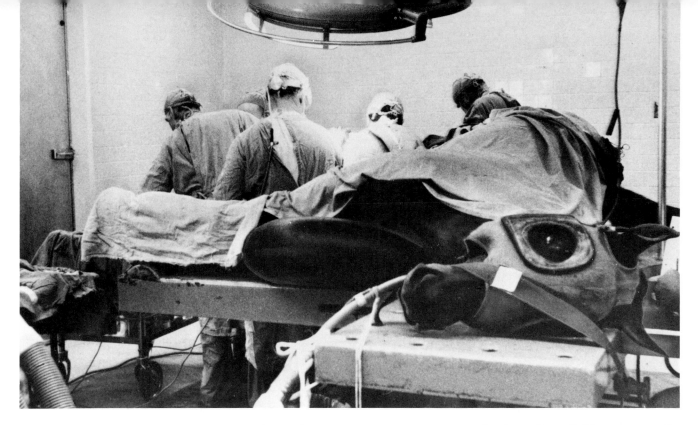

"When the men turned to the tangle of bone bits and gristle that had been the long pastern, Dr. Gerard exclaimed: 'What a mess!' "

An x-ray picture of Hoist the Flag's leg showing the T-shaped steel plate affixed to the segments of the pastern bone with half a dozen screws.

State Veterinary School at Cornell University, who had also flown in on a chartered plane; Dr. John Keefer, an orthopedic surgeon at New York Hospital who had often worked with veterinaries to save thoroughbreds; and Dr. William O. Reed, a racetrack veterinary whose emergency operating and recovery room they would use if the decision was made to operate.

Treating a thoroughbred's broken leg is extremely tedious and difficult. It isn't possible to immobilize the animal for long; if placed in a sling, the animal tends to develop colic and other digestive problems and is especially susceptible to pneumonia. There are other problems. It is difficult to keep the circulation flowing in the area of the break or fracture and to keep the area sterile. The weight upon the affected leg must be minimal. Like humans, horses tend to break casts, undoing the healing process.

On the plus side, Flag's physical condition was superb. The decision was made to go ahead with an operation. Flag was led aboard the trailer for the short ride to Dr. Reed's equine hospital on the backstretch. There the animal was further sedated, led up to a hydraulically operated, tilt-top operating table and given a knockout shot, then quickly strapped to the vertical slab. Once the horse was secured, the table was tilted back so that Flag lay on his side. Veterinary Charles Allen applied anesthesia, and the operation began at 5:00 P.M. It lasted six hours. Upon her arrival, Jane Clark had given permission to put the horse away at any point if the situation appeared too grim.

First the temporary cast was removed and the leg opened up. Dr. Jenny began with the cannon bone, employing an internal fixation technique adapted from human orthopedic surgery, an exacting business involving the use of stainless steel clamps and screws. He drilled and tapped two screw holes in the split base of the cannon bone. Then he screwed the two segments of bone together by means of a C clamp. When the men turned to the tangle of bone bits and gristle that had been the long pastern, Dr. Gerard exclaimed: "What a mess!" The bone had been shattered into seven principal segments, with shards and bits of bone down to the size of sand grains. To fill the gaps left when the detritus was cleared away, Dr. Jenny decided upon a bone graft. He opened up the colt's right hip and scooped out a quantity of strawberry-colored bone marrow to provide a matrix for healing. With great care and precision, Dr. Jenny then affixed a T-shaped steel plate to the major segments of the pastern bone with half-a-dozen screws. In other places, he used bits of steel wire. The colt was then sewn back up.

The other men had watched Dr. Jenny for signs of fatigue as the hours wore on, but he bore up well. Only once, in an aside to Dr. Delehanty, did he refer to his illness and pain. He had been, he confided, "under a good deal of stress lately."

A glass-fiber cast was applied to hold Flag's right leg so the hoof was placed in a slightly flexed or resting position. Jenny incorporated a U-shaped metal bar in the cast that permitted the colt to bear some weight without the hoof actually touching the ground.

By 11:00 P.M. the operation was over. Still unconscious, Flag was taken from the tilt table into the adjoining recovery room. Dr. Jenny slipped away with his wife to spend the night at Dr. Reed's home nearby. He was exhausted but exhilarated. "Fracture treatment is part science and part craftsmanship, on occasion elevated to the level of art," Jenny was fond of saying. The operation on Hoist the Flag would prove to be his masterpiece.

Throughout the six-hour ordeal, the Clarks, jockey Cruguet and his wife Denise, Alfred Vanderbilt, Mrs. Jenny, and a handful of others had stood by in the stark little veterinary hospital drinking coffee. Now they left to get a few hours' sleep, and Dr. Gerard, Watters, and Rob Cook stayed with the horse.

From this point on, everyone realized, much would depend upon the courage and intelligence of the patient. Fortunately, Flag had demonstrated both qualities in a brief racing career, though the cold did have faults. Flag was a "studdish," fiery colt. He bit those who came near him, except Rob Cook, who had handled the colt since he was a yearling. And when

Flag was at the top of his racing mettle, he'd even nip Rob.

In a gallop at Boxwood Farm when they were winding the colt down after his four two-year-old races, Flag bucked so hard that he split his girth and sent the exercise boy flying through the air. But Flag's main eccentricity was an aversion for oddly marked stable ponies. When he spotted one in the paddock his ears flattened and he'd lunge for the pony. As a result, Flag had to be saddled for his races in a private corner.

Flag came by some of these idiosyncrasies naturally. He is by game little Tom Rolfe, the 1965 Preakness winner, out of Wavy Navy by War Admiral. War Admiral used to try to tear down the starters' gates and on several occasions was ordered to break from outside the gate. And Flag's paternal grandsire, the great Ribot, tried to climb fences and trees when at stud in Kentucky. The sight of another horse across the fields set Ribot off, and specially high paddock fences were constructed.

Hoist the Flag was, however, to become a model patient. When he came out of anesthesia after the operation, the men restrained him. But at dawn they allowed him to get up. Remarkably, Flag sprang up on three legs with ease. Nearly twenty-four hours later he lay down to rest with his bad leg up.

Flag was moved back to Barn 38, Stall 14, where infrared lights had been installed and lanolin-treated wood shavings had been laid down instead of the more slippery straw. The feed was cut back, and Flag dropped in weight from 1100 pounds to 900 pounds. But he continued to get a gallon of apple juice mixed with his feed every day, a detail that was to help in his recovery.

Dr. Delehanty stepped into Flag's stall before flying back to Cornell, and as he started to examine the colt, Flag reached back like lightning and bit him. The veterinary hooted with laughter. "This horse has grit coming out of his ears," said Delehanty. "He's going to be all right."

Suddenly, mail began to flood into Belmont Park, much of it addressed simply to "Hoist the Flag." More than 1000 letters came in. Every writer received an answer from Jane Clark along with a postcard-sized photo of the horse.

On May 1, the ninety-seventh running of the Kentucky Derby took place in late afternoon, but no one around the Watters barn had the race tuned in. Hoist the Flag was fighting for his life. The decision to change his cast had been made early in the afternoon, and things had gone badly awry. Dr. Jenny was too ill to come for the cast change and had sent colleague Dr. John Alexander from the New Bolton Center along with a surgical team to assist Dr. Gerard at Belmont. This time, Flag was taken to a new emergency operating room that Alfred Vanderbilt had had constructed on a rush basis as a result of the Flag accident. The cast was changed under anesthesia, and everything looked fine. But when Flag awoke, his *left* hindquarters were partly paralyzed.

Just why the colt's *good* hind leg should now fail was a mystery. On the off chance that an undetected infection had broken out in the bone graft donor site on Flag's right hip, Gerard opened up the old incision and irrigated it. He reasoned that such an infection might have spread from the right hip down the spinal column to the left hip. Antibiotics were administered. Diathermy and ultrasonic treatments were given. Nothing appeared to work. For the first time, Flag began to reflect anxiety. He would struggle to his feet only to flop down again a short while later. Exhaustion set in. Flag began to suffer.

The hard decision had to be faced. Jane Clark agreed that if Flag did not pull out of it by the second morning, he should be destroyed. Gerard and Watters bedded down with Flag in his stall, Watters now living out the nightmare of every trainer with a great horse in his charge. The strain had been apparent a few days before the accident. Watters had said that he was worried about the racing strip at Churchill Downs, which, he declared, was invariably rendered hard and fast on Derby Day in the hope that a record would be broken.

"If the track is too hard, we won't ship to the Derby," he had said with finality.

At one o'clock on the second morning, the colt started to rise. The two men looked at one another. Flag gave a mighty heave and bounded to his feet. Miraculously, the muscle tone had returned to his bad hip. Flag was going to make it. Other cast changes were made without incident. The bones continued to mend. In time, Flag was taken out for little walks.

But as the months went by, the news about Jacques Jenny was not good. He had been keeping close tabs on Flag's recovery, but he was losing his own bout with cancer.

Early in November, Hoist the Flag was led aboard a cargo plane and flown to Lexington, Kentucky. Then Flag was vanned to Claiborne Farms, the vast commercial breeding establishment outside Paris, Kentucky. ("To Paris for Oo la la," said the New York *News* headline over a photograph of Flag leaving Belmont.) As Flag was led limping toward a big stone barn on a windswept hill, some broodmares cantered up to the fence to check out the new arrival. The mares must have liked what they saw, for they started whinnying. Flag reared up on heavily bandaged hind legs and whinnied excitedly. "You know why you're here, Flag," said Rob Cook with a chuckle. "You sure do."

One afternoon in mid-November, a groom led Flag around the glass-enclosed shed row of his new home for a one-and-a-half mile walk. Then he was taken outside to graze. It was a chilly day and windy, and like any high-spirited three-year-old, Flag was "spooky." When a leaf fluttered by, Flag suddenly reared and whirled. Then Jacques Jenny's masterpiece pricked his sensitive ears and gazed into the near distance where yearlings ran with the wind across the broad Kentucky meadows. A few days later, on November 20, Jacques Jenny died.

On the mend, Hoist the Flag kicks up at Claiborne Farm.

Chapter 14
Canonero Segundo

CANONERO II was a crooked-legged source of ridicule — until he won the 1971 Derby. Before the race, many American horsemen and sportswriters openly made fun of the unorthodox methods of the black Venezuelan trainer, Juan Arias, who was passed over when invitations went out for the festive pre-Derby dinner honoring trainers of entries in the race. Arias, then thirty-two, was raised in the slums of Caracas by his mother, his sister, and his grandmother, with whom he was still living in 1971. His father abandoned the family a few years after Juan arrived in the world. As a boy, Juan became intrigued with the racetrack. Whenever he could, he went to the backstretch at La Rinconada and mucked stalls without pay just to be around thoroughbreds. These were the days of the infamous dictator Marcos Perez Jimenez, who had one redeeming feature as far as Juan was concerned: Jimanez was a racing fan. Chagrined that foreign trainers carried off most of the honors at La Rinconada, Jiminez opened a government school for horse trainers, which Juan attended from 1955 through 1959. Arias soon discovered that La Rinconada's backstretch was a closed corporation. He lived through eight hand-to-mouth years.

"The only horses that I had I got by force, and they were dogs. It was terrible. I slept in the barns and didn't know where my next meal was coming from. Most of my classmates quit training pretty soon and they advised me to quit, too. I guess the only reason I kept going was because I was young and single."[1]

In 1967, the tide turned for Arias. Someone introduced him to Pedro Baptista, whose horses had been busily losing. Baptista took a liking to the slender, high-strung little horseman; he turned sixteen of his string over to Arias and gave him three months to "produce." Arias produced. Baptista's horses started bringing in bolivars by the bushel.

The following year, Arias's picture appeared in Caracas newspapers when Baptista's entry finished 1-2-3 in the Polla de Potrancas or "Prize of Fillies," winning a total of $115,000. Arias was so excited on that occasion that Baptista was afraid he would have a stroke.

Even after Canonero won the Kentucky Derby, many considered his victory a fluke. Then Canonero ran off with the Preakness in track record time.

Edward B. Benjamin of New Orleans, who bred the colt in Kentucky, summed up Canonero's story best when he said: "It was just like *National Velvet* — but no Liz Taylor." No one, it seems, wanted Canonero at first, not even Benjamin himself.

Canonero was the product of Benjamin's mare Dixieland II, whom he kept at Claiborne Farm in Paris, Kentucky, and Pretendre, a French import then standing in Lexington. Dixieland had won in England; Pretendre had been a top two-year-old there in 1965 and had finished a close second to Charlottown in the Epsom Derby the following year. Yet when Benjamin consigned Dixieland, carrying Canonero to the 1967 Keeneland Fall Breeding-Stock Sales in Lexington, the bidding petered out almost immediately. Dixieland was bid in for a mere $2700 by William Taylor, the Clairborne farm manager acting as agent for the absent Benjamin. Taylor reasoned that he wouldn't have wanted the mare and unborn foal to go so cheaply.

After the sale, Taylor phoned Benjamin and offered him Dixieland back.

"No, I don't think so," replied Benjamin. "You've got a nice young Nantallah mare there so you can keep her if you want her."

Owner Pedro Baptista gives Canonero Segundo an affectionate squeeze.

Taylor told Benjamin that he could have the mare back if he ever changed his mind. "But," said Taylor, "I didn't hear from him about her for a couple of months, until along in January, before she had foaled, he called and said:

" 'Bill, if you've still got that mare, I believe I would like to have her back.' "[2]

When Dixieland's Pretendre foal arrived he was flawed: His right foreleg was bent backward beneath the knee. Benjamin decided to sell him at the 1969 Keeneland Summer Yearling Sales, but the colt was rejected by sales officials because of his deformity. So Benjamin put him on the block in the Keeneland fall sales where conformation standards are less strict. When the rangy colt, with Hip. No. 224 pasted on his rump, was led into the sales ring, horsemen took one look at the crooked leg and went on thumbing their catalogues. After a few seconds of desultory bidding, the colt by Pretendre out of Dixieland II by Nantallah went to Luis Navas, a Venezuelan bloodstock dealer for $1200.

Navas shipped the colt and two other bargain-basement yearlings to Caracas, where he sold the three to Baptista, one of Venezuela's wealthiest men, owner of *Croma T, C/A,* a firm manufacturing a wide range of chrome products, including furniture.

"A stumpy, swarthy man with a scar on his nose, and few teeth, Baptista is considered something of an eccentric in Venezuela . . ."[3]

Baptista, proud of his Indian blood, was superstitious and ran his horses in the name of his son-in-law, Edgar Caibett, because he was convinced that they lost more often when carrying his name.

Baptista named the colt Canonero, a *canonero* being a small singing group accompanied by two guitars and a gourd. The name came to him one day when passing *el rincon canonero,* a street corner in Caracas where singers and musicians gather to make music. Neither Baptista nor his trainer Juan Arias were impressed with the big bay colt at first, for Canonero was "rather workmanlike and plain than of obvious quality." Because of his malformed right leg, the colt ran with a labored, crab-like motion that lacked grace. To make matters worse, Canonero had arrived in Caracas with a bad case of worms and a badly split right forefoot.

Arias entered Canonero in a six-furlong handicap at Caracas's beautiful La Rinconada race course — Venezuela's only major track — on August 8, 1970. To Baptista's surprise, Canonero sped home a winner in his maiden effort by a spectacular six and a half lengths. After Canonero won his second race, Baptista began to dream. He entered the colt in the six-furlong Del Mar Futurity at Del Mar racetrack in California and accompanied Arias and the horse on the flight to America. On the flight, Baptista first mentioned the Derby to Arias. In California, the II was added to Canonero's name because another horse by the name of Canonero had campaigned in Mexico City in the early 1960s. The II must have been a jinx, for Canonero finished third in a prep race and fifth in the Futurity, which was won by the fleet filly June Darling.

Baptista decided that he had been wrong about Canonero. Rather than pay to fly the colt back to Caracas, he tried to sell him in California. There were no takers. The Baptista entourage flew back to Caracas.

In Canonero's first start as a three-year-old on January 9, 1971, he won at seven eighths of a mile at La Rinconada. Baptista's Derby hopes were reborn. They were dampened somewhat on February 7, when Canonero finished eleventh, in the Clasico Gobernador del Distrito Federal at one and a quarter miles.

Nominations for the 1971 Kentucky Derby as well as the Preakness and Belmont Stakes were to close on February 15. A few days before the deadline, Charles J. "Chick" Lang, general manager of Pimlico racetrack in Baltimore, was in Miami recruiting last-minute entries among the owners of stakes horses campaigning at Hialeah. Lang, whose late father rode Reigh Count to victory in the 1928 Derby, was sitting beside the swimming pool at his Miami Springs motel with a group of horsemen one morning when he was paged to the telephone. Lang recalls:

"A man with a Spanish accent was on the line and I heard him say, 'I want to name a horse for the Preakness and the other two big races.' I said that's fine and asked the name of the horse.

"When he told me Canonero II, I thought he was kidding. I started to tell him so and even thought of hanging up, but he sounded too sincere to be one of my tipsy friends.

"I asked his name to put down as the nominee and when he said he was a friend of the owner, Mr. Baptista, I was sure somebody was putting me on. I had never heard of a horse named Canonero.

"To humor the guy, I said O.K., put down the name of the horse and as much of the breeding as the guy knew and hung up. When I rejoined my group I asked if they had heard of a colt named Canonero by a stallion named Pretendre. John Finney of Fasig-Tipton went to his room to check his records and came back saying, 'There's no such animal; it must be a joke.' So I didn't think about it until next day at Hialeah."

Still convinced that he was the butt of a joke, Lang nevertheless looked up a Churchill Downs official and gave him Canonero's nomination, phoned his own office to put him in the Preakness, and got in touch with Belmont Park to enter him in the Belmont Stakes. The next day, someone in Lang's office finally found Canonero II in the records.

Canonero II began to improve steadily. He finished third in a one-mile handicap and on March 7 beat older horses at one and a quarter miles, albeit in buggy-horse time of 2:08 2/5 carrying 115 pounds. This win was the clincher for Baptista. The colt had proven he could go a distance — a full two months before colts in the United States are asked to run that far.

By April 10, less than one month before the Derby, Canonero had won two more races and finished third twice. During one of his winning races, and one in which he finished third, he carried Derby weight of 126 pounds. Canonero's accomplishments were far more substantial than they appeared to most Americans. La Rinconada is sandier and deeper than most racetracks in the United States, a factor that produces stamina and explains in part Canonero's slow clocking when he won at one and a quarter miles. Furthermore, the track is located in the mountainous outskirts of Caracas, 3000 feet above sea level where the thin air forces development of powerful lungs. When thoroughbreds such as Canonero come down from such Olympian heights, they have a distinct, albeit temporary, advantage over animals living closer to sea level. The same is true, of course, of athletes.

Two weeks before the Derby, set for May 1, Canonero was loaded aboard a cargo plane in Caracas for the long flight to Miami, where he was to change planes for Louisville. Baptista elected to stay behind, as did his son-in-law Caibett, so Baptista sent his teen-age son, Pedro, Jr., as his representative. Things started to go wrong from the outset. Twice the plane had to turn back to Caracas, once when an engine caught fire, once because of some other mechanical difficulty. During the flight, Canonero began to fret, for the cargo included crates of noisy ducks and chickens. Arias vowed to avoid any more planes before the Derby; he would van Canonero from Miami to Louisville. At Miami he had customs problems. Baptista had neglected to send along Canonero's blood sample and other papers, so the colt had to spend four days without exercise in a quarantine stall. This setback was followed by a jouncing 1100-mile van trip from Miami to Louisville where there was yet another aggravating delay at the gates of Churchill Downs: Arias and his groom spoke only Spanish. The guards refused to let the van enter until suitable identification was made. By the time the exhausted colt was bedded down in his stall he had lost an estimated seventy to eighty pounds, his coat was lack-luster, and Arias told Derby officials the colt might not be able to start in the big race, which was now just one week away.

As little was known about Canonero in this country, Churchill Downs President Lynn Stone would have cheerfully accepted a scratch. When heavily favored Hoist the Flag broke his leg on March 31, the Derby became a wide-open race with a big field assured. Canonero was seen as another cheap horse who didn't belong, another mane and tail to clutter up the track and increase the chances of jam-ups and accidents. At first, the press paid little attention to Canonero and the Spanish-speaking entourage. Canonero was not one of the half-dozen horses considered to have a winning chance. They were the Calumet Farms' entry of Bold and Able and Eastern Fleet; Impetuosity and Twist the Axe, an entry trained by George Poole; Jim French, the game Graustark colt; and List, a sometimes dangerous stretch runner.

Arias did not rush his horse, even though time was running out. Canonero thrived in the bracing spring air and with each passing day his coat regained more of its gloss. Arias sent the colt out for long walks, long gallops, and slow workouts, an exercise boy sometimes riding him bareback in Latin American style. American horsemen shook their heads. This was not the way to get a horse ready to run one and a quarter miles against the best available competition in the country.

"They did everything wrong," said a groom who worked in the same shed row with the Venezuelan contingent. "They would work him any time they happened to get to the track. One day they put a rope around his neck and took him out of the stall. He worked a half mile in 1:53 4/5 — walking time."[4]

One day a feed man stopped by Arias's barn to ask if he would like a sack of grain.

"How much?" asked Arias through an interpreter.

"Five dollars," replied the man.

"No, no!" exclaimed Arias. "Too much. Can we have half a sack?"[5]

When newsmen asked Arias if the horse was going to work out, the Venezuelan would do a pantomime of a horse galloping. They came to look upon him as a clown. And when Arias would press his head against the big horse's chest and whisper to him intently in Spanish, they wondered whether he wasn't plain loco. Arias responded, "I find that you must treat horses like women, speaking softly to them and knowing when to give them love pats."[6]

In a final indignity, Canonero II was made a member of the six-horse mutuel field with Barbizon Streak, Knight Counter, Jr.'s Arrowhead, Fourulla, and Saigon Warrior. One trainer said angrily that he had never seen so much "garbage" in the Derby, especially the field horses. This got back to Arias.

Gustavo Avila, Venezuela's top jockey, had flown from Caracas to wear Baptista's brown silks in the Derby and work with the colt beforehand. Like Baptista, he is part Indian, a bushy-browed little man known affectionately in Caracas as *el monstruo* or "the monster" because of his success with long shots.

Because Canonero was part of the mutuel field, his odds were less than nine to one as post time neared in late afternoon on May 1. But in New York's OTB parlors, where each horse is an individual betting interest, Canonero was thirty to one.

It was warm and sunny shortly after 5 P.M when the twenty Derby entries started filing around the track from the backstretch en route to the paddock beneath the old stands. The biggest crowd in Derby history was on hand — 123,284 persons — and Lynn Stone broke Derby tradition to announce the exact crowd figure. They would push $2,648,139 through the mutuel windows on the Derby alone — the greatest amount of money ever bet on a single race in the history of the turf.

Tension was high in the number fifteen half stall where the Venezuelans were readying their big bay colt. Their nervousness transmitted itself to Canonero, who began to jump around. Arias's hands were shaking so violently he couldn't get the girth cinched. He had one of his men do it, then smoothed out the black saddlecloth with the big white number fifteen on it and soothingly patted the colt's neck.

Arias was unaware that he and the colt were being watched by Robert J. Kleberg, owner of the famous King Ranch in Texas. Kleberg had twice won the Derby — with Assault in 1946 and Middleground in 1950. "That No. 15 is just about the best-looking colt I ever saw," he said to Whitney Tower.

Kleberg checked his program and made a mental note.

At the bugle, the jockeys were tossed into their saddles, and the horses threaded their way along the path toward the track. Down at the widened foot of the homestretch where the starting gates were hooked together, starter Jim Thomson, a Scot, was getting ready to send off his fifteenth Derby field.

"That South American horse is a bit of a problem," Thomson told the *Courier-Journal*'s ubiquitous Dick Fenlon. "We're going to have to blindfold him and lead him in. We'll leave it on him until all of them are in. Then it flies off."[7]

Fourteen horses were to go in the first gate and six in the second gate. As the horses approached the gates, Thomson started barking orders.

"That List is a son of a bitch," said Thomson to his crew. "Lead him in there! In fact, all those outside

Canonero streaks past the finish line.

horses, lead them all in. Get a man on each side of the horse. Knight Counter is a watery son of a gun. He kinda squats down in there. Eddie, you go in with him." Saigon Warrior was another bad actor. In his races up to this time, starters had held his tail to keep him straight when the gates flew open.

"That Number 12 horse, if he don't go in, tail him," said Thomson of Saigon Warrior. "And if he don't tail, go in with him." Sure enough, once inside his stall, Saigon reared up. Then he reared up again. This time, jockey Bobby Parrott in his polka-dot silks went flying backward, head over heels, over the top of the back side of the gate.

"Members of Thomson's crew quickly jumped into the stall to quiet the colt. For a moment it appeared that Parrott might be injured too severely to ride. However, after stretching and exercising a bruised knee, he climbed aboard, getting a round of applause from the fans mobbed against the nearby infield fence . . ."[8]

The instant Parrot braced himself, the bell clanged, the gates flew open, and the horses burst down the long stretch through a corridor of sound. Canonero was off poorly, fifth to last as the field sorted itself out in the first few hundred strides. The Devil's red and blue of Calumet was the first to show in the two-and-a-half-furlong run past the stands into the first turn, Jorge Velasquez gunning Bold and Able along the rail from the number one post position, while Eddie Maple winged Eastern Fleet away fast from number seventeen and crossed over in spectacular fashion ahead of the field to fall in behind his stablemate. Jr.'s Arrowhead, Knight Counter, Barbizon Streak, and Unconscious trailed as the field straightened out like a comet's tail for the run down the back side. Avila had Canonero three horses out from the rail near the back of the pack and away from the heavy traffic. Leaving the backstretch, the red-blinkered Calumets were still on top. When Canonero reached

132

the far turn, still running eighteenth in the field of twenty, Avila opened up and started looping the field on the outside, picking up one horse after another. Avila whipping in roundhouse fashion, Canonero took command in the upper stretch and swept under the wire three and a quarter lengths ahead of Jim French. Bold Reason came in third, Eastern Fleet fourth. As the losing riders cantered back toward the stands, they stared in disbelief at the blinking tote board. An unsettling silence fell over the crowd: They were checking their programs to see who the number fifteen horse was. "Canonero II? Who the hell was Canonero I?" exclaimed a turf writer high in the press box.

A belated cheer went up from the stands when Avila, waving a V sign, trotted Canonero back down the track to the winner's circle. In the circle, pandemonium had broken loose. The emotional Venezuelans and their hangers-on hugged and kissed one another, crying and laughing all at once. Arias couldn't stand still. While the presentation ceremony was in progress, a friend of Baptista's in Miami phoned Caracas.

"That's a sick joke!" exclaimed Baptista when informed that he had won $145,500, the richest Derby in history. He slammed down the receiver.[9] Minutes later, calls began pouring in. One call was from a man offering $500,000 for Canonero.

Baptista's servants mixed up gallons of *vino punche,* consisting of lemon, bitters, and whiskey. Within the hour, two hundred well-wishers had appeared. The party went on for more than twenty hours. Repeated radio and television news bulletins informed Venezuela that it had won its first Kentucky Derby.

There was dancing in the streets of Caracas. At *el rincon canonero* someone quickly composed a song:

Canonero, Canonero, asombro del mundo entero,
Canonero, Canonero, sequiras siendo el primo . . .
Canonero, Canonero, surprise of the entire world,
Canonero, Canonero, you will always be first . . .[10]

The President of Venezuela sent jockey Avila a cablegram: "The great victory will stimulate Venezuela's progress in all its efforts . . ."[11]

Even so, U.S. turf writers saw Canonero's victory as "one of those things." They noted that the best horses had been caught in jam-ups in the overcrowded field; they noted the slow time of 2:03 1/5 on a fast track. The Preakness, they observed, was one and three-sixteenths miles — shorter than the Derby with its long homestretch — and was run around tighter turns than those in Louisville, both factors working against a come-from-behind horse such as Canonero.

"Nothing appeared to be in Canonero's favor.

Again, he had to make a long van ride. He bumped his head and cut himself. He ran a slight temperature. A week before the Preakness, he refused to eat his evening meal, and it turned out that he had been cutting his tongue on his teeth.

"A vet was called and two baby teeth were extracted. An important training work had to be delayed a day or two, and when it did come off, it broke watches going backwards: five furlongs in a terribly slow 1:06, galloping out in six furlongs in 1:22, clockings which would have led most trainers to feel that they should skip the Preakness and maybe even Turnip Patch Downs and take a shot at Bangkok or New Delhi."[12]

The Preakness field of eleven, included five Derby runners-up: Jim French, Bold Reason, Eastern Fleet, Impetuosity, and Vegas Vic — a sign that Canonero was still not being taken seriously by U.S. horsemen.

"They laughed at us in Louisville, and they are laughing at us in Baltimore," said Arias. "But it is we who will be laughing at the whole racing world."[13]

At the break, Eddie Maple hustled Eastern Fleet to the front and held the lead around the clubhouse turn. When he straightened his horse out for the run down the backstretch, Maple was dumfounded to discover Canonero and Avila right with him on the outside.

Baptista's son accepts the Derby cup. To his right, trainer Juan Arias and jockey Gustavo Avila smile with pride.

The pair raced down the backstretch and around the far turn nose-to-nose while the tote board blinked record-breaking fractions; many in the crowd expected one or both colts to falter. An eighth of a mile from home, Canonero took a slight lead and sped under the wire one and a half lengths in the clear in 1:54 — the fastest one and three-sixteenths miles in Preakness history, three fifths of a second faster than the previous mark set by Nashua in 1955.

"It is amazing to me," said Baptista, who had come to Baltimore for the race, "that a black man (Arias) and two Indians (Baptista and Avila) could come here and smash 200 years of tradition in racing. And now, God willing, Canonero will also win the Belmont and then — ay, yi — what a fiesta we will have in Venezuela!"[14]

Not since Carry Back had a horse so caught the imagination of the American people. Sportswriters now changed their tune. Someone nicknamed Canonero "the Caracas Cannonball." He looked, they said, like the first Triple Crown winner since Citation in 1948. Several multimillion-dollar offers would be made on the horse if he won the Triple Crown.

"We have a deal, contingent on Canonero's winning the Belmont," confirmed trainer Albert Winick to Washington *Post* columnist Gerald Strine. "Nothing has been set, however, as to whether he will be retired to our training center at Delray, Florida, or continue racing. But he must win the Triple Crown."[15]

Chartered planes loaded with Venezuelan racing fans lifted off from Caracas. The press build-up for the one-and-a-half-mile Belmont Stakes on June 4 was unprecedented in its enthusiasm. Then the word began to creep into press reports that Canonero was not well. The long flight from Venezuela, the tiring van rides, the grueling Derby and Preakness, the excitement and the tension had all begun to take their toll. First Canonero developed a skin rash, then his ankles were "burned" behind when the colt "ran down" as horsemen put it in the deep Belmont track cushion. Then it was discovered that Canonero was suffering from a case of thrush in his right hind hoof, a maladorous fungus infection akin to athlete's foot.

The public paid little attention to these reports partly because similar stories about Canonero's ailments had circulated before the Preakness and partly because Arias felt the colt would recover before the race. But Canonero missed two days of exercise and a one-and-one-eighth-mile workout that Arias considered critical.

The tension and the pressure were now getting to Baptista and the volatile Arias too. They knew their colt was not going to be fit for the Belmont. Yet he was the overwhelming favorite. Belmont Park, pre-paring for the biggest crowd in its history, would not want its drawing card scratched. It was the Majestic Prince situation all over again.

Baptista and Arias were now shouting at one another. Rumors circulated that Arias did not want to run the colt. For his part, Baptista had an offer from Winick for $3.1 million in the form of a five-year lease of Canonero at $620,000 a year. *But Canonero must win the Triple Crown.* Robert Kleberg, who had been struck by Canonero in the Derby paddock, was also maneuvering to buy Canonero, but not at that price.

"Perhaps sometime before the Belmont this Saturday, Canonero II's handlers will forego false national pride and scratch the horse," said *Sports Illustrated*. "We hope so. He is in bad shape and has been for a week . . ."

There had never been such a Belmont day: 82,694 passed the turnstiles, at least 2000 of them Venezuelans waving their nation's tricolor flags. In the paddock, Arias fought back tears. In the race, the colt went to the lead immediately, led for a mile, then faded to fourth behind the winner, Pass Catcher, a thirty-five to one shot, Jim French, and Bold Reason. A year would pass before Canonero recovered from the Triple Crown attempt.

". . . Don't be too critical of Arias and the Venezuelans for their misleading comments about Canonero II's condition during the week before the race," wrote Gerald Strine. "For a potential $3.1 million, Arias was muzzled and forced into a calculated risk. Given the identical situation, 99 percent of the American owners and trainers would have done the same thing. It is, unfortunately, the way the high-stakes game is played."[16]

One week after the Belmont, Kleberg acquired Canonero for $1.5 million. Baptista and Arias parted company.

Chapter 15
The Mistress of the Meadow

WHILE CALUMET FARMS was attempting a comeback, Meadow Stud stole the limelight. On a now memorable day, Howard Gentry, farm manager of Meadow Stud in Doswell, Virginia, took out his notebook. "Iberia arrived today with her colt at her side; 2 months, 13 days old. Colt looks poor and thin. You could run your fingers along his ribs and play a tune. Looks sick as sick. Has a temperature of 102.2. Gave him a tonic, Azimycin. Colt improving."[1] The date was June 28, 1969, and Gentry was routinely filling out his log as he had been doing for twenty-six years at Christopher T. Chenery's farm north of Richmond. Iberia, in foal to First Landing, had been sent some months earlier to Claiborne Farm in Kentucky where another Chenery stallion, Sir Gaylord, was standing. After Iberia dropped the First Landing colt at Claiborne, the mare was bred to Sir Gaylord, then shipped back to Meadow Stud with her sickly foal.

The foal, named Riva Ridge, quickly recovered. At first, no one was excited about Riva Ridge as the colt was not sturdy or handsome. Riva Ridge was an unusually pale bay later described by sportswriter Red Smith as "the color of expensive luggage." Floppy ears detracted from an aristocratic head and alert eyes. Riva's barrel was narrow and elongated. The colt's legs though, as a horseman observed, were "very slender, like deer's legs, without heavy ankles and knees; just slim, flat joints, the kind that seldom give trouble."[2] Those long legs carried Riva Ridge to the two-year-old championship in 1971, to victories in the Kentucky Derby and Belmont Stakes the following year — and probably saved Meadow Stud.

Midway through Riva's two-year-old campaign, Gentry told trainer Lucien Laurin that "we've got a better one at the farm." He was referring to Secre-

tariat, a yearling by Bold Ruler out of Chenery's mare Somethingroyal.

From 1967, when Christopher Chenery was partially paralyzed by a succession of coronary attacks, to his death at eighty-six in January 1973, Mrs. John B. Tweedy, the youngest of his three children, directed Meadow Stud and its stable. Had it not been for Helen "Penny" Tweedy's love for horses, her devotion to her father, and her steely determination to keep his royal blue and white silks flying, there might never have been a Riva Ridge or Secretariat. Family members of the Board of Meadow Stud, Inc., urged that the horses be sold, but she staunchly refused, even after the enterprise lost $85,000 her first year

Chris Chenery.

"Had it not been for Helen 'Penny' Tweedy's love for her horses, her devotion to her father, and her steely determination to keep his royal blue and white silks flying, there might never have been a Riva Ridge or Secretariat."

in control — only the second year since its incorporation in 1956 that Meadow Stud had failed to show a profit. The following year she was able to put $65,000 on the plus side of the ledger, but the doubters were still not convinced. At a family meeting in 1969, Penny Tweedy's brother, Dr. Hollis B. Chenery, chief economist of the World Bank, said the horses should be sold and the money invested in the stock market, for their value was probably close to $1,000,000.

"We probably have the legal right to do that, but we know Dad wouldn't want us to give up the horses," she said firmly. "So I don't think we have a moral right to do it."[3] Penny Tweedy's sister, Mrs. Margaret Carmichael, supported her from the beginning, and after the first year her brother did as well.

Penny Tweedy knew, however, that she was fighting a holding action, and that the fine broodmare band her father had assembled over the course of nearly three decades would probably have to go in a dispersal sale should her father die.

Riva Ridge came along, then Secretariat. Counting their syndications and winnings the Meadow pair

accounted for $13,718,305, in three years of racing for Riva and two for Secretariat.

Riva Ridge ended his career as a four-year-old in the fall of 1973 with winnings of $1,111,497 and seventeen victories in thirty starts. In his final race, he finished an exhausted last behind Hobeau Farm's four-year-old Prove Out, trained by Allen Jerkens, in the two-mile Jockey Club Gold Cup. Earlier in the fall, Riva had set a world record of 1:52 2/5 for a mile and three-sixteenths in the Brooklyn Handicap. He was syndicated for $5,210,000 and shipped to Claiborne Farm with Secretariat in mid-November.

Secretariat became the first horse since Citation in 1948 to win the Triple Crown. In his meteoric career, he won sixteen of twenty-one starts and $1,316,808, placing him fourth — behind Kelso at $1,977,896 — among all-time money winners. His most spectacular victory came in the Belmont Stakes when he set an American record of 2:24 for one and a half miles, shaving the Belmont track record by two and three-fifths seconds.

Christopher T. Chenery leads Hill Prince in after winning the 1950 Preakness with Eddie Arcaro aboard. In the Derby, Hill Prince had finished second to King Ranch's Middleground.

136

Until his death in 1969 at the age of eighty-nine, Maximillian Justice Hirsch (middle, Robert Kleberg is on right, jockey John Rotz on left) was still rising at dawn in his cottage beside Barn 1 at Belmont Park to oversee the workouts of King Ranch horses — as he'd been doing for half a century. Hirsch was born in Fredericksburg, Texas, and he remembered unfriendly Indians in the nearby hills as a child. At ten, Max started riding in quarter-horse races on the ranch of John A. Morris of the famous old New York racing family. A few years later, barefoot and in blue jeans, Max stowed away on a freight-car load of Morris racehorses bound for Maryland. The Morrises provided him with warm clothing — and he stayed on the race-track. In Hirsch's time, racing changed from sport to busi-ness, and then to big business. His foreman for fifty years, Otis "Rabbit" Jones, summed it up one day in 1968: "The sportin' atmosphere is gone. Too many folks don't have a *feel* for the horses. Now they are a machine. You got to keep some class on the backstretch somehow. Racing used to be a game; kind of a picnic. That will never be recaptured."

Among the greatest Derby trainers was Max Hirsch. Long-shot Bold Venture, his 1936 winner, sired Assault and Middleground (above), his 1946 and 1950 winners. Robert J. Kleberg bought Bold Venture for stud purposes and bred Assault and Middle-ground. Despite a permanently deformed foot, Assault won the Triple Crown for Hirsch. Assault, in fact, is one of the top horses of the century. Hirsch always felt, however, that Middleground's win over Hill Prince in 1950 gave him the most pleasure. In "Six Decades of Racing," in *Turf & Sport Digest*, he wrote: "Everyone likes to win when he isn't supposed to. I took one gamble in that race that would have made me look too foolish for words if it hadn't panned out. Eddie Arcaro was committed to ride Middleground in the Derby . . . and made no secret of the fact that he wanted to ride [Hill Prince]." Hirsch released Arcaro and gave the job to his young appren-tice jockey Billy Boland, who rode a superb race and went on to win the Belmont with Middleground after finishing second to Hill Prince in the Preakness.

The big red colt met two stinging defeats at the hands of horses trained by the remarkable Allen Jerkens. A sprinter named Onion beat him in the Whitney Stakes, and Prove Out, Riva Ridge's con-queror, beat him in the Woodward. Despite these set-backs, horsemen rank Secretariat with Sysonby, Colin, Man o' War, Citation, and Kelso, generally conceded to be the greatest horses in American racing history. In all, "Triple Sec," as one newspaper dubbed him, either tied or broke five track records and attracted an enormous television following. He finished his career in glorious fashion with two victories on grass, the one-and-a-half-mile Man o' War and the Canadian International Championship at one and five-eighths miles at Woodbine in Toronto on October 28, 1973. His syndication price of $6,080,000 set an all-time record.

On November 6, 32,990 racing fans gave Secre-tariat a thunderous ovation when Ron Turcotte jogged him in front of the Aqueduct stands between races for a last ceremonial appearance. There were speeches and the awarding of plaques, and two little girls un-folded a sheet on which they had written: "Good-bye Secretariat, We Love You."

"I was determined to keep the stable operating," says Mrs. Tweedy. "The stable had been my father's main interest for the last twenty-five years of his life. He was a self-made man who passed on some of the fruits of his labor to his children, and I didn't think we ought to change them, and certainly not while he was alive."[4]

The Chenerys are an old, resilient American family. Isaac Chenery, an Englishman, settled in what is now Belmont, Massachusetts, in 1630. In the eighteenth

The Meadow.

century, part of the family moved to Virginia. The Meadow, built in 1810, was in the Chenery family until 1922 when they came upon hard times. As a youth, Christopher Tompkins Chenery spent his summers at The Meadow, which lies twenty miles north of Richmond on the North Anna River. He had loved the old place and, like other members of the family, had been saddened when it passed into the hands of a bank. Chenery, whose father ran a dry goods store in Richmond, was graduated in 1909 from Washington and Lee University with a degree in civil engineering and membership in Phi Beta Kappa. He surveyed the Alaskan wilderness for a railway and started accumulating a sizable fortune organizing utilities holding companies. He was a bold, vigorous individual with a passion for horses, the outdoors, and physical fitness. Riding bareback, he often plunged his horses into rivers and swam with the tide.

In 1934, with his wife and daughter Penny, then fourteen, Chenery visited a cousin, Mrs. Hardenia Ferguson, living in Doswell, not far from The Meadow, which he hadn't seen for years. When they drove by, he was shocked at its condition. Shutters dangled from broken hinges; pigs and chickens wandered around the front lawn, which was graced by a gasoline pump. The land near the river was swampy and in need of draining. Even so, the old place hadn't lost its haunting charm, or its memories. "Oh, Chris, don't the old trees arch prettily over the house?" asked Cousin Hardenia.

"My father fell in love with the place all over again, right there and then," says Penny Tweedy.

Two years later, against his own practical judgment and the advice of horsemen, Chenery bought The Meadow and made plans to convert it into a thoroughbred breeding farm. At the time, he was forty-nine years old, was board chairman of Southern Natural Gas Company, and was searching for new worlds, with no thought of retirement. The Meadow tested Chenery's engineering mettle. Doswell lies in hard-scrabble southeastern Virginia, far from the lush horse country around Middleburg, Upperville, and Warrenton to the northwest. The soil had to be nurtured, the land drained, and artificial lakes created. A retaining wall built by slaves along the North Anna before the Civil War had to be rebuilt.

Composed of neat white barns and outbuildings trimmed with Chenery's royal blue racing color, the handsome old white manor house, and white-paneled fences criss-crossing 2600 acres, The Meadow is today a place of tremendous charm. But it does not present the manicured appearance of so many horse farms. Chenery put his money in the soil and in his broodmare band.

"We don't baby our horses," says farm manager Gentry, who is not related to the Kentucky Gentrys. "When they go away from here, they go away to run, not to be sold in an auction ring. You can breed a good horse on a rock pile — if it's a good horse."[5]

Forty-one stakes winners had come from Chenery's rock pile by the time of his death. He operated on a relatively small scale with phenomenal success, but until Riva Ridge came along in 1972 his Derby luck was wretched. In 1950, his Hill Prince finished second to Middleground. The colt's jockey, Eddie Arcaro, admitted to Chenery that he had waited seconds too long to make his move, gambling that the King Ranch colt would run wide on the turn for home, as was his habit. This time, however, Middleground did not run wide. In 1959, Riva Ridge's sire, First Landing, ran third behind Tomy Lee and Sword Dancer, and it was discovered that the horse was suffering from a kidney infection. In 1962, Sir Gaylord was the odds-on choice. The day before the race, Chenery was aboard a train to Louisville when he heard the radio report that his colt had broken down while galloping at the Downs. Crestfallen, his trainer, H. J. "Casey" Hayes met him at the station. Chenery took solace in the fact that his filly Cicada won the Kentucky Oaks the day before the Kentucky Derby. Had Sir Gaylord broken down one day earlier, Casey Hayes would have scratched Cicada from the Oaks and run her in the Derby, Mrs. Tweedy recalls. "He said Cicada's feed had been drawn, she knew she was going to race, and it would have upset her too much to have changed and waited until next day. We always wondered how she would have done." Cicada retired with earnings of $783,674, the greatest sum ever won by a filly until the early 1970s.

Like Colonel E. R. Bradley, Chenery was famed for the quality of his broodmares, one of the best of whom was Hildene, a daughter of Bradley's 1926 Derby winner, Bubbling Over. Chenery bought Hildene as a yearling in 1939 for $750, and for a while he was afraid that even that small amount was too much. Hildene ran eight times and quit badly eight times, though the mare did bring home third money of $100 on one occasion. At stud, she proved to be one of the foremost foundation mares of the last fifty years. Though Hildene inherited Bubbling Over's defective vision and eventually went blind, her first-generation offspring — including Hill Prince, by Princequillo, and First Landing, by Turn-to — earned nearly $2,000,000. Hildene also foaled Satsuma, the dam of Cicada.

Chenery made two other successful broodmare buys, Imperatrice for $30,000 and Iberia for $15,000. Imperatrice foaled Somethingroyal, the dam of both Sir Gaylord and Secretariat. Iberia foaled Riva Ridge.

A key factor in Chenery's success was his close relationship with Arthur Boyd Hancock, Sr., founder of Claiborne Farm, and his son, A. B. "Bull" Hancock, Jr. The elder Hancock initiated Chenery into the mysteries of thoroughbred bloodlines, helped his mares get seasons to top stallions, and his stallions get access to top mares. Located on more than 5000 acres of land in Paris, Kentucky, Claiborne is one of the biggest and most successful commercial breeding establishments in the world. When the elder Hancock became disabled, Chenery helped A. B., Jr., with business matters and financial advice as he assumed command of Claiborne. In turn, when Chenery fell ill in 1967, Bull Hancock came to Penny Tweedy's aid with advice and moral support. Nor did she forget the long association of the two families when Bull Hancock died in the fall of 1972. When the decision was made to syndicate Secretariat in early 1973 in order to pay the high taxes on her late father's estate, she gave the assignment to Seth Hancock, Bull's twenty-four-year-old son, even though many horsemen felt that he was too young and inexperienced to handle such a syndication.

Penny Tweedy believes that her father always suspected that if anyone carried on his racing stable, she would be that person. After graduation from Smith College, she had at his suggestion attended Columbia University and studied business-administration, which has come in handy. Big-time racing is big business.

When Chenery entered the hospital in 1967, the year his wife Helen died, Penny Tweedy was living in Denver with her husband and family. To manage the stud and stable, she commuted cross-country to New York to confer with Miss Elizabeth Ham, Chenery's devoted executive secretary, to the farm in Virginia to check in with Howard Gentry, and to the

Seth Hancock.

racetracks where Casey Hayes continued to campaign the Chenery string. Because her father had grown senile in his last years, she discovered the operation in a disorganized state. He had sold some of the best broodmare prospects and neglected to cull his broodmare band. During the first year following his death, when the enterprise was sliding into the red, she was strongly tempted to yield to her advisers and quit, sell the horses, and get on with her own life. Each time she got discouraged, she browsed through the old photographs at The Meadow. "Mr. and Mrs. Chenery standing in winners' circles with this major horse and that. Casey Hayes, long the trainer, seen with them, the three moving gradually beyond middle age as the Arcaros and Gilberts give way to the Shoemakers and Turcottes."[6] Then she walked into the trophy room with its heavy gold and silver cups, vases, and bowls — Hill Prince, First Landing, Sir Gaylord, Cicada.

"That blood was still running strong on the farm, so we kept going," she says.[7]

Nineteen sixty-nine was a critical turning point for Meadow Stud, Inc., though Penny Tweedy had no way of knowing it at the time. Not only had Riva Ridge appeared on the scene along with Upper Case, another good horse, but she lost — and in losing, won — a toss of the coin that would result in her ownership of Secretariat.

For several years Christopher Chenery had had an arrangement with Ogden Phipps whereby each year he would breed two of his mares to Phipps's great stallion Bold Ruler standing at Claiborne. Chenery would not pay the considerable stud fee, so Phipps in turn

would choose one of the foals. The two men had decided to flip a coin once every two years for first choice of the two foals; the loser would automatically get first choice the second year. Penny Tweedy did not think much of the arrangement. For some reason, Phipps usually seemed to get the best of the bargain. She considered putting an end to it. But out of respect to her father, as she puts it, she elected to carry it on for one more two-year period. The 1969 coin toss took place in the Belmont Park offices of Alfred Gwynne Vanderbilt, Jr., chairman of the New York Racing Association.

Penny Tweedy called "tails." The fifty-cent piece came up "heads."

The Phipps family chose the foal by Somethingroyal, a filly they named The Bride. Somethingroyal had by this time, in June, been bred back to Bold Ruler and was again in foal. Another mare, Hasty Matelda, had also been bred to Bold Ruler but was barren. Hence Penny Tweedy had the first and only choice of the 1970 offspring of this arrangement. In March 1970, the foal — Secretariat — arrived at The Meadow.

The Bride, Secretariat's full sister, has not shown much promise.

The chain of events that led to consecutive victories in the Kentucky Derby for Meadow Stable in 1972 and 1973 began with Iberia, whom Christopher Chenery bid in at the Saratoga Yearling Sales in Au-

Elizabeth Ham.

gust 1955 from the consignment of Larry MacPhail, the baseball entrepreneur. Though Iberia was by Heliopolis, a third-place finisher in the Epsom Derby, the mare wasn't much of a runner, winning only three races totaling just under $10,000 for Chenery. Iberia, though evil-tempered, was a fine broodmare, producing the stakes-winning Hydrologist, Potomac, and other winners in addition to Riva Ridge.

On April 13, 1969, Iberia foaled Riva Ridge in a black and red barn on a hillside overlooking the glorious meadows of Claiborne Farm. From the outset, it was obvious that Riva Ridge had taken after First Landing, for the colt was sweet-tempered, bright-eyed, and intelligent. And, he could run. Finally, Riva Ridge was a lucky horse. Howard Gentry's common sense and dedication had saved the foal's life. On the night before Hurricane Camille hit the Virginia coast in the summer of 1969, Gentry started to worry about Iberia and the other broodmares grazing in the low-lying fields along the river. In the hot weather, they were normally left in the fields overnight, but Gentry had heard on the radio that heavy rain — almost twenty inches — had fallen not far from Doswell. So to be on the safe side, he brought all the mares and foals onto high ground and put them in stalls for the night. During the night, water from the rain-swollen North Anna burst through the retaining wall. In the morning, a lake stood where the mares and foals had been grazing.

By September, Gentry began to suspect that Riva Ridge was something special. His log carried this notation: "Good-looking; sound; travels well; a nice way of moving. Will be bigger than half-brother Hydrologist." By the spring of 1971, when Riva was two, Penny Tweedy knew she was going to have a runner. "Long, lean, flop-eared," she wrote in her notebook. "Boys like. Will be a racehorse. Alert, quick to learn, most promising."

For a while, Riva's stablemate, Upper Case, appeared even more promising. By Round Table out of Bold Experience by Bold Ruler, Upper Case was a beautiful colt, though head-strong. When running in the fields with the other weanlings, Upper Case always ran in front. But once the two horses went into training, it became quickly apparent that Riva was by far the better horse. (In his two-year-old year, Upper Case would win one race, finish second once in four starts, winning a total of $7040.) Consequently, Riva was entered in the 1972 Derby and Upper Case was not, though Upper Case did improve tremendously as a three-year-old by which time he was of Derby caliber, having won the Florida Derby and the Wood Memorial.

Long before either of the two horses got to the races, Penny Tweedy and her father's long-time

Bold Ruler, Eddie Arcaro up, and "Sunny Jim" Fitzsimmons at Saratoga.

Meadow Stud farm manager Howard Gentry, holds Iberia, an evil-tempered animal but a fine broodmare. Besides Riva Ridge, Iberia produced the stakes-winning Hydrologist and Potomac.

Trainer Lucien Laurin gives jockey Ron Turcotte ritual last-minute instructions.

trainer came to a parting. In her view, Casey Hayes was finding it difficult to transfer his loyalty from her father to her. She turned her racing string over to young Roger Laurin, son of Lucien Laurin, a French-Canadian trainer who at that time handled the racing side of Bull Hancock's Claiborne Farm. With Roger Laurin, Penny Tweedy felt more at ease. While she had ridden since childhood and had an instinct and affection for horses, the racetrack is a world apart from the show ring and the hunting field. She had much to learn and learn fast. She felt she could ask basic questions of Laurin.

When Ogden Phipps's trainer, Eddie Neloy, died of a heart attack at Belmont Park in the spring of 1971, Laurin was offered the job. He accepted and recommended his father to Penny Tweedy.

From the outset, Penny Tweedy and Lucien Laurin hit it off, though they come from different worlds and are both extremely high-strung people. To the manner born, Penny Tweedy only occasionally flares, though like her father she has a short attention span for those who do not interest her. Laurin makes little effort to restrain his hot French-Canadian temperament. He is brutally honest about his feelings, hence his words sometimes look bad in print the next day, whereupon, like so many others in the public eye, he denies he ever uttered them.

The son of a mill hand, Laurin was born in the village of St. Paul of Joliette, fifty miles north of Montreal. His reasons for becoming a jockey in his youth were the usual ones: He was small, weighing less than

seventy-five pounds at seventeen. He rode all over Canada and the eastern United States.

"I wasn't any ball of fire," says the white-haired little man with characteristic candor, "but I did ride a lot of winners."

When weight caught up with him he turned to training, starting out at the old Pascoag racetrack in Rhode Island. It is a long road from Pascoag to Churchill Downs and the "Big Apple" in New York.

"I made the bush tracks: Wheeling, Cuba, the fairs — all over. I'm not ashamed of it. You had to keep going."

In 1966, he trained Reginald N. Webster's Amberoid, who finished in the ruck behind Kauai King in that year's Derby but went on to win the Belmont Stakes. And he handled Claiborne Farm's Dike, who finished third to Majestic Prince and Arts and Letters in the Derby three years later.

When Lucien Lauren took over Meadow Stable at Belmont Park on June 1, 1971, his son had Riva Ridge ready to run. Riva was, he told his father "a promising two-year-old." Eight days later Lucien Laurin ran Riva Ridge in his maiden race, a five-and-a-half-furlong dash, Chuck Baltazar in the saddle.

"Riva didn't know whether he was to go forward or backward when the gate opened," recalls Penny Tweedy. "He was bumped around a bit, raced greenly, and finished well back of the leaders."

Laurin quickly realized the colt needed blinkers to keep his mind on racing. In blinkers two weeks later at Belmont, Riva won his first race in commanding style. On July 9, Riva won again this time at nearby Aqueduct, and Lucien decided the horse was stakes caliber.

On July 21, Riva went to the post in the Great American at Aqueduct and finished eighth, having twisted a shoe during the running.

About this time, jockey Baltazar was suspended for an infraction aboard another horse, and Laurin replaced him with Ron Turcotte, a fellow French-Canadian. Penny Tweedy's "team," as she calls it, had now formed. Turcotte became the regular rider for Riva Ridge, Upper Case, and later for Secretariat.

Turcotte, twenty-nine, had been riding with great success for nearly a decade and was rated among the ten leading jockeys in this country. But until he rode to fame aboard Riva Ridge and Secretariat, Turcotte was practically unknown to the general public, for he lacked the flair of an Arcaro, the cantankerousness of a Hartack, the elegant style of a Baeza. He is a serious, workmanlike rider, who looks upon a race as just another job.

One of fourteen children of a lumberjack in Grand Falls, New Brunswick, Turcotte dropped out of school after the seventh grade to help support his family.

Secretariat and his team: Penny Tweedy, Lucien Laurin, Ron Turcotte, and Ed Sweat.

Ron Turcotte.

Among his tasks was to haul logs with a mare named Bess whom he dearly loved. When Turcotte turned eighteen, his father sold Bess without ceremony. Ron was so hurt that he left home the same day with fifty dollars in earnings. He hoped to find a construction job in Toronto, but at five-foot-one he was too small. When his boardinghouse landlord suggested that he try jockeying, Turcotte hitched a ride to Woodbine racetrack outside town.

"He let me out in front of the barns of E. P. Taylor's Windfields Farm. I went in and asked if I could get work. I got a job — that was in May 1960 — and I walked horses for a month, then was given two thoroughbreds and two ponies to take care of. In September, I was sent to Windfields Farm where I broke yearlings until the following March. Then I signed on with Gordon Huntley, a trainer. I rode my first race, a horse called Whispering Wind, on June 21, 1961."

He rode his first winner, Pheasant Lane, in April 1962 and swiftly became the leading rider in Canada, then traveled across the border. In 1965, he rode Tom Rolfe to a third-place finish in the Derby behind Lucky Debonair and Dapper Dan.

The other members of Penny Tweedy's team were Ed Sweat, a quiet, easygoing groom, and exercise boy

Charlie Davis, both of whom had been with Lucien Laurin for years.

Riva Ridge came into his own in August at Saratoga when he won his first big stakes race, The Flash. A last-minute virus infection kept Riva from The Hopeful, and the colt was shipped to Belmont Park, where he ran off with the biggest two-year-old classic of them all, the Futurity at six and a half furlongs, over Chevron Flight, Hold Your Peace, and Key to the Mint.

During Riva's summerlong stakes-winning spree, Laurin realized that he might have a truly exceptional horse on his hands.

"One day I sent him out to work with Three Martinis, which really is a fast horse, and which was four years old. I wanted Riva Ridge to get tired in the last eighth, but I was worried in a way about working him with such a good, older horse.

"You can ruin a horse working him. I told the boy on Three Martinis, 'I don't want you to break this other colt; when he comes to you, let them go along together.'

"The two were working along together, and the boy on Riva Ridge looked over and said to the other, 'The man wants this colt to have a work; let your horse run,' and the other guy said, 'I can't get off and carry him!'

"I don't know what it is a horse has that he can look another horse in the eye and whip him, but Riva Ridge drew off by 10 lengths in the last furlong against Three Martinis. That's when I began to think maybe I had a superhorse."[8]

When Riva romped to an eleven-length victory in the Pimlico-Laurel Futurity at one and one-sixteenths miles on October 30, all doubts vanished.

There were now important decisions to be made about Riva Ridge's future. As a two-year-old champion, Riva would automatically be the future book favorite for the 1972 Kentucky Derby.

The ink in the ledger that Elizabeth Ham kept on Meadow Stud, Inc., was pure black. Riva had won $329,929.50. And a syndicate had offered Penny Tweedy in the neighborhood of $1,000,000 for the colt. Laurin advised her to take the money, but she disagreed. Meadow Stud had been trying for at least twenty-two years to breed and race a Derby winner. She would stay in the game.

Her next decision concerned whether to run Riva in the $293,890 Garden State on November 13. Her instinct was to pass up the New Jersey race, even though Riva's grandsire, Turn-to, had won the inaugural running in 1953 and Riva's sire First Landing had won in 1958. Like the Pimlico-Laurel Futurity, the Garden State is a one-and-one-sixteenth-miles race, a long route for a two-year-old to run after a

hard summer campaign. Neither Turn-to, who bowed a tendon before the Derby, nor First Landing were the same horses at three that they had been at two, and she had often wondered whether the Garden State hadn't taken too much out of them. She asked the Jockey Club Statistical Bureau in Lexington, Kentucky, to run a computer readout on the subsequent racing careers of all Garden State winners. The readout confirmed her memory that few of them had gone on to distinguished careers at three. Only the sturdy Carry Back, winner in 1960, went on to win the Derby. (Though Needles, third to Prince John and Career Boy in the Garden State, and Tomy Lee, second to First Landing in the 1958 Garden State, both won at Louisville.) Computers did not impress Laurin. He urged her to run the colt: "He's sound now. He's ready now. Take it while you can get it."

She agreed.

The race matched Laurin *père* against Laurin *fils*, for Riva's strongest opposition was Ogden Phipps's Buckpasser filly, Numbered Account. In the paddock, Lucien's hands trembled uncontrollably as he tightened the girth on the $1,000,000 two-year-old his owner did not want to run. Riva Ridge won going away. Freetex, Key to the Mint, Numbered Account, and four others trailed. Riva emerged from the race in fine fettle and attacked his oats bin.

Riva's two-year-old earnings now totaled $503,-263.50. How best to train Riva for the Derby was now the issue.

Horsemen agree there is no more difficult race to get ready for than the Kentucky Derby. The race comes at a time of year when most of the entries have barely turned three years old. In olden times races took place in the fall, if only because crops were being gathered in the spring.

Because the universal thoroughbred birthday is January 1, Riva Ridge, for example, was officially three on January 1, 1972. In truth the horse would not be thirty-six months old until April 13, a scant three weeks before the May 6 Derby. At a time when thoroughbreds are still growing fast and their bones are still soft, they are asked for the first time to run one and a quarter miles with 126 pounds (121 pounds for fillies) on their backs against the best available (still sound) horses in the nation. The field is invariably big, and a certain number of cheap horses always clutter the race.

Ben Jones, ever the realist, used to say that he never ran a horse in the Derby unless he thought the horse had an excellent chance of winning because the risks of breaking him down were too great. There were too many other rich races later in the season to run for.

"It's a different kind of race," says Laurin. "In a way, you'd have to say it is a survival race. Everyone

144

runs hard to the first turn to get position, and then they want to protect that position so they continue to run hard. Whoever has anything left at the finish usually does well.

"What I'm saying is that you need a very fit horse to win, a horse who may be ready to run more than a mile and a quarter."[9]

The race has taken a tremendous toll of horses. In fact trainers call the Derby, the Preakness, and the Belmont Stakes "the Cripple Crown."

"I'm not high on the Derby," says trainer Johnny Nerud of Tartan Farms. "The Derby is a great publicity gimmick, but it has ruined more good young horses than any other two races put together." Nerud developed Dr. Fager, the great, weight-carrying handicap horse of 1968, winner of more than $1,000,000 in purses and holder for a time of the world's record for the mile: 1:32 1/5. Nerud is convinced that if Dr. Fager hadn't been ailing and missed the Derby, the colt probably wouldn't have been the great horse he was at age four. Nerud, also, was the trainer of Gallant Man, who finished second to Iron Liege in the 1957 Derby when Gallant Man's jockey, Willie Shoemaker, misjudged the finish line and stood up in his irons momentarily.

Indeed, the list of thoroughbreds rendered *hors de combat* by the Derby and the rest of the Triple Crown — Cavalcade, Bold Venture, Count Fleet, Pensive, Hoop Jr., Jet Pilot, Count Turf, Hill Gail, Tim Tam, Dark Star, to mention a few — is nearly as long as the list of Derby winners. The sprinter Morvich won eleven straight races at two, won the 1922 Derby, then never won another race. It took Old Rosebud two years to recover from his record-breaking Derby win in 1914. More recently, Canonero II was on the lame list for a year after the Triple Crown. Dust Commander came out of the Derby with a sore leg and was never the same again. Majestic Prince's meteoric career ended with his defeat in the Belmont; Dancer's Image was through after the Derby and Preakness; Kauai King went lame in early summer after his Derby. Many other horses, such as Graustark, broke down while training for the Derby. Many went lame during or just after the Triple Crown series.

Not that Laurin needed history to remind him of the pitfalls. In 1968 he was training Claiborne Farm's brilliant colt Drone for the Derby when he broke down at Gulfstream Park in Florida.

So great is the prize, however, that owners and trainers are rare who won't risk even an unprepared horse in the big race. As the saying goes, "You get only one shot at the Derby."

As far as Riva Ridge was concerned, Penny Tweedy was insistent that Riva have a long rest in Florida. Riva ran best when fresh, with as much rest as possible between races. Penny Tweedy and Laurin hit upon a plan that would not put Riva into serious training until February 1, 1972, with the colt's first start in the seven-furlong Hibiscus on March 22 and the Everglades, at one and one-eighth miles, on April 26, both at Hialeah. Then they would ship the horse to Keeneland for the Blue Grass Stakes at one and one-eighth miles on April 26.

Laurin planned to train Riva up to the Derby rather than run him fit with six or seven races, which had been the custom for many years. He was reverting to the pre-1940 practice of resting a horse at the farm or track during the winter and conditioning the horse in early spring. After several tune-up races, the horse was sent to the Derby. "Sunny Jim" Fitzsimmons, for example, gave William Woodward's Gallant Fox and his son Omaha only two races before their Derby victories in 1930 and 1935 respectively.

The advent of winter racing in Florida and the tactics of trainer Ben A. Jones changed that pattern. Jones was among the first to season his Derby prospects with at least half-a-dozen races.

"Jones' success caused other trainers to believe the only way to win the Derby was to race a horse up to it," says Kent Hollingsworth.

Under the earlier system, bad weather could disrupt a horse's training schedule. To avoid this problem, Laurin shipped Riva Ridge to Hialeah racetrack in Miami for rest and training. Laurin's plan struck a number of the younger turf writers as bizarre. They were convinced he was going to come up with a "short" horse on Derby Day. It gave them something to write about all spring. Laurin had been training racehorses for thirty years and hewed to his course. He knew his horse. And he knew his owner. She wanted a horse that would come through the Triple Crown races with four legs under him.

The professional horseman, observed turf writer Joe H. Palmer, must be a thoroughgoing individualist: "He has to be, for his hand is against every man, and every man's hand is against him. He must, on occasion, win at the expense of his best friend, and he must be able amicably to share the trainer's stand with a man whose horse has beaten him a nose on the post for $50,000. He must keep his own counsel too; just a fragment of knowledge carelessly given away may enable a shrewd jockey to plot a winning race against his best horse. He must stand or fall on his own knowledge and his own judgment."[10]

Every trainer frets constantly about injury to his horse. "During the dark winter mornings of early January, Laurin would not even take Riva Ridge out of his stall. He waited for full light. 'I didn't want those fool horses running into him by accident,' Laurin explained."[11] In late February and early

March, when the Florida weather grew hotter, he did take Riva out at first light if it was cool.

The rest had done the colt a lot of good. He now stood sixteen hands one and a quarter inches. A horseman who saw him for the first time on the backstretch at Hialeah was struck by the colt's greyhound-like appearance.

"Riva Ridge has been described as 'not a pretty horse' but only by observers who do not appreciate those long legs . . . He had an intelligent head and expression in his eyes, and those long front legs seemed to come out of the same hole . . . His hind legs are just as slender as his front ones, and they are right under him where they belong. His disposition couldn't be brighter, nothing seemed to annoy him, and he was always looking for his feed tub."[12]

Riva Ridge responded eagerly to the resumption of training on February 1, 1972. "Riva Ridge Sizzles Five Panels in .57 1/5" according to the *Daily Racing Form* on March 15. Translation: Riva had worked five eighths of a mile in 57-1/5 seconds, in fractions of :11 3/5, :22 1/5, :33 4/5, and :45 2/5. On that same day, Key to the Mint suffered a stifle injury, costing twenty-four days of training and a chance at the Kentucky Derby, leaving second-stringer Head of the River to carry Paul Mellon's gray and yellow silks in the classic.

Riva won his first three-year-old start in the Hibiscus on March 22. Turcotte was relieved to find that Riva was the same horse he had been at two, that the colt hadn't lost any of his competitive spirit.

"He's more relaxed this year, which is good. I can place him easy now. Last year he showed me he wouldn't pull himself up when he made the lead, but he would get a couple of lengths in front and just maintain it instead of drawing out. But if he heard anybody coming up on him, or saw them — the blinkers are slit in the back — he would put his head down and take off again."[13]

The coast appeared clear to the ninety-eighth running of the Derby. It was not, of course; it rarely is. On April 26 in the Everglades, Riva finished a tiring fourth behind Head of the River on a sloppy Hialeah track. Turcott had broken Riva along the rail, but every time he tried to break out, jockey Mickey Solomone on Hold Your Peace hemmed him in. The going along the rail was heavier than out in the track, and

Riva grew leg-weary. While changing leads coming into the homestretch, Riva slammed into the rail. The colt lost precious time in straightening out, and Head of the River won the race.

When Turcotte tried to explain his problems, Laurin cut him short: "You rode a bad race." Some sportswriters chose to recall that in the 1965 Derby, Turcotte had gotten similarly trapped aboard Raymond Guest's Tom Rolfe, winding up third behind Lucky Debonair and Dapper Dan. Laurin assured everyone that the Everglades experience would not be repeated in the Kentucky Derby.

"I'll die on the lead first, rather than have a repeat of that business, and whoever runs with me will die too," said Laurin. "Except that Riva Ridge will have a better chance of lasting all the way than anyone else . . . I wish Ron Turcotte had 'sent' him in the Everglades, to get a position on the outside, instead of staying on the rail."[14] Laurin had tipped his Derby hand, but no one was paying much attention. There would be genuine surprise when Riva ran just such a race in the Derby.

By the time Riva was shipped to Keeneland to get ready for the Blue Grass Stakes on April 26, the Florida heat had begun to bother the colt. Riva prowled his stall restlessly, as if looking for a cool spot, Ed Sweat observed. Like most thoroughbreds coming to the bracing spring air of Kentucky after Florida's heat, Riva visibly perked up. Laurin, too, perked up. Keeneland's pre-Derby meeting is like old home week for professional horsemen, having about it the picnic atmosphere of a hunt race meeting in the Virginia countryside. Keeneland is genteel, unhurried. Here the patrons mingle with jockeys and owners and trainers as the horses are saddled under the old trees behind the handsome stone clubhouse and grandstand. Despite defeat in the Everglades, Riva Ridge went off the favorite in the Blue Grass Stakes and won easily over a marginal Derby hopeful, Sensitive Music, and an indifferent field of horses.

Turf writers asserted that the race hadn't proven a stern enough trial for Riva. "Some horsemen thought Riva Ridge looked like a short horse in the Blue Grass," said Whitney Tower. "After watching him shake off his closest competitor, Sensitive Music, in mid-stretch, there was considerable argument about the quality of his performance."

For his part, Laurin was pleased that it hadn't been a hard race. The trainer's task is to bring his horse to a peak at a certain date, not one week before or one week after. Riva was ready. Now he was worried because things were going too perfectly. Prophetically, he said after the Blue Grass: "It's very premature, I know, but if you were to ask me which of the Triple Crown races I fear most, I'd say it was the Preakness. The Preakness has an altogether different kind of track."[15]

Laurin was also pleased at the way Riva Ridge had matured mentally as well as physically over the winter. The colt was even more sensible and willing than he'd been at age two. Early one morning a horse broke loose from his hot walker on the backstretch at Keeneland and galloped wild-eyed through the stable area. While other horses risked injury by rearing and plunging in fright, Riva stood in his walking ring and calmly watched the performance. In the starting gate, too, Riva kept his head when horses on either side reared or made the metal ring with flashing hoofs.

Riva has idiosyncracies, however.

"Mostly he's friendly," explained Ed Sweat one day to a reporter on the dawn patrol, "but sometimes he doesn't want nobody messing around. When he goes in the stall and stands in the middle with his head down, like this, you stand in front of him and he'll charge. Or sometimes there might be people around, and he'll just turn his back on them. Anybody goes in the stall behind him, then he'll kick.

"When he's lying down sleeping, though, you can pull at him all day and he won't move. Might raise his head and look at you, that's all."[16]

Two days after Riva's victory in the Blue Grass, Maribel Blum's Hold Your Peace, the second Derby choice, won the Stepping Stone purse at Churchill Downs. The cleverly named son of Speak John had not only proven Riva's nemesis in the Everglades but had won the Flamingo by ten lengths. Trained by Floridian Arnold Winick, Hold Your Peace was a front-runner and Riva's biggest threat. On May 2, Paul Mellon's Key to the Mint further clouded the picture by winning the Derby Trial at Churchill Downs, handing third choice No Le Hace his first defeat in five straight races, including the Louisiana and Arkansas Derbies.

Despite their successes in other big stakes races such as the Belmont, neither Mellon nor his trainer, Elliott Burch, had ever won a Kentucky Derby. Both had come agonizingly close. Burch had trained Mrs. Isabel Dodge Sloane's Sword Dancer, second to Tomy Lee in 1959. For Mellon, Burch had saddled Quadrangle, a close fifth in 1964 to Northern Dancer, and Arts and Letters, second by a nose to Majestic Prince in 1969. A Yale graduate, and the son of famous trainer Preston Burch, Elliott has a trainer-owner relationship that most other conditioners can only dream about. A shy, self-effacing man, Mellon provides Burch with the finest possible racing stock, then leaves the big decisions to Burch. It would never occur to Mellon to pressure Burch into running an unready horse in the Derby.

Key to the Mint had won the Derby Trial but was a mighty tired horse at the end, observed his jockey, Braulio Baeza. The more than twenty days' training lost after the stifle injury in Florida was evident in Key to the Mint's condition. Burch scratched the horse from the Derby, pointing him for the Preakness instead. "He's too good a horse to take chances with," said Burch. "There's a long season ahead."[17]

In Spanish, No Le Hace means the rough equivalent of "It makes no difference" and that is how his trainer, Homer Pardue, characterized the colt's loss to Key to the Mint in the Derby Trial.

"We're going to win it," said the trainer, who was born on Central Avenue beside Churchill Downs. "I'm not worried about post position. I'm not worried about the odds. I don't even care if the track is muddy or like concrete, uphill or down."[18]

The rest of the Derby field were a mixed bag. Kentuckian was owned by Preston Madden, grandson of John E. Madden and the third-generation to carry on as master of Hamburg Place in Lexington. By Madden's tremendously successful stallion, T.V. Lark, Kentuckian had finished a hard-running second to Quack, a Derby noneligible, in the California Derby, justifying a trip to the Downs in the eyes of his owner. Freetex, an erratic Florida-bred, had finished second to Riva Ridge in the Garden State the previous fall and had won the one-mile Gotham at Aqueduct at three. Juan Arias, trainer of Canonero II, was back with another long shot, a colt named Hassi's Image, who finished second to No Le Hace in the Arkansas Derby. Gustavo Avila, Canonero's jockey, was flying in from Caracas to ride a Kentucky-bred colt, Pacallo, who had been running in Puerto Rico.

The size of the field worried Laurin and the other trainers. As late as April 25 it looked as though twenty or more horses might go to the post, including two animals that had never been raced, a colt named Special Array from Maryland and One Eyed Tom from Nevada.

The problem arises nearly every year. Lynn Stone, Churchill Downs' president, says the ideal Derby field is fourteen, the number of horses that can be loaded into one starting gate. When the number exceeds fourteen, a second gate has to be used and the horses in the second gate have a distinct disadvantage.

"I frankly don't believe we could accommodate more than 22 horses," said Stone. "I like to see no more than 14. When you get 15, it means you park somebody out in the second gate. When you hook another gate on, you get the wheels of both gates plus the tongue and you're parking those horses out another 10 feet or more."[19]

With professional horsemen it is a matter of pride not to run an inferior horse in the Derby, and they try to discourage owners of such horses from running them. The dilemma is that every so often, a "no chance" horse such as Canonero II drops from the sky, so to speak, and takes it all. Sometimes, too, the owners are better judges of their horses than the trainers.

To be eligible for the Derby, a thoroughbred must be registered with the Jockey Club. The 1972 Derby eligibles came from a crop of 24,033 foals registered in 1969. At that time, it cost only $100 to nominate a horse for the Derby and another $2000 to start. Two hundred and fifty-eight thoroughbreds were nominated. The total fee was raised to $7600 for the 1974 Derby.

Some owners, mostly those new to the game, are anxious to see their silks in the Derby and to enjoy the perquisites of an owner's badge entitling them to a box seat. Still others are publicity seekers. Many sincerely believe in their horses but are misguided. In all cases, a few thousand dollars is no deterrent.

"O.K., I'll say what many of us are thinking," said Arnold Winick, trainer of Hold Your Peace. "It's as though just anybody can go out, buy a jalopy, and run in the '500' or pick up a golf bag, go to Augusta, and tee off in the Masters.

"The time is here. It is going to take someone with guts to go ahead and do what has to be done, to keep this a great race. Go ahead and write a Derby preview for those people who want to see their horses run on Derby Day, so they can get their box seat and reserved seats. But it looks like we're coming to the time when, maybe, the Derby should be an invitational race."[20]

Laurin agreed that restrictive clauses would have to be written into the race's conditions. Only Homer Pardue demurred. "Let 'em put up the $2,000 to enter and start. It's just that much more money for us."[21]

The debate had been touched off by the antics of One Eyed Tom, probably the most unlikely Derby candidate in the long history of the race. One Eyed Tom, so named because of an early eye injury, was owned and trained by Mike Hines, a former Notre Dame football player, now a divorce and bankruptcy lawyer in Las Vegas. Hines had a ranch "just a whinny away from the Sahara Hotel," where he trained the gelding, but admitted he had no idea how fast Tom could run because he had never measured

One Eyed Tom, shying from the starting gate, was one of the most unlikely Derby candidates in the long history of the race. In Louisville for the 1972 Derby, the colt had never run in a race or broken from a starting gate. Finally, Tom was scratched.

the training track on his ranch.[22] He had a 170-pound boy galloping the animal from four to six miles every day so the 126-pound Derby impost would seem light to Tom.

Tom, however, had never been schooled from a starting gate, and unless the gelding passed a starter's test, he would not be allowed to go postward in the Derby. When Tom came out on the track for his test, a knot of Derby trainers, exercise boys, and newsmen gathered to watch. Tom's exercise boy took him into the gate five times, and each time the frightened gelding reacted differently. Once Tom walked out. Another time he bolted and executed a neat U-turn. Once he shied away from the contraption. When it was over, his rider's legs were streaked with green paint from the gate. Tom had flunked. After a few days, Tom got the hang of the gate. But by this time, peer pressure had taken its effect on Hines. Tom was scratched.

Downs' officials had a still more serious worry. The trainer of an equally unqualified horse, Special Array, had announced at Pimlico that he was heading for the Derby, "no matter what," providing, of course, he could get his horse off the track veterinary's unsound list. Special Array's owner of record was Bronislava Derivan, wife of trainer Frank Deri-

van of Parkville, Maryland, a teacher of retarded children. Their daughter Yvonne served as exercise girl, and their son Ronald had been the breeder. At the age of twenty-three Ronald had died of asthma after extracting a promise from his father that Special Array would be entered in "the three big ones" — the Derby, Preakness, and Belmont. Special Array was out of the mare Keen Array by Special Pleading, he by Citation.

When Derivan entered Special Array in his maiden start, an allowance race at Pimlico less than two weeks before the Derby, the track veterinary ordered the colt scratched because he was so lame. Special Array never made it to Churchill Downs.

The field shook down to sixteen starters; Freetex on the rail, No Le Hace on the outside in the second starting gate, and the stalls between filled out by Sensitive Music, Hold Your Peace, Introductivo, Dr. Neale, Our Trade Winds, Big Brown Bear, Kentuckian, Riva Ridge, Pacallo, Hassi's Image, Majestic Needle, Head of the River, and Big Spruce. For the fourth time in twenty-two years, a Chenery horse was going off the favorite in the Kentucky Derby. Second choice was Hold Your Peace and third choice was No Le Hace, despite the colt's unfavorable post position.

Christopher Chenery, who was in the hospital, had always warned his daughter to be ready for heartbreaking disappointments in racing, and his words came back to her as race time approached. To help break the Derby jinx, she decided to wear her lucky dress, a sleeveless white shift with blue figures. She wore as well the racehorse pin her mother had given her, and to please her late mother's friends, she wore white gloves.

Derby Day, May 6, broke sunny and clear. By 7:00 A.M., when *Daily Racing Form* writer Joe Hirsch arrived at the backstretch, he found cars lined up the length of Longfield Avenue waiting for the parking lots to open. Lines were also rapidly forming at the turnstiles, especially at the one marked "centerfield." Many of the early arrivals had folding chairs that they set up in front of the track's television monitors. In this way they could say they had gone to the Derby and also seen it.

This would be the biggest Derby Day to date, with an American racetrack attendance record of 130,564. As early as 9:00 A.M., observed Red Smith, "foot traffic was moving like wet cement through the tunnels to the centerfield." By 11:30 A.M., when the first of the day's ten races went off, 45,000 people occupied the centerfield. The crowd would bet a record $2,885,325 on the Derby and $7,164,717 on the total race card. Both the crowd and betting figures were nearly double those of ten years earlier. The Derby had been growing steadily and would continue to grow in popularity. Another $2,452,403 would be bet in New York's seventy-one Off-Track Betting parlors.

When Turcotte rode the fourth race to get the feel of the track, he discovered that though it was officially rated "fast," it was cuppy and tiring along the rail. He made a mental note to keep Riva five or six feet out from the rail.

The gate clanged open for the Derby at 5:34 P.M., and Riva broke alertly. A quick glance to his left told Turcotte that Marquez on Hold Your Peace was not going to try for the lead. With Riva rolling along well, Turcotte in a split second abandoned his plan to lie third or fourth in the early running. He booted Riva right to the lead to the astonishment of many and flashed past the quarter mile in 23-4/5, Majestic Needle hard on his heels. As the horses leaned into the first turn, Marquez moved Hold Your Peace into second place where he could keep an eye on Turcotte. By now the field was stringing out. No Le Hace was back in the pack.

Thinking, wrongly as it turned out, that Riva was loafing in the lead, Marquez made a move and drove his colt to Riva's quarter, whereupon Turcotte let out a notch and Riva bounded away to a one-length lead. Riva was moving far faster than Marquez had thought, registering a very respectable 23-4/5 for the second quarter and 1:11 4/5 for the six furlongs. At the far turn, Marquez made a second move and again Riva spurted away, flying into the homestretch three lengths in the lead as Hold Your Peace began to shorten stride.

Now No Le Hace came on, picking up tiring horses, taking over second at the eighth pole, but the horse was too late. Riva cruised under the wire, still under restraint, by three and a quarter lengths, No Le Hace a similar distance ahead of Hold Your Peace. Riva's time was 2:01 4/5, the seventh fastest in Derby history, not spectacular except for the fact that Turcotte had had a tight hold throughout.

"The key to the Derby was Riva Ridge's ability to string together quarters of almost metronomic regularity — 23 4/5, 23 4/5, 24 1/5, and 25 4/5," observed the *Daily Racing Form*'s John McEvoy. "The last was the slowest, but he was under no pressure to do better."

Riva Ridge became only the thirteenth horse in Derby history to win wire to wire, and after twenty-two years, Christopher Chenery won the Derby at last.

The sunshine glanced off the big gold cup as Governor Wendell Ford of Kentucky made the presentation on the white platform behind the winner's circle. The lovely blond owner hugged her trainer and kissed her jockey, projecting her excitement to millions of television viewers. At the victory party in the Chur-

chill Downs directors' room a short while later, waiters served champagne, Veuve Cliquot Ponsardin 1966, six glasses to a silver tray.

"Well, is he *still* a short horse?" asked Laurin, confronting one of his most persistent critics among the racing press.

As soon as the Tweedy party returned to their rooms in one of Louisville's many Holiday Inns — the old Brown Hotel where Chris Chenery had hosted gay, pre-Derby parties was gone — Elizabeth Ham put through a call to Mrs. Mignon Lokensgard, one of Christopher Chenery's nurses at the New Rochelle Medical Center in New York. "I had a feeling that this might have gotten through to him," recalls Miss Ham. "I asked her what had happened, and she said: 'I think he knows.'" Mrs. Lokensgard had turned on the television set in Chenery's room during the Derby. Chenery paid little attention, but when he saw his daughter appear on the screen clutching the gold cup, he stirred in his bed. "Mr. Chenery, Mr. Chenery," exclaimed the nurse. "You have just won the Kentucky Derby!" Mrs. Lokensgard wiped away the tears that had suddenly started to roll down his cheeks.

While Secretariat was winning everything in sight as a two-year-old in the summer and fall of 1972, Riva Ridge fell into a losing streak. Here Penny Tweedy gives her colt a consoling pat before yet another losing effort in the International at Laurel in the fall. After winning the Kentucky Derby, Belmont Stakes, and Hollywood Derby, Riva won no more races that year, and Mrs. Tweedy conceded they should have used more "restraint." She stirred up an angry controversy with Monmouth Park officials in New Jersey when she charged, after a Riva losing effort, that traces of tranquilizing drugs had been found in the colt's system when she got him back to Saratoga. She sticks by her guns to this day. Monmouth officials discount her charge. In July 1973, Riva set a world record of 1:52 2/5 for one and three-sixteenths miles in Aqueduct's Brooklyn Handicap. At the same time, Riva whipped old rival Key to the Mint and became an equine millionaire. On September 15, 1973, he finished second to stablemate Secretariat in the Marlboro Cup at Belmont Park in his only race against him.

Chapter 16
The Horse with the Nielsen Rating

EARLY IN 1973, thirty-two investors paid $190,000 a share — $6,080,000 — to syndicate Secretariat. The colt then weighed 1200 pounds, putting his value at $345 an ounce, higher than the price of gold.

When the investors signed the syndication agreement, Secretariat had yet to make his debut as a three-year-old, and they knew that history was littered with the names of red-hot two-year-olds whose flames sputtered out at three. Thoroughbred breeding history was similarly cluttered with names of truly great race horses — Calumet's Citation, for one — who were tremendous disappointments at stud. Some, like his fleet stablemate Coal Town, failed totally as sires.

The thirty-two syndicators of Secretariat have been tremendously lucky so far. Secretariat won the Triple Crown, a title no other horse had been able to win for a quarter century.

Shortly after the syndication agreement was announced, and before Secretariat had begun his three-year-old campaign, Warner L. Jones, one of the syndicate members, said, "the reason I went in on Secretariat is that I think he could be another Man o' War." The Louisville breeder added, "The way I look at it, every foal by Secretariat that hits the ground will be worth $100,000, and I consider this an investment like American Tel and Tel or Exxon."

Jones believes he can recoup his $190,000 with the sale of the first two or three Secretariat yearlings even if they eventually prove they can't run a lick. And

if the son of the late Bold Ruler proves anywhere near as successful in the breeding shed as such professionals expect, Jones should wind up eventually with nine or ten immensely valuable four-legged properties.

Warner Jones is a tough, self-made member of the tight little circle of men including Leslie Combs II, John R. Gaines, Dr. William W. Lockridge, Preston Madden, the late Bull Hancock, and Hancock's son Seth, who control syndication of about one fifth of America's most valuable thoroughbred stallions.

Secretariat more than rewarded Jones's confidence with his 1973 performance on the track.

On May 5, the big colt came from behind in a long, steady drive to win the Kentucky Derby in

Warner Jones.

LEFT:
"Secretariat had become the first horse since Citation in 1948 to win the Triple Crown."

153

Groom Ed Sweat grabs Secretariat's bridle to take off blinkers a few minutes after the colt had won the Gotham tying the track record. Trouble lay ahead in the Wood Memorial.

1:59 2/5, three-fifths of a second faster than Northern Dancer's record, set in 1964.

Arnold Kirkpatrick, editor of *The Thoroughbred Record* noted that Secretariat had "accelerated in each successive quarter, his individual fractions by interpolation having been as follows:

:25 1/5   :24 1/5   :23 3/5   :23 2/5   :23

"No matter how you look at it, Secretariat's was the most impressive Kentucky Derby ever run, and the longer you look at it, the more impressive it becomes."[1]

Sigmund Sommer's Sham finished second, two and one-half lengths back, also racing past the finish line in under two minutes flat, fully eight lengths ahead of the field, despite a mouth severely bloodied in an accident at the starting gate.

Nineteen million saw the ninety-ninth Kentucky Derby on television. Not since the gray Native Dancer thrilled TV viewers with his races in the early 1950s had there been such intense interest in a horse. Secretariat became the horse with the Nielsen rating.

In the Preakness, he looped his field on the club house turn and led to the wire. And on June 9, he won the Belmont by an awesome thirty-one lengths — nearly one-sixteenth of a mile — in 2:24 3/5, shaving Gallant Man's 1957 record by two and three-fifths seconds.

At the Keeneland Yearling Sales in July, a colt by Secretariat's sire Bold Ruler went to a Japanese-dominated syndicate for $600,000 — the highest price ever paid for a yearling.

The bidding on the Bold Ruler colt opened at $500,000 and lasted just two minutes and forty seconds. Moments after Lexington bloodstock agent Jim Scully had bid in the colt, a Louisiana oil man leaned over to him and his client, Zenya Yoshida, Japan's leading thoroughbred breeder: "Would you fellas take a hundred thousand dollar profit on that colt? I mean it. I'll give you $700,000 for him."[2] Scully declined.

The demand for thoroughbred yearlings has appeared insatiable in recent years, thanks in great measure to the infusion of foreign money in the market, yet racing attendance and mutuel handle have been dropping as the result of the economy, and overexpansion of racing and off-track betting. Secretariat came galloping onto the scene at a time when the sport needed him.

154

In many respects, Secretariat's career parallels that of Man o' War to an amazing degree. When Big Red started racing, his name on a program was enough to fill the grandstand. "In time, policemen had to be assigned to prevent souvenir hunters from snatching hairs from his mane and tail, and his thundering hoofs became as much a part of the Golden Age of Sport as the crack of Babe Ruth's bat or Bill Tilden's whistling serves."[3]

When Secretariat started running in his three Derby prep races in New York in the Spring — the Bay Shore, the Gotham, and the Wood Memorial — he packed the grandstands as Man o' War had done in 1919 and 1920. In his three-year-old debut on March 17 at Aqueduct, Secretariat bulled courageously through a fast-closing gap between two horses to win the seven-furlong dash by 4-1/2 lengths. The crowd went wild. When Ron Turcotte took Secretariat to the front at the halfway mark in the Gotham, an unearthly roar went up from the stands, drowning out the whine of jet aircraft at nearby JFK airport.

"He is the Triple Threat of the Triple Crown," enthused the *Daily Racing Form*'s Charlie Hatton. "He runs in front, comes from behind, handles classic weight, and runs up a tin roof and over broken bottles."

During the colt's three-year-old campaign, three secretaries were kept busy answering as many as 200 letters a day addressed to Penny Tweedy and the horse. At the paddock rail, racegoers strained to touch him, and a ripple of applause followed Secretariat as the colt left the paddock for the course and cantered postward. It looked as though Penny Tweedy would have to rename her colt Secretariat, Inc.: Las Vegas, Madison Avenue, and CBS-TV discovered "The Horse of the Century." So did artists, sculptors, writers, and photographers. T-shirt manufacturers, medallion makers, and scores of others proposed schemes to commercialize the $6,080,000 colt. One enterprising man bought hundreds of two-dollar win tickets on Secretariat's Triple Crown races, framed them with a picture of the horse, and sold them for $350 apiece.

So many autograph seekers pursued Penny Tweedy that she had trouble moving around at the track. Television crews focused cameras on her while she watched Secretariat's races. A force of Pinkertons guarded the colt's stall on a round-the-clock basis. The many requests to view Secretariat in his stall had to be severely limited, else there would have been a Radio City-like queue outside his barn most of the day. Before the Belmont Stakes, when it was apparent Secretariat would sweep the Triple Crown, his picture appeared on the covers of *Time*, *Newsweek*, *The National Observer*, and *Sports Illustrated*. Secretariat was now a "cover horse." In late June, Representative Hugh L. Carey, a New York congressman, rose from his seat in the House of Representatives to declare Secretariat, "Rex Americana Equinus, King of the Sport of Kings." Columnist Art Buchwald said Secretariat would make a fine addition to the troubled White House staff of Richard Nixon because the horse was universally respected.

"The emotional involvement of people in Secretariat has been intense," says Penny Tweedy. When her big red colt was upset by Onion at Saratoga in August 1973, many people wrote in to say that they had noticed on the televised account of the race that the colt did not appear well. "It's as though they were justifying one of their children. It was very touching."

A few days later, Secretariat did come down with a fever and virus.

On September 15, 1973, Secretariat won the biggest promotion of all, the $250,000 Marlboro Cup, beating stablemate Riva Ridge in the first commercially sponsored event in New York racing history.

Had Penny Tweedy not thought it inappropriate, the colt could have earned close to that doing two "walk-ons" a day around a fountain in front of a Las Vegas hotel for a couple of weeks.

To sift such proposals for "good taste," Mrs. Tweedy employed the William Morris Agency, and to advise her on her common-law property rights involving use of Secretariat's name, she consulted the Wall Street law firm of Hughes, Hubbard, and Reed.

Secretariat looks the part of the super-horse. He's big, bigger even than Man o' War. When seen for the first time walking down the track to the paddock with groom Eddie Sweat at his head, Secretariat strikes one as more like a hunter or a warhorse than a racer. The blanketed figure appears almost to swagger, swaying to the right and left on the front end, walking strangely stiff-legged behind, his legs wrapped in royal blue and white walking bandages equipped with zippers.

When stripped for saddling, Secretariat reveals heavily muscled hindquarters, the key to his fantastically powerful propulsion system. His shoulders are ideally long and sloping, his chest deep. His proportions are heroic. He stands sixteen hands two inches, weighs in the neighborhood of 1200 pounds, with a girth measuring seventy-five and three-quarter inches to Man o' War's seventy-two inches.

He's golden-red in color, with a wispy white blaze running down his forehead to his nose and three flashy white stockings.

"It's as though God wanted to make a perfect racehorse," rhapsodized Pimlico's Chick Lang.

Secretariat is a prodigious "doer," consuming sixteen quarts of oats a day, two more than Riva, and all the hay he can eat. He eats almost continuously,

Riva Ridge (left) sometimes resents all the attention focused on his more glamorous young stablemate, Secretariat (right). They're shown arriving at JFK airport in New York in March 1973 to open their spring campaigns.

but tidily — some oats, then a sip of bottled water, some hay. His diet includes oats cooked into a mash, carrots, vitamins, and "sweet feed," or grains covered with molasses.

When the hayrack is removed the morning of a race, most horses grow edgy, for they sense what's coming. Secretariat usually takes a nap.

"Secretariat is just like a big kid who doesn't know his own strength," says Penny Tweedy. "He's a very happy horse, not mean, but he's awfully strong and an awful tease.

"Riva is a friendly horse, too, and competitive. But Secretariat is more competitive about everything. He insists on being fed first. He bucks and kicks the side of the stall and we think, 'Oh dear, he's going to get hurt.' So we feed him first, then Riva, then the rest of the horses."

When sick, Secretariat becomes irritable, sometimes going so far as to cock a warning hind foot at his stoical groom, as if to say: "Bug off, and leave me alone, Eddie," says Penny Tweedy.

Penny Tweedy feels Riva resents his precocious stablemate in the next stall. "He used to be the center of attention himself, and you could tell he liked it." Increasingly during the spring of 1973, Riva would turn his rump to the stall door when the crowds formed around Secretariat. Penny Tweedy and Lucien Laurin decided that Riva needed a tonic in the form of a win. They shipped him to Suffolk Downs, where he ran off with the Massachusetts Handicap and received an enthusiastic reception from the crowd.

Groom Eddie Sweat is a short, stocky man from Holly Hill, South Carolina, as is Charlie Davis, Secretariat's exercise boy. Both men are strong, quiet, and affectionate around the horses. When Riva Ridge started to paw the ground nervously before a race at Saratoga in the summer of 1973, Sweat kept jiggling his bit to distract the colt. Davis scratched Riva's ear and said soothingly: "O.K. old boy, now you stop that." Riva relaxed and, a few minutes later, won the race.

Whereas Sweat never uses two words when one will do, Davis is outgoing, happy-go-lucky, and a flamboyant dresser. When he rides his stable pony into the paddock for Secretariat's races, eyes invariably turn his way: His outfit is generally more eye-catching than the jockey's silks.

Secretariat was foaled a little after midnight on March 30, 1970, at Meadow Stud. From the beginning, much was expected of him. His breeding was impeccable, his conformation stunning.

"Wow!" exclaimed Penny Tweedy when she first saw him. For a long time, she called him her "wow colt." Now she calls him "sexy."

Early in October, Howard Gentry wrote in his note-

156

book: "About the best colt we've ever had at the farm."

Secretariat's sire, Bold Ruler, raced under the colors of Mrs. Henry Carnegie Phipps's Wheatley Stable and was trained by Sunny Jim Fitzsimmons. Though Bold Ruler finished a tiring fourth in the 1957 Derby, he was among the best horses of an exceptional generation. As a stud, Kentuckians speak of Bold Ruler in the same breath as the immortal Lexington. Bold Ruler led the sire list for seven years, 1963 through 1969, and his progeny had won a record $14,236,613 through 1972. In July 1971, Bold Ruler succumbed to cancer of the throat at age seventeen, having covered his last mares a few months earlier.

Bold Ruler tended to produce offspring who were precocious and fast at age two and sometimes tailed off at age three when asked to go a distance. Hence the commonly voiced belief that Bold Rulers couldn't "get" a distance. "Everybody scared me to death about Bold Ruler," said Lucien Laurin.

Charles F. Stone of *The Blood-Horse* asserts that the Bold Ruler theory has always "stood firmly on shaky ground." Stone remembers that Bold Ruler had gone on to win at the one-and-one-quarter-mile Derby distance later in his three-year-old year, had won at that distance twice the following year, and had "sired eleven horses that won stakes races at the Derby distance."

Secretariat's dam Something Royal has proven an outstanding broodmare; her offspring include Sir Gaylord who sired Sir Ivor, an Epsom Derby winner. Her sire, Princequillo, has produced many distance horses.

When Penny Tweedy's "wow colt" was turned over to Laurin for training, he found the colt so good-looking he was afraid he'd never be able to run. Secretariat later dispelled such thoughts. Secretariat's courage was tested in his maiden start at Aqueduct on July 4, 1972. When the gates clanged open, another horse slammed so hard into Secretariat that he almost went down. Then he was bumped into the fence at the three-eighths pole. Rallying from these two experiences, frightening for a first-time starter, Secretariat closed fast, making up seven to eight lengths to finish fourth.

Secretariat's experiences in his first race affected his running style for more than a year. After leaving the gate with his field, Secretariat would drop back to avoid the heavy traffic and the possibility of getting knocked again. For a long time, too, Secretariat hit the after-burner at the three-eighths pole.

Secretariat won his first race by six lengths on July 15 and seven straight races thereafter, looping wide on the turns and swarming over the fields, cooking them in his run between the half-mile pole and the

Charlie Davis.

Pancho Martin.

Riva Ridge's precocious stablemate pounds down the track at Belmont Park in March 1973 with the Kentucky Derby in his sights. Secretariat had been named "Horse of the Year" in 1972, stealing some of the limelight from Riva.

quarter pole. Secretariat won the Hopeful, Futurity, Laurel Futurity, and the Garden State. He finished his year with seven wins in nine starts, having been disqualified after winning the Champagne because he had swerved into a horse after Turcotte tapped him with a whip for the first time. Secretariat's bankroll totaled $456,404.

Early in 1973, Laurin announced he would get Secretariat ready for the Derby with three races — as he had with Riva — but that he would take the New York route: the Bay Shore, Gotham, and Wood Memorial. After tying the Aqueduct track record in the Gotham mile with ease, things looked rosy indeed for the Wood Memorial, a critical race as Secretariat would be asked to go one and one-eighth miles for the first time. Furthermore, the Santa Anita Derby winner Sham, a top horse, would be in the race, and his trainer, Frank "Pancho" Martin, was proclaiming loudly that his colt was going to whip Secretariat's ears off.

A few days before the Wood, Laurin asked Turcotte to work Secretariat a mile in 1:38. As Turcotte came barreling down the track, a loose horse suddenly appeared ahead of him and a group of green horses were in his path, so he eased back on his horse and finished in 1:42.

Laurin then had to fly to Florida to attend a funeral, signals somehow got crossed, and Secretariat was not given another short, sharp workout to make up for the slow work. Such oversights give trainers gray hair. The incident may have cost Secretariat the Wood.

Laurin also conditions horses for Edwin Whittaker, who wanted to run his horse Angle Light in the Wood, so the trainer named him as an entry with Secretariat in this race. Whittaker understandably was not interested in having his horse exercised to help Secretariat win, and Laurin instructed jockey Jacinto Vazquez to go on with Angle Light and win it any way he knew how. When Pancho Martin realized Laurin was saddling an entry he announced that *he* would run two horses besides Sham — Knightly Dawn and Beautiful Music.

The strain of the upcoming Derby was beginning to tell on both trainers. Laurin was taking sleeping pills for the first time in his life. Of Cuban descent, Martin, like Laurin, is a first-rate trainer and a high-strung individual. Martin lost his temper the morning of the race when he read in Charlie Hatton's *Daily Racing Form* column that Laurin had said, "The only way they can beat him is to steal it." "Stealing a race" is common enough racetrack parlance for clever tactics, but Martin read into it an insinuation that he was planning gang tactics against Secretariat. He angrily scratched the two extra horses and proclaimed that he would beat Secretariat so soundly Laurin would have no excuses. "He's got more excuses than China has rice — and China has a hell of a lot of rice," said Martin.[4]

Laurin refused to be drawn into a fight.

Sigmund Sommer said he was glad Martin had scratched the two horses and that he expected Laurin to scratch Angle Light. Angle Light stayed in the race. Vazquez took the Whittaker colt to the front, set a slow pace, and stole the race. The jockey on Sham was so busy watching and waiting for Secretariat's big run that by the time he set sail for Angle Light, it was too late.

After ten straight victories, Secretariat, the "super-horse," had been beaten. Laurin had to appear in the winner's circle as Angle Light's trainer, but he was unable to summon a smile for photographers.

Penny Tweedy after Secretariat wins the Triple Crown.

Ron Turcotte and Secretariat win the Belmont Stakes — and the Triple Crown.

The first Saturday in May 1973: A record 134,476 packed Churchill Downs to see the ninety-ninth running of the Kentucky Derby won by Secretariat. The crowd bet $3,284,962 on the Derby and $7,627,965 total for the day, both new highs.

It was now Martin's turn to make excuses. If Sham's regular rider, Laffit Pincay, Jr., had been available, Sham would have won, he said. And it naturally dawned on him that if the speedy Knightly Dawn had been in the race, he could have forced "an honest" pace. Angry, he vowed never to speak to Laurin again.

Turf writers now abandoned Secretariat. The *Daily Racing Form* handicapper picked Sham. Whitney Tower picked Sham. The talk of a super-horse had probably been premature, said the Washington *Post's* Gerald Strine. An upset was likely, said Andrew Beyer of the Washington *Star-News*. Sham, they enthused, was looking more and more like the Kentucky Derby horse. And indeed, he was. The big colt had won five of his ten races, and his volatile trainer had brought him to the peak of his form in a series of California races. The colt was, the headline writers couldn't resist saying, "no pretense" — Sham being by Pretense out of Sequoia by Princequillo. Sham's workouts had been sharp and fast.

Sham had been bred by Bull Hancock, who always ran some horses in his own colors and had desperately wanted to win a Kentucky Derby. Had Hancock not died and had 1973 not been Secretariat's year, he might well have realized his dream. Sommer, a New York real estate man, had bought Sham for $200,000 at the November 1972 dispersal sale of Hancock's racing stock after his death at sixty-two of cancer.

At Churchill Downs, Sham was assigned a stall in Barn 42, just seven stalls away from Secretariat and Angle Light. Martin and Laurin were not speaking, and neither man crossed the invisible line dividing their territorial prerogative. Martin, however, kept poisoning the atmosphere by jabbing his cigar in the direction of Meadow Stable and elaborating on his reasons for disliking Laurin. Martin stepped up the tempo. Sham, he insisted, was going to leave the great Secretariat up the track. Some writers exploited the one-sided feud: the Cuban refugee trainer versus the high society trainer; Penny Tweedy versus Sig Sommer, the self-made man.

Things became even more unpleasant. Word began to circulate that Secretariat was in trouble. Jimmy Jones of Calumet fame was on the grounds conditioning a Derby longshot named Restless Jet, owned by his wife and three other women. In talks with reporters, he made no secret of his feeling that Secretariat was an overrated horse who couldn't have warmed up Citation. Jimmy said to a reporter:

"I keep hearing that there is some heat in his leg somewhere and he is being treated with icepacks. Lucien denies it, but some people around the stables insist it's true. And Secretariat did run in the Wood as if something was pinching him."[5]

Said Andrew Beyer: "Rumors continue to swirl that he trained last week with the aid of Butazolidin. None of these stories has been confirmed and Laurin adamantly denies them all. But when a horse has recently been syndicated for more than $6,000,000, it is not considered good form to reveal afterwards that he is suffering from physical problems."[6]

Sham picked up further support when Jimmy "the Greek" Snyder, the noted oddsmaker, said that while the "numbers" favored Secretariat, his body wisdom told him otherwise. "I don't know why, but I don't like Secretariat."[7]

Laurin's emotions are close to the surface, and the commotion began to upset him. He had his own doubts. He thought the Wood Memorial was a fluke, a race to be thrown out, as the saying goes. On the other hand, how does a trainer know until the horse runs? The syndicators, he knew, were just as anxious for the answer as he was. Sham was a top horse, and Laffit Pincay, Jr., was the nation's leading jockey. And this was the Derby.

During Derby week, the stables along the Churchill Downs backstretch begin stirring with life at dawn. Down the shed rows in the glare of bare light bulbs, drowsy grooms pad from stall to stall. Someone flips on a transistor radio. A groom shoves a horse's rump as he enters the stall: "Move ovuh, you big dude." From warm piles of muck, steam drifts into the frosty air. There's the aroma, too, of wintergreen and antiseptic and strong black coffee. The sun begins to climb in the sky. Owners, trainers, jockeys, and newsmen arrive in their cars, clustering later in little groups in front of the stark cinder-block barns.

A television camera crew sets up in front of Secretariat while the colt is walked around the shed row. Secretariat pauses to nibble the microphone. Across the way, a network radio man records the sound of another Derby hopeful munching grass. The sound of thrumming hooves comes from the track. Solemn-faced trainers clutch their watches. In the background across the infield, the twin spires break the flat monotony of the stands. Grooms slap water on the gleaming flanks of thoroughbreds back from their works, skimming the water off with swift flicks of metal sweat scrapers. For owners, trainers, and jockeys, the hours begin to drag after midmorning, and there is time to worry about all the things that can cause a horse to lose.

To distract themselves, Penny Tweedy and Lucien Laurin set out every day for the Bluegrass country around Lexington to look at horse farms. At night, Penny has dinner with Ron Turcotte, on whom the responsibility of riding a $6,000,000 Derby favorite lies heavily.

Derby Day itself dawns more quietly. Except for

At the start, Ron Turcotte lets Secretariat — wearing saddle-cloth No. 1A — drift back as Shecky Greene takes the lead.

Secretariat is last in the first run by the grandstand as Shecky
Greene stays on the front end.

Turcotte (far right in checked silks) starts to pick up horses on the clubhouse turn with Shecky Greene still in front at the three-furlong mark, followed by Gold Bag, Royal and Regal, Sham, Angle Light, and the rest of the field.

Secretariat has made his move. At the three-eighths pole, Shecky Greene on the rail has started to fade, as Sham takes the lead, with Secretariat swinging wide to take third.

As Sham races past the quarter-pole, Turcotte takes the whip to Secretariat and the issue is drawn.

Driving for the wire, Secretariat leads Sham, and now Laffit
Pincay, Jr., goes to the whip.

168

Turcotte has put his whip away as Secretariat hurtles toward the finish line two and a half lengths ahead of Sham, who led Our Native by eight lengths, with Forego fourth.

It's Secretariat. The time: 1:59 2/5, a Derby record, three fifths of a second faster than Northern Dancer's mark set in the 1964 race.

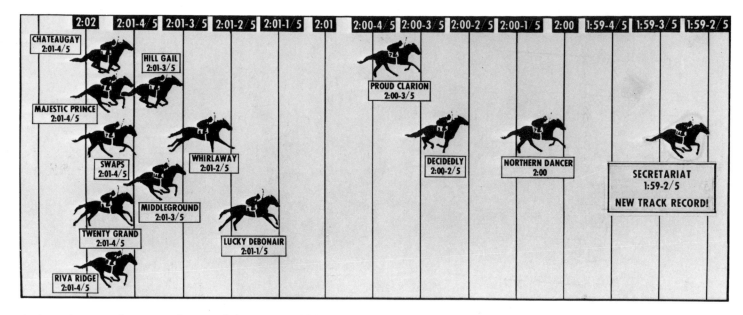

| 2:02 | 2:01-4/5 | 2:01-3/5 | 2:01-2/5 | 2:01-1/5 | 2:01 | 2:00-4/5 | 2:00-3/5 | 2:00-2/5 | 2:00-1/5 | 2:00 | 1:59-4/5 | 1:59-3/5 | 1:59-2/5 |

CHATEAUGAY 2:01-4/5

HILL GAIL 2:01-3/5

MAJESTIC PRINCE 2:01-4/5

PROUD CLARION 2:00-3/5

SWAPS 2:01-4/5

WHIRLAWAY 2:01-2/5

DECIDEDLY 2:00-2/5

NORTHERN DANCER 2:00

SECRETARIAT 1:59-2/5 NEW TRACK RECORD!

MIDDLEGROUND 2:01-3/5

TWENTY GRAND 2:01-4/5

LUCKY DEBONAIR 2:01-1/5

RIVA RIDGE 2:01-4/5

A chart showing where great horses of the past would have finished in Secretariat's Derby.

a few veterans like Red Smith and Joe Hirsch, most newsmen stay in bed. There have been parties the night before, and there are no more workouts to witness, no more interviews to conduct. Millions of words and thousands of feet of film have been broadcast.

Churchill Downs president Lynn Stone and his staff have been preparing for a year. "Basically, it's a problem of crowd control," he explains. The crowd never does get completely controlled. A bunch of kids hopped the fence in 1875, and they've been coming over the fence ever since. A few young men parachuted into the infield not long ago.

As she has for four decades, Mrs. Kingsley Walker, a Louisville florist, prepares the blanket of roses for the winning horse and the bouquet for the jockey. Head gardener Donald Lord has replanted more than 60,000 flowers from the greenhouses to the Downs' sixty flower beds. Jim Thomson, the Scotsman who has been sending Derby fields away from the starting gate since 1957 is ready. Track superintendent Thurman Pangburn has the track fast.

Going postward with Secretariat, Angle Light, and Sham were Shecky Greene, a speed horse; Navajo; Royal and Regal, winner of the Florida Derby; My Gallant, winner of the Blue Grass; Gold Bag; Our Native; Restless Jet; Forego; Twice a Prince; and Warbucks.

A dangerous situation developed at the start as the horses were being loaded into the gate. Twice a Prince refused to enter his stall. Once inside, he reared up, catching one leg in the gate momentarily and throwing jockey Angel Santiago, riding in his first Derby. The horse thrashed around, his shoes clanging against the metal of the gate. In the next stall, jockey Don Brumfield dismounted from Our Native when Twice a Prince kicked his horse. Our Native was led out the front of the gate. In the excitement, Sham, trapped in the gate without an assistant starter to hold him, slammed his head against the gate, nearly tearing out two front teeth. Luckily, Secretariat hadn't been loaded in the gate yet, so Turcotte was able to walk the colt around away from the confusion. Finally, an assistant starter got Twice a Prince out of the gate and walked the horse around for a moment to try to calm him down. Santiago remounted and the horse was led back into the gate. All the horses were in now. Seconds later they were off.

Jockey Walter Blum dashed Shecky Greene right to the front. Secretariat broke slowly and settled down in last place in the run past the stands and into the clubhouse turn.

"God Almighty," Laurin thought to himself. "Don't tell me it's going to be another of them."[8]

"Secretariat began to pick up horses, on the outside, on the first turn, and once he straightened for the backstretch the question over whether he would fire was resolved. He began a long, steady yet spectacular run that carried him quickly to the middle of the pack. The question then became: Would he stay?

Ron Turcotte on Secretariat (left) looks across at Eddie Maple on Riva Ridge as the Marlboro Cup field rounds the turn for home. Riva Ridge was leading at the time, but the colt wasn't in front for long. "I took a peek over my shoulder," said Riva's jockey later, "and I saw him coming — a big red head and body coming right at me. That was Secretariat, and there was nothing I could do about it. My horse was still going strong, right to the finish. He ran as hard as any horse ever did. But it was no use. It was a helpless feeling."

Ron Turcotte jogs Secretariat back after winning the $250,000 Marlboro Cup at Belmont by three and a half lengths over stablemate Riva Ridge. The big colt set a world record of 1:45 1/5 for one mile and one-eighth.

"Pincay had Sham in contention from soon after the start, and he did not let Shecky Greene . . . get out of touch. Sham was in second position after six furlongs and went after Shecky rounding the far turn . . . His horse quickly rushed by Shecky Greene, although the latter hung on gamely and still was third at the eighth pole.

"As Sham moved into command easily, Secretariat was continuing his looping run on the outside. He was a running horse, and suddenly as they straightened away for the stretch run it became the two-horse race predicted for the Wood Memorial. Turcotte drove the favorite to the flank of Sham; he felt he could go on by, but was not sure. 'Riders like Pincay . . . are so cool that they always will have some horse left, so you never know for sure what is going to happen until you challenge them.'

"Secretariat came to the leader, his handsome head held low, heavy muscles grouping and stretching beneath the glistening coat. Turcotte reached back and hit him three times . . . He had his horse measured by about the three-sixteenths pole, and although Sham — the taste of blood in his mouth — held on with courage, Secretariat rather quickly drew out. The power which had carried him wide on the turn held its momentum as he and Sham ran a classic in a non-American way — the last part faster than the first part."[9]

Blood was hemorrhaging from Sham's mouth when they brought the game colt back to Barn 42, and one of the grooms sickened at the sight. A veterinary finally stopped the bleeding and cauterized the wound.

At the other end of the barn, a station wagon arrived with champagne for the winner's stable help. Ed Sweat wouldn't touch it; he had a horse to take care of, but he posed for photographers with an empty glass. Charlie Davis had some, though, and then some more.

When he is excited, Secretariat's exercise boy starts to stutter, and Sweat sometimes has to stand by to interpret. But on May 5, 1973, with the shadows lengthening over the Downs, Charlie Davis needed no interpreter:

"How, how, how, *sweet* it is!"

RIGHT:
Secretariat steps down the track into history.

174

Appendix I
Kentucky Derby Records

THE WINNERS

Ninety-one colts, seven geldings, and one filly have won the Derby. Regret (1915) was the filly. The geldings were Vagrant (1876), Apollo (1882), Macbeth (1888), Old Rosebud (1914), Exterminator (1918), Paul Jones (1920), Clyde Van Dusen (1929).

BIRTHPLACE

Tomy Lee (1959), Omar Khayyam (1917), and Northern Dancer (1964) are the only winners not foaled in the United States. Northern Dancer was foaled in Canada. The other two were foaled in England. Tomy Lee was brought to this country as a weanling, Omar Khayyam as a yearling. Cavalcade (1934) and Pensive (1944) are sons of mares bred to stallions in England and brought to America while the mares were carrying the Derby winners.

Seventy-six winners were foaled in Kentucky. Lord Murphy, Kingman, and Typhoon II were foaled in Tennessee; Assault and Middleground in Texas; Spokane in Montana (while that state was still part of the Northwest Territory); Elwood in Missouri; Wintergreen in Ohio; Regret and Cavalcade in New Jersey; Decidedly, Swaps and Morvich in California; Reigh Count and Secretariat in Virginia; Lawrin in Kansas; Dust Commander in Illinois; Needles and Carry Back in Florida, and Kauai King in Maryland.

COLOR

Determine, 1954 winner, was the first gray to win the Derby, Decidedly was the second. Bay horses have won the Derby 46 times. Chestnuts have won 32 times, browns 14 times, and blacks 4 times.

OWNERS

Eight Winners: Calumet Farm — Whirlaway (1941), Pensive (1944), Citation (1948), Ponder (1949), Hill Gail (1952), Iron Liege (1957), Tim Tam (1958), and Forward Pass (1968). The late Warren Wright owned Calumet the first four times the stable won; Mrs. Wright was owner in 1952, later won as Mrs. Gene Markey in 1957, 1958, 1968.

Four Winners: E. R. Bradley — Behave Yourself (1921), Bubbling Over (1926), Burgoo King (1932), Brokers Tip (1933).

TRAINERS

Six Winners: Ben A. Jones — Lawrin (1938), Whirlaway (1941), Pensive (1944), Citation (1948), Ponder (1949), Hill Gail (1952).

Four Winners: H. J. Thompson — Behave Yourself (1921), Bubbling Over (1926), Burgoo King (1932), Brokers Tip (1933).

Three Winners: James Fitzsimmons — Gallant Fox (1930), Omaha (1935), Johnstown (1939). Max Hirsch — Bold Venture (1936), Assault (1946), Middleground (1950).

JOCKEYS

Five Winners: Eddie Arcaro — Lawrin (1938), Whirlaway (1941), Hoop Jr. (1945), Citation (1948), Hill Gail (1952). Bill Hartack — Iron Liege (1957), Venetian Way (1960), Decidedly (1962), Northern Dancer (1964), Majestic Prince (1969).

Three Winners: Isaac Murphy — Buchanan (1884), Riley (1890), Kingman (1891). Earle Sande — Zev (1923), Flying Ebony (1925), Gallant Fox (1930). Bill Shoemaker — Swaps (1955), Tomy Lee (1959), Lucky Debonair (1965).

Two Winners: Willie Simms — Ben Brush (1896), Plaudit (1898). Jimmy Winkfield — His Eminence (1901), Alan-A-Dale (1902). Johnny Loftus — George Smith (1916), Sir Barton (1919). Albert Johnson — Morvich (1922), Bubbling Over (1926). Linus McAtee — Whiskery (1927),

Clyde Van Dusen (1929). Charles Kurtsinger — Twenty Grand (1931), War Admiral (1937). Conn McCreary — Pensive (1944), Count Turf (1951). Bobby Ussery — Proud Clarion (1967), Dancer's Image (1968) disqualified. Ismael Valenzuela — Tim Tam (1958), Forward Pass (1968) placed first. Ron Turcotte — Riva Ridge (1972), Secretariat (1973).

NEGRO JOCKEYS: Isaac Murphy, Willie Simms, Jimmy Winkfield (see records above). O. Lewis — Aristides (1875). Billy Walker — Baden-Baden (1877). G. Lewis — Fonso (1880). Babe Hurd — Apollo (1882). Erskine Henderson — Joe Cotton (1885). Isaac Lewis — Montrose (1887). Alonzo Clayton — Azra (1892). J. Perkins — Halma (1895).

APPRENTICE JOCKEYS: Ira Hanford on Bold Venture (1936) and Bill Boland on Middleground (1950).

FEMALE JOCKEYS: Diane Crump, finished 15th aboard Fathom (1970) in 17-horse field.

MOST APPEARANCES: Eddie Arcaro rode in the Derby for the 21st time in 1961, a record number of mounts for any rider in the race. Bill Shoemaker has ridden in the Derby 17 times.

BREEDERS

EIGHT WINNERS: Calumet Farm — Whirlaway (1941), Pensive (1944), Citation (1948), Ponder (1949), Hill Gail (1952), Iron Liege (1957), Tim Tam (1958), Forward Pass (1968). All eight Calumet-bred Derby winners were foaled in the same barn at that farm near Lexington, Kentucky.

FIVE WINNERS: A. J. A. Alexander — Baden-Baden (1877), Fonso (1880), Joe Cotton (1885), Chant (1894), His Eminence (1901). (*Author's Note:* Some horsemen credit O. H. Chenault as breeder of His Eminence on technical ground that he bought the colt's dam before he was foaled.) John E. Madden — Old Rosebud (1914), Sir Barton (1919), Paul Jones (1920), Zev (1923), Flying Ebony (1925). Madden bred Sir Barton in partnership with Vivian Gooch of England. All five Madden-bred Derby winners were foaled in the same barn at Hamburg Place near Lexington, Kentucky.

FOUR WINNERS: E. R. Bradley — Behave Yourself (1921), Bubbling Over (1926), Burgoo King (1932), Brokers Tip (1933). Bradley owned Idle Hour Stock Farm in Fayette County, Kentucky and bred Burgoo King in partnership with H. N. Davis.

SIRES

TRIPLE: Reigh Count (1928) sired Count Fleet (1943) who sired Count Turf (1951). Pensive (1944) sired Ponder (1949) who sired Needles (1956).

THREE WINNERS: Falsetto — Chant (1894), His Eminence (1901), Sir Huon (1906). Virgil — Vagrant (1876), Hindoo (1881), Ben Ali (1886). Sir Gallahad III — Gallant Fox (1930), Gallahadion (1940), Hoop Jr. (1945). Bull Lea — Citation (1948), Hill Gail (1952), Iron Liege (1957).

TWO WINNERS: King Alfonso — Fonso (1880), Joe Cotton (1885). Longfellow — Leonatus (1883), Riley (1890). Broomstick — Meridian (1911), Regret (1915). McGee — Donerail (1913), Exterminator (1918). The Finn — Zev (1923), Flying Ebony (1925). Black Toney — Black Gold (1924), Brokers Tip (1933). St. Germans — Twenty Grand (1931), Bold Venture (1936). Man o' War — Clyde Van Dusen (1929), War Admiral (1937). Blenheim II — Whirlaway (1941), Jet Pilot (1947). Bold Venture (1936) — Assault (1946), Middleground (1950).

DERBY WINNERS: Halma (1895) sired Alan-A-Dale (1902). Bubbling Over (1926) sired Burgoo King (1932). Reigh Count (1928) sired Count Fleet (1943). Gallant Fox (1930) sired Omaha (1935). Bold Venture (1936) sired Assault (1946) and Middleground (1950). Pensive (1944) sired Ponder (1949). Count Fleet (1943) sired Count Turf (1951). Ponder (1949) sired Needles (1956). Determine (1954) sired Decidedly (1962). Swaps (1955) sired Chateaugay (1963).

SECOND IN DERBY: Falsetto (1879) sired three winners, Chant (1894), His Eminence (1901), Sir Huon (1906). Himyar (1878) sired Plaudit (1898). Native Dancer (1953) sired Kauai King (1966).

THIRD IN DERBY: Free Knight (1886) sired Elwood (1904), First Landing (3rd 1959) sired Riva Ridge (1972).

UNPLACED IN DERBY: Bob Miles (1884) sired Manuel (1899). Insco (6th, 1931) sired Lawrin (1938). Bull Lea (8th, 1938) sired Citation (1948), Hill Gail (1952), and Iron Liege (1957). Bold Ruler (4th 1957) sired Secretariat (1973).

OLDEST: Falsetto, 30 years old when Sir Huon won in 1906.

YOUNGEST: Pensive, 8 years old when Ponder won in 1949. Gallant Fox, 8 years old when Omaha won in 1935. Royal Coinage, 8 years old when Venetian Way won in 1960. Raise A Native, 8 years old when Majestic Prince won in 1969.

STARTERS

Largest field to start in the Derby was 22 in 1928; the smallest fields were in 1892 and 1905, which had three starters each. The largest number of nominees to the Derby was 258 in 1972; the smallest was 32 in 1913.

FAVORITES

ODDS-ON: In 27 runnings of the Derby there has been an odds-on favorite (a horse, which if he won, would pay less than even money). Of these 15 have won, eight have been second. The others finished worse than third.

POST-TIME: Himyar went to post at 1 to 4 in the 1878 Derby. He finished second. Count Fleet (1943) and Citation (1948, coupled with Coal Town) won at 40 cents to $1. Bimelech also was a 40 cents to $1 favorite, finished second in 1940.

PAY-OFF: Citation (coupled with Coal Town) and Count Fleet each paid $2.80 when they won. These were the smallest winning prices since pari-mutuel betting on the Derby was introduced. Hindoo (1881), Halma (1895), and Agile (1905) each paid 1 to 3 to win the Derby. Donerail (1913) paid $184.90 for each $2 win ticket, record pay-off in the mutuels on the Derby.

TIME

FASTEST: Spokane (1889) 2:34 1/2 at mile and one-half. Secretariat (1973) 1:59 2/5 at mile and one-quarter.

Venetian Way's 2:02 2/5 was the fastest Derby time for an "off" track. The track was listed as "good" on Derby Day, 1960.

SLOWEST: Kingman (1891) 2:52 1/4 at mile and one-half. Stone Street (1908) 2:15 1/5 for mile and one-quarter.

Statistics courtesy of Churchill Downs

FASTEST WINNERS

1973	Secretariat	1:59 2/5
1964	Northern Dancer	2:00
1962	Decidedly	2:00 2/5
1967	Proud Clarion	2:00 3/5
1965	Lucky Debonair	2:01 1/5
1941	Whirlaway	2:01 2/5

FINAL QUARTER-MILES

1973	Secretariat	shaded :23 1/5
1941	Whirlaway	shaded :23 3/5
1949	Ponder	shaded :23 4/5
1967	Proud Clarion	shaded :24
1964	Northern Dancer	:24
1969	Majestic Prince	shaded :24 1/5

FINAL HALF-MILES

1973	Secretariat	:46 2/5
1967	Proud Clarion	shaded :47 4/5
1941	Whirlaway	shaded :48
1971	Canonero II	shaded :48 1/5
1962	Decidedly	shaded :48 3/5
1956	Needles	shaded :48 4/5

Courtesy *The Blood-Horse*

Churchill Downs has had only nine presidents in its 100-year history. The first was Col. M. Lewis Clark, who served from 1875–1894. Then came William Schulte (1895–1901), Charles Grainger (1902–1917); Johnson Camden (1918–1927); Samuel Culbertson (1928–1937); Col. Matt Winn (1938–1949); Bill Corum (1950–1958); Wathen Knebelkamp (1959–1969) and the current president, Lynn Stone.

Appendix II
Race Charts, 1875-1973

99th Kentucky Derby, May 5, 1973

1¼ miles. (2:00). Ninety-ninth running Kentucky Derby. Scale weights. $125,000 added. 3-year-olds. By subscription of $100 each in cash, which covers nomination for both the Kentucky Derby and Derby Trial. All nomination fees to Derby winner, $2,500 to pass the entry box, Thursday, May 3, $1,500 additional to start, $125,000 added, of which $25,000 to second, $12,500 to third, $6,250 to fourth, $100,000 guaranteed to winner (to be divided equally in event of a dead-heat). Weight, 126 lbs. The owner of the winner to receive a gold trophy. Closed with 218 nominations. Value of race, $198,800. Value to winner $155,050; second, $25,000; third, $12,500; fourth, $6,250. Mutuel Pool, $3,284,962.

Horses	Eqt A Wt	PP	¼	½	¾	1	Str	Fin	Jockeys	Owners	Odds to $1
Secretariat	b 3 126	10	11^h	6½	5^1	2½	1½	1²½	R Turcotte	Meadow Stable	a-1.50
Sham	b 3 126	4	5^1	3^2	2^1	1½	2^6	2^8	L Pincay Jr	S Sommer	2.50
Our Native	b 3 126	7	6½	8½	8^1	5^h	3^h	3½	D Brumfield	Pr'ch'd-Thom's-R'g't	10.60
Forego	3 126	9	9^{1}½	9½	6½	6^2	4½	4²½	P Anderson	Lazy F Ranch	28.60
Restless Jet	3 126	1	7½	7^h	10½	7½	6^{1}½	5²¼	M Hole	Elkwood Farm	28.50
Shecky Greene	b 3 126	11	1^{1}½	1^3	1^{1}½	3^3	5^1	6^{1}½	L Adams	J Kellman	b-5.70
Navajo	b 3 126	5	10^{1}½	10^1	11^4	8½	8^2	7no	W Soirez	J Stevenson-R Stump	52.30
Royal and Regal	3 126	8	3^1	4^3	4^3	4^1	7½	8^{3}½	W Blum	Aisco Stable	28.30
My Gallant	b 3 126	12	8^h	11^{1}½	12^3	11^2	10½	9^h	B Baeza	A I Appleton	b-5.70
Angle Light	3 126	2	4^h	5^{1}½	7^1	10^{1}½	9^{1}½	10^{1}¾	J LeBlanc	E Whittaker	a-1.50
Gold Bag	b 3 126	13	2^h	2^h	3½	9^1	11^1	11no	E Fires	R Sechrest-Gottdank	68.30
Twice a Prince	b 3 126	6	13	13	13	13	12^2	12^{1}½	A Santiago	Elmendorf	62.50
Warbucks	3 126	3	12^1	12^3	9^h	12^{1}½	13	13	W Hartack	E E Elzemeyer	7.20

a-Coupled, Secretariat and Angle Light; b-Shecky Greene and My Gallant.

Time, :23 2/5, :47 2/5, 1:11 4/5, 1:36 1/5, 1:59 2/5 (new track record). Track Fast.

$2 Mutuel Prices—Secretariat (a-Entry) $5.00 to win, $3.20 to place, $3.00 to show. Sham $3.20 to place, $3.00 to show. Our Native $4.20 to show.

Ch. c, by Bold Ruler—Somethingroyal, by Princequillo. Trainer, L. Laurin, Bred by Meadow Stud, Inc. (Va.).

In gate—5:37. Off at 5:37 Eastern Daylight Time. Start good. Won handily.

Secretariat relaxed nicely and dropped back last leaving the gate as the field broke in good order, moved between horses to begin improving position entering the first turn, but passed rivals from the outside thereafter. Turcotte roused him smartly with the whip in his right hand leaving the far turn and **Secretariat** strongly raced to the leaders, lost a little momentum racing into the stretch where Turcotte used the whip again, but then switched it to his left hand and merely flashed it as the winner willingly drew away in record breaking time. **Sham**, snugly reserved within striking distance after brushing with **Navajo** at the start, raced around rivals to the front without any need of rousing and drew clear between calls entering the stretch, was under a strong hand ride after being displaced in the last furlong and continued resolutely to dominate the remainder of the field. **Our Native,** reserved in the first run through the stretch, dropped back slightly on the turn, came wide in the drive and finished well for his placing. **Forego,** taken to the inside early, veered slightly from a rival and hit the rail entering the far turn, swung wide entering the stretch and vied with **Our Native** in the drive. **Restless Jet** saved ground in an even effort. **Shecky Greene** easily set the pace under light rating for nearly seven furlongs and faltered. **Navajo** was outrun. **Royal and Regal** raced well for a mile and had nothing left in the drive. **My Gallant** was not a factor. **Angle Light** gave way steadily in a dull effort and was forced to check when crowded by **Gold Bag** on the stretch turn. **Gold Bag** had good speed and stopped. **Twice a Prince** reared and was hung in the gate briefly before the start and then showed nothing in the running. **Warbucks** was dull.

98th Kentucky Derby, May 6, 1972

1¼ miles. Scale weights, $125,000 added and $5,000 gold cup. Value to winner $140,300; second, $25,000; third, $12,500; fourth, $5,000. Mutuel pool $2,885,325.

Horses	Eq't Wt	PP	¼	½	¾	1	Str	Fin	Jockeys	Owners	Odds to $1
Riva Ridge	wb 126	9	1½	1¹½	1¹½	1¹½	1³	1³¾	R Turcotte	Meadow Stable	1.50
No Le Hace	wb 126	16	6²	6⁵	5³	3³	3⁵	2³½	P Rubbicco	J R Straus	4.50
Hold Your Peace	wb 126	3	3¹½	2½	2⁵	2⁸	2³	3³½	C Marquez	Maribel G Blum	3.90
Introductivo	wb 126	4	8²	7²	7ʰ	8¹	4³	4²	R Breen	Mr-Mrs CJ Rob'tson Sr	52.90
Sensitive Music	wb 126	2	10²	9³	9⁵	4¹	5¹½	5¾	J L Rotz	F H Lindsay	31.00
Freetex	wb 126	1	11³	11⁴	6ʰ	7ʰ	6²	6¹	C Baltazar	Middletown Stable	15.90
Big Spruce	w 126	15	12½	13²	11¹	13²	7²	7½	L Adams	Elmendorf	f-8.90
Head of the River	w 126	14	9ʰ	10ʰ	10⁴	9³	8⁶	8⁵	M Hole	Rokeby Stable	19.00
Big Brown Bear	w 126	7	14ʰ	12¹	14⁵	12ʰ	10²	9¹¾	R Broussard	Mr-Mrs A E Reinhold	27.80
Kentuckian	wb 126	8	15⁴	14¹	12²	11⁵	11³	10¾	D Brumfield	P W Madden	16.70
Hassi's Image	wb 126	11	5³	4½	3²	6²	9¹½	11²	H Gustines	Hassi Shina	31.00
Majestic Needle	wb 126	12	2½	3²	4²	5²	12½	12ⁿᵒ	M Mang'llo	R E Lehmann	f-8.90
Our Trade Winds	w 126	6	16	16	16	15²	13½	13½	J Nichols	R Mitchell	f-8.90
Napoise	wb 126	13	13¹½	15⁷	15²	16	14⁵	14⁴½	R Kotenko	R E Lehmann	f-8.90
Dr. Neale	w 126	5	4ʰ	5³	8¹	10¹½	16	15ⁿᵏ	W Leeling	C E Nicholas	f-8.90
Pacallo	wb 126	10	7¹	8¹	13²	14³	15¹	16	G Avila	Walnut Hill Farm	54.50

f—Mutuel field

Time, :23 4/5, :47 3/5, 1:11 4/5, 1:36, 2:01 4/5. Track fast.

$2 mutuels paid: Riva Ridge, straight $5.00; place $3.80; show $3.00. No Le Hace, place $4.40; show, $3.40; Hold Your Peace, show, $3.60.

Winner—B. c., by First Landing—Iberia, by Heliopolis. Trainer, Lucien Laurin. Bred in Kentucky by Meadow Stud, Inc.

Riva Ridge quickly recovered after being bumped at the start to assume command, continued slightly wide while under patient handling, disposed of **Hold Your Peace** when ready while drifting out through the upper stretch and encountered little difficulty in holding **No Le Hace** safe. The latter, unhurried for a mile, moved up along the outside thereafter, commenced swerving again through the closing drive and was clearly best of the others. **Hold Your Peace** away in good order to prompt the pace while in hand, raced slightly wide to maintain a striking position, dropped to the inside in the upper stretch when the winner drifted out but lacked a further response. **Introductivo** improved his racing position steadily in the late stages but could not menace the top trio. **Sensitive Music** passed tiring horses. **Freetex** was without speed. **Big Spruce** was always outrun. **Head of the River** failed to enter contention. **Kentuckian** lacked speed. **Hassi's Image** swerved sharply to the inside at the start, bumping with **Pacallo**, continued in a forward position while saving ground and stopped badly after going seven furlongs. **Majestic Needle** dropped back steadily. **Dr. Neale** could not keep pace. **Pacallo** failed to menace after being bumped at the start.

The Winner's Pedigree

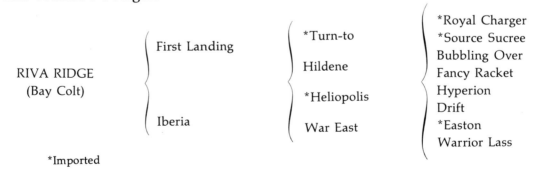

RIVA RIDGE
(Bay Colt)

First Landing
- *Turn-to
  - *Royal Charger
  - *Source Sucree
- Hildene
  - Bubbling Over
  - Fancy Racket

Iberia
- *Heliopolis
  - Hyperion
  - Drift
- War East
  - *Easton
  - Warrior Lass

*Imported

97th Kentucky Derby, May 1, 1971

1¼ miles. Scale Weights. $125,000 added and $5,000 gold cup. Value to winner $145,500; second $25,000; third $12,500; fourth $5,000. Mutuel pool $2,648,139.

Horses	Wt	PP	¼	½	¾	1	Str	Fin	Jockeys	Owners	Odds to $1
Canonero II	126	12	16^1	18^5	15^3	4½	1^3	1^{3¼}	G Avila	E Caibett	f-8.70
Jim French	126	10	10^h	11^2	10^2	7^2	5½	2^2	A C'dero Jr	F J Caldwell	4.80
Bold Reason	126	14	18^6	16½	12^2	9^2	6^2	3^{nk}	J Cruguet	W A Levin	18.30
Eastern Fleet	126	17	6^2	3^h	2^{1½}	2^{1½}	2^h	4^h	E Maple	Calumet Farm	a-3.80
Unconscious	126	8	7^2	6^2	5^1	5^h	4½	5^{1¾}	L Pincay Jr	A A Seeligson Jr	2.80
Vegas Vic	126	7	13^3	13^3	13^1	13½	7^1	6^{nk}	H Grant	Betty Sechrest-C Fritz	19.30
Tribal Line	126	15	15^2	14^h	17^6	8½	8^2	7no	D E Whited	J E-T A Grissom	80.80
Bold and Able	126	1	1^h	1^2	1^{1½}	1^h	3^h	8^3	J Velasquez	Calumet Farm	a-3.80
List	126	18	17^h	17½	14^2	14^{1½}	9^2	9^3	J Nichols	Mrs J W Brown	8.60
Twist the Axe	126	11	9½	10^1	7^1	6^{1½}	10^2	10^{1½}	G Patterson	Pastorale Stable	c-5.10
Going Straight	126	2	11^2	8^h	6^h	10^3	12^2	11^h	O Torres	Donamire Farm	45.60
Royal Leverage	126	5	19^8	15^2	16^1	18^5	11^h	12^2	M Fromin	P Teinowitz	b-41.60
Impetuosity	126	20	8½	9^2	8^2	15^1	13^h	13^{1½}	E Guerin	W P Rosso	c-5.10
Helio Rise	126	16	12½	12^1	9^h	11^1	14^1	14^3	K Knapp	R W, V-RT Wilson Jr	58.20
On the Money	126	9	20	20	20	17½	15^{1½}	15^1	M Solomone	Teinowitz-Schmidt	b-41.60
Barbizon Streak	126	6	2^h	5^1	11^1	12^1	16^6	16^{18}	D Brumfield	Mrs H J Udouj	f-8.70
Knight Counter	126	13	4^2	4^{1½}	3^1	3^1	17^6	17^{11}	M Mang'llo	R Huffman	f-8.70
Jr's Arrowhead	126	4	3^h	2^1	4^1	16^{1½}	18^2	18^6	A Rini	Walnut Hill Farm	f-8.70
Fourulla	126	19	5^h	7½	18^3	19^4	19^4	19^{14}	D MacBeth	A H Sullivan	f-8.70
Saigon Warrior	127	3	14^3	19^9	19^5	20	20	20	R Parrott	C M Day	f-8.70

f-Mutuel field. a-Coupled, Eastern Fleet and Bold and Able; c-Twist the Axe and Impetuosity; b-Royal Leverage and On the Money.

Time, :23, :46 4/5, 1:11 3/5, 1:36 1/5, 2:03 1/5. Track fast.

$2 mutuels paid: Canonero II (field), straight $19.40, place $8.00; show $4.20; Jim French, place $6.20, show $4.40; Bold Reason, show $12.60.

Winner- B. c., by *Pretendre—Dixieland II, by Nantallah. Trainer, Juan Arias. Bred by E. B. Benjamin (Ky.)

In gate—5:42. Off at 5:42½ Eastern Daylight Time. Start good. Won ridden out.

Canonero II., void of speed and unhurried for three-quarters, was forced to come to the extreme outside to launch his bid upon leaving the backstretch, continued to circle his field entering the stretch to take command with a bold rush in the upper stretch and was under intermittent urging to prevail. **Jim French,** allowed to settle in stride, moved up along the inside when launching his bid on the second turn, was forced to come out between horses entering the stretch, commenced lugging in to brush with **Barbizon Streak,** continued gamely to move through close quarters in midstretch, but could not reach the winner. **Jim French** came back with a cut on the coronet band of his right rear. **Bold Reason,** badly outrun for six furlongs, moved between horses until forced to steady when blocked in the upper stretch, dropped to the inside when clear and finished with good courage. **Eastern Fleet,** away alertly to gain a forward position along the inside, moved through in slightly close quarters leaving the backstretch, moved to the fore between calls in the upper stretch, commenced drifting out in the closing drive and gave way willingly. **Unconscious,** never far back while along the inner railing, continued to save ground while moving into serious contention on the final turn, came out for the drive and had little left when the real test came. **Bold and Able** was sent to the fore at once, bore out entering the first turn, came back to the inside when clear to make the pace to the top of the stretch, at which point he dropped back steadily. **List** failed to enter contention while closing some ground in the late stages. **Twist the Axe,** in hand early, moved up along the outside after three quarters to loom boldly on the final turn, but could not sustain his bid. **Impetuosity,** breaking smartly from his outside position, continued slightly wide to midway down the backstretch where he was dropped in to move up between horses, was forced to check sharply when **Jr's Arrowhead** dropped over at the half-mile ground, losing his action, and failed to recover when clear. **Barbizon Streak,** away in good order, was caught in close quarters entering the first turn, continued slightly wide and commenced dropping back after five furlongs. **Knight Counter** was bumped and forced out entering the first turn. **Jr's Arrowhead** came away alertly to gain a striking position along the outside, commenced lugging in at the half-mile ground and dropped back steadily. **Fourulla** bore out badly entering the first turn.

Overweight—Saigon Warrior, 1 pound.   Scratched—Sole Mio.

The Winner's Pedigree

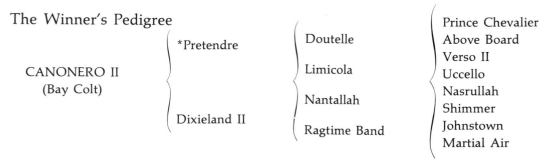

			Prince Chevalier
	*Pretendre	Doutelle	Above Board
CANONERO II			Verso II
(Bay Colt)		Limicola	Uccello
			Nasrullah
	Dixieland II	Nantallah	Shimmer
			Johnstown
		Ragtime Band	Martial Air

96th Kentucky Derby, May 2, 1970

1¼ miles. Scale Weights. $125,000 added and $5,000 gold cup. Value of race $170,300. Value to winner $127,800; second $25,000; third $12,500; fourth $5,000. Mutuel pool $2,383,912.

Horses	Wt	PP	¼	½	¾	1	Str	Fin	Jockeys	Owners	Odds to $1
Dust Com'nder	126	2	9^{2}	6½	5^{2}	7^{1}	$1^{1\frac{1}{2}}$	1^{5}	M Manganello	R E Lehmann	15.30
My Dad George	126	12	16^{3}	14^{2}	14^{1}	5^{h}	3^{3}	2½	R Broussard	R M Curtis	2.80
High Echelon	126	11	17	17	17	15^{2}	5^{2}	3^{h}	L Adams	Ethel D Jacobs	a-4.90
Naskra	126	14	10^{2}	10^{2}	$10^{2\frac{1}{2}}$	8^{2}	4^{h}	4^{1}	B Baeza	Her-Jac-Stable	15.90
Silent Screen	126	6	6^{3}	3^{h}	3^{1}	1^{1}	2^{1}	$5^{2\frac{1}{2}}$	J L Rotz	Elberon Farm	5.70
Admiral's Shield	126	15	14^{2}	16^{5}	16^{2}	16	7^{3}	6^{h}	J Nichols	W C Robinson Jr	29.70
Corn off the Cob	126	17	5^{h}	5^{2}	$6^{1\frac{1}{2}}$	$3^{1\frac{1}{2}}$	6^{3}	7^{3}	A Cordero Jr	Fence Post Farm	13.10
Personality	126	16	7^{h}	$9^{1\frac{1}{2}}$	11½	9^{h}	8^{h}	$8^{2\frac{1}{2}}$	E Belmonte	Ethel D Jacobs	a-4.90
Native Royalty	126	8	$8^{1\frac{1}{2}}$	8^{1}	8^{1}	4½	9^{2}	$9^{2\frac{1}{4}}$	I Valenzuela	Happy Valley Farm	f-10.10
Robin's Bug	126	7	3^{h}	4^{2}	4^{h}	$10^{1\frac{1}{2}}$	10^{3}	10½	L Moyers	W J Hickey-R F Kuhn	f-10.10
Terlago	126	13	$4^{1\frac{1}{2}}$	$7^{1\frac{1}{2}}$	7^{h}	11^{2}	11^{2}	$11^{1\frac{1}{4}}$	W Shoemaker	S J Agnew	7.40
Dr. Behrman	126	3	11^{2}	11^{1}	12^{1}	14½	12^{2}	12^{2}	C Baltazar	Lin-Drake Farm	f-10.10
Action Getter	126	9	$15^{1\frac{1}{2}}$	15^{h}	15½	13^{2}	13^{1}	$13^{2\frac{1}{2}}$	M Venezia	E V Benjamin-J Jones Jr	f-10.10
George Lewis	126	1	$2^{1\frac{1}{2}}$	2^{4}	$2^{1\frac{1}{2}}$	2½	14^{1}	14^{h}	W Hartack	Mr-Mrs A Magerman	9.40
Fathom	126	10	12½	13^{3}	9^{1}	12^{3}	15^{3}	$15^{3\frac{1}{2}}$	D Crump	W L L Brown	f-10.10
Rancho Lejos	126	5	1^{3}	1^{3}	1^{1}	6^{2}	16	16	R Campas	S Carson-I Apple	f-10.10
Holy Land	126	4	13^{4}	12½	13½	Fell			H Pilar	Mrs J S Dean Jr	15.90

a-Coupled, High Echelon and Personality: f-Mutuel field.

Time, :23 1/5, :46 4/5, 1:12, 1:37 2/5, 2:03 2/5. Track Good.

$2 mutuels paid: Dust Commander, straight $32.60, place $12.60, show $7; My Dad George, place $5, show $3.20; High Echelon (a-Entry), show $4.40.

Winner—Ch.c., by Bold Commander—Dust Storm, by Windy City II. Trainer Don Combs; Bred by Pullen Bros. (Ill.)

Dust Commander, soundly bumped at the start to be hard held early, commenced to advance along the inside after a half mile, continued to save ground to the final turn where he was forced to come out between horses to launch his rally, remained slightly wide into the stretch and responding to pressure was up leaving the furlong marker and drew well clear under intermittent urging. **My Dad George,** slow to begin and unhurried for three quarters, commenced to advance from between horses upon leaving the backstretch, cut back to the inside on the final turn to loom boldly in the upper stretch but could not sustain his bid. **High Echelon,** badly outrun for a mile, came to the extreme outside to circle his field entering the stretch and finished boldly. **Naskra,** in hand while being outrun, launched a bid from between horses on the second turn to loom menacingly a furlong away but could not sustain his rally. **Silent Screen,** soundly bumped and knocked off stride soon after the start, was forced to be sent along to remain in contention, continued along the outside to take command boldly on the final turn, drew off in the upper stretch only to falter when subjected to extreme pressure. **Admiral's Shield** found his best stride too late. **Corn off the Cob,** in hand early, moved up strongly to loom a contender on the final turn but had little left when the real test came. **Personality** failed to enter contention. **Native Royalty,** unhurried while being outrun early, launched a bid from the outside leaving the backstretch to loom boldly a quarter mile away but had little left when the real test came. **Robin's Bug** stopped badly after showing good speed for three quarters. **Terlago** dropped back steadily. **George Lewis** gave way suddenly after prompting the issue to the top of the stretch. **Rancho Lejos** broke alertly to swerve to the inside into horses, ducked out abruptly while being straightened into **Silent Screen,** continued on the lead to midway of the second turn where he collapsed suddenly. **Holy Land** clipped horse's heels while in close quarters midway of the second turn and fell.

Scratched—Protanto.

The Winner's Pedigree

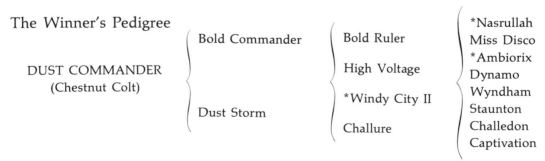

DUST COMMANDER (Chestnut Colt)	Bold Commander	Bold Ruler	*Nasrullah
			Miss Disco
		High Voltage	*Ambiorix
			Dynamo
	Dust Storm	*Windy City II	Wyndham
			Staunton
		Challure	Challedon
			Captivation

95th Kentucky Derby, May 3, 1969

1¼ miles, Scale Weights, $125,000 added and $5,000 gold cup. Value to winner $113,200; second, $25,000; third $12,500; fourth $5,000. Mutuel pool $2,625,524.

Horses	Wt	PP	¼	½	¾	1	Str	Fin	Jockeys	Owners	Odds to $1
Majestic Prince	126	8	4h	3½	3½	2³	1½	1nk	W Hartack	Frank McMahon	1.40
Arts and Letters	126	3	2h	4³	4⁴	1½	2²	2½	B Baeza	Rokeby Stable	4.40
Dike	126	7	7⁸	6h	5⁴	3²	3⁷	3¹⁰	J Velasquez	Claiborne Farm	4.20
Traffic Mark	126	2	8	8	8	6⁴	4¹½	4¹¾	P I Grimm	Mr-Mrs R F Roberts	45.20
Top Knight	126	1	3h	2h	1¹	4⁵	5⁸	5¹³	M Ycaza	S B Wilson Estate	2.30
Ocean Roar	126	6	1⁴	1²	2½	5h	6⁴	6⁹	R L Stewart	L Miller	28.00
Fleet Allied	126	5	6⁵	7⁷	6²	7⁸	7¹⁰	7⁸	D Hall	Mr-Mrs V Kanowsky	57.00
Rae Jet	126	4	5¹	5¹	7½	8	8	8	R C Howard	R E Harris	70.90

Time, :23 3/5, :48, 1:12 2/5, 1:37 3/5, 2:01 4/5. Track fast.

$2 mutuels paid: Majestic Prince straight $4.80, place $3.40, show $2.60; Arts and Letters place $4.20, show $3; Dike show $2.80.

Winner—Ch.c., by Raise a Native-Gay Hostess. Trainer Johnny Longden; Bred by Leslie Combs II.

Majestic Prince swerved out a bit through run to the first turn, dropped over while moving at the leaders after three furlongs, continued along the outside to hold his position, rallied when sharply roused on the second turn to wear down **Arts and Letters** nearing the furlong marker and was fully extended to prevail. **Arts and Letters** in hand early, continued along the inside in a brilliant move to take over the lead on the stretch turn, rallied gamely when headed and gave way grudgingly. **Dike,** slow to settle in stride and unhurried for three-quarters, came out to launch his bid on the final turn to loom boldly in midstretch, only to hang slightly through the closing drive. **Traffic Mark** passed only tiring horses. **Top Knight** forwardly placed from the start, moved strongly along the inside to take command midway down the backstretch, drifted out on rounding the second turn and succumbed suddenly. **Ocean Roar** stopped badly after making the pace for five furlongs. **Fleet Allied** dropped back after encountering slightly close quarters entering the first turn and failed to threaten. **Rae Jet** was squeezed back when caught in a speed jam entering the first turn and soon lost contact with the field.

The Winner's Pedigree

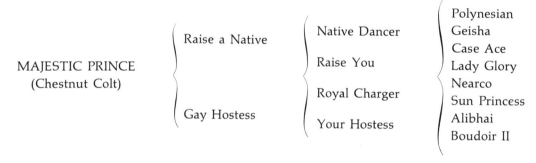

MAJESTIC PRINCE (Chestnut Colt)

Raise a Native
— Native Dancer
— — Polynesian
— — Geisha
— Raise You
— — Case Ace
— — Lady Glory

Gay Hostess
— Royal Charger
— — Nearco
— — Sun Princess
— Your Hostess
— — Alibhai
— — Boudoir II

94th Kentucky Derby, May 4, 1968

1¼ miles, Scale Weights, $125,000 added and $5,000 gold cup. Value to winner $122,600; second $25,000, third $12,500, fourth $5,000.

Horses	Wt	PP	½	¾	1	Str	Fin	Jockeys	Owners	Odds to $1
**Dancer's Image	126	12	14	10½	8hd	1¹	1¹½	R Ussery	Peter Fuller	3.60
Forward Pass	126	13	4⁴	3⁴	2²	2½	2nk	I Valenzuela	Calumet Farm	2.20
Francie's Hat	126	10	11²	7²	7²	4²	3²½	E Fires	Saddle Rock Farm	23.50
T. V. Commercial	126	2	8¹	9¹	6½	5hd	4¹	H Grant	Bwamazon Farm	24.00
Kentucky Sherry	126	4	1²	1²	1hd	3²	5¹	J Combest	Mrs J W Brown	f-14.70
Jig Time	126	3	6½	6½	4hd	6hd	6½	R Broussard	Cragwood Stable	36.30
Don B	126	7	5²	5¹	5½	7⁴	7⁵	D Pierce	D B Wood	35.50
Trouble Brewing	126	5	9¹	11²	13⁴	12⁴	8nk	B Thornburg	Coventry Rock Farm	f-14.70
Proper Proof	126	11	12¹	12²	11²	8¹½	9⁴	J Sellers	Mrs M Fisher	9.90
Te Vega	126	6	13hd	13¹	12²	9²	10¾	M Manganello	F C Sullivan	f-14.70
Captain's Gig	126	9	2hd	2¹	3²	10²	11¹½	M Ycaza	Cain Hoy Stable	6.10
Iron Ruler	126	1	7½	8½	9hd	11¹	12³	B Baeza	October House Fm.	5.70
Verbatim	126	8	10hd	14	14	14	13no	A Cordero	Jr Elmendorf	37.40
Gleaming Sword	126	14	3½	4hd	10²	13¹	14	E Belmonte	C V Whitney	31.20

Times, :22 1/5, :45 4/5, 1:09 4/5, 1:36 1/5, 2:02 1/5. Track Fast.

$2 mutuels paid: **Dancer's Image, straight $9.20, place $4.40, show $4.00; **Forward Pass, place $4.20, show $3.20; Francie's Hat, show $6.40.

f-Field.

**Winner-gr c., by Native Dancer-Noors Image. Trainer L. C. Cavalaris, Jr. Bred by Peter Fuller.

Dancer's Image void of speed through early stages after being bumped at start, commenced a rally after three-quarters to advance between horses on second turn, cut back to inside when clear entering stretch at which point his rider dropped his whip. Responding to a vigorous hand ride the colt continued to save ground to take command nearing furlong marker and was hard pressed to edge **Forward Pass.** The latter broke alertly only to be bumped and knocked into winner, continued gamely while maintaining a forward position along outside, moved boldly to take command between calls in upper stretch and held on stubbornly in a prolonged drive. **Francie's Hat** allowed to settle in stride, commenced a rally after three quarters and finished full of run. **T. V. Commercial** closed some ground in his late rally but could not seriously menace. **Kentucky Sherry** broke in stride to make the pace under good rating, saved ground to stretch where he drifted out while tiring. **Jig Time** faltered after making a menacing bid on second turn. **Proper Proof** was always outrun. **Captain's Gig** tired badly after prompting the issue for three-quarters. **Iron Ruler** failed to enter contention. **Gleaming Sword** broke alertly but sharply to inside to bump with **Forward Pass** continued in a forward position for five furlongs and commenced dropping back steadily.

The Winner's Pedigree

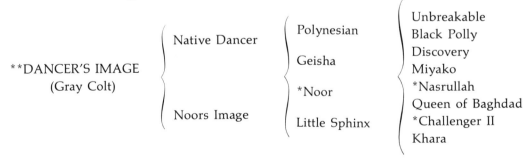

**DANCER'S IMAGE
(Gray Colt)

Native Dancer
- Polynesian
  - Unbreakable
  - Black Polly
- Geisha
  - Discovery
  - Miyako

Noors Image
- *Noor
  - *Nasrullah
  - Queen of Baghdad
- Little Sphinx
  - *Challenger II
  - Khara

93rd Kentucky Derby, May 6, 1967

1¼ Miles. Scale weights: $125,000 added and $5,000 Gold Cup. 3-year-olds. Value to winner $119,700; second $25,000; third $12,500; fourth $5,000. Mutuel Pool, $1,933,028.

Horses	Eq't WT	PP	¼	½	¾	1	Str	Fin	Jockeys	Owners	Odds to $1
Proud Clarion	b 126	7	9⁵	9³	8¹	5ʰ	2²	1¹	R Ussery	Darby Dan Farm	30.10
Barbs Delight	b 126	5	1¹	1¹½	1²	1¹	1ʰ	2³	K Knapp	Hug'let Jr-Spald'g-St'e Jr	15.70
Damascus	126	2	6ʰ	4¹	4¹	4²	3⁴	3¹¼	W Sh'maker	Mrs E W Bancroft	1.70
Reason to Hail	b 126	13	8²	8²	6½	6²	5²	4½	W Blum	Miss P Jacobs	20.70
Ask the Fare	b 126	14	5ʰ	7½	9¹	8³	4ʰ	5²¼	D Holmes	Holiday Stable	66.40
Successor	b 126	6	10²	10¹½	12¹	12³	6¹	6¹	B Baeza	Wheatly Stb.-O M Phipps	4.60
Gen'man James	b 126	10	13⁴	12²	7²	7¹½	7¹	7¹½	R J Camp'll	M G Phipps	37.10
Ruken	b 126	1	12ʰ	13⁶	10½	9²	9²	8ʰ	F Alvarez	L Rowan	4.80
Diplomat Way	b 126	4	3½	3²	3⁴	2½	8ʰ	9ⁿᵒ	J Sellers	H Peltier	7.10
Sec'd Enc'ntr	b 126	12	14	14	14	14	13⁵	10²	B Phelps	Harris-Pierce Jr	f-17.30
Dawn Glory	b 126	8	2²	2½	2ʰ	3ʰ	10²	11¹	E Fires	Establo Eden	f-17.30
Dr. Isby	126	3	11²	11¹	11¹	11½	11²	12ⁿᵏ	W Hartack	P L Grissom	11.00
Field Master	126	9	4¹½	5¹	13¹⁵	13¹⁰	12⁶	13⁷	A Pineda	Mr-Mrs J H Seley	f-17.30
Lightning Orphan	126	11	7²	6¹½	5½	10¹	14	14	D Brumfield	Reverie Knoll Farm	78.20

f—Mutuel field.

Time, :22 1/5, :46 3/5, 1:10 4/5, 1:36, 2:00 3/5. Track fast.

$2 Mutuel Prices—Proud Clarion $62.20 straight, $27.80 place, $12.00 show; Barbs Delight $16.00 place, $7.60 show; Damascus $3.40 show.

Winner: B. c., by Hail to Reason—Breath O'Morn, by Djeddah. Trainer, L. Gentry. Bred by J. W. Galbreath (Kentucky).

In gate—4:31. Off at 4:31½ Eastern Standard Time. Start good. Won driving.

Proud Clarion taken in hand at the start and brought to the inside at once, continued to save ground to the half-mile ground, was eased out thereafter to launch his bid, was forced to circle his field when rallying entering the stretch, engaged **Barbs Delight** a furlong away and proved best in a stiff drive. The latter, sent to the fore at once, raced along the inner railing while being well rated, responded gamely when challenged to turn back **Damascus** in the upper stretch and held on well in a prolonged drive. **Damascus,** reserved off the pace for three-quarters, loomed boldly along the outside on the final turn to continue gamely to midstretch where he appeared to hang under extreme pressure. **Reason to Hail** improved his racing position steadily from between horses in the late stages but could not menace the top trio. **Ask the Fare** failed to seriously threaten. **Successor** was always outrun and without apparent excuse. **Ruken,** void of early speed, appeared in close quarters while along the inside through the run down the backstretch and could not menace. **Diplomat Way** raced with the top flight to the top of the stretch and weakened badly. **Dawn Glory** tired after prompting the issue for seven furlongs. **Dr. Isby** was always far back. **Field Master** swung wide on the initial turn. **Lightning Orphan** raced wide.

The Winner's Pedigree

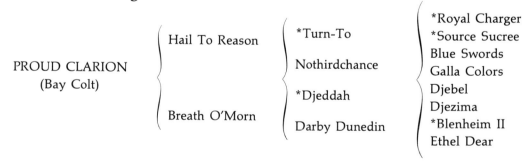

PROUD CLARION
(Bay Colt)

Hail To Reason

Breath O'Morn

*Turn-To

Nothirdchance

*Djeddah

Darby Dunedin

*Royal Charger
*Source Sucree
Blue Swords
Galla Colors
Djebel
Djezima
*Blenheim II
Ethel Dear

92nd Kentucky Derby, May 7, 1966

1¼ MILES. Scale Weights: $125,000 added and $5,000 Gold Cup. 3-year-old. Value to winner $120,500; second $25,000; third $12,500; fourth $5,000.

Horses	Eq't A Wt	PP	¼	½	¾	1	Str	Fin	Jockeys	Owners	Odds to $1
Kauai King	b 3 126	12	1¹	1³	1²	1¹	1¹½	1½	D Brumfield	Ford Stable	2.40
Advocator	b 3 126	5	6ʰ	5²	3²	2¹	3¹	2ⁿᵒ	J Sellers	Ada L Rice	16.90
Blue Skyer	b 3 126	2	11²	8¹	8²	3¹	4¹½	3¾	E Fires	Padgett-Grant	f-17.00
Stupendous.......	b 3 126	3	9²	6ʰ	4ʰ	4¹	2½	4ⁿᵏ	B Baeza	Wheatley Stable	5.40
Abe's Hope.......	b 3 126	13	10ʰ	12¹½	9ʰ	5½	5²	5¹	W Sh'maker	Grand Prix Stable	3.20
Rehabilitate.......	b 3 126	4	14³	11½	13ʰ	12³	6²	6¹½	R Turcotte	R Lehman	f-17.00
Amberoid.........	3 126	1	15	15	12²	8¹½	7³	7⁸	W Boland	R N Webster	6.10
Fleet Shoe........	b 3 126	7	13½	14²	14ʰ	11³	8³	8⁶	L Gilligan	G Putnam	33.50
Exhibitionist	b 3 126	8	5ʰ	7²	7½	9ʰ	10²	9¹½	E Belmonte	Mrs E D Jacobs	20.10
Sky Guy..........	3 126	10	4²	4¹	5²	7½	11¹	10ⁿᵏ	L Adams	W G Helis Jr	68.40
Williamston Kid ...	3 126	15	12¹	13½	11¹	10¹	12⁴	11¹²½	R L Stev'on	Ternes-Bartlett	19.00
Quinta	b 3 126	14	2¹½	2⁴	2³	6½	9¹	12¹²½	P Kallai	Bokum II-Scott II	63.70
Tragniew	3 126	11	8²	10ʰ	10¹	13¹	13²	13³	D Pierce	B J Richards	11.80
Beau Sub	3 126	9	7½	9½	15	14⁵	14⁶	14¹⁴	R Parrott	Clear Springs Stable	f-17.00
Dominar..........	b 3 126	6	3²	3¹	6ʰ	15	15	15	W Harmatz	Flying M Stable	f-17.00

f—Mutuel field.

Time—:22 4/5, :46 1/5, 1:10 3/5, 1:35, 2:02. Track Fast.

$2 mutuels Paid—Kauai King $6.80 to win, $4.20 to place, $3.60 to show. Advocator $13.00 to place, $8.60 to show. Blue Skyer (In a betting field with Rehabilitate, Beau Sub and Dominar) $5.40 to show.

Winner—Dk. b. or br. c. by Native Dancer-Sweep-In, by Blenheim II. Trainer Henry Forrest. Bred by Pine Brook Farm.

In gate—4:32 Off at 4:32 Eastern Standard Time. Start good. Won driving.

Kauai King broke in stride to gain a narrow advantage, continued well out in the track through the initial stretch run, cut to the inside entering the first turn to draw off under patient handling, continued along the inner railing while coasting on the lead, responded when soundly shaken up a quarter out to turn back a bold bid from **Stupendous** in the upper stretch and was under hard left-handed whipping to hold **Advocator** safe. The latter, away in good order, but reserved off the pace for three-quarters, moved up boldly along the outside on the second turn, dropped back a bit in the midstretch, but came again to finish strongly. **Blue Skyer** allowed to settle in stride and unhurried for six furlongs, rallied along the extreme outside leaving the backstretch, cut between horses entering the stretch and closed boldly under extreme pressure. **Stupendous,** in hand for a half-mile, advanced steadily along the inside thereafter to loom boldly through the upper stretch, but appeared to hang through the closing drive. **Abe's Hope,** slow to begin, was forced to come wide when launching his rally on the second turn, remained on the outside entering the stretch and was gaining slowly at the finish. **Rehabilitate** closed a big gap following a sluggish beginning. **Amberoid** stumbled at the start and was far back throughout. **Sky Guy** broke out at the start into **Tragniew.** The latter was bumped at the start and could not threaten.

The Winner's Pedigree

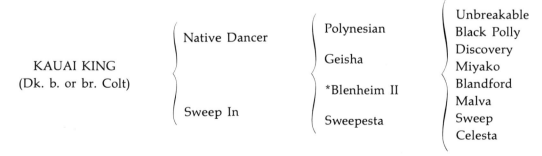

KAUAI KING
(Dk. b. or br. Colt)

Native Dancer

Sweep In

Polynesian

Geisha

*Blenheim II

Sweepesta

Unbreakable
Black Polly
Discovery
Miyako
Blandford
Malva
Sweep
Celesta

91st Kentucky Derby, May 1, 1965

1¼ MILES. Scale weights: $125,000 added and $5,000 Gold Cup. 3-year-olds. Value to winner $112,000; second, $25,000; third, $12,500; fourth, $5,000.

Horses	Eq't A WT	PP	¼	½	¾	1	Str	Fin	Jockeys	Owners	Odds to $1
Lucky Debonair	3 126	8	3h	2²½	2½	2²	1³	1nk	W Sh'maker	Mrs Ada L Rice	4.30
Dapper Dan	b 3 126	1	11	11	11	7¹	5½	2²	I Valenzuela	O Phipps	30.00
Tom Rolfe	3 126	9	7²	5¹	3¹½	4¹½	3h	3¹	R Turcotte	Powhatan	5.60
Native Charger	b 3 126	4	4³	4¹½	4½	3½	4¹	4nk	J L Rotz	Warner Stable	6.40
Hail to All	3 126	7	9²	10²	9¹½	8h	6¹½	5²¼	M Ycaza	Mrs B Cohen	3.80
Mr. Pak	3 126	10	8²	8²½	7²	6½	8⁴	6h	J Nichols	Mrs M Keim	53.80
Swift Ruler	3 126	11	10h	9½	8½	10²	7½	7³	L Spraker	E Allen	34.90
Flag Raiser	b 3 126	5	1²	1h	1h	1h	2h	8²½	R Ussery	I Bieber	17.90
Carp'nt'r's Rule	b 3 126	6	6¹½	7²	10³	11	9¹	9½	W Harmatz	P L Grissom	78.70
Bold Lad	b 3 126	3	5h	6¹½	6½	5h	10½	10²	W Hartack	Wheatley Sta	2.00
Narushua	3 126	2	2h	3h	5²	9½	11	11	T Dunlavy	J W Mecom	92.00

Time, :23 1/5, :47 1/5, 1:11 4/5, 1:37, 2:01 1/5. Track fast.

$2 Mutuels Paid—Lucky Debonair $10.60, $5.40 place, $4.20 show; Dapper Dan—$26.00 place, $12.60 show; Tom Rolfe $4.80 show.

Winner—B. c., by Vertex—Fresh as Fresh, by Count Fleet. Trainer, F. Catrone. Bred by Danada Farm.

Lucky Debonair broke alertly to show the way through the opening furlong, dropped back a bit when Shoemaker took a snug hold nearing the sixteenth marker, moved up again to engage **Flag Raiser** midway of the first turn, continued to duel with that one while along the outside to the final quarter where he moved to the fore when sharply roused, moved off to a lengthy advantage through the upper stretch but was fully extended to turn back a belated bid from **Dapper Dan.** The latter, away slowly and unhurried for six furlongs, moved up along the inside on leaving the backstretch, angled out sharply to launch his closing rally on the final turn and, responding to strong handling, was slowly getting to the winner. **Tom Rolfe,** in hand for a half mile, moved up boldly along the inside to engage the top flight at the half mile ground, dropped back a bit on rounding the second turn only to come again while under extreme pressure and finished gamely. **Native Charger,** bumped while between horses entering the first turn, quickly recovered to remain in contention while along the outside to loom menacingly on the stretch turn and finished evenly in a good effort. **Hail to All,** slow to begin as usual, launched a rally on rounding the second turn and finished boldly while between horses through the closing drive. **Mr. Pak** finished well. **Swift Ruler** failed to reach contention. **Flag Raiser** came out soon after the start to bump with **Carpenter's Rule** but was quickly straightened away to take a clear lead in the initial run through the stretch, came to the inside thereafter to be well-rated only to weaken badly through the closing drive. **Carpenter's Rule** was bumped soon after the start and failed to reach contention. **Bold Lad** in hand while being outrun early and saving ground, was angled to the outside soon after entering the backstretch to reach a contending position at the half mile ground, then continued well to the top of the stretch while he gave way badly in the final drive. **Narushua** showed forwardly for three-quarters and tired badly.

The Winner's Pedigree

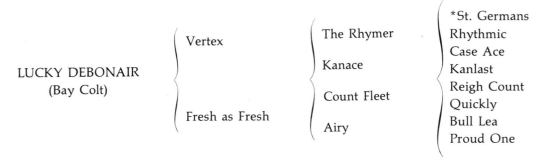

LUCKY DEBONAIR
(Bay Colt)

Vertex

Fresh as Fresh

The Rhymer

Kanace

Count Fleet

Airy

*St. Germans
Rhythmic
Case Ace
Kanlast
Reigh Count
Quickly
Bull Lea
Proud One

90th Kentucky Derby, May 2, 1964

$125,000 Added and $5,000 Gold Cup. 3-year-olds. Scale Weights. Value of race $156,800. Value to winner $114,300; second, $25,000; third, $12,500; fourth, $5,000. Mutuel Pool, $2,144,079.

Horses	Eq't WT	PP	¼	½	¾	1	Str	Fin	Jockeys	Owners	Odds to $1
N'thern Dancer	b 126	7	7²½	6ʰ	6²	1ʰ	1²	1ⁿᵏ	W Hartack	Windfields Farm	3.40
Hill Rise	126	11	6¹½	7²½	8ʰ	4ʰ	2½	2³¼	W Sh'm'kr	El Peco Ranch	1.40
The Scoundrel	b 126	6	3½	4ʰ	3¹	2¹	3²	3ⁿᵒ	M Ycaza	R C Ellsworth	6.00
Roman Brother	126	12	9²	9½	9²	6²	4½	4ⁿᵏ	W Chmbrs	Harbor View Frm	30.60
Quadrangle	b 126	2	5¹	5¹½	4ʰ	5¹½	5¹	5³	R Ussery	Rokeby Stables	5.30
Mr. Brick	126	1	2³	1½	1½	3¹	6³	6¾	I Valenz'la	R Sturgis	15.80
Mr. Moonlight	126	5	8²	8¹	7ʰ	7³	7⁴	7⁵	J Combest	Mrs M Dent	54.40
Dandy K.	126	9	12	12	12	8ʰ	8¹½	8²¼	M Solom'ne	C Carmine	17.40
Ishkoodah	b 126	8	11²	11²	11²	9²	9³	9⁴	R Baldwin	Tumblewood St.	29.20
Wil Rad	126	3	4ʰ	3½	5ʰ	11½	11⁷	10ⁿᵒ	J Vasquez	Clark-Radkovich	57.70
Extra Swell	b 126	4	10½	10ʰ	10½	12	10ʰ	11¹⁴	M Volzke	Mr-Mrs E Davis	152.20
Royal Shuck	b 126	10	1ʰ	2²	2ʰ	10ʰ	12	12	H Bolin	E A Dust	179.40

Time: 22 2/5, :46, 1:10 3/5, 1:36, 2:00 (new track record). Track fast.

$2 Mutuels Paid—Northern Dancer $8.80, $3.60 place, $3.00 show; Hill Rise $3.00 place, $2.60 show; The Scoundrel $3.20 show.

Winner—B. c., by Nearctic—Natalma, by Native Dancer. Trainer, H. A. Luro. Bred by E. P. Taylor.

Northern Dancer, in good order to gain a contending position along the inside, continued to save ground while under snug restraint, moved up steadily after six furlongs, but was forced to come out midway of the second turn, responded to gain command a quarter out and prevailed under strong left-handed whipping. **Hill Rise,** unhurried, was bumped twice through the stretch run the first time, continued along the outside thereafter to commence a rally at the half-mile ground, lost additional ground in a wide spread leaving the backstretch, rallied to strong handling on entering the stretch and was slowly getting to the winner. **The Scoundrel** broke in stride, swerved out to bump with **Hill Rise** in the run to the initial turn, continued in a forward position to gain command between calls on the second turn and weakened gradually through the closing drive. **Roman Brother,** allowed to settle in stride, commenced to advance along the inner railing after seven furlongs and finished strongly even though in slightly close quarters. **Quadrangle,** brushed and squeezed back at the start, wanted for racing room entering the first turn, continued well to the top of the stretch where he lacked a closing rally. **Mr. Brick** broke alertly but sharply to the outside brushing with **Quadrangle,** continued to make the pace under good rating and gave way suddenly after going a mile. **Mr. Moonlight** swerved to the outside for no apparent reason nearing the half-mile ground and could not threaten thereafter. **Dandy K.** was outrun, as was **Ishkoodah. Wil Rad** was through early. **Royal Shuck** showed speed for three-quarters and stopped badly.

The Winner's Pedigree

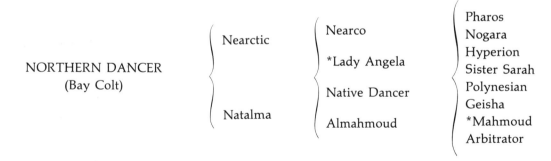

NORTHERN DANCER (Bay Colt)	Nearctic	Nearco	Pharos
			Nogara
		*Lady Angela	Hyperion
			Sister Sarah
	Natalma	Native Dancer	Polynesian
			Geisha
		Almahmoud	*Mahmoud
			Arbitrator

89th Kentucky Derby, May 4, 1963

$125,000 added and $5,000 Gold Cup. 3-year-olds. Scale weights. Value of race $151,400. Value to winner $108,900; second, $25,000; third $12,500; fourth $5,000. Mutuel Pool, $1,818,087.

Horses	Eq't A Wt	PP	¼	½	¾	1	Str	Fin	Jockeys	Owners	Odds to $1
Chateaugay	3 126	1	6^1	6^h	6^3	4^2	1^1	1$^{11/4}$	B Baeza	Darby Dan Farm	9.40
Never Bend	3 126	6	1½	1^1	1^1	1^1	2^2	2^{nk}	M Ycaza	Cain Hoy Stable	3.10
Candy Spots	b 3 126	9	3^2	3$^{21/2}$	3^3	3^h	3^2	3$^{43/4}$	W Sh'maker	R C Ellsworth	1.50
On My Honor	b 3 126	8	9	9	9	7^3	6^2	4$^{11/4}$	P Frey	Ambush Stable	30.80
No Robbery	b 3 126	7	2^3	2^2	2^2	2^2	4^2	5$^{11/4}$	J L Rotz	Greentree Stable	2.70
Bonjour	b 3 126	3	5^2	4½	4^2	6^7	5$^{11/2}$	6^3	I Val'nzuela	Miss P Jacobs	9.30
Gray Pet	b 3 126	5	4^1	5^4	5^2	5^h	7^6	7^6	A Gomez	Walnut Hill Farm	40.00
Investor	b 3 126	2	8^1	8½	8½	9	8^2	8$^{31/2}$	F Callico	J J Cherock	37.40
Royal Tower	b 3 126	4	7^3	7^5	7^3	8^2	9	9	G Hern'dez	B J Ridder	138.70

Time, :23, :46 2/5, 1:10, 1:35 2/5, 2:01 4/5. Track fast.

$2 Mutuels Paid—Chateaugay, $20.80, $7.00 place, $3.60 show; Never Bend, $5.00 place, $3.40 show; Candy Spots, $2.80 show.

Winner:—Ch. c, by Swaps—Banquet Bell, by Polynesian. Trainer, J. P. Conway. Bred by J. W. Galbreath.

Chateaugay, taken well back shortly following the start and held in reserve through the opening six furlongs, was eased to the extreme outside soon after leaving the backstretch, moved with a rush to wear down **Never Bend** through the upper stretch and prevailed in a long drive. **Never Bend** rushed to the lead at once, saved ground under patient handling, drifted out slightly while under pressure in midstretch and held on stubbornly after giving way to the winner. **Candy Spots,** kept much closer to the pace than before, was forced to check momentarily while racing up onto **No Robbery's** heels entering the first turn, remained slightly wide to the second turn where he commenced to advance along the inside, was checked momentarily nearing the three furlongs marker, and once again when blocked along the inside nearing the quarter pole, rallied willingly when clear in the stretch and finished strongly along the outside. **On My Honor,** badly outrun for a mile, came slightly wide in his belated bid and closed some ground. **No Robbery** prompted the issue from the start, raced slightly wide while going kindly to the final turn where he attempted to get out a bit. Rotz immediately straightened the colt to bring him back towards the inside, and he continued gamely to the upper stretch where he commenced to falter when put to a drive. **Bonjour** maintained a striking position to the final turn and tired. **Gray Pet** was outrun. **Investor** and **Royal Tower** were far back throughout.

The Winner's Pedigree

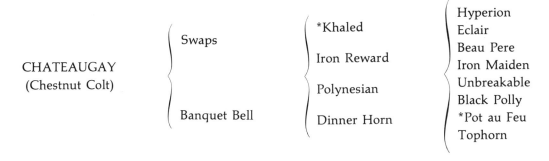

CHATEAUGAY (Chestnut Colt)	Swaps	*Khaled	Hyperion
			Eclair
		Iron Reward	Beau Pere
			Iron Maiden
	Banquet Bell	Polynesian	Unbreakable
			Black Polly
		Dinner Horn	*Pot au Feu
			Tophorn

88th Kentucky Derby, May 5, 1962

$125,000 added and $5,000 gold cup. 3-year-olds. Scale weights. Value to winner $119,650; second, $25,000; third, $12,500; fourth, $5,000. Mutuel Pool $1,553,916.

Horses	Eq't A Wt	PP	¼	½	¾	1	Str	Fin	Jockeys	Owners	Odds to $1
Decidedly	b 126	4	10²	9½	8¹	5¹½	3½	1²¼	W Hartack	El Peco Ranch	8.70
Roman Line	b 126	14	7½	6²	6²	4¹½	1ʰ	2ⁿᵏ	J Combest	T A Grissom	26.30
Ridan	126	13	5¹	2ʰ	2¹	3²	2ʰ	3ⁿᵏ	M Ycaza	Jolley-Woods Greer	1.10
Sir Ribot	126	5	2¹	8¹½	7²	6²	5²	4¹½	R York	Mr-Mrs F Turner Jr	13.00
Sunrise County	b 126	2	4²	3¹½	1ʰ	2½	4²	5²	W Sh'maker	T B Martin	2.80
Crimson Satan	b 126	11	14½	14ʰ	12¹	10³	6²	6¹¾	B Phelps	Crimson King Farm	21.50
Green Hornet	126	6	11½	13⁴	13⁴	12¹½	9³	7¾	J Longden	Mrs J W Brown	49.50
Good Fight	126	12	9¹½	10²	10ʰ	9¹½	10¹½	8ʰ	R Brouss'rd	F-B Farm	f-28.70
Admiral's Voyage	126	3	3¹	4²	3¹	1ʰ	7³	9⁴½	B Baeza	F W Hooper	12.10
Royal Attack	b 126	8	8½	5ʰ	5½	8²	8²	10⁵	E Burns	N S McCarthy	81.30
Touch Bar	b 126	10	15	15	15	15	14	11²½	J J Rivera	Estopinal-Arnaud	f-28.70
Lee Town	b 126	7	1²	1¹½	4¹½	7½	12⁸	12⁸	W Carstens	J V P Stable	f-28.70
Mister Pitt	b 126	9	13¹	11²	11²	11²	11³	13⁷	W Harmatz	Golden Tri Stable	123.30
Sharp Count	b 126	1	6ʰ	7½	9¹½	13¹	13¹	14	E Curry	Reverie Knoll Farm	f-28.70
Prego	b 126	15	12³	12ʰ	14¹	14²	Pull. up.		L Adams	R Lehman	28.90

f—Mutuel field.

Time, :22 3/5, :45 4/5, 1:10 1/5 1:35 1/5, 2:00 2/5 (new track record). Track fast.

$2 Mutuels Paid—Decidedly, $19.40, $8.20 place, $4.20 show; Roman Line, $19.20 place, $7.60 show; Ridan, $3.00 show.

Winner—Gr.c. by Determine—Gloire Fille, by War Glory. Trainer, H. A. Luro. Bred by G. A. Pope, Jr.

Went to Post—4:33½. Off at 4:34 Eastern Standard Time.

Start good. **Decidedly,** taken in hand at the start to be held in reserve for six furlongs, came to the outside thereafter to commence his bid, continued wide to engage the leaders through the upper stretch, moved to the fore leaving the furlong marker and was under pressure to draw off. **Roman Line,** steadied while maintaining a striking position from the outset, rallied from between horses in the late stages to gain command a furlong out but had little left to contain the belated bid of the winner. **Ridan** allowed to settle through the opening quarter mile, moved with a rush along the outside thereafter to prompt the issue in the run down the backstretch, attempted to bear out rather badly on leaving the backstretch but continued gamely to midstretch where he faltered under extreme pressure. **Sir Ribot,** away in good order, appeared to run up onto horses' heels entering the first turn, came out thereafter and finished strongly. **Sunrise County,** never far back while going much more kindly than before, dueled vigorously for the lead to the final sixteenth where he gave way suddenly while under pressure. **Crimson Satan,** shuffled back when bumped at the start, rallied after six furlongs and finished full of run. **Green Hornet** turned in a good closing rally. **Admiral's Voyage** tired suddenly after vying for the lead to the top of the stretch. **Touch Bar** broke sharply to the outside. **Lee Town** tired badly. **Mister Pitt** broke sharply to the outside. **Prego** appeared to throw a stifle entering the stretch and was immediately pulled up.

Scratched—Sir Gaylord, Donut King, Cicada.

The Winner's Pedigree

DECIDEDLY (Gray Colt)

- Determine
  - *Alibhai
    - Hyperion
    - Teresina
  - Koubis
    - *Mahmoud
    - Brown Biscuit
- Gloire Fille
  - War Glory
    - Man o' War
    - Annette K.
  - Belle Femme
    - *Beau Pere
    - French Vamp

87th Kentucky Derby, May 6, 1961

$125,000 added and $5,000 Gold Cup. 3-year-olds. Scale weights. Value to winner $120,500; second, $25,000; third, $12,500; fourth, $5,000. Mutuel Pool, $1,483,164.

Horses	Eq't A Wt	PP	¼	½	¾	1	Str	Fin	Jockeys	Owners	Odds to $1
Carry Back	126	14	11²	11¹½	11½	6¹½	4³	1¾	J Sellers	Mrs K Price	2.50
Crozier	b 126	11	3²	2ʰ	3⁶	3⁶	1½	2²	B Baeza	F W Hooper	3.50
Bass Clef	126	9	15	15	15	9¹	5½	3²¼	R Baldwin	Mrs V E Smith	f-16.50
Dr. Miller	b 126	15	12½	14³	14¹	14³	7³	4¹	W Sh'maker	Mrs E D Jacobs	8.60
Sherluck	126	3	9²	7½	6²	4²	6²	5¹¼	E Arcaro	J Sher	5.70
Globemaster	126	8	1¹½	1³	1½	2³	3³	6¾	J L Rotz	L P Sasso	8.70
Four-and-Twenty	b 126	4	2¹	3⁵	2²	1ʰ	2¹	7½	J Longden	Albert Ranches Ltd	a-5.30
Flutterby	b 126	13	10½	10²½	10½	10ʰ	9½	8¹	H Moreno	Albert Ranches Ltd	a-5.30
Loyal Son	b 126	5	13ʰ	12½	12½	11½	10³	9ʰ	L Hansman	Eastwood Stable	71.40
On His Metal	126	2	14½	13³	13²	12¹	8¹	10⁵	D Dodson	J G Brown	53.60
Light Talk	126	12	5²	4ʰ	5³	5²	11¹	11¹½	R Nono	Jacnot Stable	64.90
Ambiopoise	b 126	10	8²	8²	8²	8²	12²	12²¼	R Ussery	R Lehman	16.20
Ronnie's Ace	b 126	6	6²	9²	7¹	13³	13¹	13¹¼	A Maese	Clark-Radkovich	f-16.50
Dearborn	b 126	1	4ʰ	5²	4ʰ	7ʰ	14³	14½	B Phelps	E A Dust	82.40
Jay Fox	b 126	7	7ʰ	6ʰ	9ʰ	15	15	15	L Gilligan	Brae Burn Farm	f-16.50

f—Mutuel field.   a—Coupled, Four-and-Twenty and Flutterby.

Time, :23 4/5, :47 3/5, 1:11 2/5, 1:36 1/5, 2:04. Track good.

$2 Mutuels Paid—Carry Back $7.00 straight, $4.20 place, $3.20 show; Crozier $4.60 place, $4.20 show; Bass Clef (f-Field) $5.60 show.

Winner—Br. c., by Saggy—Joppy, by Star Blen. Trained by J. A. Price. Bred by J. A. Price.

In gate—4:31. Off at 4:31½ Central Daylight Time. Start good. Won driving.

Carry Back, slow to begin as usual, was kept wider than necessary when his rider elected to find the better going, lost additional ground to avoid any possible interference on rounding the second turn, rallied when roused at the top of the stretch to come on strongly and wore down **Crozier** even though being carried out slightly by that one in midstretch. **Crozier,** restrained off the early pace while placed along the inner rail, was forced to steady momentarily nearing the half-mile ground when blocked, came to the outside when clear to move steadily at the leaders, wore down that pair in the upper stretch while under pressure, commenced drifting out through the closing furlongs but could not withstand the winner. **Bass Clef,** badly outrun for the first mile, cut between horses when rallying thereafter, and while running a weaving course through the stretch run he closed a big gap. **Dr. Miller** made a very strong closing rally but the move was just too late to be effective. **Sherluck,** allowed to settle in stride while placed along the inner rail, commenced a sustained drive on leaving the backstretch to loom boldly on entering the front straightaway at which point he commenced to hang while under extreme pressure. **Globemaster,** allowed to take a clear advantage at once, saved ground while being rated, rallied momentarily when challenged leaving the half-mile marker to continue gamely to the top of the stretch where he stopped abruptly. **Four-and-Twenty,** brought off the inner rail while seeking better footing at the start, prompted the pace for six furlongs, moved along the outside to assume command on the second turn and then tired very suddenly in midstretch. **Flutterby** was far back throughout with no visible excuse. **Light Talk** dropped back steadily. **Ambiopoise** was out run from the start.

The Winner's Pedigree

			Equipoise
CARRY BACK	Saggy	Swing and Sway	Nedana
(Brown Colt)			Hyperion
		*Chantress	Surbine
	Joppy	Star Blen	*Blenheim II
			*Starweed
		Miss Fairfax	Teddy Beau
			Bellicent

86th Kentucky Derby, May 7, 1960

$125,000 added and $5,000 Gold Cup. 3-year-olds. Weight for age. Gross value, $158,950. Gross to winner $116,450. Net to winner $114,850; second, $25,000; third, $12,500; fourth, $5,000. Mutuel Pool, $1,490,199.

Horses	Eq't A Wt	PP	¼	½	¾	1	Str	Fin	Jockeys	Owners	Odds to $1
Venetian Way.......	126	9	4^2	$4^{2½}$	2^2	2^5	1^2	$1^{3½}$	W Hartack	Sunny Blue Farm	6.30
Bally Ache..........	b 126	3	1^h	$1^{1½}$	1^2	1^1	2^6	$2^{7½}$	R Ussery	Edgehill Farm	1.70
Victoria Park........	b 126	11	9^4	8^3	8^3	5^3	4^3	$3^{2¼}$	M Ycaza	Windfields Farm	16.60
Tompion............	b 126	13	$3^{1½}$	3^h	3^2	3^2	3^h	4no	W Sh'maker	C V Whitney	1.10
Bourbon Prince.....	b 126	10	$12^{1½}$	12^5	10^3	8^5	5^1	$5^{5½}$	C Rogers	Mrs A L Rand	77.00
Cuvier Relic	126	4	5^h	5^h	6½	7^1	6^3	6^5	J Sellers	S I Crew	22.90
Tony Graff..........	b 126	6	13	13	13	13	10^5	$7^{1½}$	W Ch'mbers	A Graffagnini	67.90
Spring Broker.......	b 126	1	8^h	9^2	9^2	9^6	9^3	$8^{1½}$	J L Rotz	M H Van Berg	f-40.60
Divine Comedy......	b 126	12	6^3	6^2	4^1	4^1	7^h	$9^{1¼}$	I Valenz'ela	Llangollen Farm	61.60
Fighting Hodge	126	7	7^h	7½	7^1	6^h	8^2	10^7	D Pierce	Mrs C S Hodge	f-40.60
Yomolka............	b 126	2	10^h	10^h	11^h	11^1	11^1	$11^{4¼}$	P I Grimm	Valley Farm	137.60
Lurullah	b 126	5	11^3	11^3	12^9	12^1	12^6	12^{16}	S Brooks	T A Grissom	74.20
Henrijan	b 126	8	2½	2^2	5^h	10^2	13	13	A Valenz'la	Mr-Mrs S H Elmore	f-40.60

f-Mutuel field.

Time, :23 2/5, :46 4/5, 1:11, 1:36-3/5, 2:02 2/5. Track good.

$2 Mutuels Paid—Venetian Way, $14.60 straight, $4.60 place, $3.40 show: Bally Ache, $3.00 place, $3.00 show; Victoria Park, $5.00 show.

Winner—Ch. c. by Royal Coinage—Firefly, by Papa Redbird, trained by V. J. Sovinski; bred by J. W. Greathouse.

Went to Post—4:31. Off at 4:31 Central Daylight Time.

Start good. Won ridden out. **Venetian Way,** away alertly, remained within striking distance while under snug restraint to the second turn, where he was sent up along the outside, displaced **Bally Ache** for the lead at the top of the front stretch and drew into his commanding advantage while being ridden out. **Bally Ache** displayed his customary speed, shook off **Henrijan** after a quarter mile, was cleverly rated thereafter and, while unable to handle the winner, he was easily best of the others. **Victoria Park,** allowed to settle in stride, was eased to the outside after six furlongs to commence his bid which fell far short. **Tompion,** off in good order, raced in perfect position to the final turn, where he flattened out badly when put to a drive. **Bourbon Prince** made an ineffectual late rally. **Cuvier Relic** could not keep pace. **Tony Graff** was void of early speed. **Divine Comedy** maintained a striking position along the outside for six furlongs and then tired badly. **Lurullah** appeared in close quarters shortly following the start. **Henrijan** stopped badly after forcing the issue for nearly five furlongs.

Scratched—Hillsborough.

The Winner's Pedigree

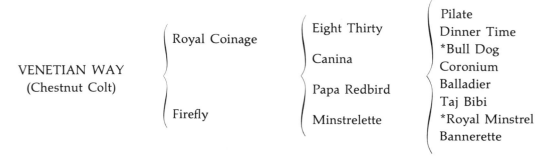

VENETIAN WAY (Chestnut Colt)	Royal Coinage	Eight Thirty	Pilate
			Dinner Time
		Canina	*Bull Dog
			Coronium
	Firefly	Papa Redbird	Balladier
			Taj Bibi
		Minstrelette	*Royal Minstrel
			Bannerette

85th Kentucky Derby, May 2, 1959

$125,000 added and $5,000 Gold Cup. 3-year-olds. Weight for age. Net value to winner $119,650; second $25,000; third $12,500; fourth $5,000.

Horses	Wt	PP	¼	½	¾	Mi	Str	Fin	Jockeys	Owners	Odds to $1
*Tomy Lee	126	9	2²	2¹½	1ʰᵈ	2¹½	2²	1ⁿᵒ	W Sh'maker	Mr-Mrs F Turner Jr	3.70
Sword Dancer	126	14	4ʰᵈ	4ʰᵈ	4²	1½	1ʰᵈ	2²¼	W Boland	Brookmeade Stable	8.80
First Landing	126	3	7¹	8½	5ʰᵈ	4½	3¹½	3¹	E Arcaro	Meadow Farm	3.60
Royal Orbit	126	17	10¹½	12³	11³	8²	6ʰᵈ	4ʰᵈ	W Harmatz	J Braunstein Est	46.60
Silver Spoon	121	4	9¹	9²	6½	3²	3ʰᵈ	5²¼	R York	C V Whitney	10.80
Finnegan	126	8	6²	6¹	7ʰᵈ	5¹½	7²	6½	J Longden	Neil McCarthy	10.60
Dunce	126	7	14½	13²	12³	11½	8¹	7¹½	S Brooks	Claiborne F	f-7.30
Open View	126	13	5²	5⁴	3²	6²	5½	8³	K Korte	Elkcam Stable	†17.20
Atoll	126	5	3½	3ʰᵈ	3½	7¹	9¹½	9ⁿᵒ	S Boulmetis	Elkcam & Chesler	†17.20
Rico Tesio	126	1	17	17	17	13²	11¹	10¹½	M Ycaza	Briardale Farm	48.10
Festival King	126	15	8½	7ʰᵈ	9²	9²	10ʰᵈ	11½	W Carstens	C B Fishbach	f-7.30
John Bruce	126	11	16½	16¹½	15½	14³	14¹	12ⁿᵒ	K Church	K G Marshall	34.50
Easy Spur	126	6	13³	10ʰᵈ	10¹	10¹½	13½	13ʰᵈ	W Hartack	Spring Hill F	7.90
The Chosen One	126	16	11¹	14⁴	14⁴	12½	12½	14⁴½	J Combest	Mrs S H Sadacca	f-7.30
Our Dad	126	1	12½	11½	13²	15²	15⁴	15¹	P Anderson	Patrice Jacobs	f-8.00
*Die Hard	126	12	15²	15½	16½	16³	16⁸	16⁶	J Sellers	Jacnot Stable	f-7.30
Troilus	126	10	1½	1¹½	2½	17	17	17	C Rogers	B Sharp	7.30

f—Mutuel field.   †Coupled.

Time, :24 1/5, 47 3/5, 1:11 3/5, 1:36, 2:02 1/5. Track fast.

$2 Mutuels Paid—*Tomy Lee $9.40 straight, $4.80 place, $3.80 show; Sword Dancer $9.00 place, $6.20 show; First Landing $4.00 show.

Winner—B. c. by *Tudor Minstrel—Auld Alliance, by Brantome. Trained by Frank Childs. Bred in England by D. H. Wells.

Start good, won driving. **Tomy Lee** snugged in off early pace of **Troilus**, moved from between horses with **Sword Dancer** to assume a slight advantage at half-mile ground, continued slightly wide to be headed on final bend, respond to strong handling and while drifting out, and being carried in, through stretch run he proved narrowly best. **Tomy Lee** survived a claim of foul lodged by rider of runner-up for allegedly having carried that one wide from 5/16ths marker to final sixteenth. **Sword Dancer** moved to a contending position along outside at once, continued wide to move readily and take command nearing final quarter mile, was carried wide into stretch to continue to show the way and while lugging in he just failed to last. **First Landing** loomed up boldly when called upon entering stretch, but could not improve his position. **Royal Orbit** taken in hand when in position early, commenced to move after going three-quarters to make a bold bid through midstretch but was not quite good enough. **Silver Spoon** moved rapidly in run down backstretch to leaders to maintain a striking position to midstretch where she could not gain under further urging.

The Winner's Pedigree

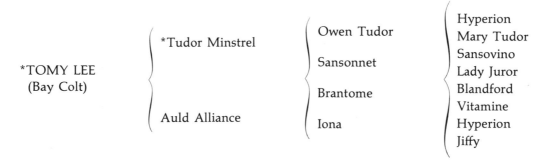

*TOMY LEE (Bay Colt)	*Tudor Minstrel	Owen Tudor	Hyperion
			Mary Tudor
		Sansonnet	Sansovino
			Lady Juror
	Auld Alliance	Brantome	Blandford
			Vitamine
		Iona	Hyperion
			Jiffy

84th Kentucky Derby, May 3, 1958

$125,000 Added and $5,000 Gold Cup. 3-year-olds. Weight for Age. Net value to winner $116,400; second $25,000; third $12,500; fourth $5,000.

Horses	Eq't A Wt	PP	St	½	¾	1	Str	Fin	Jockeys	Owners	Odds to $1
Tim Tam	w 126	2	8	8¹	5¹	4ʰᵈ	2³	1½	I Valenzuela	Calumet Farm	2.10
Lincoln Road	wb 126	7	1	1²	1²	1¹½	1²	2½	C Rogers	Sunny Blue Farm	46.90
Noureddin	wb 126	11	11	12⁴	12³	8½	3²	3⁶	J Combest	Crabgrass S	15.40
Jewel's Reward	w 126	3	6	6¹½	6ʰᵈ	5¹	4ʰ	4ⁿᵒ	E Arcaro	Maine Chance F	#-2.00
Martin's Rullah	wb 126	5	12	13¹¹	13¹⁰	10³	9³	5³	C McCreary	Mr & Mrs G Lewis	43.10
Chance it Tony	w 126	10	13	11¹½	9ʰ	11²	8²	6¹¾	L Batchellor	Mrs A Canulli	245.00
A Dragon Killer	w 126	9	9	9²	10ʰ	7²	7½	7ʰ	L Hansman	Mrs S H Sadacca	294.40
Gone Fishin'	w 126	4	5	4¹½	2½	2ʰ	5½	8¹	R Neves	L Langollen F	20.10
Benedicto	w 126	14	10	10²	8½	6ʰ	6³	9²	R Dever	Bellardi & Harkins	f-59.30
Ebony Pearl	w 126	13	4	3½	3¹½	3⁴	10³	10²½	M Ycaza	Maine Chance F	#-2.00
Red Hot Pistol	w 126	8	3	5³	4ʰ	13	12²	11¹½	D Dodson	Mrs S E Wilson Jr	f-59.30
Silky Sullivan	w 126	12	14	14	14	12²	11¹	12¹½	W Sh'maker	Ross & Klipsten	2.10
Flamingo	wb 126	6	7	7¹	11³	9³	13	13	G Glisson	C V Whitney	49.50
Warren G.	wb 126	1	2	2	7		eased		K Church	W G Reynolds	122.30

#—Coupled Jewel's Reward and Ebony Pearl.

f—Field

Time, :23 1/5, :47 3/5, 1:13 1/5, 1:38 2/5, 2:05. Track muddy.

$2 Mutuels paid—Tim Tam, $6.20 straight, $3.80 place, $3.00 show; Lincoln Road, $26.80 place, $11.40 show; Noureddin, $5.60 show.

Winner—Dk. b. c. by Tom Fool—Two Lea, by Bull Lea. Trained by H. A. Jones. Bred by Calumet Farm.

Start good. Won driving. **Tim Tam** unhurried while being outrun early, commenced to advance along inside after going a half mile, moved through in close quarters on final bend and when brought out between horses for drive he was fully extended to wear down **Lincoln Road** near the end. **Lincoln Road** made the pace under a well judged ride, saved ground much of way and held on stubbornly in a long drive. **Noureddin** far back through first six furlongs, circled his field when commencing his bid on second turn, lost additional ground on entering stretch and finished fastest of all in middle of track to be easily best of others. **Jewel's Reward** in hand while maintaining a striking position along outside, commenced to advance while continuing slightly wide on final bend but could not gain through final furlong when put to extreme pressure. **Martin's Rullah** closed a big gap in late stages but could not seriously menace top trio. **Gone Fishin'** loomed boldly on entering stretch but had little left when real test came. **Ebony Pearl** stopped badly after making a menacing bid on stretch turn. **Silky Sullivan** broke well but was allowed to stride while saving ground until final turn where he made only a brief and ineffectual bid of less than a sixteenth mile and refused to extend himself thereafter.

The Winner's Pedigree

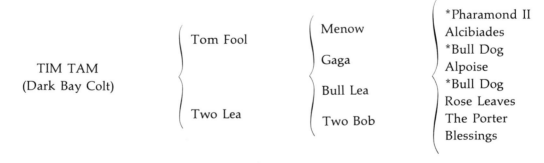

TIM TAM (Dark Bay Colt)	Tom Fool	Menow	*Pharamond II
			Alcibiades
		Gaga	*Bull Dog
			Alpoise
	Two Lea	Bull Lea	*Bull Dog
			Rose Leaves
		Two Bob	The Porter
			Blessings

83rd Kentucky Derby, May 4, 1957

$125,000 added and $5,000 Gold Cup. 3-year-olds. Weight for age. Net value to winner $107,950; second, $25,000; third, $12,500; fourth, $5,000. Mutuel Pool, $1,401,017.

Horses	Eq't A Wt	PP	St	½	¾	1	Str	Fin	Jockeys	Owners	Odds to $1
Iron Liege	w 126	6	4	3^3	$2^{1}\!/_2$	$2^{1}\!/_2$	$1^{1}\!/_2$	1no	W Hartack	Calumet Farm	8.40
Gallant Man	w 126	4	6	7^2	7^1	$5^{1}\!/_2$	$3^{1}\!/_2$	$2^{2}\!/_4$	W Sh'maker	R Lowe	3.70
Round Table	wb 126	3	5	4^3	4^3	4^2	4^h	3^3	R Neves	Kerr Stable	3.60
Bold Ruler	w 126	7	3	2^h	$3^{1}\!/_2$	$3^{1}\!/_2$	5^3	$4^{1}\!/_4$	E Arcaro	Wheatley Stable	1.20
Federal Hill	wb 126	2	1	$1^{1}\!/_2$	$1^{1}\!/_2$	1^h	2^h	$5^{3}\!/_4$	W Carstens	C Lussky	7.90
Indian Creek	wb 126	5	7	$6^{2}\!/_2$	$6^{1}\!/_2$	7^3	7^3	6^1	G Taniguchi	Mrs A L Rice	73.10
Mister Jive	wb 126	1	2	5^3	$5^{2}\!/_2$	$6^{1}\!/_2$	$6^{1}\!/_2$	$7^{3}\!/_2$	H Woodh'se	J L Applebaum	55.90
Better Bee	w 126	9	9	9	9	8^3	8^6	8^{10}	J Adams	W S Miller	42.40
Shan Pac	wb 126	8	8	$8^{1}\!/_2$	$8^{1}\!/_2$	9	9	9	J R Adams	T A Grissom	46.50

Time, :23 3/5, :47, 1:11 2/5, 1:36 4/5, 2:02 1/5. Track fast.

$2 Mutuels Paid—Iron Liege, $18.80 straight, $9.40 place, $6.20 show; Gallant Man, $5.00 place, $4.00 show; Round Table, $4.00 show.

Winner—B. c. by Bull Lea—Iron Maiden, by War Admiral, trained by H. A. Jones; bred by Calumet Farm.

In gate—4:32. Off at 4:32 Central Daylight Time.

Start good. Won driving; second and third the same. **Iron Liege,** away alertly, saved ground while racing nearest **Federal Hill** to the mile, took command during the drive and, responding to strong handling, held **Gallant Man** safe but won with little left. **Gallant Man,** in hand and saving ground to the last three-eighths mile, moved up determinedly in the early stretch, reached the lead between calls and was going stoutly when his rider misjudged the finish and he could not overtake **Iron Liege** when back on stride. **Round Table,** well placed and racing evenly to the stretch, closed willingly under punishment but could not reach the leaders. **Bold Ruler,** a sharp factor from the outset but racing well out in the track, failed to stay when set down through the stretch. **Federal Hill** took command at once, set the pace until inside the stretch, then gave way when challenged by **Iron Liege. Indian Creek** was never prominent and had no mishap. **Mister Jive** could not keep up. **Better Bee** was never dangerous. **Shan Pac** was over-matched.

Scratched—Gen. Duke, 126.

The Winner's Pedigree

			*Teddy
		*Bull Dog	Plucky Liege
	Bull Lea		Ballot
		Rose Leaves	*Colonial
IRON LIEGE			Man o' War
(Bay Colt)		War Admiral	Brushup
	Iron Maiden		*Sir Gallahad III
		Betty Derr	Uncle's Lassie

82nd Kentucky Derby, May 5, 1956

$125,000 added and $5,000 Gold Cup. 3-year-olds. Weight for age. Net value to winner $123,450; second, $25,000; third, $12,500; fourth, $5,000.

Horses	Eq't A Wt	PP	St	½	¾	1	Str	Fin	Jockeys	Owners	Odds to $1
Needles	w 126	1	12	16^3	16^6	$7^{1/2}$	$2^{1/2}$	$1^{3/4}$	D Erb	D & H Stable	1.60
Fabius	w b 126	12	2	3^2	$2^{1/2}$	$1^{1/2}$	1^h	$2^{1/2}$	W Hartack	Calumet Farm	c-4.00
Come On Red	w 126	10	14	14^1	10^1	$4^{1/2}$	$3^{1/2}$	$3^{3/4}$	A Popara	Helen W Kellogg	f-29.00
Count Chic	w b 126	5	15	11^2	12^2	9^3	$4^{1/2}$	$4^{1/2}$	S Brooks	Mr & Mrs D Lozzi	8.00
Pintor Lea	w b 126	3	11	$12^{1/2}$	$11^{1/2}$	$6^{1/2}$	5^1	$5^{1/2}$	R L Baird	Calumet Farm	c-4.00
Career Boy	w b 126	2	13	15^3	$13^{1/2}$	10^2	$8^{1/2}$	$6^{2/2}$	E Guerin	C V Whitney	a-4.90
No Regrets	w b 126	7	6	5^1	4^h	2^h	$7^{1/2}$	$7^{1/2}$	D Dodson	W E Britt	52.80
Head Man	w b 126	4	4	4^h	3^h	5^1	6^1	$8^{3/4}$	E Arcaro	C V Whitney	a-4.90
King O' Swords	w b 126	16	9	$7^{1/2}$	6^1	8^1	9^1	9^1	R B'gmnke	Rev Knoll Farm	f-29.00
High King	w 126	6	17	17	17	17	12^4	10^{nk}	W M Cook	J Gavegnano	79.50
Jean Baptiste	w b 126	14	16	$13^{1/2}$	$15^{1/2}$	$12^{1/2}$	$11^{1/2}$	11no	J Nichols	Mrs L P Tate	f-29.00
Terrang	w b 126	11	1	$2^{2/2}$	$1^{1/2}$	3^1	10^2	12^5	W Sh'maker	Rex C Elsworth	8.30
Black Emperor	w b 126	13	10	10^2	14^2	11^3	13^3	13^5	J Adams	Hasty House Farm	26.40
Besomer	w b 126	9	8	$8^{1/2}$	$8^{1/2}$	14^h	14^2	$14^{1/2}$	N Shuk	Companas Stable	71.20
Invalidate	w b 126	15	3	6^2	7^1	16^3	15^4	15^2	L Gilligan	T A Grissom	f-29.00
Ben A Jones	w b 126	8	5	1^h	5^3	13^2	17	16^1	P J Bailey	G & M Stable	53.80
Countermand	w b 126	17	7	9^4	9^h	$15^{1/2}$	16^2	17	A Kirkland	Brandywine Stable	12.00

a-Coupled, Fabius and Pintor Lea; c-Career Boy and Head Man.
(The owner of the winner to receive a gold trophy.)

Time, :23 4/5, :47 1/5, 1:11 3/5, 1:36 4/5, 2:03 2/5. Track fast.

$2 Mutuels Paid—Needles, $5.20 straight, $3.60 place, $3.40 show; Fabius (c-Entry) $3.80 place, $3.60 show; Come on Red (f-Field) $6.60 show.

Winner—B. c., by Ponder—Noodle Soup, by Jack High, trained by H. L. Fontaine; bred by W. E. Leach.

Went to Post—4:33. Off at 4:33½ Central Daylight Time.

Start good. Won driving; second and third the same. **Needles,** well handled, saved ground when outrun to the last three-eighths mile, was sent to the middle of the track for the stretch run and, responding readily to urging, wore down **Fabius** and won going away. **Fabius,** well placed from the start, took command approaching the stretch, held on gamely when set down in the drive but was unable to withstand **Needles. Come On Red,** far back early, moved up boldly entering the stretch, finished willingly under punishment but was not good enough for the top pair. **Count Chic,** unable to keep up early, made a good bid in the early stretch, then failed to rally when hard urged in the drive. **Pintor Lea** gradually worked his way forward to the stretch, remained next to the inner rail for the drive but could not threaten the leaders. **Career Boy** lacked early foot but finished fairly well. **No Regrets** tired after showing early speed. **Head Man** raced forwardly placed to the mile but had nothing left for the stretch run. **King O' Swords** bumped with **Invalidate** at the start and failed to recover. **High King** was never dangerous. **Jean Baptiste** raced far back throughout. **Terrang** had early speed but failed to stay. **Black Emperor** was far back the entire trip. **Besomer** was through early. **Invalidate** had brief speed after bumping with **King O' Swords** at the break. **Ben A. Jones** had brief speed. **Countermand** could not keep up.

Scratched—Reaping Right, 126.

The Winner's Pedigree

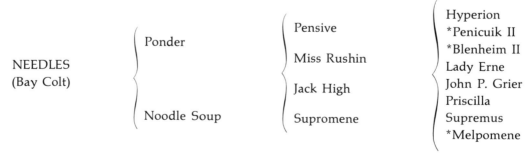

NEEDLES (Bay Colt)
- Ponder
  - Pensive
    - Hyperion
    - *Penicuik II
  - Miss Rushin
    - *Blenheim II
    - Lady Erne
- Noodle Soup
  - Jack High
    - John P. Grier
    - Priscilla
  - Supromene
    - Supremus
    - *Melpomene

81st Kentucky Derby, May 7, 1955

$125,000 added and $5,000 Gold Cup. 3-year-olds. Weight for age. Net value to winner $108,400 ($100,000 guaranteed); second $25,000; third $12,500, fourth $5,000.

Horses	Eq't A Wt	PP	St	½	¾	1	Str	Fin	Jockeys	Owners	Odds to $1
Swaps	w 126	8	4	1¹	1¹	1½	1½	1¹½	W Sh'maker	R C Ellsworth	2.80
Nashua	w 126	5	1	3¹	3¹	2¹	2⁴	2⁶½	E Arcaro	Belair Stud	1.30
Summer Tan	w b 126	10	6	4⁶	4⁵	3⁴	3²	3⁴	E Guerin	Mrs J W Galbreath	4.90
Racing Fool	w 126	7	5	5¹	5¹	5¹	4³	4½	H Moreno	Cain Hoy Stable	a-5.70
Jean's Joe	w b 126	9	9	10	8³	6½	5²	5¹½	S Brooks	Murcain Stable	16.20
Flying Fury	w 126	2	10	8³	9¹	9²	6½	6¾	C McCreary	Cain Hoy Stable	a-5.70
Honeys Alibi	w 126	4	2	6³	6³	7¹	7½	7³½	W Harmatz	W-L Ranch Co	55.60
Blue Lem	w b 126	1	7	9½	10	10	9⁴	8¹½	C Rogers	H C Fruehauf	23.30
Nabesna	w b 126	3	8	7³	7¹½	8¹	8¹	9¹⁰	J Adams	C Mooers	52.80
Trim Destiny	w 126	6	3	2²½	2ʰ	4ʰ	10	10	L C Cook	G R White	50.90

a—Coupled Racing Fool and Flying Fury.

Time, :23 3/5, :47 2/5, 1:12 2/5, 1:37, 2:01 4/5. Track fast.

$2 Mutuels Paid—Swaps, $7.60 straight, $3.40 place, $2.60 show; Nashua $3.00 place, $2.40 show; Summer Tan $3.00 show.

Winner—Ch.c. by *Khaled—Iron Reward, by *Beau Pere, trained by M. A. Tenney; bred by R. C. Ellsworth.

Went to Post—4:31. Off at 4:31½, Central Daylight Time.

Start good from stall gate. Won driving; second and third the same. **Swaps,** alertly ridden, took command soon after the start, raced **Trim Destiny** into defeat before reaching the upper turn, responded readily when challenged by **Nashua** during the stretch run and drew clear in the last sixteenth mile. **Nashua,** well placed from the outset, was kept in hand to the last three-eighths mile, moved up boldly on the outside of **Swaps** for the stretch run but was not good enough for the latter, although much the best of the others. **Summer Tan,** never far back and reserved to the last half-mile, made a mild bid approaching the stretch, then faltered. **Racing Fool,** in hand to the stretch, was unable to threaten the leaders when set down for the drive. **Jean's Joe** lacked early foot and was never dangerous. **Flying Fury** was sluggish and was never prominent. **Honeys Alibi** was outrun and had no mishaps. **Blue Lem** raced far back the entire trip. **Nabesna** was through early. **Trim Destiny** raced nearest **Swaps** for three-quarters mile, then gave way.

The Winner's Pedigree

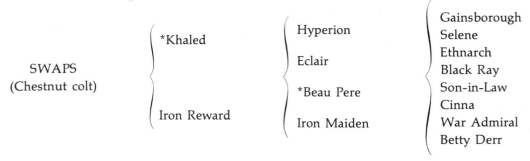

SWAPS (Chestnut colt)
- *Khaled
  - Hyperion
    - Gainsborough
    - Selene
  - Eclair
    - Ethnarch
    - Black Ray
- Iron Reward
  - *Beau Pere
    - Son-in-Law
    - Cinna
  - Iron Maiden
    - War Admiral
    - Betty Derr

80th Kentucky Derby, May 1, 1954

$100,000 added and $5,000 Gold Cup. 3-year-olds. Weight for age. Net value to winner $102,050; second, $10,000; third, $5,000; fourth, $2,500.

Horses	Eq't Wt.	PP	St	½	¾	1	Str	Fin	Jockeys	Owners	Odds to $1
Determine	wb 126	7	5	3^3	$3\frac{1}{2}$	$2\frac{1}{2}$	$1\frac{1}{2}$	$1^1\frac{1}{2}$	R York	A J Crevolin	b-4.30
Hasty Road	wb 126	1	1	$1^1\frac{1}{2}$	1^2	1^2	$2^2\frac{1}{2}$	$2^2\frac{1}{2}$	J Adams	Hasty House Fm	a-5.30
Hasseyampa	wb 126	12	12	$12^1\frac{1}{2}$	8^3	$5\frac{1}{2}$	3^h	$3^2\frac{1}{2}$	A Kirkland	Walmac Farm	25.60
Goyamo	wb 126	5	16	16^6	15^1	$10^1\frac{1}{2}$	$6\frac{1}{2}$	4^{nk}	E Arcaro	R Martin-A Jones	4.90
Admiral Porter	wb 126	8	3	$4^1\frac{1}{2}$	$4^1\frac{1}{2}$	4^h	4^2	5^1	P J Bailey	Sunny Blue Fm	54.10
Correlation	wb 126	4	15	$15^1\frac{1}{2}$	16^{10}	9^1	5^1	$6^3\frac{1}{4}$	W Sho'aker	R S Lytle	3.00
Fisherman	w 126	16	7	6^1	$6\frac{1}{2}$	$6\frac{1}{2}$	7^2	$7^2\frac{1}{2}$	H Woodh'se	C V Whitney	6.30
James Session	w 126	10	8	8^h	$13\frac{1}{2}$	13^1	13^1	8^n	L Risley	Mr-Mrs H James	71.10
Allied	wb 126	3	10	10^1	7^h	$8\frac{1}{2}$	9^1	9^h	S Brooks	A J Crevolin	b-4.30
Gov Browning	wb 126	2	14	14^6	14^2	$11\frac{1}{2}$	$10\frac{1}{2}$	10^1	D Erb	Martin-McKin'y	f-16.20
Super Devil	w 126	9	11	$11\frac{1}{2}$	9^1	$12\frac{1}{2}$	11^h	11^{nk}	R L Baird	Rebel Stable	f-16.20
Red Hannigan	wb 126	13	13	13^2	12^2	$14^1\frac{1}{2}$	14^3	12^{nk}	W Boland	Woodley Ln Fm	f-16.20
Black Metal	wb 126	15	6	$5\frac{1}{2}$	5^h	$7^1\frac{1}{2}$	12^h	13^2	A DeSpirito	Maine Chance Fm	13.20
Timely Tip	w 126	14	2	2^3	2^3	3^1	8^2	$14^2\frac{1}{2}$	H Craig	A L Birch	53.70
Sea O Erin	wb 126	6	4	7^3	$11\frac{1}{2}$	$15^1\frac{1}{2}$	$15\frac{1}{2}$	15^3	C McCreary	Hasty House Fm	a-5.30
King Phalanx	w 126	11	17	17	17	$16\frac{1}{2}$	$16\frac{1}{2}$	16^1	D Dodson	S E Wilson Jr	32.30
Mel Leavitt	wb 126	17	9	9^1	10^2	17	17	17	R McLa'lin	J W Brown	f-16.20

f-Mutuel field. b-Coupled, Determine and Allied; a-Hasty Road and Sea O Erin.

Time, :23 3/5, :47 3/5, 1:12, 1:37, 2:03. Track fast.

$2 Mutuels Paid—Determine (b-Entry) $10.60 straight; $5.60 place; $4.80 show; Hasty Road (a-Entry) $6.80 place, $5.60 show; Hasseyampa, $12.00 show

Winner—Gr. c, by *Alibhai—Koubis, by *Mahmoud, trained by W. Molter; bred by Dr. E. Asbury.

Went to Post—4:34. Off at 4:35 Central Daylight Time.

Start good. Won driving; second and third the same. **Determine,** roughed immediately after the start in the jam caused by **Hasty Road** and **Timely Tip,** recovered under good handling and raced within striking distance of the leader to the stretch, responded to brisk urging during the drive and, taking command, won going away. **Hasty Road** began fast, bore to the outside in the run to the first turn, retained a clear lead until reaching the stretch, then was unable to withstand the winner. **Hasseyampa** gradually worked way forward while racing in the middle of the track, closed strongly under punishment but was unable to reach the top pair. **Goyamo** saved ground while working way forward to the stretch, was sent between horses for the drive and, blocked near the furlong pole, was unable to get to the leaders when finally clear. **Admiral Porter** gave good effort and had no mishap. **Correlation,** bumped immediately after the break, was far back to the last half mile, then finished strongly. **Fisherman** raced well to the mile, then weakened. **James Session** was outrun. **Allied** tired. **Gov. Browning** was never prominent and had no excuse. **Timely Tip** bore to the inside after the start, causing a jam, then raced well to the stretch before tiring badly. **Super Devil** was through early. **Red Hannigan** showed nothing. **Sea O Erin** had brief speed. **Black Metal** failed to stay after beginning alertly. **Mel Leavitt** could not keep up.

Scratched—Close Out, 126.

The Winner's Pedigree

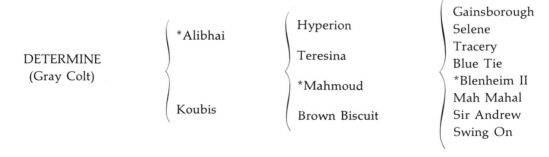

DETERMINE (Gray Colt)	*Alibhai	Hyperion	Gainsborough
			Selene
		Teresina	Tracery
			Blue Tie
	Koubis	*Mahmoud	*Blenheim II
			Mah Mahal
		Brown Biscuit	Sir Andrew
			Swing On

79th Kentucky Derby, May 2, 1953

$100,000 added and $5,000 Gold Cup. 3-year-olds. Weight for age. Net value to winner $90,050; second $10,000; third $5,000; fourth $2,500. Trainer awards: First $3,000; second $2,000; third $1,000. Breeder awards: First $2,000; second $1,000; third $500.

Horses	Eq't A Wt	PP	St	½	¾	1	Str	Fin	Jockeys	Owners	Odds to $1
Dark Star	w 126	10	3	$1^{1\frac{1}{2}}$	$1^{\frac{1}{2}}$	$1^{1\frac{1}{2}}$	$1^{1\frac{1}{2}}$	1^h	H Moreno	Cain Hoy Stable	24.90
Native Dancer	w 126	6	6	8^3	$4^{\frac{1}{2}}$	4^2	2^1	2^5	E Guerin	A G Vanderbilt	a-.70
Invigorator	w 126	4	5	$7^{\frac{1}{2}}$	$6^{\frac{1}{2}}$	6^1	4^1	3^2	W Sh'maker	Saxon Stable	40.90
Royal Bay Gem	w 126	11	11	11	8^2	$7^{1\frac{1}{2}}$	$7^{1\frac{1}{2}}$	$4^{1\frac{1}{2}}$	J Combest	E Constantin Jr	6.80
Correspondent	w 126	2	2	2^2	2^1	$2^{\frac{1}{2}}$	3^1	$5^{1\frac{3}{4}}$	E Arcaro	Mrs G Guiberson	3.00
Straight Face	w b 126	9	7	4^3	3^1	$3^{\frac{1}{2}}$	5^h	6^{nk}	T Atkinson	Greentree Stable	10.40
Social Outcast	w 126	8	10	$10^{\frac{1}{2}}$	$10^{1\frac{1}{2}}$	8^2	8^2	7^2	J Adams	A G Vanderbilt	a-.70
Money Broker	w b 126	7	9	$5^{\frac{1}{2}}$	$5^{\frac{1}{2}}$	5^h	6^3	$8^{2\frac{3}{4}}$	A Popara	G & G Stable	45.80
Ram O' War	w b 126	3	8	$9^{\frac{1}{2}}$	11	10^1	9^1	9^{nk}	D Dodson	B S Campbell	85.10
Curragh King	w b 126	5	4	6^2	9^1	11	11	10^h	D Erb	E M Goemans	99.10
Ace Destroyer	w b 126	1	1	$3^{\frac{1}{2}}$	7^2	9^3	10^1	11	J D Jessop	Mr-Mrs T M Dan'l	91.80

a-Coupled, Native Dancer and Social Outcast.

Time, :23 4/5, :47 4/5, 1:12 1/5, 1:36 3/5, 2:02. Track fast.

$2 Mutuels Paid—Dark Star, $51.80 straight, $13.60 place, $7.00 show; Native Dancer (a-Entry), $3.20 place, $2.80 show; Invigorator, $9.40 show.

Winner—Br. c, by *Royal Gem II.—Isolde, by *Bull Dog, trained by E. Hayward; bred by W. L. Jones, Jr.

Went to Post—4:32. Off at 4:32½ Central Daylight Time.

Start good from stall gate. Won driving; second and third the same. **Dark Star,** alertly ridden, took command soon after the start, set the pace to the stretch under steady rating, then responded readily when set down in the drive and lasted to withstand **Native Dancer,** but won with little left. **Native Dancer,** roughed at the first turn by **Money Broker,** was eased back to secure racing room, raced wide during the run to the upper turn, then saved ground entering the stretch and finished strongly, but could not overtake the winner, although probably best. **Invigorator,** in close quarters entering the backstretch, raced well when clear and closed willingly under urging, but could not threaten the top pair. **Royal Bay Gem,** away sluggishly, was forced to lose ground while working way forward and could not reach the leaders when set down through the stretch. **Correspondent,** bumped after the break by **Ace Destroyer,** recovered under good handling and raced nearest **Dark Star** to the stretch, but had nothing left for the drive. **Straight Face** raced prominently to the mile, then weakened. **Social Outcast** lacked early speed and was never dangerous. **Money Broker** swerved into **Native Dancer** at the first turn, raced well to the stretch, then gave way. **Ram O' War** was far back the entire trip. **Curragh King** was through early. **Ace Destroyer** began fast, bumped **Correspondent** and displayed early speed, but failed to stay.

Scratched—Spy Defense, 126

The Winner's Pedigree

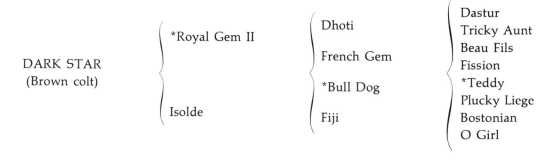

	*Royal Gem II	Dhoti	Dastur
			Tricky Aunt
		French Gem	Beau Fils
DARK STAR			Fission
(Brown colt)		*Bull Dog	*Teddy
	Isolde		Plucky Liege
		Fiji	Bostonian
			O Girl

78th Kentucky Derby, May 3, 1952

$100,000 added and $10,000 Gold Cup. 3-year-olds. Weight for age. Net value to winner $96,300; second $10,000; third $5,000; fourth $2,500. Trainer awards: First $3,000, second $2,000; third $1,000. Breeder awards: First $2,000; second $1,000; third $500.

Horses	Eq't A wt	PP	St	½	¾	1	Str	Fin	Jockeys	Owners	Odds to $1
Hill Gail ....w 126		1	1	$2\frac{1}{2}$	$1\frac{1}{2}$	1^5	1^3	1^2	E Arcaro	Calumet Farm	1.10
Sub Fleet..........w 126		9	8	$6\frac{1}{2}$	$5\frac{1}{2}$	$3\frac{1}{2}$	2^6	$2^{8\frac{3}{4}}$	S Brooks	Dixiana	22.90
Blue Man..........w 126		14	16	13^2	$12\frac{1}{2}$	6^1	6^2	$3\frac{1}{2}$	C McCreary	White Oak Stable	4.40
Master Fiddle......wb 126		13	14	$10\frac{1}{2}$	$9\frac{1}{2}$	5^2	$4\frac{1}{2}$	$4^{1\frac{1}{4}}$	D Gorman	Myhelyn Stable	a-9.30
Count Flame.......wb 126		4	10	14^4	14^3	13^1	8^3	$5\frac{1}{2}$	W Sh'maker	J J Amiel	a-9.30
Arroz..............w 126		16	13	11^h	10^h	10^2	7^3	$6^{1\frac{1}{4}}$	R York	Mrs G Guiberson	31.70
Happy Go Lucky ...wb 126		12	7	$3\frac{1}{2}$	3^h	4^2	3^h	$7^{2\frac{1}{2}}$	A Ferrai'olo	H G Backman	54.60
Hannibal ....wb 126		15	3	1^2	2^3	$2^{1\frac{1}{2}}$	$5\frac{1}{2}$	8^3	W J P'more	B Sharp	76.80
Cold Command .....w 126		11	6	15^2	16	11^2	$11\frac{1}{2}$	$9\frac{3}{4}$	G Porch	C V Whitney	8.50
Smoke Screen......w 126		10	15	16	15^1	12^2	12^4	10^{nk}	J Adams	Reverie Knoll	103.70
Gushing Oil........wb 126		7	11	$12\frac{1}{2}$	13^2	$8\frac{1}{2}$	$9\frac{1}{2}$	11^{nk}	Atkinson	S E Wilson Jr	6.70
Pintor ....w 126		6	9	$8\frac{1}{2}$	7^2	7^1	10^1	$12^{1\frac{1}{4}}$	H Mora	Montpelier Stable	42.50
Shag Tails.........wb 126		5	4	4^3	4^2	$9\frac{1}{2}$	13^3	13^2	J Nazareth	M Shagrin	f-18.80
Eternal Moon ......wb 126		8	12	9^6	$11\frac{1}{2}$	14^5	14^3	$14^{1\frac{1}{2}}$	J R Layton	Emerald Hill	f-18.80
Brown Rambler ....wb 126		3	2	5^2	6^3	16	15^{10}	15^{18}	D Dodson	Mildred F U'wood	f-18.80
Swoop ....w 126		2	5	7^2	$8\frac{1}{2}$	15^2	16	16	K Church	High Tide Stable	f-18.80

f-Mutuel field. a-Coupled, Master Fiddle and Count Flame.

Time, :12 2/5, :23 3/5, :34 4/5, :46 4/5, :59, 1:11, 1:23 3/5, 1:35 2/5, 1:48 2/5, 2:01 3/5. Track fast.

$2 Mutuel Paid—Hill Gail, $4.20 straight, $4.00 place, $3.20 show; Sub Fleet, $14.60 place, $7.80 show; Blue Man, $3.60 show.

Winner—Dk.b. c. by Bull Lea—Jane Gail, by *Blenheim II, trained by B. A. Jones; bred by Calumet Farm.

Went to Post—4:37. Off at 4:38 Central Daylight Time.

Start good from stall gate. Won ridden out; second and third driving. **Hill Gail** swerved to the outside after the break, crowding **Swoop** and **Brown Rambler,** raced nearest **Hannibal** for five-eighths of a mile, then assumed command and entered the stretch with a clear lead, but was ridden out to withstand **Sub Fleet.** The latter, on the outside until settled along the backstretch, steadily worked his way forward hereafter, finished willingly under punishment, but could not reach the winner. **Blue Man,** away slowly and on the outside throughout, made up ground steadily, but could not reach the leaders, giving a game effort. **Master Fiddle** lacked early speed and was in tight quarters approaching the three-quarters mile marker, raced well when clear, but was unable to seriously threaten the top ones. **Count Flame** lacked early foot, but closed determinely. **Arroz** had a rough trip. **Happy Go Lucky** was through after the mile. **Hannibal** gave way after racing prominently to the stretch. **Cold Command,** roughed soon after the start, failed to recover. **Smoke Screen** showed nothing. **Gushing Oil,** forced back during the run to the first turn, was unable to reach serious contention. **Pintor** tired during the stretch run. **Shag Tails** was through early. **Eternal Moon** had no mishap. **Brown Rambler** and **Swoop,** crowded immediately after the break, were far back thereafter.

Scratched—Top Blend.

The Winner's Pedigree

			*Teddy
		*Bull Dog	Plucky Leige
	Bull Lea		Ballot
		Rose Leaves	*Colonial
HILL GAIL			Blandford
(Dark Bay colt)		*Blenheim II	Malva
	Jane Gail		Ladkin
		Lady Higloss	Hi Gloss

77th Kentucky Derby, May 5, 1951

$100,000 added and $5,000 Gold Cup. 3-year-olds. Weight for age. Net value to winner $98,050; second $10,000; third $5,000; fourth $2,500. Trainer awards: first, $3,000; second $2,000; third, $1,000. Breeder awards: first, $2,000, second, $1,000; third, $500.

Horses	Eq't A Wt	PP	St	½	¾	1	Str	Fin	Jockeys	Owners	Odds to $1
Count Turf	wb 126	9	18	11^3	$6^{1½}$	4^1	$1^{2½}$	1^4	C McCreary	J J Amiel	f-14.60
Royal Mustang	wb 126	16	4	4^1	$4½$	$6½$	5^2	2^h	P J Bailey	S E Wilson Jr	a-53.00
Ruhe	wb 126	10	12	7^h	$10½$	7^h	$6^{1½}$	$3^{2½}$	J D Jessop	Mrs E Denemark	10.80
Phil D	w 126	18	5	1^h	$1½$	2^1	$3½$	4^h	R York	W C Martin	f-14.60
Fanfare	w 126	5	1	$5½$	$7½$	5^2	$4½$	$5^{¾}$	S Brooks	Calumet Farm	6.30
Battle Morn	wb 126	11	14	18^1	15^h	$10½$	10^2	$6^{1½}$	E Arcaro	Cain Hoy Stable	2.80
Anyoldtime	w 126	1	2	10^h	9^2	$9½$	$8½$	7^{nk}	R L Baird	W M Peavey	b-68.90
Pur Sang	w 126	20	8	$12½$	$11^{1½}$	$11^{1½}$	$9½$	$8^{1½}$	J Adams	Springbrook Farm	f-14.60
Hall of Fame	wb 126	17	6	2^2	$2^{1½}$	3^1	7^3	$9½$	T Atkinson	Greentree Stable	c-8.70
Timely Reward	w 126	3	11	$14½$	14^h	15^1	$13^{1½}$	10^1	J Stout	Mrs W Gilroy	8.60
Counterpoint	w 126	2	7	8^h	5^h	12^1	$11½$	11^2	D Gorman	C V Whitney	d-5.90
Repetoire	wb 126	19	20	$3^{2½}$	3^h	1^1	2^1	12^{nk}	P McLean	Mr & Mrs S C Mikell	8.40
King Clover	wb 126	12	9	$9½$	8^1	8^3	14^2	$13½$	F Bone	C C Boshamer	f-14.60
Sonic	w 126	6	3	$6½$	$12½$	$14½$	$15½$	$14½$	W Boland	King Ranch	8.30
Sir Bee Bum	w 126	13	15	17^6	18^4	17^2	16^3	15^n	D Madden	W M Peavey	b-68.90
Snuzzle	w 126	14	17	15^h	17^2	13^2	17^3	16^4	G Porch	Brown Hotel Stable	120.70
Fighting Back	wb 126	8	10	13^1	$13½$	16^1	12^h	$17^{2½}$	W L John'n	Murlogg Farm	f-14.90
Big Stretch	wb 126	15	19	$16½$	16^h	18^5	18^{15}	18^{10}	D Dodson	Greentree Stable	c-8.70
Golden Birch	wb 126	4	13	19^8	19^{10}	19^4	19^5	19^5	C Swain	S E Wilson Jr	a-53.00
Mameluke	wb 126	7	16	20	20	20	20	20	R Adair	C V Whitney	d-5.90

f-Mutuel field. a—Coupled, Royal Mustang and Golden Birch; b—Anyoldtime and Sir Bee Bum; c—Hall of Fame and Big Stretch; d—Counterpoint and Mameluke.

Time, :12, :23 2/5, :34 3/5, :47 2/5, :59 3/5, 1:12 2/5, 1:24 4/5, 1:37, 1:49 4/5, 2:02 3/5. Track fast.

$2 mutuels paid—Count Turf (Field), $31.20 straight, $14.00 place, $6.60 show; Royal Mustang (a-Entry), $53.00 place, $24.80 show; Ruhe, $7.80 show.

Winner—B.c., by Count Fleet—Delmarie, by Pompey, trained by S. Rutchick; bred by Dr. and Mrs. F. P. Miller.

Went to Post—4:38. Off at 4:39 1/2 Central Daylight Time.

Start good from stall gate. Won driving; second and third the same. **Count Turf**, away well and kept in a forward position from the beginning, raced by **Repetoire** entering the stretch, responded to brisk urging and won going away. **Royal Mustang**, never far back, saved ground until the stretch, was forced a bit wide on the turn, then came again under strong handling, but could not get to the winner. **Ruhe** lacked early speed, but steadily improved position after the opening half, was sent around horses entering the stretch and could not overtake **Royal Mustang**. **Phil D.** was hustled to the front early, engaged **Hall of Fame** for three-quarters, then weakened. **Fanfare**, in hand until reaching the last three-eighths, was moving up strongly during the stretch run when crowded, came again, but could not threaten the leaders. **Battle Morn**, reserved to the half, was hustled along thereafter, but could not reach serious contention and had no excuse. **Anyoldtime**, on the inside throughout, raced evenly. **Pur Sang** was never dangerous. **Hall of Fame** gave way after racing well to the stretch. **Timely Reward** began slowly and could not secure a good position. **Counterpoint** tired badly after racing prominently to the upper turn. **Repetoire** was on the outside for the good line break, moved up fast and tired badly after racing prominently to the mile. **King Clover** had no mishap. **Sonic** was through after a half mile. **Fighting Back** showed nothing. **Big Stretch** was far back throughout. **Mameluke** quit badly after showing brief speed and pulled up sore.

The Winner's Pedigree

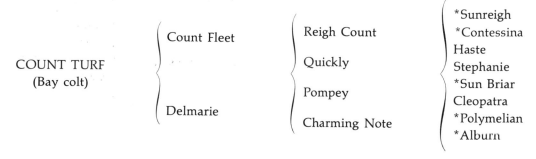

COUNT TURF (Bay colt)

- Count Fleet
  - Reigh Count
    - *Sunreigh
    - *Contessina
  - Quickly
    - Haste
    - Stephanie
- Delmarie
  - Pompey
    - *Sun Briar
    - Cleopatra
  - Charming Note
    - *Polymelian
    - *Alburn

76th Kentucky Derby, May 6, 1950

$100,000 added and $5,000 Gold Cup. 3-year-olds. Weight for age. Net value to winner $92,650; second $10,000; third $5,000; fourth $2,500. Trainer awards: first, $3,000; second $2,000; third, $1,000. Breeder awards: first, $2,000; second, $1,000; third, $500.

Horses	Wt	PP	St	½	¾	1	Str	Fin	Jockeys	Owners	Odds $1 Str't
Middleground	126	14	7	5½	3½	2^{1}	1½	$1^{1\frac{1}{4}}$	Boland	King Ranch	a-7.90
Hill Prince	126	5	9	$8^{1\frac{1}{2}}$	6½	5^{2}	$3^{1\frac{1}{2}}$	2½	Arcaro	C T Chenery	2.50
Mr. Trouble	126	2	5	3^{1}	1½	3^{hd}	2^{1}	$3^{2\frac{3}{4}}$	Dodson	C V Whitney	b-6.20
Sunglow	126	8	3	9½	8½	7½	4½	4^{5}	Robertson	Brookmeade	27.20
Oil Capitol(dh)	126	6	1	6^{3}	5^{1}	4^{1}	6^{1}	5	Church	T Gray	8.70
Hawley(dh)	126	13	6	4^{hd}	4^{hd}	9^{1}	7^{hd}	5¾	Glisson	C Mooers	82.80
Lotowhite	126	9	4	11^{3}	9^{1}	10^{1}	9^{2}	$7^{1\frac{1}{2}}$	Scurlock	H P Headley	37.20
On The Mark	126	11	12	$10^{1\frac{1}{2}}$	10^{5}	8½	8½	$8^{1\frac{1}{2}}$	Guerin	King Ranch	a-7.90
Your Host	126	1	2	1^{2}	$2^{1\frac{1}{2}}$	1½	5½	9^{4}	Longden	W M Goetz	1.60
Hallieboy	126	7	13	12^{1}	13½	13^{1}	13^{1}	$10^{1\frac{1}{2}}$	Atkins	W T Fugate	69.20
Dooly	126	3	8	14	12^{2}	12½	11^{hd}	11no	Brooks	C V Whitney	b-6.20
Trumpet King	126	4	10	7^{hd}	11½	11^{hd}	10½	12^{2}	Woodhouse	Willorene Farm	106.40
Stranded	126	10	14	13½	14	14	12^{1}	$13^{1\frac{1}{2}}$	Baird	Am'crombie & Smith	120.90
Black George	126	12	11	2^{3}	7½	6^{1}	14	14	Nelson	W H Veeneman	27.00

(dh) Oil Capitol and Hawley deadheated for fifth. a—coupled Middleground and On The Mark. b—coupled Mr. Trouble and Dooly.

Time: :11 4/5, :22 4/5, :34 2/5, :46 3/5, :59 2/5, 1:11 2/5, 1:24, 1:36 4/5, 1:49, 2:01 3/5. Track fast.

$2 mutuels paid—Middleground (coupled with On The Mark) $17.80 straight; $5.40 place; $3.80 show. Hill Prince $3.80 place, $3.20 show. Mr. Trouble (coupled with Dooly) $3.60 show.

Winner—Ch. c. by Bold Venture-Verguenza, by Chicaro, trained by Max Hirsch; bred by King Ranch.

Went to Post—4:31. Off at 4:32½ Central Daylight Time.

Start good from stall gate. Won driving; second and third the same. **Middleground,** never far back and saving ground under a steady ride, moved up boldly at the stretch turn and, after taking command, held **Hill Prince** safe. The latter, on the inside from the start, was in close quarters at the upper turn, continued willingly when clear and, after suffering some interference from the tiring **Your Host,** closed resolutely, but could not overtake **Middleground. Mr. Trouble,** a sharp factor from the start, was much used engaging **Your Host** until inside the stretch, then failed to rally when set down in the drive. **Sunglow** began fast, dropped back after the start, then recovered and moved up steadily, but could not better his position when hard ridden during the final furlong. **Oil Capitol** began fast, raced well after the break and made a good bid nearing the stretch, then tired, but deadheated with **Hawley** for fifth. **Hawley** tired after showing early speed, but finished on equal terms with **Oil Capitol. Lotowhite** was outrun. **Your Host** began alertly, gave way to **Mr. Trouble** after three-quarters of a mile, then came again to assume command, but tired badly during the stretch run. **On The Mark** was never dangerous. **Hallieboy** showed nothing. **Dooly** was through early. **Trumpet King** could not keep up. **Stranded** was never a factor. **Black George** failed to stay after showing early speed.

Scratched-Greek Ship.

The Winner's Pedigree

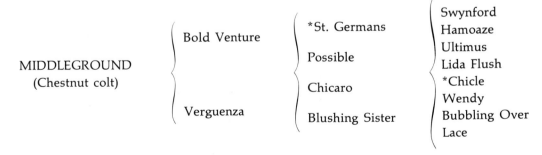

MIDDLEGROUND (Chestnut colt)	Bold Venture	*St. Germans	Swynford
			Hamoaze
		Possible	Ultimus
			Lida Flush
	Verguenza	Chicaro	*Chicle
			Wendy
		Blushing Sister	Bubbling Over
			Lace

75th Kentucky Derby, May 7, 1949

$100,000 added and $10,000 Gold Cup. 3-year-olds. Weight for age. Net value to winner $91,600; second $10,000; third $5,000; fourth $2,500. Trainer awards: First, $3,000; second, $2,000; third, $1,000. Breeder awards: first $2,000; second $1,000; third $500.

Horse	Eqt Wt	PP	St	½	¾	1	Str	Fin	Jockeys	Owners	Odds $1 Str't
Ponder	w 126	2	14	14	12^2	6^1	3^1	1^3	Brooks	Calumet Farm	16.00
Capot	wb 126	9	5	2^2	2^1	2^1	1^3	$2^{4½}$	Atkinson	Greentree Stable	a-13.10
Palestinian	wb 126	13	9	7^1	3^h	3^2	$2½$	3^2	W'dhouse	I Bieber	8.30
Old R'ckport	wb 126	15	13	9^1	6^1	4^3	5^5	$4^{4½}$	Glisson	C Mooers	4.90
Halt	wb 126	10	12	11^h	13^{10}	9^3	7^2	5^1	McCreary	Woodvale Farm	14.20
Olympia	w 126	4	1	$1^{1½}$	1^1	1^1	$4½$	$6^{4½}$	Arcaro	F W Hooper	.80
Model Cadet	w 126	16	8	8^2	$4½$	$5^{2½}$	$6½$	$7½$	Scurlock	Mrs A L Rice	66.00
Duplicator	wb 126	14	11	12^3	10^1	$8½$	8^4	8^5	James	Mr & Mrs J H Seley	146.30
Johns Joy	wb 126	7	3	$5^{1½}$	5^1	7^h	9^6	9^7	Adams	J A Kinard Jr	15.50
Ky. Colonel	wb 126	3	4	10^2	11^h	12^1	10^8	10^{nk}	Peterson	J A Goodwin	41.60
Lextown	w 126	11	6	3^h	9^1	$11½$	11^1	11^1	Richard	Lexbrook Stable	f-97.30
Jacks Town	wb 126	1	2	$6½$	8^h	10^2	12^4	12^5	Taylor	Afton Villa Farm	90.20
Wine List	wb 126	12	7	$4½$	7^1	13^8	13	13	Dodson	Greentree Stable	a-13.10
Senecas Coin	wb 126	8	10	13^1	14	14	Pulled Up		Duff	Mrs A Roth	f-97.30

f—Mutuel field. a—Capot and Wine List coupled as Greentree Stable entry.

Time, :11, :22 2/5, :33 3/5, :46 2/5, :59 3/5, 1:12 3/5, 1:25, 1:38 3/5, 1:51 2/5, 2:04 1/5. Track fast.

$2 Mutuels Paid—Ponder, $34 straight, $11.60 place, $6.20 show; Greentree entry, $9.60 place, $5.80 show; Palestinian, $4.80 show.

Winner—Dk. b. c. by Pensive—Miss Rushin, by *Blenheim II, trained by B. A. Jones; bred by Calumet Farm.

Went to Post—4:31. Off at 4:32½.

Start good from stall gate. Won driving; second and third the same. **Ponder,** away slowly, gradually worked his way forward while racing on the extreme outside, responded to brisk urging entering the stretch and, after wearing down the leaders, won, but had little left. **Capot,** forwardly placed from the start, went to the front when settled in the stretch, held on willingly, but was unable to withstand **Ponder,** although easily best of the others. **Palestinian,** well ridden, saved ground to the stretch, then made a bold bid when set down in the drive, bur faltered during the last sixteenth. **Old Rockport,** on the inside and never far back, could not get to the leaders when hard ridden through the stretch. **Halt** lacked early speed and passed tired horses during the last three-eighths. **Olympia** made the pace until inside the stretch, then gave way. **Model Cadet** moved up after going the first half mile, then tired. **Duplicator,** on the outside throughout, never seriously threatened.

The Winner's Pedigree

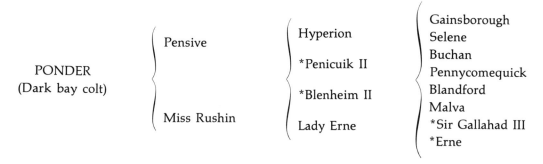

			Gainsborough
		Hyperion	Selene
	Pensive		Buchan
		*Penicuik II	Pennycomequick
PONDER			Blandford
(Dark bay colt)		*Blenheim II	Malva
	Miss Rushin		*Sir Gallahad III
		Lady Erne	*Erne

209

74th Kentucky Derby, May 1, 1948

$100,000 added and $5,000 Gold Cup. 3-year-olds. Weight for age. Net value to winner $83,400; second $10,000; third $5,000; fourth $2,500. Trainer awards: First $3,000; second $2,000; third $1,000. Breeder awards: First $2,000; second $1,000; third $500.

Horses	Eq't Wt	PP	St	½	¾	1	Str	Fin	Jockeys	Owners	Odds $1 Str't
Citation	w 126	1	2	2^h	2^3	2^5	1^2	$1^{3\frac{1}{2}}$	E Arcaro	Calumet Farm	a-.40
Coaltown	wb 126	2	1	1^6	$1^{3\frac{1}{2}}$	$1^{\frac{1}{2}}$	2^4	2^3	N L Pierson	Calumet Farm	a-.40
My Request	w 126	6	3	4^h	4^3	$3^{1\frac{1}{2}}$	3^1	$3^{1\frac{1}{2}}$	D Dodson	B F Whitaker	3.80
Billings	w 126	5	6	$5^{\frac{1}{2}}$	$3^{\frac{1}{2}}$	4^8	4^{15}	4^{20}	M Peterson	Walmac Stable	14.70
Grandpere	w 126	4	4	3^2	6	6	$5^{\frac{1}{2}}$	5^{nk}	J Gilbert	Mrs J P Adams	17.80
Escadru	wb 126	3	5	6	5^6	$5^{1\frac{1}{2}}$	6	6	A Kirkland	W L Brann	7.10

a-Citation and Coaltown coupled as Calumet Farm entry.

Time, :12 1/5, :23 2/5, :34 3/5, :46 3/5, :59 1/5, :1:11 2/5, 1:24 3/5, 1:38, 1:51 2/5, 2:05 2/5. Track sloppy.

$2 Mutuels Paid—Calumet Farm entry (Citation and Coaltown), $2.80 straight. No place or show betting.

Winner—B.c. by Bull Lea—*Hydroplane II, by Hyperion, trained by B. A. Jones; bred by Calumet Farm.

Went to Post—4:32. Off at 4:32 1/2.

Start good from stall gate. Won handily; second and third driving. **Citation,** away forwardly, and losing ground while racing back of **Coaltown** to the stretch, responded readily to a steady hand ride after disposing of the latter and drew clear. **Coaltown** began fast, established a clear lead before going a quarter and, making the pace on the inside in the stretch, continued willingly, but was not good enough for **Citation,** although easily the best of the others. **My Request,** bothered slightly after the start, was in hand while improving his position to the stretch, then failed to rally when set down for the drive. **Billings** suffered interference after the break when **Grandpere** bore to the outside, was in close quarters on the first turn when caught between **Escadru** and **Citation,** then could not better his position when clear. **Grandpere** broke into **Billings** at the start, displayed speed for a half mile, then gave way. **Escadru,** forced to take up when in close quarters entering the backstretch, could not reach serious contention thereafter and tired badly after going three-quarters of a mile.

Scratched—Galedo.

The Winner's Pedigree

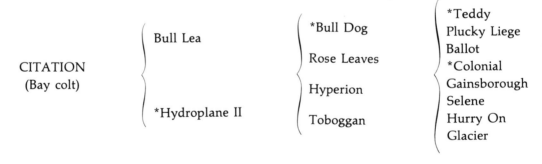

CITATION
(Bay colt)

Bull Lea

*Hydroplane II

*Bull Dog

Rose Leaves

Hyperion

Toboggan

*Teddy
Plucky Liege
Ballot
*Colonial
Gainsborough
Selene
Hurry On
Glacier

73rd Kentucky Derby, May 3, 1947

$100,460 added and $5,000 Gold Cup. 3-year-olds. Weight for age. Net value to winner $92,160; second $10,000; third $5,000; fourth $2,500. Trainer awards: First $3,000; second $2,000; third $1,000. Breeder awards: First $2,000; second $1,000; third $500.

Horses	Eq't Wt	PP	St	½	¾	1	Str	Fin	Jockeys	Owners	Odds $1 Str't
Jet Pilot	w 126	13	1	1¹½	1¹	1¹½	1¹½	1ʰ	Guerin	Maine Chance Farm	5.40
Phalanx	w b 126	8	13	13	10²	5¹½	5½	2ʰ	Arcaro	C V Whitney	2.00
Faultless	w 126	3	2	6²½	6¹½	4½	3ʰ	3¹	Dodson	Calumet Farm	6.30
On Trust	w b 126	9	5	2ʰ	2¹	3¹	2ʰ	4²¼	Longden	E O Stice & Sons	6.70
Cosmic B'mb	w b 126	1	4	3½	3¹½	6²½	6½	5²	Clark	W Helis	31.90
Star Reward	w 126	5	3	5¹	4ʰ	2ʰ	4¹	6¹	Brooks	Dixiana	11.20
Bullet Proof	w 126	4	6	9ʰ	7½	7³	7⁵	7⁵	Wright	Mrs M E Whitney	13.10
W L Sickle	w b 126	7	11	8²	8½	8ʰ	8½	8ʰ	Campbell	W-L Ranch	‡16.50
Stepfather	w b 126	6	9	12¹	9¹	9³	9²	9⁶	Westrope	W-L Ranch	‡16.50
Liberty Road	w b 126	12	10	10¹	11¹	11⁵	10¹	10½	Jessop	Brookmeade Stable	45.20
Riskolater	w b 126	10	12	11¹	12½	10⁵	11⁶	11⁶	Balz'etti	Circle M Farm	15.00
Double Jay	w b 126	2	7	4³	5½	12⁶	12⁶	12¹⁵	Gilbert	Ridgewood Stable	47.30
Jett-Jett	w 126	11	8	7ʰ	13	13	13	13	Hanka	W M Peavey	†99.40

‡Coupled, W. L. Sickle and Stepfather. †Mutuel field.

Time, :12 1/5, :24, :36, :49, 1:01 2/5, 1:14 2/5, 1:27 1/5, 1:40 2/5, 1:53, 2:06 4/5. Track slow.

$2 Mutuels Paid—Jet Pilot, $12.80 straight, $5.20 place, $4.00 show; Phalanx, $4.00 place, $3.00 show; Faultless, $4.60 show.

Winner—Ch.c. by *Blenheim II—Black Wave, by *Sir Gallahad III., trained by Tom Smith; bred by A. B. Hancock & Mrs. R. A. Van Clief.

Went to Post—4:47½. Off at 4:50½. Central Standard Time.

Start good from stall gate. Won driving; second and third the same. **Jet Pilot,** alertly handled, assumed command at once, made the pace to the stretch under good rating and, responding readily when hard ridden in the drive, lasted to withstand **Phalanx.** The latter, away very sluggishly and outrun during the first half mile, worked his way forward steadily thereafter and, taken out for the stretch run, finished fast and was getting to the winner at the end. **Faultless,** never far back and steadied along to the stretch, responded readily when set down in the drive, then closed strongly in a sharp effort. **On Trust,** forwardly placed from the beginning and in a good effort, failed to rally when roused for the drive and faltered near the finish. **Cosmic Bomb** a sharp factor early, engaged **Jet Pilot** for five furlongs, then weakened. **Star Reward** made a good bid approaching the stretch, then gave way. **Bullet Proof** went evenly and had no mishap. **W L Sickle** was never prominent. **Stepfather,** away slowly, was never a serious factor. **Liberty Road** was far back the entire trip. **Riskolater** was off sluggishly and was never a serious factor. **Double Jay** had brief speed and pulled up sore. **Jett-Jett** unseated his rider at the post, ran off a quarter and showed nothing in the running.

Scratched—(22173) Balheim, 126.

The Winner's Pedigree

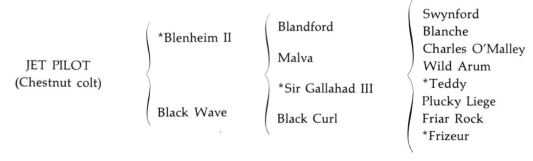

JET PILOT (Chestnut colt)	*Blenheim II	Blandford	Swynford
			Blanche
		Malva	Charles O'Malley
			Wild Arum
	Black Wave	*Sir Gallahad III	*Teddy
			Plucky Liege
		Black Curl	Friar Rock
			*Frizeur

72nd Kentucky Derby, May 4, 1946

$100,000 added and $5,000 Gold Cup. 3-year-olds. Weight for age. Net value to winner $96,400; second $10,000; third $5,000; fourth $2,500. Trainer awards: First $3,000; second $2,000; third $1,000. Breeder awards: First $2,000; second $1,000; third $500.

Horses	Eq't Wt	PP	St	½	¾	1	Str	Fin	Jockeys	Owners	Odds $1 Str't
Assault	wb 126	2	3	5½	4hd	3½	12½	18	Mehrtens	King Ranch	8.20
Spy Song	w 126	6	2	12	1½	1½	22	2hd	Longden	Dixiana	7.80
Hampden	wb 126	17	14	61	5hd	42½	52	31	Jessop	Foxcatcher Farm	5.80
Lord Boswell	w 126	3	1	9½	7½	91½	3½	41½	Arcaro	Maine Chance Farm	‡1.10
Knockdown	w 126	11	4	2½	2½	21½	4½	54	Permane	Maine Chance Farm	‡1.10
Alamond	wb 126	7	8	11½	8½	112	61	61	Kirkland	A C Ernst	65.30
Bob Murphy	wb 126	13	16	13½	11½	62	7½	7½	Bodiou	D Ferguson	†31.80
Pellicle	wb 126	8	11	122	9½	8hd	8hd	81½	Hettinger	H P Headley	16.10
Perf't Bahram	w 126	5	12	153	132	10½	11½	9½	Atkinson	Maine Chance Farm	‡1.10
Rippey	w 126	14	7	4hd	61	5hd	91	101	Zufelt	W Helis	10.20
Jobar	w 126	16	17	17	164	164	164	111½	Layton	H W Fielding	†31.80
Dark Jungle	wb 126	12	6	31½	3hd	7½	10½	122	LoTurco	Lucas B Combs	60.70
Alworth	wb 126	4	10	101	121	13hd	133	13½	Scurlock	Mrs R D Patterson	†31.80
With Pl'sure	wb 126	10	9	7½	101	142	142	14½	Wahler	Brolite Farm	48.30
M'rine V't'ry	wb 126	15	15	141	143	153	15½	151	Padgett	Bobanet Stable	45.00
Wee Admir'l	wb 126	9	5	81½	161	12½	122	163	Watson	R S McLaughlin	59.40
Kendor	wb 126	1	13	166	151	17	17	17	Johnson	Mrs D Hollingsworth	†31.80

‡Coupled, Lord Boswell, Knockdown and Perfect Bahram. †Mutuel field.

Time, :12, :23 2/5, :35 2/5, :48, 1:01 1/5, 1:14 1/5, 1:27 2/5, 1:40 4/5, 1:53 3/5, 2:06 3/5. Track slow.

$2 Mutuels Paid—Assault, $18.40 straight, $9.60 place, $6.80 show; Spy Song, $9.00 place, $6.60 show; Hampden, $5.20 show.

Winner—Ch. c. by Bold Venture—Igual, by Equipoise, trained by M. Hirsch; bred by King Ranch.

Went to Post—5:17. Off at 5:20 Central Daylight Time.

Start good from stall gate. Won driving; second and third the same. **Assault,** forwardly placed and saving ground from the beginning, came through on the inside entering the stretch, quickly disposed of **Spy Song** and drew out to win with little left. **Spy Song** assumed command early, made the pace until reaching the stretch, then gave way to the winner, but continued resolutely to hold **Hampden.** The latter, on the extreme outside at the beginning, raced in the middle of the track the entire trip, was pulled up sharply when his rider misjudged the finish, then came again when roused, but could not better his position. **Lord Boswell,** in hand for six furlongs, was blocked near the upper turn, came again when clear, but could not overhaul the leaders when hard ridden through the stretch. **Knockdown** forced the pace to the mile, then gave way.

The Winner's Pedigree

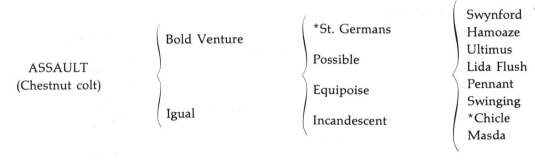

ASSAULT (Chestnut colt)

Bold Venture — *St. Germans (Swynford, Hamoaze); Possible (Ultimus, Lida Flush)

Igual — Equipoise (Pennant, Swinging); Incandescent (*Chicle, Masda)

71st Kentucky Derby, June 9, 1945

$75,000 added and $5,000 Gold Cup. 3-year-olds. Weight for age. Net value to winner $64,850; second $8,000; third $3,000; fourth $1,000. Trainer awards: First $3,000; second $2,000; third $1,000. Breeder awards: First $2,000; second $1,000; third $500.

Horses	Eq't Wt	PP	St	¼	½	¾	Str	Fin	Jockeys	Owners	Odds $1 Str't
Hoop Jr	w 126	12	2	1¹	1¹	1¹	1⁶	1⁶	Arcaro	F W Hooper	3.70
Pot O'Luck	w 126	7	15	14¹½	10½	8²	5²	2¾	Dodson	Calumet Farm	3.30
D'by Dieppe	wb 126	9	16	12ʰᵈ	9¹	6½	3½	3ⁿᵏ	Calvert	Mrs W G Lewis	5.60
Air Sailor	w 126	5	5	5½	5²	3⁴	4²	4⁴	Haas	T D Buhl	20.90
Jeep	wb 126	3	6	7½	7½	5ʰ	6⁴	5³	Kirkland	C V Whitney	6.80
Bymeabond	wb 126	10	1	2½	2³	2½	2ʰ	6³	F A Smith	J K Houssels	†6.80
Sea Swallow	wb 126	2	3	6½	8½	10³	7½	7½	Woolf	Mrs C S Howard	†6.80
Fighting Step	w 126	13	11	4²	4¹	4¹	8¹	8½	South	Murlogg Farm	19.80
Burn'g Dream	w 126	6	7	10½	11½	11⁴	9⁴	9²	Snider	E R Bradley	15.80
Alexis	w 126	11	4	3½	3½	7½	11⁶	10½	Scawth'n	Christiana Stables	12.20
Foreign Ag't	wb 126	4	9	9¹	6ʰᵈ	9½	10½	11⁵	Knott	Lookout Stock Farm	25.90
Misweet	w 121	1	8	8ʰ	13¹	13¹	13⁴	12⁵	Craig	A Rose	†6.80
Tiger Rebel	w 126	8	10	11¹	12⁴	12⁵	12ʰᵈ	13¹½	Layton	Brent & Talbot	†6.80
Bert G	wb 126	14	14	15⁴	15¹⁵	15²⁰	14¹	14¹⁰	Summers	T L Graham	‡†6.80
Jacobe	wb 126	15	12	13¹½	14⁴	14⁴	15²⁰	15⁸	Lindberg	A R Wright	†6.80
Kenilw'th L'd	wb 126	16	13	16	16	16	16	16	Weid'm'n	T L Graham	‡†6.80

†Mutuel field. ‡Coupled, Bert G. and Kenilworth Lad.

Time, :23 1/5, :48, 1:14, 1:41, 2:07. Track muddy.

$2 Mutuels Paid—Hoop Jr., $9.40 straight, $5.20 place, $4.00 show; Pot O' Luck, $4.80 place, $3.60 show; Darby Dieppe, $4.00 show.

Winner—B. c. by *Sir Gallahad III.—One Hour, by *Snob II, trained by I. H. Parke; bred by R. A. Fairbairn.

Went to Post—6:17. Off at 6:22.

Start good from stall gate. Won easily; second and third driving. **Hoop Jr.,** away well, opened up a clear advantage in the first three-sixteenths-mile, was taken in hand to make the pace under a steadying hold to the stretch, responded with much energy when called upon and won with something left. **Pot O' Luck,** away slowly, started up after reaching the final five furlongs, lost ground on the final turn but cut to the inside while closing fast and overtook **Air Sailor** and **Darby Dieppe** in swift succession near the end. **Darby Dieppe** bettered his position gradually from a sluggish start but weakened suddenly near the end. **Air Sailor** went forwardly placed on the outside from the start, rallied only mildly and also faltered in the late stages. **Jeep,** always clear as he raced wide, did not respond when called upon. **Bymeabond,** taken to the inside early, forced the early pace in hand, made a bold bid on the stretch turn but gave way steadily in the last quarter-mile. **Sea Swallow** had no mishap. **Fighting Step** weakened after racing well to the final quarter-mile and swerved in the last furlong. **Burning Dream** raced wide and never threatened. **Alexis,** kept up under pressure, flattened out badly before going a mile. **Foreign Agent** dropped out of contention on the second turn.

The Winner's Pedigree

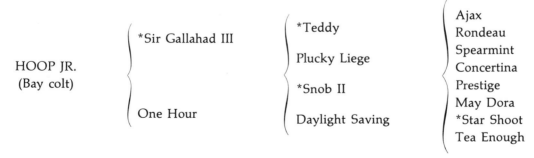

HOOP JR.
(Bay colt)

*Sir Gallahad III

One Hour

*Teddy

Plucky Liege

*Snob II

Daylight Saving

Ajax
Rondeau
Spearmint
Concertina
Prestige
May Dora
*Star Shoot
Tea Enough

70th Kentucky Derby, May 6, 1944

$75,000 added and $5,000 Gold Cup. 3-year-olds. Weight for age. Net value to winner $64,675; second $8,000; third $3,000; fourth $1,000. Trainer awards: First $3,000; second $2,000; third $1,000. Breeder awards: First $2,000; second $1,000; third $500.

Horses	Eq't Wt	PP	St	½	¾	1	Str	Fin	Jockeys	Owners	Odds $1 Str't
Pensive	w 126	4	4	13¹	10ʰ	5½	3½	1⁴½	McCreary	Calumet Farm	7.10
Broadcloth	wb 126	9	7	3½	3²	1½	1ʰ	2¹	Woolf	Mrs G Poulsen	7.40
Stir Up	wb 126	5	5	4¹½	4¹	2²	2ʰ	3ʰ	Arcaro	Greentree Stable	1.40
Shut Up	wb 126	10	12	14³	13¹½	7½	5²	4ʰ	Eccard	Erlanger Stable	†7.70
Brief Sigh	wb 126	13	3	9½	8¹½	3½	4¹½	5¾	Nodarse	River Divide Farm	†7.70
Gay Bit	w 126	7	16	16	16	16	6¹½	6¹	Westrope	Bobanet Stable	25.80
Bell Buzzer	wb 126	3	15	15¹	15³	13²	9²	7¹½	Thompson	D Ferguson	†7.70
Gr'ps Image	wb 126	14	10	11¹	12½	9²	8ʰ	8⁴	Grohs	Mrs A J Abel	20.00
Skytracer	wb 126	2	1	7½	6ʰ	6½	7½	9²	Caffarella	M B Goff	8.40
Chal'nge Me	wb 126	1	2	6¹½	7½	10³	10⁵	10½	W Garner	Brolite Farm	8.90
Alorter	wb 126	6	6	5ʰ	5ʰ	11²	11⁴	11⁵	Adams	A C Ernst	19.50
Comenow	wb 126	16	11	2¹	2¹½	4½	12¹½	12²	Layton	Philip Godfrey	†7.70
Val'y Flares	wb 126	11	14	8½	11¹½	12¹	13²	13²	Burns	B R Patno	†7.70
Diavolaw	wb 126	12	9	1¹	1½	8½	14½	14¹	Molbert	W C Hobson	†7.70
Rock'd Boy	wb 126	8	8	10¹	9ʰ	14¹½	15¹½	15⁵	Bailey	W C Davis	†7.70
Amer. Eagle	wb 126	15	13	12²	14²	15⁴	16	16	Higley	J V Maggio	†7.70

†Mutuel field.

Time, :12, :23 3/5, :35, :47 1/5, 1:12 2/5, 1:25, 1:38 1/5, 1:51 2/5, 2:04 1/5. Track good.

$2 Mutuels Paid—Pensive, $16.20 straight, $7.20 place, $4.60 show; Broadcloth, $6.80 place, $4.60 show; Stir Up, $3.00 show.

Winner—Ch.c. by Hyperion—*Penicuik II, by Buchan, trained by B. A. Jones; bred by Calumet Farm.

Went to Post—5:17. Off at 5:19½. Central War Time.

Start good from stall gate. Won ridden out; second and third driving. **Pensive** worked his way forward on the outside, was sent to the inside when the leaders swung wide approaching the stretch, came willingly when put to strong pressure, wore down the leaders swiftly and won drawing away. **Broadcloth** took command after three-quarters, was unable to draw clear and failed to withstand the winner. **Stir Up** moved forward with **Broadcloth,** was forced to lose some ground when challenging for the lead. **Shut Up** worked his way forward through the field and closed with a rush. **Brief Sigh** tired in the drive.

Scratched—Peace Bells, 121; Autocrat, 126; Comanche Peak, 126.

The Winner's Pedigree

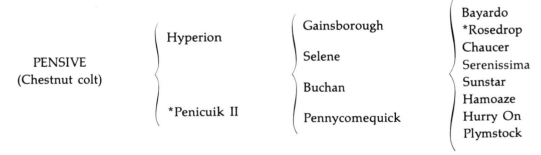

PENSIVE
(Chestnut colt)

Hyperion

*Penicuik II

Gainsborough

Selene

Buchan

Pennycomequick

Bayardo
*Rosedrop
Chaucer
Serenissima
Sunstar
Hamoaze
Hurry On
Plymstock

69th Kentucky Derby, May 1, 1943

$75,000 added and $5,000 Gold Cup. 3-year-olds. Weight for age. Net value to winner $60,725; second $8,000; third $3,000; fourth $1,000. Trainer awards: First $3,000; second $2,000; third $1,000. Breeder awards: First $2,000; second $1,000; third $500.

Horses	Eq't Wt	PP	St	½	¾	1	Str	Fin	Jockeys	Owners	Odds $1 Str't
Count Fleet........	wb 126	5	1	1ʰ	1²	1²	1²	1³	Longden	Mrs J Hertz	.40
Blue Swords.......	wb 126	1	2	4½	4¹½	2¹½	2²	2⁶	Adams	A T Simmons	9.00
Slide Rule.........	wb 126	2	6	6½	3ʰ	4¹½	3³	3⁶	McCreary	W E Boeing	10.80
Amber Light.......	wb 126	7	5	5¹⅓	5³	3½	4²	4½	Robertson	Dixiana	17.50
Bankrupt..........	w 126	6	9	9³	9¹	7½	6½	5¹½	Zufelt	T B Martin	†21.90
No Wrinkles.......	w 126	10	7	8³	7½	6¹	7ʰ	6ʰ	Adair	Milky Way Farm	34.60
Dove Pie..........	wb 126	4	10	10	10	8²	8¹	7³	Eads	J W Rodgers	86.50
Gold Shower.......	w 126	9	4	2⁴	2¹	5³	5½	8¹⁰	Atkinson	V S Bragg	12.10
Modest Lad........	wb 126	3	8	7ʰ	6ʰ	9⁴	9⁴	9⁸	Swain	Mrs H Finch	71.20
Burnt Cork	wb 126	8	3	3¹	8¹½	10	10	10	Gonzalez	E Anderson	†21.90

†Mutuel field.

Time, :12 2/5, :23 1/5, :34 2/5, :48 3/5, :59 2/5, 1:12 3/5, 1:25, 1:37 3/5, 1:50 2/5, 2:04 2/5. Track fast.

$2 Mutuels Paid—Count Fleet, $2.80 straight, $2.40 place, $2.20 show; Blue Swords, $3.40 place, $3.00 show; Slide Rule, $3.20 show.

Winner—Br.c. by Reigh Count—Quickly, by Haste, trained by G. D. Cameron; bred by Mrs. J. Hertz.

Went to Post—5:30½. Off at 5:31½.

Start good from stall gate. Won handily; second and third driving. **Count Fleet** began fast, was hustled along, shook off the bid of **Gold Shower** and won handily. **Blue Swords** was in hand until reaching the last half-mile, came determinedly, but was not good enough. **Slide Rule** was blocked when approaching the final turn and, taken out for the drive, could not reach the leaders. **Amber Light** made a game bid entering the stretch but tired.

Scratched—Twoses, Ocean Wave.

The Winner's Pedigree

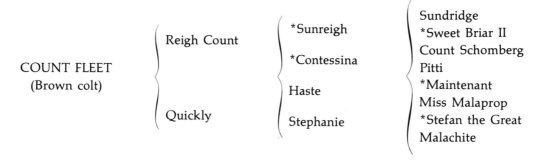

COUNT FLEET
(Brown colt)

Reigh Count — *Sunreigh — Sundridge / *Sweet Briar II

*Contessina — Count Schomberg / Pitti

Quickly — Haste — *Maintenant / Miss Malaprop

Stephanie — *Stefan the Great / Malachite

68th Kentucky Derby, May 2, 1942

$75,000 added and Gold Cup. 3-year-olds. Weight for age. Net value to winner $64,225; second $8,000; third $3,000; fourth $1,000. Trainer awards: First $3,000; second $2,000; third $1,000. Breeder awards: first $2,000; second $1,000; third $500.

Horses	Eq't Wt	PP	St	½	¾	1	Str	Fin	Jockeys	Owners	Odds $1 Str't
Shut Out	w 126	3	1	4²	3¹½	3ʰ	1½	1²¼	Wright	Greentree Stable	‡1.90
Alsab	wb 126	7	5	10¹	8¹	4½	4²	2ʰ	James	Mrs A Sabath	5.10
Val'a Orp'n	wb 126	14	10	2ʰ	2½	2²	2ʰ	3¹½	Bierman	Valdina Farm	§9.90
With Regards	w 126	15	4	1²	1¹	1½	3²	4½	Longden	Mr & Mrs T D Grimes	5.40
First Fiddle	wb 126	2	11	11½	10ʰ	9ʰ	6³	5³	McCreary	Mrs E Mulrenan	†9.20
Devil Diver	wb 126	5	2	5¹½	5¹½	5¹½	5²	6¹½	Arcaro	Greentree Stable	‡1.90
Fair Call	wb 126	1	7	6¹	6¹½	6¹	7¹	7ⁿᵏ	Lingberg	Mill River Stable	†9.20
Dogpatch	wb 126	10	3	3ʰ	4½	7ʰ	8½	8ʰ	Skelly	Milky Way Farm	59.70
Hollywood	w 126	6	14	14⁵	13¹	12²	10¹	9¹	Woolf	Valdina Farm	§9.90
Sw'p S'ger	wb 126	4	15	15	15⁵	13³	11²	10½	Shelhamer	T D Buhl	†9.20
Apache	w 126	13	6	7¹	7½	8½	9¹	11¹	Stout	Belair Stud	16.90
Sir War	wb 126	8	8	9¹½	11½	11²	12⁴	12⁴	Adams	Circle M Ranch	†9.20
Fairy Man'h	wb 126	9	13	12¹	9ʰ	10¹	13²	13⁶	Gilbert	Foxcatcher Farm	39.90
Requested	w 126	12	9	8¹½	12½	14⁶	14⁵	14⁵	Haas	B F Whitaker	5.10
B't a. Spur	wb 126	11	12	13½	15	15	15	15	Craig	E C A Berger	†9.20

†Mutuel field. ‡Coupled as Greentree Stable entry. §Valdina Farm Entry.

Time, :12 1/5, :35 2/5, :47 2/5, 1:00, 1:12 3/5, 1:25 4/5, 1:39, 1:50 4/5, 2:04 2/5. Track fast.

$2 Mutuels Paid—Greentree Entry (Shut Out and Devil Diver), $5.80 straight, $3.40 place, $3.00 show; Alsab, $6.20 place, $4.80 show; Valdina Farm Entry (Valdina Orphan and Hollywood), $5.20 show.

Winner—Ch. c. by Equipoise—Goose Egg, by *Chicle, trained by John M. Gaver; bred by Greentree Stable.

Went to Post—5:31. Off at 5:33.

Start good from stall gate. Won ridden out; second and third driving. **Shut Out,** taken in hand after being hustled along for three-eighths, went close to the pace under smooth rating, responded when called upon and, wearing down the leaders, continued strongly while drawing out through the last eighth. **Alsab,** taken to the outside after a half-mile, started up after three-quarters and closed resolutely to head **Valdina Orphan** in the final stride. **Valdina Orphan** forced a fast pace under clever rating, rallied when placed to strong pressure entering the stretch and held on gamely.

Scratched—First Prize, Sun Again.

The Winner's Pedigree

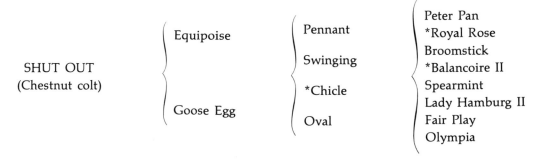

SHUT OUT
(Chestnut colt)

Equipoise
  Pennant
    Peter Pan
    *Royal Rose
  Swinging
    Broomstick
    *Balancoire II

Goose Egg
  *Chicle
    Spearmint
    Lady Hamburg II
  Oval
    Fair Play
    Olympia

67th Kentucky Derby, May 3, 1941

$75,000 added and Gold Cup. 3-year-olds. Weight for age. Net value to winner $61,275; second $8,000; third $3,000; fourth $1,000. Trainer awards: First $3,000; second $2,000; third $1,000. Breeder awards: First $2,000; second $1,000; third $500.

Horses	Eq't Wt	PP	St	½	¾	1	Str	Fin	Jockeys	Owners	Odds $1 Str't
Whirlaway	wb 126	4	6	8^1	$6^{1½}$	4^1	1^3	1^8	Arcaro	Calumet Farm	2.90
Staretor	w 126	2	1	7^2	$4^{1½}$	5^3	$2^½$	2^{nk}	Woolf	H S Nesbitt	36.00
M'rk't Wise	wb 126	7	5	6^2	8^4	6^3	5^3	3^2	Anderson	L Tufano	19.10
Porter's Cap	wb 126	9	4	2^h	3^5	$2^{1½}$	3^h	4^1	Haas	C S Howard	3.30
Little Beans	wb 126	5	10	10^{12}	9^5	8^5	7^2	5^1	Moore	Mrs L Palladino	12.10
Dispose	w 126	11	2	1^2	1^2	1^h	4^h	$6^{1½}$	Bierman	King Ranch	7.20
Blue Pair	wb 126	3	3	3^5	2^h	$3^½$	$6^½$	$7^½$	James	Mrs V S Bragg	20.60
Our Boots	wb 126	10	9	4^3	$5^½$	7^2	8^5	8^3	McCreary	Woodvale Farm	3.90
Rob't Morris	w 126	8	8	$5^{1½}$	7^1	9^6	9^8	9^{12}	Richards	J F Byers	13.90
Valdina Paul	wb 126	6	7	9^3	10^{15}	10^{15}	10^{15}	10^{12}	H Lem'ns	Valdina Farm	†24.30
Swain	wb 126	1	11	11	11	11	11	11	Adams	C Putnam	†24.30

†Mutuel field.

Time, :23 3/5, :46 3/5, 1:11 3/5, 1:37 2/5, 2:01 2/5 (new track record). Track fast.

$2 Mutuels Paid—Whirlaway, $7.80 straight, $5.00 place, $4.40 show; Staretor, $35.20 place, $17.00 show; Market Wise, $10.80 show.

Winner—Ch.c. by *Blenheim II.—Dustwhirl, by Sweep, trained by B. A. Jones; bred by Calumet Farm.

Went to Post—5:53. Off at 5:54½.

Start good and slow. Won easily; second and third driving. **Whirlaway,** eased back when blocked in the first eighth and taken to the inside approaching the first turn, started up after reaching the final half-mile, was taken between horses on the final turn, responded with much energy to take command with a rush and, continuing with much power, drew out fast in the final eighth. **Staretor,** away slowly, made his move gradually, drifted out slightly before straightening up in the stretch and held on well in the final drive. **Market Wise,** also well back early, rallied after reaching the last five-sixteenths and finished with courage. **Porter's Cap,** a strong factor from the start, tired after reaching the last three-sixteenths.

The Winner's Pedigree

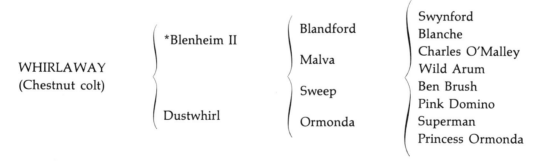

WHIRLAWAY (Chestnut colt)	*Blenheim II	Blandford	Swynford
			Blanche
		Malva	Charles O'Malley
			Wild Arum
	Dustwhirl	Sweep	Ben Brush
			Pink Domino
		Ormonda	Superman
			Princess Ormonda

66th Kentucky Derby, May 4, 1940

$75,000 added and Gold Cup. 3-year-olds. Weight for age. Net value to winner $60,150; second $8,000; third $3,000; fourth $1,000. Trainer awards: First $3,000; second $2,000; third $1,000. Breeder awards: First $2,000; second $1,000; third $500.

Horses	Eq't Wt	PP	St	½	¾	1	Str	Fin	Jockeys	Owners	Odds $1 Str't
Gallahadion........	wb 126	1	4	3^h	2^h	4^1	3^2	$1^{1\frac{1}{2}}$	Bierman	Milky Way Farms	35.20
Bimelech..........	w 126	2	1	$2\frac{1}{2}$	3^h	1^h	$1\frac{1}{2}$	2^n	F A Smith	E R Bradley	.40
Dit...............	wb 126	6	5	4^1	4^1	3^3	$2\frac{1}{2}$	3^1	Haas	W A Hanger	6.70
Mioland..........	wb 126	3	3	5^2	$5\frac{1}{2}$	5^2	4^1	4^2	Balaski	C S Howard	6.40
Sirocco	wb 126	5	6	6^1	6^3	6^5	6^6	5^2	Longden	Dixiana	42.70
Roman...........	wb 126	4	2	$1^{1\frac{1}{2}}$	$1^{1\frac{1}{2}}$	2^h	5^h	6^6	McCombs	J E Widener	24.20
Royal Man........	wb 126	7	7	7^2	7^h	$7\frac{1}{2}$	7^3	7^3	Gilbert	Tower Stable	61.20
Pictor	w 126	8	8	8	8	8	8	8	Woolf	W L Brann	18.00
Photo for second											

Time, :11 3/5, :23 2/5, :35 3/5, :48, 1:02 3/5, 1:12 4/5, 1:25 1/5, 1:38 3/5, 1:51 3/5, 2:05. Track fast.

$2 Mutuels Paid—Gallahadion, $72.40 straight, $13.80 place, $4.80 show; Bimelech, $3.20 place; $2.40 show; Dit, $2.80 show.

Winner—B. c. by *Sir Gallahad III.—Countess Time, by Reigh Count, trained by R. Waldron; bred by R. A. Fairbairn.

Went to Post—4:48. Off at 4:50.

Start good and slow. Won driving; second and third same. **Gallahadion,** away well, moved forward with **Bimelech,** responded to strong urging when wearing down **Bimelech,** drew out, but won with little left. **Bimelech,** first in motion, went wide throughout, moved into command nearing the final quarter-mile, bore out on the stretch turn, held the lead approaching the final furlong, but was unable to hold the winner. **Dit,** steadied along early, was forced wide entering the stretch.

Scratched—True Star.

The Winner's Pedigree

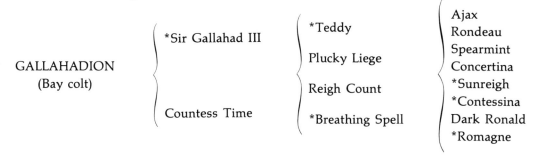

GALLAHADION (Bay colt)	*Sir Gallahad III	*Teddy	Ajax
			Rondeau
		Plucky Liege	Spearmint
			Concertina
	Countess Time	Reigh Count	*Sunreigh
			*Contessina
		*Breathing Spell	Dark Ronald
			*Romagne

65th Kentucky Derby, May 6, 1939

$50,000 added and $5,000 Gold Cup. 3-year-olds. Weight for age. Net value to winner $46,350; second $6,000; third $3,000; fourth $1,000. 115 nominations.

Horses	Eq't Wt	PP	St	½	¾	1	Str	Fin	Jockeys	Owners	Odds $1 Str't
Johnstown	wb 126	5	2	1²	1⁴	1⁴	1⁵	1⁸	Stout	Belair Stud	.60
Challedon	w 126	7	5	7⁵	5½	4⁶	3¹	2¹	Seabo	W L Brann	6.60
H'her Broom	w 126	2	6	4½	6¹	3ʰ	4⁶	3½	James	J H Whitney	12.00
Viscounty	wb 126	3	8	6¹	4¹	2¹	2ʰ	4⁶	Bierman	Valdina Farms	52.20
Technician	wb 126	6	4	5¹	7⁸	5½	5⁵	5⁸	Adams	Woolford Farm	5.80
El Chico	w 126	1	1	2½	2½	6⁴	6³	6³	Wall	W Ziegler Jr	8.20
T M Dors't	wb 126	8	3	3³	3¹	7¹²	7¹⁵	7	Haas	J W Brown	64.90
On Location	wb 126	4	7	8	8	8	8	P. up	Robertson	Milky Way Farms	97.70

Time, :23 2/5, :47 2/5, 1:12 4/5, 1:38, 2:03 2/5. Track fast.

$2 Mutuels Paid—Johnstown, $3.20 straight, $3.00 place, $2.80 show; Challedon, $3.60 place, $3.20 show; Heather Broom, $3.00 show.

Winner—B.c. by Jamestown—La France, by *Sir Gallahad III., trained by J. Fitzsimmons; bred by A. B. Hancock.

Went to Post—4:29. Off at 4:29½.

Start bad and slow. Won easily; second and third driving. **Johnstown** swerved to the inside as he took command, made the pace for a mile, was lightly roused in the stretch and quickly increasing his advantage, won with speed in reserve. **Challedon** was between horses in the early running and began to move up after reaching the last five-eighths. **Heather Broom** dropped back when racing wide on the first turn, rallied after going seven-eighths and outfinished **Viscounty.**

Scratched—Challenge, Xalapa Clown.

The Winner's Pedigree

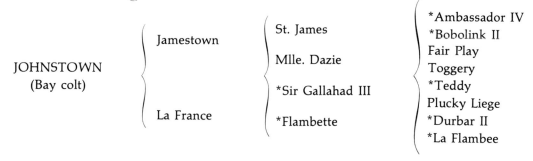

	Jamestown	St. James	*Ambassador IV
			*Bobolink II
JOHNSTOWN		Mlle. Dazie	Fair Play
(Bay colt)			Toggery
	La France	*Sir Gallahad III	*Teddy
			Plucky Liege
		*Flambette	*Durbar II
			*La Flambee

64th Kentucky Derby, May 7, 1938

$50,000 added and $5,000 Gold Cup. 3-year-olds. Weight for age. Net value to winner $47,050; second $6,000; third $3,000; fourth $1,000. 103 nominations.

Horses	Eq't Wt	PP	St	½	¾	1	Str	Fin	Jockeys	Owners	Odds $1 Str't
Lawrin	w 126	1	5	5^h	$5\frac{1}{2}$	2^h	1^3	1^1	Arcaro	Woolford Farm	8.60
Dauber	wb 126	3	10	$9\frac{1}{2}$	$8\frac{1}{2}$	6^4	3^1	2^5	Peters	Foxcatcher Farms	9.70
Can't Wait	wb 126	7	4	4^1	$3^1\frac{1}{2}$	3^3	4^4	3^n	Balaski	M Selznick	24.20
Menow	wb 126	10	7	1^2	$1^1\frac{1}{2}$	$1^1\frac{1}{2}$	2^2	4^{nk}	Workm'n	H P Headley	8.50
The Chief	w 126	9	8	$6\frac{1}{2}$	6^1	5^h	5^4	5^6	Westrope	M Howard	12.00
Fighting Fox	w 126	5	6	2^3	2^h	$4\frac{1}{2}$	6^3	6^3	Stout	Belair Stud	1.40
Co-Sport	wb 126	2	9	$8^1\frac{1}{2}$	9^2	9^5	7^2	7^2	Woolf	B Friend	89.50
Bull Lea	wb 126	6	1	7^4	$7\frac{1}{2}$	8^3	8^1	8^h	Anderson	Calumet Farm	2.90
Elooto	wb 126	4	2	10	10	10	10	9^2	Faust	Blue Ridge Farm	122.30
Mou'n Ridge	w 126	8	3	$3^1\frac{1}{2}$	4^1	7^2	$9^1\frac{1}{2}$	10	Robertson	Milky Way Farms	105.20

Time, :23 1/5, :47 2/5, 1:12 2/5, 1:38 1/5, 2:04 4/5. Track fast.

$2 Mutuels Paid—Lawrin, $19.20 straight, $8.80 place, $4.80 show; Dauber, $12.00 place, $6.00 show; Can't Wait, $8.20 show.

Winner—Br. c. by Insco—Margaret Lawrence, by Vulcain, trained by B. A. Jones; bred by H. M. Woolf.

Went to Post—4:32. Off at 4:36½.

Start good and slow. Won driving; second and third same. **Lawrin**, saving much ground, responded willingly when called upon, came through on the inside when wearing down **Menow**, opened up a commanding advantage approaching the final eighth, then bore out through the last sixteenth, but held **Dauber** safe. The latter, badly outrun early, began to improve his position when racing wide on the stretch turn, continued near the middle of the track while closing with fine speed and was getting to the winner. **Can't Wait**, rated under steady reserve for about three-quarters, outfinished **Menow** in the last stride. The latter made a good pace under steady rating, swerved out on the stretch turn and tired under pressure thereafter. **The Chief** ran an even race. **Fighting Fox** did not respond when urged and gave way badly after a mile.

The Winner's Pedigree

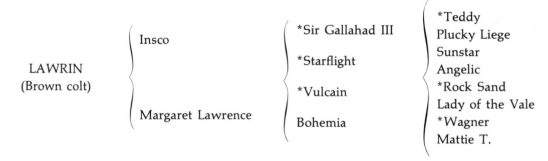

LAWRIN
(Brown colt)

Insco
 *Sir Gallahad III — *Teddy / Plucky Liege
 *Starflight — Sunstar / Angelic

Margaret Lawrence
 *Vulcain — *Rock Sand / Lady of the Vale
 Bohemia — *Wagner / Mattie T.

63rd Kentucky Derby, May 8, 1937

$50,000 added and $5,000 Gold Cup. 3-year-olds. Weight for age. Net value to winner $52,050; second $6,000; third $3,000; fourth $1,000. 103 nominations.

Horses	Eq't Wt	PP	St	½	¾	1	Str	Fin	Jockeys	Owners	Odds $1 Str't
War Admiral	w 126	1	2	$1^{1\frac{1}{2}}$	1^{1}	$1^{1\frac{1}{2}}$	1^{3}	$1^{1\frac{3}{4}}$	Kurts'er	Glen Riddle Farms	1.60
Pompoon	w 126	14	6	5^{2}	4^{1}	2^{2}	2^{5}	2^{8}	Rich'rds	J H Louchheim	8.00
R'g Reward	wb 126	17	7	8½	6½	8^{3}	5^{3}	3^{3}	Rob'tson	Milky Way Farms	‡4.60
Melodist	w 126	3	10	6^{h}	5^{1}	5^{h}	4^{h}	4^{1}	Longden	Wheatley Stable	15.10
Sceneshifter	wb 126	12	13	10½	12½	11^{h}	$7^{1\frac{1}{2}}$	5^{2}	Stout	M Howard	§11.20
Heelfly	w 126	10	1	$3^{1\frac{1}{2}}$	2½	3^{3}	3½	6^{h}	Wright	Three D's Stock F	16.20
Dellor	wb 126	2	4	$7^{1\frac{1}{2}}$	9½	6½	6½	7½	James	J W Parrish	13.70
Burn'g Star	wb 126	15	15	14^{1}	13^{1}	13^{1}	10^{1}	8^{h}	Parke	Shandon Farm	†9.30
C'rt Scandal	wb 126	6	11	12½	8^{h}	9^{3}	12^{1}	9^{1}	Steffen	T B Martin	†9.30
Clodion	wb 126	13	14	13^{2}	14½	12^{2}	9^{h}	10^{1}	Anders'n	W A Carter	†9.30
Fairy Hill	wb 126	4	3	$2^{1\frac{1}{2}}$	3^{3}	4½	$8^{1\frac{1}{2}}$	$11^{1\frac{1}{2}}$	Peters	Foxcatcher Farms	44.60
M'ry Maker	wb 126	7	19	17^{2}	11^{1}	10½	11½	12½	Dabson	Miss E G Rand	†9.30
No Sir	wb 126	19	17	16^{h}	17^{1}	17½	$13^{1\frac{1}{2}}$	13^{h}	LeBlanc	Miss M Hirsch	†9.30
Grey Gold	wb 126	11	18	19^{2}	$19^{1\frac{1}{2}}$	19^{1}	14½	14^{1}	Rosen	E W Duffy	†9.30
Military	wsb 126	5	9	$15^{1\frac{1}{2}}$	15^{1}	15^{1}	15^{1}	15½	Corbett	Milky Way Farms	‡4.60
S'set Trail II	wb 126	18	20	20	20	20	$16^{1\frac{1}{2}}$	16^{2}	Dotter	R Walsh	†9.30
Fencing	wsb 126	8	12	9½	10½	16^{h}	17^{2}	17^{5}	Westr'pe	M. Howard	§11.20
Bernard F	wb 126	16	16	18^{5}	18^{3}	19½	18^{3}	18^{1}	Hardy	I J Collins	†9.30
Sir Damion	wb 126	20	8	11½	16^{h}	14^{3}	19^{4}	19^{12}	Yager	Marshall Field	†9.30
Billionaire	wb 126	9	5	4^{h}	7½	7^{2}	20	20	Woolf	E R Bradley	16.50

†Mutuel field. ‡Coupled in betting as Milky Way Farms entry. §Coupled in betting as M. Howard entry.

Time, :23 1/5, :46 4/5, 1:12 2/5, 1:37 2/5, 2:03 1/5. Track fast.

$2 Mutuels Paid—War Admiral, $5.20 straight, $4.20 place, $3.40 show; Pompoon, $9.40 place, $6.00 show; Reaping Reward (coupled with Military as Milky Way Farms entry), $3.80 show.

Winner—Br.c. by Man o' War—Brushup, by Sweep, trained by G. Conway; bred by S. D. Riddle.

Went to Post—4:42. Off at 4:50½.

Start good and slow. Won easily; second and third driving. **War Admiral,** fractious at post, was away fast, was sent clear of his company, was taken under restraint after racing a quarter-mile, set the pace easily to the final half-mile, increased his advantage gradually on the stretch turn and won in hand. **Pompoon,** forced wide throughout, was reserved off the pace, offered good response when called upon, held on with fine courage, but did not seriously threaten the winner. **Reaping Reward,** in close quarters early, dropped back on the stretch turn, but came again, only to tire in the late stages. **Melodist,** a factor from the start, tired when the real test came. **Sceneshifter** lost much ground on the final turn, then closed well in a splendid effort. **Heelfly,** fractious at the post but away fast, tired in the stretch.

The Winner's Pedigree

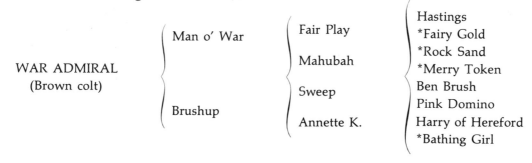

WAR ADMIRAL (Brown colt)	Man o' War	Fair Play	Hastings
			*Fairy Gold
		Mahubah	*Rock Sand
			*Merry Token
	Brushup	Sweep	Ben Brush
			Pink Domino
		Annette K.	Harry of Hereford
			*Bathing Girl

62nd Kentucky Derby, May 2, 1936

$40,000 added and $5,000 Gold Cup. 3-year-olds. Weight for age. Net value to winner $37,725; second $6,000; third $3,000; fourth $1,000. 102 nominations.

Horses	Eq't Wt	PP	St	½	¾	1	Str	Fin	Jockeys	Owners	Odds $1 Str't
Bold Venture	w 126	5	13	8¹½	1¹	1¹½	1¹	1ʰ	Hanford	M L Schwartz	20.50
Brevity	wb 126	10	10	9¹½	6¹½	3¹	2²	2⁶	Wright	J E Widener	.80
Indian Br'm	wb 126	2	7	6ʰ	3²	2¹½	3⁵	3³	Burns	A C T Stock Farm	5.10
Coldstream	w 126	13	6	2ʰ	4¹	5³	5³	4⁵	Wall	Coldstream Stud	15.20
Bien Joli	wb 126	6	2	4ʰ	7¹	6³	6²	5ʰ	Balaski	E R Bradley	14.90
Holl Image	wb 126	14	12	12¹	11¹	11¹½	7³	6⁴	Fisher	Superior Stable	†43.40
He Did	wsb 126	3	1	1²	2½	4⁴	4ʰ	7ʰ	Kurts'g'r	Mrs S B Mason	33.80
Teufel	wb 126	8	9	11½	10¹	8ʰ	8¹	8ʰ	Lit'nb'ger	Wheatley Stable	‡10.60
Gold Seeker	wb 121	12	14	13	12²	10½	10⁴	9⁴	Peters	Foxcatcher Farms	†43.40
Merry Pete	wb 126	1	8	7¹½	8³	7¹	9ʰ	10⁶	Malley	Belair Stud	‡10.60
The Fighter	w 126	7	3	5ʰ	9ʰ	12⁶	11⁴	11⁵	Robertson	Milky Way Farms	§16.50
Grand Slam	wb 126	9	5	3²	5ʰ	9²	12⁸	12¹⁰	Workman	Bomar Stable	19.10
Sangreal	wb 126	11	11	10²	13	13	13	13	Garner	Milky Way Farms	§16.50
Granville	wb 126	4	4	Lost rider.					Stout	Belair Stud	‡10.60

†Mutuel field. ‡Coupled in betting as Wheatley Stable and Belair Stud entry. §Coupled in betting as Milky Way Farms entry.

Time, :23 3/5, :47 4/5, 1:12 3/5, 1:37 4/5, 2:03 3/5. Track fast.

$2 Mutuels Paid—Bold Venture, $43.00 straight, $11.80 place, $6.60 show; Brevity, $5.00 place, $4.00 show; Indian Broom, $3.80 show.

Winner—Ch.c. by *St. Germans—Possible, by Ultimus, trained by M. Hirsch; bred by M. L. Schwartz.

Went to Post—4:41. Off at 4:45½.

Start good and slow. Won driving; second and third same. **Bold Venture,** in close quarters immediately after the start, began to improve his position fast on the outside after about three eighths, took an easy lead approaching the final half-mile and, holding on with fine courage under strong handling, withstood **Brevity's** bid. The latter, probably best and knocked to his knees within a few strides after the start, had to race wide thereafter, closed resolutely and was wearing down the winner. **Indian Broom,** blocked in the first quarter, raced to a contending position, made a bid entering the stretch, then weakened.

Scratched—Banister, Dnieper, Seventh Heaven, Forest Play, Silas.

The Winner's Pedigree

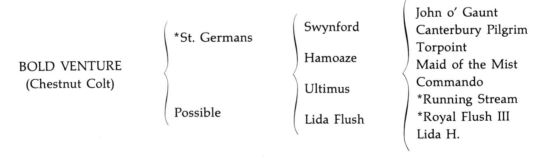

BOLD VENTURE (Chestnut Colt)	*St. Germans	Swynford	John o' Gaunt
			Canterbury Pilgrim
		Hamoaze	Torpoint
			Maid of the Mist
	Possible	Ultimus	Commando
			*Running Stream
		Lida Flush	*Royal Flush III
			Lida H.

222

61st Kentucky Derby, May 4, 1935

$40,000 added and $5,000 Gold Cup. 3-year-olds. Weight for age. Net value to winner $39,525; second $6,000; third $3,000; fourth $1,000. 110 nominations.

Horses	Eq't Wt	PP	St	½	¾	1	Str	Fin	Jockeys	Owners	Odds $1 Str't
Omaha..........	wb 126	10	12	9½	5¹	1²	1¹½	1¹½	Saunders	Belair Stud	4.00
Ro. Soldier	wb 126	3	10	11¹	8¹½	4ʰ	2²	2⁴	Balaski	Sachsenmaier & Reu'r	6.20
Whiskolo	w 126	8	15	12½	10¹½	2¹	3²	3¹½	Wright	Milky Way Farms	†8.40
Nellie Flagg......	w 121	9	1	8¹½	7½	5³	4³	4ʰ	Arcaro	Calumet Farm	3.80
Blackbirder.......	wb 126	13	14	14¹	11¹	11²	5¹	5²	Garner W	Mrs C Hainesworth	†8.40
Psychic Bid.......	wb 126	7	11	4ʰ	4¹	7¹	6³	6⁴	Jones	Brookmeade Stable	49.20
Morpluck........	wsb 126	11	16	16¹	13²	12²	7ʰ	7ʰ	Garner M	J H Louchheim	†8.40
Plat Eye..........	w 126	15	4	1½	1½	3¹	8¹	8¹	Coucci	Greentree Stable	16.40
McCarthy.........	wb 126	4	18	18	15¹	14⁴	14¹	9³	Finnerty	Morrison & Keating	†8.40
Com'nwealth......	wb 126	17	17	17⁴	12¹	9ʰ	10²	10²	Woolf	Mrs W M Jeffords	9.50
Sun Fairplay......	wb 126	5	3	10¹	9¹½	13³	11¹	11³	Renick	Fairfields Stable	52.30
Today............	wb 126	16	6	6¹	6½	8¹	9²	12⁶	Work'an	C V Whitney	8.40
Whopper	wsb 126	2	9	5½	3½	6½	12¹	13¹½	Landolt	H P Headley	†8.40
Bluebeard	wb 126	6	2	7¹	14¹½	15¹	15¹	14¹½	Schutte	Mrs R B Fairbanks	†8.40
Tutticurio........	wb 126	18	13	13ʰ	16⁴	16³	16⁴	15¹	Corbett	Brandon Stable	†8.40
Boxthorn	wb 126	12	8	3½	2¹	10ʰ	13¹	16²	Meade	E R Bradley	5.00
St Bernard	w 126	1	5	2ʰ	18	18	18	17½	Keester	E G Shaffer	†8.40
Weston...........	wb 126	14	7	15ʰ	17¹	17¹	17¹	18	Young	Braedalbane Stable	†8.40

†Mutuel field.

Time, :23, :47 3/5, 1:13 2/5, 1:38 2/5, 2:05. Track good.

$2 Mutuels Paid—Omaha, $10.00 straight, $5.00 place, $3.80 show; Roman Soldier, $6.40 place, $4.20 show; Whiskolo (Field), $3.40 show.

Winner—Ch. c. by Gallant Fox—Flambino, by Wrack, trained by J. Fitzsimmons; bred by Belair Stud.

Went to Post—5:13. Off at 5:15½.

Start good and slow. Won easily; second and third driving. **Omaha** escaped interference in the early crowding, was taken to the outside after the first quarter, raced to the lead gradually after reaching the half-mile post and held sway thereafter, winning easily. **Roman Soldier** worked his way to the outside after reaching the backstretch, responded well when called upon, but could not menace the winner. **Wiskolo** raced to a contending position with a rush, lost ground on the far turn and tired in the last three-sixteenths. **Nellie Flag** suffered interference soon after the start, was again impeded on the first turn and could not improve her position when clear in the last five-sixteenths.

Scratched—Color Bearer, Chanceview, Prince Splendor, Calumet Dick.

The Winner's Pedigree

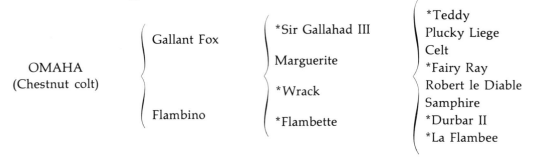

OMAHA (Chestnut colt)
- Gallant Fox
  - *Sir Gallahad III
    - *Teddy
    - Plucky Liege
  - Marguerite
    - Celt
    - *Fairy Ray
- Flambino
  - *Wrack
    - Robert le Diable
    - Samphire
  - *Flambette
    - *Durbar II
    - *La Flambee

60th Kentucky Derby, May 5, 1934

$30,000 added and $5,000 Gold Cup. 3-year-olds. Weight for age. Net value to winner $28,175; second $5,000; third $2,500; fourth $1,000. 124 nominations.

Horses	Eq't Wt	PP	St	½	¾	1	Str	Fin	Jockeys	Owners	Odds $1 Str't
Cavalcade	w 126	8	11	7^1	$5^{1/2}$	3^1	2^3	$1^{2\,1/2}$	Garner	Brookmeade Stable	‡1.50
Discovery	wb 126	6	4	3^2	$3^{1/2}$	1^2	1^{nk}	2^4	Bejshak	A G Vanderbilt	12.10
Agrarian	w 126	9	7	$10^{1/2}$	$8^{1/2}$	8^1	5^h	3^n	Kurts'g'r	Mrs F J Heller	14.90
Mata Hari	wb 121	3	1	1^h	1^h	2^h	3^4	4^n	Gilbert	Dixiana	6.30
Peace Ch'nce	w 126	2	12	$12^{1\,1/2}$	10^h	$9^{1/2}$	6^1	$5^{1\,1/2}$	Wright	J E Widener	9.70
Spy Hill	w 126	11	10	9^1	$7^{1/2}$	7^h	7^2	6^4	Coucci	Greentree Stable	33.30
Time Clock	wb 126	1	13	13	11^6	11^8	12^{10}	7^h	Bellizzi	Brookmeade Stable	‡1.50
Sing'g Wood	w 126	7	5	$4^{1/2}$	$4^{1/2}$	$4^{1/2}$	$4^{1/2}$	8^h	Jones	Mrs J H Whitney	24.10
Bazaar	w 121	12	9	6^1	$6^{1/2}$	$6^{1/2}$	8^2	9^6	Meade	E R Bradley	5.10
Speedmore	w 126	5	2	8^h	$9^{1/2}$	$10^{1/2}$	$10^{1\,1/2}$	$10^{1\,1/2}$	Horn	J H Louchheim	†10.40
Sgt. Byrne	wb 126	10	6	2^3	2^2	$5^{1\,1/2}$	9^4	11^3	Renick	J Simonetti	†10.40
Sir Thomas	wb 126	4	8	$11^{1\,1/2}$	13	12^4	11^2	12^{10}	Pascuma	A B Gordon	36.20
Quasimodo	wb 126	13	3	5^1	$12^{1/2}$	13	13	13	Burke	Mrs B Franzheim	†10.40

†Mutuel field. ‡Coupled in betting as Brookmeade Stable entry.

Time, :23, :47 1/5, 1:12 1/5, 1:37 2/5, 2:04. Track fast.

$2 Mutuels Paid—Cavalcade (coupled with Time Clock as Brookmeade Stable entry), $5.00 straight, $4.00 place, $3.20 show; Discovery, $9.20 place, $5.80 show; Agrarian, $5.00 show.

Winner—Br.c. by *Lancegaye—*Hastily, by Hurry On, trained by R.A. Smith; bred by F.W. Armstrong.

Went to Post—5:13. Off at 5:21½.

Start good and slow. Won handily; second and third driving. **Cavalcade,** away slowly, was not permitted to make up much ground for a half-mile, then began moving up leaving the backstretch, where he came through between horses, wore down **Discovery** and drew out for a handy win. **Discovery,** away fast, drew into an easy lead approaching the stretch, and held on well, but was overmatched. **Agrarian** closed resolutely.

Scratched—Riskulus, Blue Again, Prince Pompey, Fogarty, Thomasville, Howard.

The Winner's Pedigree

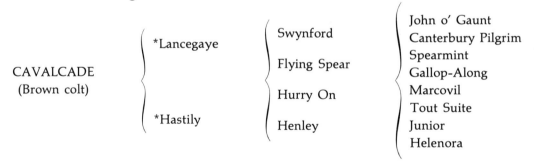

CAVALCADE
(Brown colt)

*Lancegaye
 Swynford
  John o' Gaunt
  Canterbury Pilgrim
 Flying Spear
  Spearmint
  Gallop-Along

*Hastily
 Hurry On
  Marcovil
  Tout Suite
 Henley
  Junior
  Helenora

59th Kentucky Derby, May 6, 1933

$50,000 added and $5,000 Gold Cup. 3-year-olds. Weight for age. Net value to winner $48,925; second $6,000; third $3,000; fourth $1,000. 118 nominations.

Horses	Eq't Wt	PP	St	½	¾	1	Str	Fin	Jockeys	Owners	Odds $1 Str't
Brokers Tip	wb 126	11	11	11^1	8½	4^2	2^{1}½	1^n	Meade	E R Bradley	8.93
Head Play	w 126	7	5	3½	1½	1^1	1^h	2^4	Fisher	Mrs S B Mason	5.64
Charley O	wb 126	1	6	7^h	6^1	2^{1}½	3^4	3^{1}½	Corbett	R M Eastman Estate	6.02
Ladysman	wb 126	4	7	5½	7^3	5^{1}½	5^{1}½	4^n	Workm'n	W R Coe	‡1.43
Pomponious	w 126	12	12	10½	9½	6½	6^3	5^3	Bejshak	W R Coe	‡1.43
Spicson	wb 126	9	13	13	12^3	10^{1}½	7^1	6^{1}½	Fischer	L M Severson	†25.85
Kerry P'tch	wb 126	5	1	6^{1}½	5½	3^h	4^h	7^2	Schaefer	L Rosenberg	26.89
Mr. Khayyam	w 126	13	9	9^1	11^3	9^h	9^2	8½	Walls	Catawba Stable	§4.09
Inlander	wb 126	6	8	8^2	10^2	8^1	8^2	9^{1}½	Bellizzi	Brookmeade Stable	44.27
Strideaway	wb 126	8	4	12½	13	12^3	10^3	10^5	Beck	Three D's Stock Farm	†25.85
Dark Win'r	wb 126	3	10	4^2	4^h	7^2	11^8	11^{12}	Jones	W S Kilmer	†25.85
Isaiah	wb 126	10	2	2^{1}½	3½	11^2	12^8	12	McCros'n	J W Parrish	66.86
G'd Advice	wb 126	2	3	1^h	2^h	13	13	P. up.	Legere	Catawba Stable	§4.09

†Mutuel field. ‡Coupled in betting as W. R. Coe entry. §Coupled in betting as Catawba Stable entry.

Time, :23 1/5, :47 1/5, 1:12 4/5, 1:40 2/5, 2:06 4/5. Track good.

$2 Mutuels Paid—Brokers Tip, $19.86 straight, $6.28 place, $4.54 show; Head Play, $5.52 place, $4.08 show; Charley O., $3.84 show.

Winner—Br.c. by Black Toney—*Forteresse, by Sardanapale, trained by H. J. Thompson; bred by Idle Hour Stock Farm.

Went to Post—5:10. Off at 5:18.

Start good out of machine. Won driving; second and third same. **Brokers Tip,** much the best, began slowly, saved ground when leaving backstretch, but lost some on the stretch turn, then went to the inside and, overcoming interference, was up to win in the final strides after a long and tough drive. **Head Play,** rated close to the pace, went to front easily, bore out when increasing his lead on the stretch turn and bumped the winner. **Charley O.,** in hand for three-quarters, challenged gamely, then tired, but held **Ladysman** safe. The latter raced wide most of the way and failed to rally when hard urged.

Scratched—Pompoleon, Sarada, Fingal, Warren Jr., Captain Red, Boilermaker, Silent Shot, At Top, Fair Rochester.

The Winner's Pedigree

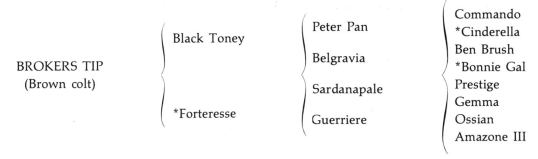

BROKERS TIP (Brown colt)	Black Toney	Peter Pan	Commando
			*Cinderella
		Belgravia	Ben Brush
			*Bonnie Gal
	*Forteresse	Sardanapale	Prestige
			Gemma
		Guerriere	Ossian
			Amazone III

58th Kentucky Derby, May 7, 1932

$50,000 added and $5,000 Gold Cup. 3-year-olds. Weight for age. Net value to winner $52,350; second $6,000; third $3,000; fourth $1,000. 115 nominations.

Horses	Eq't Wt	PP	St	½	¾	1	Str	Fin	Jockeys	Owners	Odds $1 Str't
Burgoo King	w 126	13	4	3^1	3^2	2^3	1^4	1^5	James	E R Bradley	‡5.62
Economic	wb 126	10	2	1^2	$1^{1½}$	1^h	$2^{1½}$	2^h	Horn	J H Louchheim	16.93
Stepenf'chit	wb 126	4	12	$9^½$	5^1	$4^{1½}$	4^1	$3^½$	Ensor	Mrs J H Whitney	§3.28
Br'don Mint	wb 126	11	3	$2^½$	2^h	3^1	3^h	4^n	Ellis	Brandon Stable	†6.68
Over Time	wb 126	5	13	13^h	8^2	6^3	5^h	5^n	Sande	Mrs J H Whitney	§3.23
Tick On	wb 126	6	14	12^1	10^2	5^2	6^6	6^4	Wall	Loma Stable	1.84
Our Fancy	wb 126	3	1	4^h	$7^½$	8^2	7^h	7^1	Allen	J B Respess	†6.68
Gallant Sir	wb 126	19	18	$11^{1½}$	6^h	7^3	8^2	8^2	Woolf	Northway Stable	†6.68
Hoops	wb 126	8	9	14^2	11^2	10^4	9^1	$9^½$	Fischer	W F Knebelkamp	28.62
Cold Check	wb 126	12	5	$7^½$	4^h	9^1	10^2	$10^{1½}$	Garner W	J W Parrish	45.88
Adobe Post	wb 126	7	20	$16^½$	15^h	16^h	13^1	11^3	Landolt	Knebelkamp & Morris	28.52
Crys'l Prince	w 126	1	8	20	14^1	12^h	$12^½$	12^3	Corbett	P C Thompson	†6.68
Oscillation	w 121	2	7	6^1	9^h	11^1	11^h	13^2	Neal	Longridge Stable	†6.68
Pr Hotspur	wb 126	17	16	18^1	16^1	17^2	16^2	$14^{1½}$	And'son	J Leiter Estate	78.37
Cee Tee	w 126	14	11	15^1	18^2	15^h	15^1	15^4	McCros'n	Dixiana	†6.68
Cathop	w 126	20	19	19^1	$17^{1½}$	18^8	17^2	$16^½$	Pichon	R M Eastman	†6.68
Lucky Tom	wb 126	16	17	8^h	13^2	14^1	14^1	17^8	Pasc'ma	J J Robinson	10.64
Thistle Ace	wb 126	9	10	$10^½$	19	19	19	18^8	Elston	G Collins	†6.68
Brother Joe	w 126	18	6	5^h	12^h	13^1	18^h	19	Fator	E R Bradley	‡5.62
Lib Limited	wb 126	15	15	17^h	Broke down				Garner M	Three D's Stock Farm	†6.68

†Mutuel field. ‡Coupled in betting as E. R. Bradley entry. §Coupled in betting as Mrs. J. H. Whitney entry.

Time, :24 1/5, :48 1/5, 1:13, 1:38 4/5, 2:05 1/5. Track fast.

$2 Mutuels Paid—Burgoo King (coupled with Brother Joe as E. R. Bradley entry), $13.24 straight, $5.08 place, $4.00 show; Economic, $15.62 place, $8.54 show; Stepenfetchit (coupled with Over Time as Mrs. J. H. Whitney entry), $3.52 show.

Winner—Ch. c. by Bubbling Over—Minawand, by Lonawand, trained by H. J. Thompson; bred by H. N. Davis and Idle Hour Stock Farm.

Went to Post—5:04. Off at 5:19½.

Start good out of machine. Won easily; second and third driving. **Burgoo King,** away fast and well rated, followed the pace closely until reaching the final three-eighths, where he easily wore down **Economic** and won easily. **Economic** set the pace under good rating, was no match for the winner, but outlasted **Stepenfetchit.** The latter saved ground in the early stages, was under restraint until reaching the closing half-mile and rallied mildly when taken to the outside in the stretch.

The Winner's Pedigree

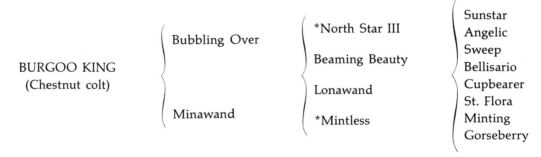

BURGOO KING
(Chestnut colt)

- Bubbling Over
  - *North Star III
    - Sunstar
    - Angelic
  - Beaming Beauty
    - Sweep
    - Bellisario
- Minawand
  - Lonawand
    - Cupbearer
    - St. Flora
  - *Mintless
    - Minting
    - Gorseberry

57th Kentucky Derby, May 16, 1931

$50,000 added and $5,000 Gold Cup. 3-year-olds. Weight for age. Net value to winner $52,350; second $6,000; third $3,000; fourth $1,000. 130 nominations.

Horses	Eq't Wt	PP	St	½	¾	1	Str	Fin	Jockeys	Owners	Odds $1 Str't
Tw'y Grand	wb 126	5	9	10^{1}½	6^1	2^2	1^1	1^4	Kurts'er	Greentree Stable	‡.88
Sweep All	wb 126	1	10	4^1	3^{1}½	1½	2^3	2^3	Coltiletti	Dixiana	26.96
Mate	w 126	10	11	7^h	4^h	3^h	3^4	3^4	Ellis	A C Bostwick	2.83
Spanish Play	w 126	6	4	8^{1}½	8^1	6^{1}½	5^2	4^{1}½	Allen	Knebelkamp & Morris	45.09
Boys Howdy	w 126	7	3	2^1	5^1	5^1	4^h	5^6	Riley	H C Hatch	23.26
Insco	wb 126	12	6	9^h	11^1	8^3	6^3	6^1	O'Donnell	G Watkins	†22.91
Pittsburgher	w 126	9	7	11^3	10^1	9½	8^h	7^h	Corbett	Shady Brook F S'ble	8.49
The Mongol	w 126	3	1	5^h	9^h	11^1	9½	8^1	McCoy	Hamburg Place	†22.91
Ladder	wb 126	4	2	3½	1½	4^3	7^1	9^h	Schaefer	W J Salmon	26.00
An's Aweigh	wb 126	2	12	12	12	10^{1}½	10^6	10^2	Steffen	Greentree Stable	‡.88
Surf Board	w 126	8	8	6^h	7^1	7½	11½	11^8	Watters	Greentree Stable	‡.88
Pr D'Amour	wb 126	11	5	1^h	2½	12	12	12	James	J Leiter	76.23

†Mutuel field. ‡Coupled in betting as Greentree Stable entry.

Time, :23 1/5, :47 2/5, 1:12, 1:37 2/5, 2:01 4/5, (new track record). Track fast.

$2 Mutuels Paid—Twenty Grand (coupled with Anchors Aweigh and Surf Board as Greentree Stable entry) $3.76 straight, $3.00 place, $2.60 show; Sweep All, $15.58 place, $7.16 show; Mate, $3.62 show.

Winner—B.c. by *St. Germans—Bonus, by *All Gold, trained by J. Rowe, Jr.; bred by Greentree Stable.

Went to Post—5:02. Off at 5:03½

Start good out of machine. Won easily; second and third driving. **Twenty Grand,** slow to begin, was sent up slowly after a half, raced strongly on the outside and, wearing down **Sweep All,** drew away fast and won with speed in reserve. **Sweep All** broke slowly, but saved ground, followed the leaders in the backstretch, raced into a good lead on the stretch turn, but could not withstand the winner's rush. **Mate** improved his position fast in the first quarter, saved ground on the second turn, but failed to rally under vigorous driving in the stretch. **Spanish Play** closed with good courage.

Scratched—Equipoise, Up, Don Leon.

The Winner's Pedigree

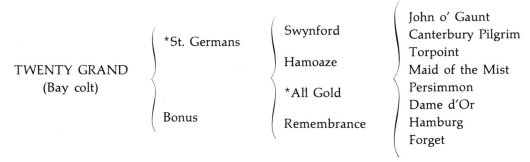

			John o' Gaunt
TWENTY GRAND (Bay colt)	*St. Germans	Swynford	Canterbury Pilgrim
		Hamoaze	Torpoint
			Maid of the Mist
	Bonus	*All Gold	Persimmon
			Dame d'Or
		Remembrance	Hamburg
			Forget

56th Kentucky Derby, May 17, 1930

$50,000 added and $5,000 Gold Cup. 3-year-olds. Weight for age. Net value to winner $50,725; second $6,000; third $3,000; fourth $1,000. 150 nominations.

Horses	Eq't Wt	PP	St	½	¾	1	Str	Fin	Jockeys	Owners	Odds $1 Str't
Gallant Fox	wb 126	7	8	4¹	1¹	1²	1²	1²	Sande	Belair Stud	1.19
Gal't Knight	wb 126	8	7	7¹	6½	3³	2½	2²	Schutte	Audley Farm	22.73
Ned O.	w 126	3	3	12½	13ʰ	9½	4ʰ	3¹	Mooney	G W Foreman	25.79
Gone Away	wb 126	10	14	14½	11½	7½	5²	4⁴	M Garner	W Zeigler Jr	52.92
C'k Brigade	ws 126	6	13	6¹	4ⁿᵏ	2ʰ	3ʰ	5½	Ellis	T M Cassidy	16.62
Longus	wb 126	1	15	15	14⁴	10ʰ	7¹	6²	O'Brien	R C Stable	†18.12
Uncle Luther	w 126	2	12	8½	8ʰ	6½	6¹	7²	Creese	L Stivers	†18.12
Tannery	w 126	12	2	3¹	3¹	5ʰ	8½	8ʰ	W Garner	E F Prichard	3.12
B'y Limited	wb 126	14	11	10½	12½	12²	10²	9½	Walls	Three D's Stock Farm	‡50.43
Alcibiades	w 126	4	4	1²	2½	4ʰ	9ʰ	10ʰ	Jones	H P Headley	†18.12
Kilkerry	w 126	9	9	11½	10ʰ	11½	11⁴	11⁶	May	Three D's Stock Farm	‡50.43
Br'z'g Thru	wb 126	13	6	13¹	9²	14ʰ	13¹	12⁵	Smith	E R Bradley	§8.75
B'keye Poet	wb 126	15	5	2ʰ	5½	8½	12²	13¹	Legere	E R Bradley	§8.75
High Foot	w 126	5	1	5ʰ	7¹	13½	14⁸	14⁸	Meyer	Valley Lake Stable	22.88
Dick O'Hara	w 126	11	10	9²	15	15	15	15	Barrett	P H Joyce	†18.12

†Mutuel field. ‡Coupled as Three D's Stock Farm Stable entry. §E. R. Bradley entry.

Time, :23 3/5, :47 4/5, 1:14, 1:40 4/5, 2:07 3/5. Track good.

$2 Mutuels Paid—Gallant Fox, $4.38 straight, $3.76 place, $3.42 show; Gallant Knight, $14.60 place, $8.78 show; Ned O., $10.14 show.

Winner—B.c. by *Sir Gallahad III.—Marguerite, by Celt, trained by J. Fitzsimmons; bred by Belair Stud.

Went to Post—5:00. Off at 5:02½.

Start good out of machine. Won easily; second and third driving. **Gallant Fox,** in extremely close quarters for the first three-eighths, raced into the lead on the outside after straightening out in the backstretch, held command under restraint thereafter and won with something in reserve. **Gallant Knight** began slowly, worked his way up with a big loss of ground, offered a mild challenge entering the final eighth, but tired badly near the end. **Ned O.** began improving his position after five-eighths, lost ground on the last turn, but finished resolutely. **Gone Away,** on the extreme outside throughout, moved up fast on the stretch turn, but quit in the final eighth.

Scratched—Busy, 126.

The Winner's Pedigree

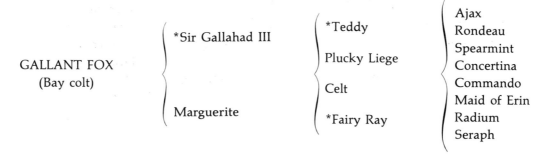

GALLANT FOX
(Bay colt)

*Sir Gallahad III

Marguerite

*Teddy

Plucky Liege

Celt

*Fairy Ray

Ajax
Rondeau
Spearmint
Concertina
Commando
Maid of Erin
Radium
Seraph

55th Kentucky Derby, May 18, 1929

$50,000 added and $5,000 Gold Cup. 3-year-olds. Weight for age. Net value to winner $53,950; second $6,000; third $3,000; fourth $1,000. 159 nominations.

Horses	Eq't Wt	PP	St	½	¾	1	Str	Fin	Jockeys	Owners	Odds $1 Str't
C V Dusen	wb 126	20	7	$1^{1/2}$	1^3	1^2	1^3	1^2	McAtee	H P Gardner	3.00
Naishapur	wb 126	4	2	12^h	12^2	8^3	$5^{1/2}$	2^3	Allen	Wilshire Stable	5.57
Panchio	wb 126	13	1	4^2	3^3	2^h	$2^{1/2}$	3^n	Coltiletti	Three D's Stock Farm	†§8.44
Blue Larkspur	w 126	21	4	3^h	$4^{1/2}$	$5^{1/2}$	3^h	$4^{1/2}$	M Garner	E R Bradley	‡1.71
Windy City	w 126	19	9	8^h	8^1	7^3	$8^{1/2}$	5^h	Pool	F M Grabner	22.84
Voltear	wb 126	1	8	5^h	5^2	6^h	7^h	6^h	O'Donnell	Dixiana	18.42
The Nut	wb 126	18	3	17^1	10^1	4^h	6^1	7^1	Robertson	Warm Stable	40.62
Folking	wb 126	14	18	2^3	$2^{1/2}$	$3^{1/2}$	4^3	8^1	Pascuma	H T Archibald	†8.44
Karl Eitel	wb 126	10	16	7^1	$7^{1/2}$	9^h	9^h	9^4	Jones	J J Coughlin	28.80
Upset Lad	w 126	5	13	$10^{1/2}$	17^1	14^1	13^1	10^6	Chiavetta	Belle Isle Stable	†8.44
Calf Roper	wb 126	9	15	16^1	15^1	10^3	10^3	11^h	Hardy	Three D's Stock Farm	†§8.44
Minotaur	wb 126	7	14	10^1	9^2	11^2	$11^{1/2}$	12^h	Halbert	J R Thompson	30.80
Bay Beauty	wb 126	15	10	11^1	$11^{1/2}$	12^h	17^1	13^4	Horvath	E R Bradley	‡1.71
Chicatie	wb 126	3	12	14^1	14^h	13^1	13^1	$14^{1/2}$	W Garner	Fair Stable	87.09
Paul Buny'n	wb 126	12	17	19^2	19^1	18^2	15^1	$15^{1/2}$	Clelland	L M Severson	†8.44
Essare	wb 126	6	5	$6^{1/2}$	6^1	15^h	14^1	16^3	Connelly	Jacques Stable	†8.44
L B'd'lbane	wb 126	8	11	13^1	13^1	16^1	16^2	17^2	Crump	D Breckinridge	†8.44
Ben M'hree	wb 126	16	21	20^3	18^h	17^1	18^1	18^1	Abel	CC &G Y Hieatt	†8.44
Chip	wb 126	11	20	21	20^3	19^3	19^3	19^6	Heupel	Mrs E L Swikard	†8.44
Prince Pat	wb 126	17	19	18^h	21	21	20^4	20^4	Laidley	Three D's Stock Farm	†§8.44
Paraphrase	wb 126	2	6	$9^{1/2}$	16^h	20^1	21	21	Fronk	H P Headley	†8.44

†Mutuel field. ‡Coupled in betting as E. R. Bradley entry. §Coupled in betting as Three D's Stock Farm entry.

Time, :24, :49, 1:15 2/5, 1:42 4/5, 2:10 4/5. Track muddy.

$2 Mutuels Paid—Clyde Van Dusen, $8.00 straight, $3.70 place, $3.06 show; Naishapur, $4.72 place, $3.26 show; Panchio (coupled with Calf Roper as Three D's Stock Farm entry and in the field), $3.50 show.

Winner—Ch.g. by Man o' War—Uncle's Lassie, by Uncle, trained by C. Van Dusen; bred by H. P. Gardner.

Went to Post—4:58. Off at 5:11.

Start good and slow. Won easily; second and third driving. **Clyde Van Dusen** took the lead after the first quarter, saved ground while setting the pace and responded to light shaking up to the stretch to hold his opponents safe. **Naishapur**, slow to start and racing wide, began moving up after going five-eighths and, after being blocked in the stretch, where he swerved, finished with a rush when clear. **Panchio** was prominent for the entire race and, benefited by a strong ride, outfinished **Blue Larkspur**. The latter ran well to the stretch turn, where he dropped back, but came again gamely after going to the inside in the stretch and just failed to get up for third place. **Windy City** raced well and held on gamely. **Voltear** tired in the final drive. **Ben Machree** finished with a rush. **Karl Eitel** tired. **Minotaur** was always far back. **Essare** showed early speed. **Folking** was done after reaching the stretch.

Scratched—Ervast, 126; Boris, 126; The Choctaw, 126; St. Ignatius, 126; Hiram Kelly, 126.

The Winner's Pedigree

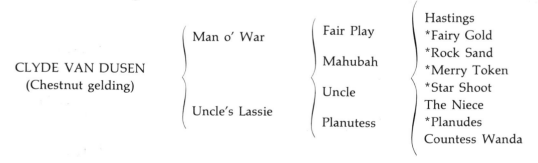

CLYDE VAN DUSEN
(Chestnut gelding)

Man o' War
- Fair Play
  - Hastings
  - *Fairy Gold
- Mahubah
  - *Rock Sand
  - *Merry Token

Uncle's Lassie
- Uncle
  - *Star Shoot
  - The Niece
- Planutess
  - *Planudes
  - Countess Wanda

54th Kentucky Derby, May 19, 1928

$50,000 added and $5,000 Gold Cup. 3-year-olds. Weight for age. Net value to winner $55,375; second $6,000; third $3,000; fourth $1,000. 196 nominations.

Horses	Eq't Wt	PP	St	½	¾	1	Str	Fin	Jockeys	Owners	Odds $1 Str't
Reigh Count	w 126	4	3	5ʰ	5ʰ	2¹½	1ʰ	1³	Lang	Mrs J Hertz	‡2.06
Misstep	w 126	1	1	1¹	1¹	1¹½	2⁴	2²	Garner	Le Mar Stock Farm	10.20
Toro	w 126	7	6	6ʰ	6ʰ	3½	3½	3⁴	Ambrose	E B McLean	4.75
Jack Higgins	w 126	8	7	8²	7²	4ʰ	4⁶	4¹½	Allen	W J Curran	†4.42
Reigh Olga	w 126	5	4	7½	8½	7¼	5⅜	5²	Pool	O Lehmann	‡2.06
Lawley	w 126	9	15	16¹	16½	9½	6⁵	6²	Thurber	Viking Stable	†4.42
Don Q.	w 126	2	20	20¹	20¹	22	7¹	7²	Walls	Sagamore Stable	†4.42
Bobashela	w 126	20	11	11¹	11¹	5ʰ	11¹	8²	Fisher	Audley Farm	§12.08
Blackwood	wb 126	10	2	2¹½	2¹½	8½	8¹	9½	Chiavetta	Bloomfield Stable	†4.42
M'tie Flynn	wb 126	6	5	3¹	3¹½	6²	16¹	10ʰ	Fronk	S Peabody	14.18
Sun Beau	wb 126	18	16	18¹	18¹	14¹	10¹	11ʰ	Craigmyle	W S Kilmer	38.42
Bar None	wb 126	13	19	21¹	21¹	12¹	9²	12½	Kederis	Longridge Stable	†4.42
Distraction	wb 126	19	21	22	22	19¹	17½	13¹	McAuliffe	Wheatley Stable	11.51
Petee-Wr'k	wb 126	15	17	14¹	14¹	10¹	18¹	14³	Johnson	J R Macomber	†4.42
Typhoon	wb 126	17	22	19½	19²	18¹	12²	15¹	Barnes	Kenton Farm Stable	41.21
Replevin	wb 126	11	9	12ʰ	12ʰ	16¹	13¹	16¹	Peterson	F Johnson	†4.42
Cartago	wb 126	3	10	9¹	9¹	15¹	19²	17ʰ	Horvath	R E Leichleiter	†4.42
Bonivan	126	21	8	4ʰ	4ʰ	20⁴	15²	18²	Landolt	A A Kaiser	†4.42
Charmarten	wb 126	22	18	17½	17¹	13½	14½	19²	Butwell	Wild Rose Farm Stable	†4.42
Vito	126	12	13	10½	10½	11¹	20¹	20²	Kummer	A H Cosden	¶39.04
Sortie	wb 126	14	12	15¹	15¹	17½	21⁸	21¹²	Weiner	A C Schwartz	¶39.04
Strolling Player	126	16	14	12ʰ	13ʰ	21ʰ	22	22	Fields	Salubria Stable	§12.08

†Mutuel field. ‡Coupled in betting as Mrs. J. D. Hertz and O. Lehmann entry. §Coupled in betting as Audley Farm Stable and Salubria Stable entry. ¶Coupled in betting as A. H. Cosden and A. C. Schwartz entry.

Time, :24 1/5, :49 3/5, 1:15 4/5, 1:43 2/5, 2:10 2/5. Track heavy.

$2 Mutuels Paid—Reigh Count (coupled with Reigh Olga as Mrs J. D. Hertz and O. Lehmann entry), $6.12 straight, $5.78 place, $3.98 show; Misstep, $8.28 place, $5.90 show; Toro, $3.76 show.

Winner—Ch.c. by *Sunreigh—*Contessina, by Count Schomberg, trained by B. S. Michell; bred by Willis Sharpe Kilmer.

Went to Post—5:05. Off at 5:11.

Start good and slow. Won easily; second and third driving. **Reigh Count** was ridden vigorously in the early running and responded nobly, racing into a forward position in the first half-mile, then forced the pace and, under strong riding in the stretch, took the lead and drew away to win with speed in reserve. **Misstep** began fast next to the inner rail, showed fine speed and, setting a fast pace for the going, finished well, but was easily held safe. **Toro** suffered slightly from some interference, but when clear in the stretch came steadily and was running fast at the end.

Scratched—Colonel Shaw, 126; Mop Up, 126; Rumpelstiltskin, 126; Dowagiac, 126.

The Winner's Pedigree

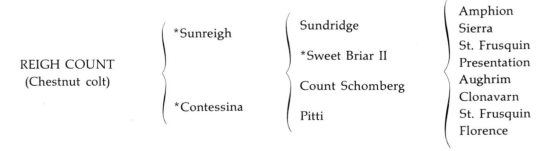

REIGH COUNT
(Chestnut colt)

*Sunreigh
— Sundridge — Amphion / Sierra
— *Sweet Briar II — St. Frusquin / Presentation

*Contessina
— Count Schomberg — Aughrim / Clonavarn
— Pitti — St. Frusquin / Florence

53rd Kentucky Derby, May 14, 1927

$50,000 added and $5,000 Gold Cup. 3-year-olds. Weight for age. Net value to winner $51,000; second $6,000; third $3,000; fourth $1,000. 162 nominations.

Horses	Eq't Wt	PP	St	½	¾	1	Str	Fin	Jockeys	Owners	Odds $1 Str't
Whiskery ....wb 126		7	6	5^h	3^h	$3^{1½}$	3^2	1^h	McAtee	H P Whitney	‡2.40
Osmand...........w 126		10	4	2^1	2^3	2½	1^h	$2^{1½}$	Sande	J E Widener	§6.90
Jock..............w 126		1	3	1^5	1^5	1½	2½	3^1	Lang	E B McLean	¶37.80
Hydromel........wsb 126		5	8	6^h	7^1	4^{nk}	4½	4^h	W Garner	J N Camden	16.00
Bostonian ....w 126		12	11	9^2	8½	7½	6^4	5^4	Abel	H P Whitney	‡2.40
B'dy Bauer ....wb 126		4	10	10^{nk}	$9^{1½}$	5^3	$5^{1½}$	6^2	G Johns'n	Idle Hour Stock Farm	‖15.40
Royal Julian ....w 126		2	1	$7^{1½}$	5^h	6½	7^{nk}	7^4	Lilley	W H Whitehouse	†14.70
Fred Jr...........wb 126		13	15	15	14^2	9^1	9^3	8^6	Burger	S W Grant	18.30
Scapa Flow........wb 126		15	7	3^h	4½	8^2	8½	9^2	Coltiletti	W M Jeffords	7.00
Bl. Panther ....wb 126		6	5	8^h	10^1	10^1	10^1	10^8	Schaefer	W J Salmon	†14.70
Kiev...............wb 126		8	14	11^h	11^2	12^2	12^2	11^2	M Garner	J E Widener	§6.90
R. Stocking.......wb 126		3	2	$4^{1½}$	6^h	11½	11^2	12^3	Pool	J W Parrish	4.70
Rip Rap ....wb 126		11	13	12^1	12^1	13^4	14^4	13^4	O'Donnell	Sage Stable	11.60
Bewithus ....wb 126		9	9	13½	15	14^2	13^1	14^5	A Johnson	Idle Hour Stock Farm	‖15.40
War Eagle........wb 126		14	12	14½	13^2	15	15	15	Ambrose	E B McLean	¶37.80

†Mutuel field. ‡H. P. Whitney entry, §J. E. Widener entry, ¶E. B. McLean entry; ‖Idle Hour Stock Farm entry.

Time, :23 1/5, :47 1/5, 1:12 2/5, 1:38 4/5, 2:06. Track slow.

$2 Mutuels Paid—Whiskery (coupled with Bostonian as H. P. Whitney entry), $6.80 straight, $3.80 place, $3.40 show; Osmond (coupled with Kiev as J. E. Widener entry), $6.40 place, $5.80 show; Jock (coupled with War Eagle as E. B. McLean entry), $14.20 show.

Winner—Br.c. by Whisk Broom II—Prudery, by Peter Pan, trained by F. Hopkins; bred by H. P. Whitney.

Went to Post—5:09. Off at 5:11.

Start good and slow. Won driving; second and third same. **Whiskery** moved up steadily, though racing a trifle wide and, holding on gamely, wore down **Osmand** in the last sixteenth. The latter, always well up for the entire distance, held on much gamer than expected in the final drive. **Jock** began fast, showed high speed but tired in the last eighth. **Hydromel** showed a fine performance and continued gamely in the stretch. **Bostonian** was far out of it for a half-mile and closed a big gap. **Buddy Bauer** also closed a big gap from a slow beginning.

Scratched—Saxon, 126; My Son, 126; Mr. Kirkwood, 126.

The Winner's Pedigree

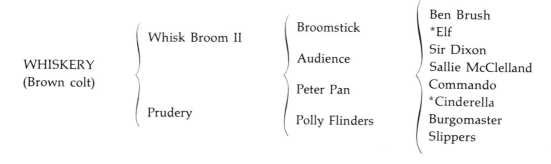

WHISKERY (Brown colt)	Whisk Broom II	Broomstick	Ben Brush
			*Elf
		Audience	Sir Dixon
			Sallie McClelland
	Prudery	Peter Pan	Commando
			*Cinderella
		Polly Flinders	Burgomaster
			Slippers

52nd Kentucky Derby, May 15, 1926

$50,000 added and $5,000 Gold Cup. 3-year-olds. Weight for age. Net value to winner $50,075; second $6,000; third $3,000; fourth $1,000. 164 nominations.

Horses	Eq't Wt	PP	St	½	¾	1	Str	Fin	Jockeys	Owners	Odds $1 Str't
Bub'g Over	wb 126	11	1	1^1	1^1	1^1	1^2	1^5	Johnson	Idle Hour Stock Farm	†1.90
B'g'nbag'ge	wb 126	3	3	7^h	6^2	5^5	2^1	2^3	Blind	Idle Hour Stock Farm	†1.90
Rock Man	w 126	2	2	3^h	3^3	2^h	3^4	3^n	Coltiletti	Sagamore Stable	42.10
Rhinock	w 126	12	8	8^h	10^h	9^1	5^5	4^4	Garner	Parkview Stable	14.60
Pompey	w 126	9	5	$2½$	2^h	3^h	$4½$	5^2	Fator	W R Coe	2.10
Espino	wb 126	6	6	9^1	5^h	7^2	7^4	6^6	Smith	W Zeigler Jr	39.70
Light C'bine	wb 126	1	4	6^h	11^1	10^h	8^1	7^5	Griffin	I B Humphreys	61.00
Canter	w 126	8	11	4^h	4^h	4^h	6^2	8^2	Turner	J E Griffith	24.10
Blondin	wsb 126	4	9	10^1	$7½$	11^1	9^1	9^h	McAtee	H P Whitney	9.30
Display	wb 126	10	13	12^5	12^8	8^2	11^1	10^h	Maiben	W J Salmon	16.20
Recollection	wb 126	7	12	13	13	12^1	12^1	11^h	Callahan	Kohn & Theisen	†11.40
Ch'p de Mars	w 126	5	7	5^h	8^1	$6½$	$10½$	12^1	Pool	Keeneland Stud Farm	†11.40
Rovcrofter	w 126	13	10	11^1	9^1	12^4	13	13	Scobie	G F Croissant	†11.40

†Mutuel field. ‡Coupled in betting as Idle Hour Stock Farm Stable entry.

Time, :23, :47, 1:12 1/5, 1:38 1/5, 2:03 4/5. Track fast.

$2 Mutuels Paid—E. R. Bradley's Idle Hour Stock Farm Stable entry (Bubbling Over and Bagenbaggage), $5.80 straight, $5.80 place, $4.60 show; Rock Man, $30.00 show.

Winner—Ch.c. by *North Star III.—Beaming Beauty, by Sweep, trained by H. J. Thompson; bred by Idle Hour Stock Farm.

Went to Post—5:05. Off at 5:09 New York Time.

Start good and slow. Won easily; second and third driving. **Bubbling Over** raced into the lead at once and setting a great pace under restraint, showed the way until the stretch, where his rider permitted him to sprint away from the others and win away off by himself. **Bagenbaggage,** began slowly but, making up ground gamely, passed the others and finished a fast-going second. **Rock Man** raced prominently from the start, but was tiring and just lasted to save third place. **Rhinock** came with a surprisingly rush near the end. **Pompey** was done after racing well for three-quarters and had no mishap. **Espino** raced well. **Canter** was close up for most of the way, but quit in the stretch.

Scratched—Boot to Boot, 126; Take a Chance, 126; Bolton, 126; Rasuli, 126.

The Winner's Pedigree

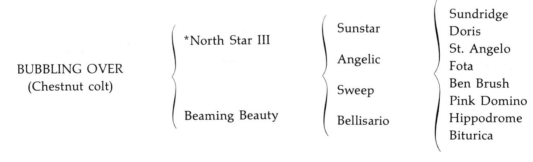

BUBBLING OVER
(Chestnut colt)

*North Star III

Beaming Beauty

Sunstar

Angelic

Sweep

Bellisario

Sundridge
Doris
St. Angelo
Fota
Ben Brush
Pink Domino
Hippodrome
Biturica

51st Kentucky Derby, May 16, 1925

$50,000 added and $5,000 Gold Cup. 3-year-olds. Weight for age. Net value to winner $52,775; second $6,000; third $3,000; fourth $1,000. 139 nominations.

Horses	Eq't Wt	PP	St	½	¾	1	Str	Fin	Jockeys	Owners	Odds $1 Str't
Fly'g Ebony	wb 126	6	4	$1^{1/2}$	$2^{1/2}$	2^3	1^h	$1^{1 1/2}$	Sande	G A Cochran	†3.15
Captain Hal	w 126	11	5	$2^{1 1/2}$	$1^{1 1/2}$	1^h	$2^{1/2}$	2^n	Heupel	A A Kaiser	5.60
Son of John	w 126	12	8	3^h	3^2	3^2	3^2	3^4	Turner	D W Scott	‡16.40
Single Foot	w 126	3	1	5^1	$5^{1 1/2}$	$4^{1/2}$	$4^{1/2}$	4^1	Johnson	J E Griffith	30.15
Step Along	wsb 126	9	7	$6^{1/2}$	6^h	6^h	5^1	5^2	Pool	F M Grabner	‡16.40
Swope	wb 126	4	9	8^h	7^2	7^1	6^1	6^n	Legere	H C Fisher	†3.15
P of B'rbon	wb 126	14	15	9^2	$10^{1/2}$	8^1	7^1	$7^{1/2}$	Schut'ger	Lexington Stable	§†3.15
Needle Gun	wb 126	2	3	4^h	$4^{1/2}$	$9^{1/2}$	9^1	8^5	Ponce	W Zeigler Jr	†3.15
Ky. Cardinal	w 126	13	10	10^1	11^1	10^1	8^h	9^h	Garner	G F Croissant	7.50
B. Compan'n	w 126	19	16	11^1	14^2	11^1	10^1	10^h	Ambrose	S A Cowan	†3.15
B'way Jones	w 126	8	11	$12^{1/2}$	13^1	12^1	12^h	11^{nk}	Meyer	Idle Hour Stock Farm	50.85
Quatrain	wb 126	17	13	14^1	12^1	14^2	13^1	$12^{1/2}$	Bruening	F Johnson	1.95
Almadel	wb 126	20	17	19^1	9^1	13^1	14^2	13^4	McD'm't	H P Headley	26.45
Backbone	w 126	18	18	18^1	19^1	16^2	15^2	14^2	McAtee	H P Whitney	¶16.20
Sw'p'g Away	w 126	10	19	13^2	18^1	15^1	17^1	$15^{1 1/2}$	Robinson	Xalapa Farm Stable	§†3.15
Elector	wb 126	7	20	20	20	20	$19^{1/2}$	16^2	Mooney	La Brae Stable	†3.15
The Bat	wb 126	1	6	15^1	15^h	17^1	16^1	$17^{1 1/2}$	Parke	H P Whitney	¶16.20
Lee O Cot'r	wb 126	15	12	7^1	$8^{1/2}$	$5^{1/2}$	11^4	18^6	Fronk	R W Collins	†3.15
Voltaic	w 126	16	14	$16^{1/2}$	16^1	18^1	18^2	19^{20}	Coltiletti	R L Gerry	160.75
Chief Uncas	w 126	5	2	17^1	17^1	19^1	20	20	McCleary	A A Busch	†3.15

†Mutuel field. ‡D. W. Scott and F. M. Grabner entry; §Lexington Stable and Xalapa Farm Stable entry; ¶H. P. Whitney entry.

Time, :23 2/5, :47 3/5, 1:12 3/5, 1:39 3/5, 2:07 3/5. Track sloppy.

$2 Mutuels Paid—Flying Ebony (Field), $8.30 straight, $3.80 place, $2.80 show; Captain Hal, $5.50 place, $4.40 show; Son of John (coupled with Stepalong as D. W. Scott and F. M. Grabner entry), $5.50 show.

Winner—Blk.c. by The Finn—Princess Mary, by Hessian, trained by W. B. Duke; bred by J. E. Madden.

Went to Post—4:32. Off at 4:36.

Start good and slow. Won easily; second and third driving. **Flying Ebony,** well ridden and away forwardly, set the early pace, then followed **Captain Hal** closely and, after a sharp drive through the stretch outstayed the latter and won going away. **Captain Hal** showed fine speed and raced into a good lead, but tired slightly and appeared to have suffered from some interference when **Flying Ebony** came over in the last eighth. **Son of John** raced prominently all the way and was in close quarters through the last eighth. **Single Foot** raced well all the way. **Step Along** closed a considerable gap. **Swope** raced well. **Quatrain** began slowly and was far back all the way. **Almadel** was always outrun. **Kentucky Cardinal** was always beaten. **Needle Gun** ran fairly well.

Scratched—Reminder, 126; Chantey, 126; Reputation, 126; King Nadi, 126; Elsass, 126.

The Winner's Pedigree

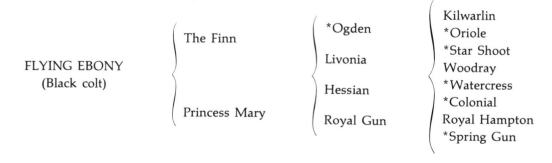

			Kilwarlin
		*Ogden	*Oriole
	The Finn		*Star Shoot
		Livonia	Woodray
FLYING EBONY			*Watercress
(Black colt)		Hessian	*Colonial
	Princess Mary		Royal Hampton
		Royal Gun	*Spring Gun

50th Kentucky Derby, May 17, 1924

$50,000 added and $5,000 Gold Cup. 3-year-olds. Weight for age. Net value to winner $52,775; second, $6,000; third, $3,000; fourth, $1,000. 152 nominations.

Horses	Eq't Wt	PP	St	½	¾	1	Str	Fin	Jockeys	Owners	Odds $1 Str't
Black Gold	w 126	1	3	5h	6h	3½	3²	1½	Mooney	Mrs R M Hoots	1.75
Chilhowee	w 126	13	6	4¹	3h	4¹½	1h	2n	Johnson	Gallaher Bros	15.25
Beau Butler	wb 126	10	8	15h	11nk	10¹	10h	3h	Lyke	Idle Hour Stock Farm	‡10.25
Altawood	w 126	7	19	19	14¹	7⁴	5²	4h	McDer'tt	C B Head	19.10
Bracadale	wb 126	12	4	1½	1³	1²	2½	5⁸	Sande	Rancocas Stable	§3.40
Transmute	w 126	2	1	6¹	4h	2²	4³	6h	McAtee	H P Whitney	¶10.25
Revenue Ag't	w 126	5	9	10½	8¹	8h	7¹	7h	Hurn	G A Cochran	26.75
Thorndale	wb 126	6	11	7¹	7¹½	5³	6½	8²	Marinelli	B Block	†10.70
Klondyke	w 126	3	13	8h	10h	9¹	9⁴	9⁴	Parke	H P Whitney	¶10.25
Mad Play	wb 126	9	14	11h	9½	6½	8h	10½	Fator	Rancocas Stable	§3.40
K'g Gorin II	w 126	4	12	12²	17²	12¹	13¹	11²	Garner	P Coyne	36.60
Cann'n Shot	wb 126	8	18	18¹½	19	11½	12¹	12¹½	Ellis	C A Hartwell	†10.70
Modest	ws 126	16	15	13¹	18²	14h	11½	13¹	Wallace	E B McLean	†10.70
Diogenes	w 126	15	10	16h	15¹	13¹	14¹	14²	Ponce	Mrs W M Jeffords	†10.70
Nautical	w 126	19	7	9h	16h	15¹	15h	15½	Lang	J S Cosden	†10.70
Mr Mutt	w 126	17	17	17¹	13½	17¹	16¹	16²	Merimee	H C Fisher	35.00
Baffling	wb 126	18	2	2½	2½	16½	17h	17¹	Carroll	Idle Hour Stock Farm	‡10.25
Wild Aster	w 126	11	5	3¹	5¹	18¹	18²	18⁴	Coltiletti	Greentree Stable	†10.70
Bob Tail	w 126	14	16	14¹	12½	19	19	19	Blind	Idle Hour Stock Farm	‡10.25

†Mutuel field. ‡Coupled in betting as Idle Hour Stock Farm Stable entry. §Coupled in betting as Rancocas Stable entry. ¶Coupled in betting as H. P. Whitney entry.

Time, :23 2/5, :47 3/5, 1:13, 1:39 1/5, 2:05 1/5. Track fast.

$2 Mutuels Paid—Black Gold, $5.50 straight, $5.40 place, $4.40 show; Chilhowee, $12.30 place, $7.30 show; E. R. Bradley's Idle Hour Stock Farm Stable entry (Beau Butler, Baffling and Bob Tail), $4.70 show.

Winner—Blk.c. by Black Toney—Useeit, by Bonnie Joe, trained by H. Webb; bred by Mrs. R. M. Hoots.

Went to Post—4:43. Off at 4:45.

Start good and slow. Won driving; second and third same. **Black Gold,** well ridden and prominent in the early racing, moved up resolutely after reaching the stretch and disposed of the others in the last seventy yards. **Chilhowee** ran a good race and headed **Bracadale** in the last eighth, but tired slightly near the end. **Beau Butler** closed a great gap and ran an excellent race. **Altawood** closed an immense gap after making a slow beginning. **Bracadale** tired after leading to the stretch. **Transmute** was done after going the first three-quarters. **Mad Play** was always outrun. **Baffling** ran a good three-quarters. The others were never prominent.

Scratched—Glide, 121.

The Winner's Pedigree

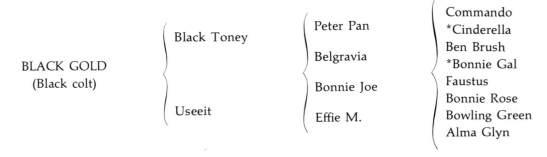

			Commando
		Peter Pan	*Cinderella
	Black Toney		Ben Brush
		Belgravia	*Bonnie Gal
BLACK GOLD			Faustus
(Black colt)		Bonnie Joe	Bonnie Rose
	Useeit		Bowling Green
		Effie M.	Alma Glyn

234

49th Kentucky Derby, May 19, 1923

$50,000 added. 3-year-olds. Weight for age. Net value to winner $53,600 and $5,000 gold cup; second $6,000; third $3,000; fourth $1,000. 145 nominations.

Horses	Eq't Wt	PP	St	½	¾	1	Str	Fin	Jockeys	Owners	Odds $1 Str't
Zev	wb 126	10	5	1^2	1^2	$1\frac{1}{2}$	1^2	$1^{1\frac{1}{2}}$	Sande	Rancocas Stable	19.20
Martingale	wb 126	19	12	2^2	$2\frac{1}{2}$	2^h	2^1	2^1	Kummer	J S Cosden	‡19.75
Vigil	wb 126	5	14	$10\frac{1}{2}$	8^1	$6\frac{1}{2}$	5^1	3^1	Marinelli	W J Salmon	15.25
Nassau	w 126	8	4	3^1	3^h	$3^{1\frac{1}{2}}$	3^1	4^n	Garner	F Johnson	3.25
Chittagong	wb 126	1	2	9^2	7^1	4^1	6^1	$5^{1\frac{1}{2}}$	Heupel	J Hertz	†5.85
Enchantm't	wb 126	11	11	6^h	4^1	$5\frac{1}{2}$	$4\frac{1}{2}$	6^2	McAtee	H P Whitney	§2.30
Rialto	w 126	17	15	$12\frac{1}{2}$	10^1	8^h	$7\frac{1}{2}$	7^2	Coltiletti	Greentree Stable	§2.30
Aspiration	wb 126	9	7	7^1	$5\frac{1}{2}$	7^{nk}	9^1	$8^{1\frac{1}{2}}$	Kennedy	B Block	††29.20
Prince K.	w 126	4	1	4^1	$9\frac{1}{2}$	9^h	$11\frac{1}{2}$	$9\frac{1}{2}$	Kelsay	Marshall Bros	†5.85
Br't Tom'w	wb 126	7	3	14^h	11^2	10^{nk}	8^1	$10\frac{1}{2}$	Ponce	Idle Hour Stock Farm	28.05
In Memoriam	w 126	21	10	11^h	$12\frac{1}{2}$	$11\frac{1}{2}$	16^1	$11\frac{1}{2}$	Mooney	C Weidemann	†5.85
Bo McMillan	w 126	20	8	5^1	6^3	12^1	15^h	12^1	Connelly	T J Pendergast	11.95
Better Luck	w 126	6	18	8^1	15^1	14^h	$17\frac{1}{2}$	13^1	Johnson	B Block	††29.20
Wida	w 126	12	9	15^1	$13\frac{1}{2}$	13^h	14^h	14^8	Yerrat	T E Mueller	†5.85
Picketer	w 126	18	16	13^1	14^2	15^1	$10\frac{1}{2}$	15^2	Corcoran	H P Whitney	§2.30
Gen Thatch'r	w 126	16	17	16^1	16^2	17^1	13^1	16^2	Rob'son	Nevada Stock Farm	12.80
Calcutta	wb 126	14	13	18^1	17^1	$16\frac{1}{2}$	$19\frac{1}{2}$	17^1	Yeargin	G R Allen	†5.85
The Clown	w 126	2	21	$17\frac{1}{2}$	19^2	19^1	$18\frac{1}{2}$	18^4	Lunsf'rd	Audley Farm	†5.85
Golden Rule	w 126	15	6	19^1	$18\frac{1}{2}$	18^h	$12\frac{1}{2}$	19^{10}	Lang	J S Cosden	‡19.75
Cherry Pie	w 126	3	20	21	21	20^1	20^4	20^2	Penman	Greentree Stable	§2.30
Pravus	wb 126	13	19	20^1	$20\frac{1}{2}$	21	21	21	Owens	F Wieland	†5.85

†Mutuel field. ‡Coupled in betting as J. S. Cosden entry. §Coupled in betting as Greentree Stable and H. P. Whitney entry. ††Coupled in betting as B. Block entry.

Time, :23 2/5, :47 2/5, 1:12 2/5, 1:39, 2:05 2/5. Track fast.

$2 Mutuels Paid—Zev, $40.40 straight, $30.60 place, $18.40 show; J. S. Cosden entry (Martingale and Golden Rule), $25.80 place, $16.60 show; Vigil, $12.30 show.

Winner—Br.c. by The Finn—Miss Kearney, by *Planudes, trained by D. J. Leary; bred by J. E. Madden.

Went to Post—4:47. Off at 4:53.

Start good and slow. Won easily; second and third driving. **Zev** broke forwardly and, showing high speed, raced into a good lead at once and, withstanding a drive through the stretch, gamely held **Martingale** safe at the end. **Martingale** was in closest pursuit nearly throughout and held his position well in the stretch drive. **Vigil** began slowly and had to race wide, but closed a big gap and may have been best. **Nassau** raced well and saved much ground on the last turn. **Chittagong** ran a fine race. **Enchantment** tired. **Rialto** closed a big gap. **Prince K.** quit. **Beau McMillan** was away poorly. **Cherry Pie** had little chance from the start.

Scratched—Anna M. Humphrey, 121; Chickvale, 126; Everhart, 126.

The Winner's Pedigree

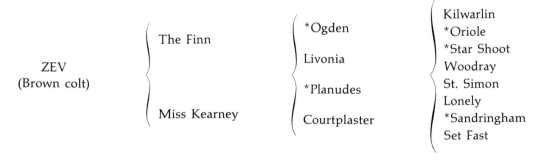

			Kilwarlin
		*Ogden	*Oriole
	The Finn		*Star Shoot
		Livonia	Woodray
ZEV			St. Simon
(Brown colt)		*Planudes	Lonely
	Miss Kearney		*Sandringham
		Courtplaster	Set Fast

48th Kentucky Derby, May 13, 1922

$50,000 added, also $5,000 gold cup and $2,000 other gold trophies. 3-year-olds. Weight for age. Net value to winner $46,775; second $6,000; third $3,000; fourth $1,000. 92 nominations.

Horses	Eq't Wt	PP	St	½	¾	1	Str	Fin	Jockeys	Owners	Odds $1 Str't
Morvich	w 126	4	2	$1^{1}\frac{1}{2}$	$1^{1}\frac{1}{2}$	$1^{1}\frac{1}{2}$	$1^{1}\frac{1}{2}$	$1^{1}\frac{1}{2}$	Johnson	B Block	1.20
Bet Mosie	w 126	7	8	$8\frac{1}{2}$	6^3	$5\frac{1}{2}$	4^1	2^h	Burke	Idle Hour Stock Farm	†2.90
John Finn	ws 126	1	4	5^1	5^1	6^2	2^h	3^1	Pool	G F Baker	22.60
Deadlock	w 126	6	6	4^1	$4\frac{1}{2}$	$4^{1}\frac{1}{2}$	3^h	4^4	Mooney	R H Shannon	6.90
My Play	w 126	3	1	2^h	2^h	3^1	5^2	5^4	Rob'son	Lexington Stable	19.05
Letterman	w 126	9	9	$7\frac{1}{2}$	$7\frac{1}{2}$	7^1	7^1	6^1	Rice	Greentree Stable	24.80
Surf Rider	w 126	8	7	6^1	8^1	$8^{1}\frac{1}{2}$	8^1	$7\frac{1}{2}$	Scobie	Montfort Jones	35.75
Startle	w 121	2	3	3^2	3^1	2^h	$6\frac{1}{2}$	8^{nk}	Connelly	H H Hewitt	13.90
By Gosh	w 126	10	10	9	9	9	9	9	Barnes	Idle Hour Stock Farm	†2.90
Busy Amer'n	wb 126	5	5	Broke down					Barrett	Idle Hour Stock Farm	†2.90

†Coupled in betting as Idle Hour Stock Farm Stable entry.

Time, :23 4/5, :47 3/5, 1:13, 1:39 1/5, 2:04 3/5. Track fast.

$2 Mutuels Paid—Morvich, $4.40 straight, $4.30 place, $3.50 show; E. R. Bradley's Idle Hour Stock Farm Stable entry (Bet Mosie, By Gosh, and Busy American), $2.90 place, $2.70 show; John Finn, $6.60 show.

Winner—Br.c. by Runnymede—Hymir, by Dr. Leggo, trained by F. Burlew; bred by A. B. Spreckels.

Went to Post—4:50. Off at 4:53.

Start good and slow. Won easily; second and third driving. **Morvich** ran as if he outclassed the others, was kept in the lead under hard restraint for the first mile and drew away in the stretch to win under a pull. **Bet Mosie** was ridden wide on the turns and lost much ground, but closed a big gap and finished gamely. **John Finn** raced prominently all the way and finished resolutely. **Deadlock** raced well, but tired in the last quarter. **My Play** ran well, but finished quite lame. **Startle** was done after going three-quarters. **Busy American** broke down in the first quarter.

Scratched—Banker Brown, 126.

The Winner's Pedigree

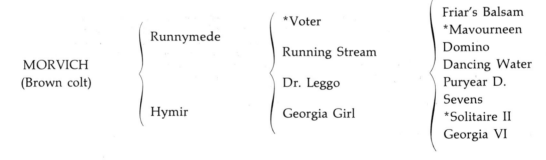

	Runnymede	*Voter	Friar's Balsam
MORVICH			*Mavourneen
(Brown colt)		Running Stream	Domino
			Dancing Water
	Hymir	Dr. Leggo	Puryear D.
			Sevens
		Georgia Girl	*Solitaire II
			Georgia VI

47th Kentucky Derby, May 7, 1921

$50,000 added. 3-year-olds. Weight for age. Net value to winner $38,450 and $5,000 gold cup; second $10,000; third $5,000; fourth $2,000. 109 nominations.

Horses	Eq't Wt	PP	St	½	¾	1	Str	Fin	Jockeys	Owners	Odds $1 Str't
Behave Y'self	w 126	1	9	8½	8¹	6½	1½	1ʰ	Thomp'n	E R Bradley	†8.65
Bl'k Servant	w 126	7	2	1¹	1ʰ	1½	2½	2⁶	Lyke	E R Bradley	†8.65
Prudery	w 121	2	4	5½	4½	3ʰ	3ʰ	3½	Kummer	H P Whitney	‡1.10
Tryster	w 126	10	8	6ʰ	5½	5ʰ	4¹	4⁴	Coltiletti	H P Whitney	‡1.10
Careful	w 121	3	7	4ʰ	3ʰ	4ʰ	5²	5⁴	Keogh	W J Salmon	13.60
Coyne	w 126	5	3	7²	6ʰ	7²	7¹	6¹	Garner	Harned Bros	11.20
Leonardo II	w 126	4	5	3½	2³	2½	6½	7½	Schut'r	Xalapa Farm Stable	§4.30
Uncle Velo	ws 126	12	1	11¹	10²	9¹½	8²	8²	Pool	G F Baker	65.30
Bon Homme	wb 126	11	6	10¹	11⁶	11²	10¹	9⁶	Rob'son	Xalapa Farm Stable	§4.30
Planet	wb 126	6	12	12	12	12	11¹½	10⁵	King	H P Headley	81.30
Star-Voter	w 126	8	11	9¹	7¹	8ʰ	9²	11¹	Ensor	J K L Ross	8.55
Muskall'nge	wb 126	9	10	2¹	9¹	10¹	12	12	Carroll	H C Fisher	96.25

†Coupled in betting as E. R. Bradley entry. ‡Coupled in betting as H. P. Whitney entry. §Coupled in betting as Xalapa Farm Stable entry.

Time, :23 1/5, :46 4/5, 1:11 3/5, 1:38 3/5, 2:04 1/5. Track fast.

$2 Mutuels Paid—E. R. Bradley entry (Behave Yourself and Black Servant), $19.30 straight, $13.00 place, $5.60 show; H. P. Whitney entry (Prudery and Tryster), $3.30 show.

Winner—Br.c. by Marathon—Miss Ringlets, by Handball, trained by H. J. Thompson; bred by E. R. Bradley.

Went to Post—4:50. Off at 4:56.

Start good and slow. Won driving; second and third same. **Behave Yourself** began slowly, but saved much ground on the last two turns and, gaining steadily in the stretch, outstayed **Black Servant** in a game finish. The latter showed fine speed in pacemaking and disposed of **Leonardo II.** before going three-quarters, then held on well in the final drive, but tired near the end. **Prudery** made a wide turn into the stretch and finished gamely. **Tryster** was far back in the early running, but finished fast and gaining. **Leonardo II.** tired after going well for the first mile. **Careful** was done after going three-quarters. **Coyne** ran fairly well.

Scratched—Gray Lag, 126; Billy Barton, 126; Firebrand, 126.

The Winner's Pedigree

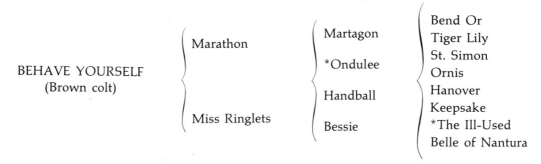

			Bend Or
		Martagon	Tiger Lily
	Marathon		St. Simon
		*Ondulee	Ornis
BEHAVE YOURSELF			Hanover
(Brown colt)		Handball	Keepsake
	Miss Ringlets		*The Ill-Used
		Bessie	Belle of Nantura

46th Kentucky Derby, May 8, 1920

$30,000 added. 3-year-olds. Weight for age. Net value to winner $30,375; second $4,000; third $2,000; fourth $275. 107 nominations.

Horses	Eq't Wt	PP	St	½	¾	1	Str	Fin	Jockeys	Owners	Odds $1 Str't
Paul Jones	w 126	2	1	1¹½	1½	1²	1ʰ	1ʰ	Rice	Ral Parr	‡16.20
Upset	w 126	5	4	3ʰ	3ʰ	2½	2ʰ	2⁴	Rodrig'z	H P Whitney	††1.65
On Watch	wb 126	13	16	13½	7¹	3½	3¹	3⁴	Barrett	G W Loft	§4.30
Damask	b 126	8	9	7ʰ	4ʰ	4¹	4¹	4²	Ambrose	H P Whitney	††1.65
Donnacona	w 126	7	10	6ʰ	6½	5½	5²	5⁴	O'Brien	G W Loft	§4.30
Blazes	w 126	15	7	8½	5¹	6½	6¹	6½	Kummer	Ral Parr	‡16.20
By Golly	w 126	4	5	2ʰ	8¹	8¹½	8¹	7ʰ	Lyke	E R Bradley	†13.20
Wildair	w 126	14	8	4½	2ʰ	7¹	7½	8ʰ	Fator	H P Whitney	††1.65
Bersagliere	wb 126	9	3	10½	11½	9¹	9¹	9½	Murray	C A Cochran	22.75
Patches	wb 126	6	12	14¹	10ʰ	10²	10ʰ	10⁴	Hanover	F C Bain	†13.20
Herron	w 126	1	6	9ʰ	13²	11¹½	11²	11½	Butwell	E Alvarez	†13.20
Sandy Beal	w 126	10	14	15²	14²	12¹	12¹	12½	Williams	W S Murray	12.50
Prince Pal	w 126	3	2	5¹	12ʰ	13²	13²	13²	Schut'r	Simms & Oliver	18.90
David Har'm	wb 126	11	11	11½	9½	14²	14²	14¹½	Fairb'er	W R Coe	‡‡35.20
Cleopatra	wb 121	12	13	12ⁿᵏ	15⁴	15⁵	15¹	15⁵	McAtee	W R Coe	‡‡35.20
Peace Pen'nt	wb 126	17	15	16¹⁰	16²⁰	16²⁰	16²⁰	16²⁰	Garner	W F Polson	6.35
Sterling	wb 126	16	17	17	17	17	17	17	Callahan	C C Van Meter	33.00

†Mutuel field. ‡Coupled in betting as Ral Parr entry. ††Coupled in betting as H. P. Whitney entry. §Coupled in betting as G. W. Loft entry. ‡‡Coupled in betting as W. R. Coe entry.

Time, :23 4/5, :48 1/5, 1:14 4/5, 1:42, 2:09. Track slow.

$2 Mutuels Paid—Ral Parr entry (Paul Jones and Blazes), $34.40 straight, $12.30 place, $6.60 show; H. P. Whitney entry (Upset and Damask), $3.20 place, $3.00 show; G. W. Loft entry (On Watch and Donnacona), $4.00 show.

Winner—Br.g. by *Sea King—May Florence, by Hamburg, trained by William Garth; bred by J. E. Madden.

Went to Post—5:08. Off at 5:12.

Start good and slow. Won driving; second and third same. **Paul Jones** was away fast, raced into the lead at once and, holding on in game style, outstayed **Upset** in the final drive. The latter moved up menacingly after going a half-mile and, saving ground when coming into the stretch, appeared a winner a sixteenth out, but tired right at the end. **On Watch** came from far back in the last half-mile and finished well. **Damask** raced forwardly, but tired in the stretch. **By Golly** quit. **Donnacona** had no mishap. **Peace Pennant** was always far back. **Sandy Beall** retired after going a half-mile and so did **Bersagliere**.

Scratched—Golden Broom, 126; Kinnoul, 126; Simpleton, 126; Ethel Gray, 121; Westwood, 126.

The Winner's Pedigree

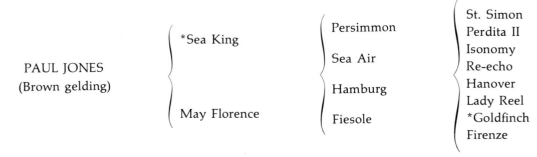

PAUL JONES (Brown gelding)	*Sea King	Persimmon	St. Simon
			Perdita II
		Sea Air	Isonomy
			Re-echo
	May Florence	Hamburg	Hanover
			Lady Reel
		Fiesole	*Goldfinch
			Firenze

45th Kentucky Derby, May 10, 1919

$20,000 added. Net value to winner $20,825; second $2,500; third $1,000; fourth $275. 75 nominations.

Horses	Eq't Wt	PP	St	½	¾	1	Str	Fin	Jockeys	Owners	Odds $1 Str't
Sir Barton	wb 112½	1	1	1^2	$1\frac{1}{2}$	1^2	$1\frac{1}{2}$	1^5	Loftus	J K L Ross	‡2.60
Billy Kelly	w 119	11	8	$3\frac{1}{2}$	3^4	2^3	2^4	2^1	Sande	J K L Ross	‡2.60
Under Fire	w 122	7	11	$9\frac{1}{2}$	$9\frac{1}{2}$	$6\frac{1}{2}$	3^1	3^1	Garner	P Dunne	19.15
Vulcanite	w 110	6	10	$10\frac{1}{2}$	5^h	$4\frac{1}{2}$	4^1	4^6	Howard	W F Polson	70.00
Senn's Park	wb 122	8	9	6^2	$4\frac{1}{2}$	$5\frac{1}{2}$	5^1	5^1	Lunsf'rd	O A Bianchi	†14.10
Be Frank	w 119	2	6	7^h	$7\frac{1}{2}$	$7\frac{1}{2}$	$6\frac{1}{2}$	$6\frac{1}{2}$	Butwell	C M Garrison	27.45
Sailor	wb 119	10	12	12	10^2	$10\frac{1}{2}$	$8\frac{1}{2}$	7^8	McIntyre	J W McClelland	§2.10
St Bernard	w 119	4	2	5^h	6^1	9^1	7^2	8^2	Pool	B J Brannon	†14.10
Regalo	w 117	9	7	8^2	$8^{1\frac{1}{2}}$	8^1	9^2	9^4	Murphy	Gallaher Bros	6.05
Eternal	w 122	5	3	$2\frac{1}{2}$	$2\frac{1}{2}$	$3\frac{1}{2}$	10^5	10^{10}	Schutt'r	J W McClelland	§2.10
Frogtown	w 119	12	4	11^2	$11\frac{1}{2}$	11^2	11^{10}	11^{20}	Morys	W S Kilmer	22.45
Vindex	w 122	3	5	4^{nk}	12	12	12	12	Knapp	H P Whitney	8.15

Time. :24 1/5, :48 2/5, 1:14, 1:41 4/5, 2:09 4/5. Track heavy.

Sir Barton and Billy Kelly coupled in betting as J. K. L. Ross entry; Sailor and Eternal coupled as J. W. McClelland entry; Sennings Park and St. Bernard coupled in betting as field horses.

$2 Mutuels Paid—J. K. L. Ross Entry (Sir Barton and Billy Kelly), $7.20 straight, $6.70 place, $6.00 show; Under Fire, $10.80 show.

Winner—Ch.c. by *Star Shoot—Lady Sterling, by Hanover, trained by H. G. Bedwell; bred by Madden and Gooch.

Went to Post—5:10. Off at 5:14.

Start good and slow. Won easily; second and third driving. **Sir Barton** raced into the lead at once and, well ridden, led under restraint until reaching the stretch, where he was shaken up and easily held **Billy Kelly** safe in the eighth. **Billy Kelly** held to his task well, was under restraint in the early running and finished gamely. **Under Fire** gained steadily from a slow beginning and finished fast and gamely. **Vulcanite** ran well and finished close up. **Eternal** was done after going three-quarters. **Regalo** ran disappointingly. **Sennings Park** tired in the stretch.

Scratched—Corson, 122; Clermont, 122. Overweight—Sir Barton, 2½ pounds.

The Winner's Pedigree

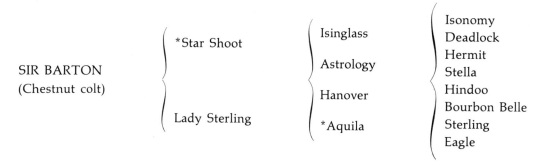

	*Star Shoot	Isinglass	Isonomy
SIR BARTON			Deadlock
(Chestnut colt)		Astrology	Hermit
			Stella
	Lady Sterling	Hanover	Hindoo
			Bourbon Belle
		*Aquila	Sterling
			Eagle

44th Kentucky Derby, May 11, 1918

$15,000 added. Net value to winner $14,700; second $2,500; third $1,000; fourth $275. 70 nominations.

Horses	Eq't Wt	PP	St	½	¾	1	Str	Fin	Jockeys	Owners	Odds $1 Str't
Exterminator.......	w 114	5	5	5^1	$4\frac{1}{2}$	1^h	2^4	1^1	Knapp	W S Kilmer	29.60
Escoba..........	wb 117	1	2	$3^1\frac{1}{2}$	2^h	2^1	1^n	2^8	Notter	K D Alexander	4.25
Viva America	w 113	2	1	$1^1\frac{1}{2}$	$1^1\frac{1}{2}$	3^4	3^2	3^4	War'on	C T Worthington	29.00
War Cloud........	w 117	4	7	4^h	5^2	4^4	4^3	4^2	Loftus	A K Macomber	1.45
Lucky B..........	w 117	6	4	6^h	7^8	$5\frac{1}{2}$	5^6	5^6	McCabe	O A Bianchi	6.15
J T Clark.........	wb 117	8	8	7^3	6^3	7^6	7^3	6^{12}	Morys	J W Schorr	8.90
Sew'l Combs	wb 117	3	3	2^{nk}	3^1	6^2	$6\frac{1}{2}$	7^1	Gentry	Gallaher Bros	8.75
Am'n Eagle.......	wsb 117	6	6	8	8	8	8	8	Sande	T C McDowell	19.25

Time, :24 1/5, :49 1/5, 1:16 1/5, 1:43 3/5, 2:10 4/5. Track muddy.

$2 Mutuels Paid—Exterminator, $61.20 straight, $23.10 place, $12.40 show; Escoba, $4.90 place, $4.60 show; Viva America, $13.20 show.

Winner—Ch.g. by McGee—Fair Empress, trained by H. McDaniel; bred by F. D. Knight.

Went to Post—5:19. Off at 5:21.

Start good and slow. Won handily; second and third driving. **Exterminator** moved up fast after going three-quarters and, slipping through on the inner rail, raced into the lead and outstayed **Escoba.** The latter faced forwardly from the start, made a resolute effort in the last eighth, but tired in the last sixteenth. **Viva America** showed the most early speed, but found the distance a trifle too far. **War Cloud** met with much interference on the first two turns, but remained close up to the last quarter, where he tired. **Sewell Combs** raced well for three-quarters. **James T. Clark** was sharply cut off when he moved up fast at the half-mile ground.

Scratched—Aurum, 117; Jim Heffering, 117.

Overweight—Viva America, 1 pound.

The Winner's Pedigree

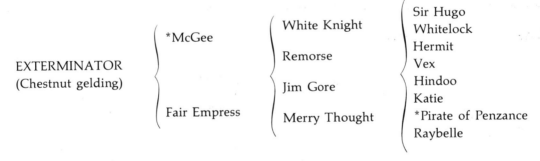

```
                                        ┌ White Knight ┌ Sir Hugo
                         ┌ *McGee       │              └ Whitelock
                         │              │ Remorse      ┌ Hermit
EXTERMINATOR             │              │              └ Vex
(Chestnut gelding)       │              │ Jim Gore     ┌ Hindoo
                         └ Fair Empress │              └ Katie
                                        │ Merry Thought ┌ *Pirate of Penzance
                                        └               └ Raybelle
```

43rd Kentucky Derby, May 12, 1917

$15,000 added. Net value to winner $16,600; second $2,500; third $1,000; fourth $275. 76 nominations.

Horses	Eq't Wt	PP	St	½	¾	1	Str	Fin	Jockeys	Owners	Odds $1 Str't
Omar Kh'm	wb 117	8	11	10^h	10^1	6½	2^1	1^2	Borel	Billings & Johnson	12.80
Ticket	wb 117	3	1	3^h	3½	4½	1½	2½	J M'Tag't	A Miller	1.45
Midway	wb 117	1	12	12^1	9^1	8½	3^h	3^4	Hunt	J W Parrish	14.65
Rickety	w 117	11	5	7½	5^1	1^h	4½	4^1	Robins'n	H P Whitney	4.55
War Star	wb 110	9	6	5^{1}½	6^1	5½	5^h	5^h	Buxton	A K Macomber	†8.65
Manis'r Toi	wb 117	14	15	13½	11½	10^1	6^1	6^h	Keogh	E Herz	15.45
Skeptic	w 117	4	14	6^1	4^h	9^1	7^1	7^{1}½	Martin	H H Hewitt	‡16.45
Guy F'tune	wb 117	2	2	14^1	12^1	12^1	11^1	8½	Connelly	Pastime Stable	‡16.45
Star Mast'r	wb 117	12	9	4½	2^h	2^h	8^{11}	9^h	Loftus	A K Macomber	†8.65
Star Gazer	wb 110	13	10	1½	1½	3^h	9½	10^2	Crump	A K Macomber	†8.65
Cudgel	wb 117	5	13	11^1	7^1	13^1	12½	11^5	Murphy	J W Schorr	23.00
Green Jones	w 117	7	3	9^h	13^1	11½	13^1	12^8	Goose	W H Baker	‡16.45
T O'T Wave	wb 117	10	4	15	14^2	14^1	14^1	13^4	Morys	Beverwyck Stable	‡16.45
Berlin	wb 117	6	7	2½	8^h	8½	10^1	14^{12}	Andress	J S Ward	16.20
Acabado	wb 114	15	8	15	15	15	15	15	Schutt'r	Wickliffe Stable	75.45

Time, :23 3/5, :47 3/5, 1:12 4/5, 1:38, 2:04 3/5. Track fast.

War Star, Star Master and Star Gazer coupled in betting as A. K. Macomber entry; Skeptic, Guy Fortune, Green Jones and Top o' the Wave coupled in the field.

$2 Mutuels Paid—Omar Khayyam, $27.60 straight, $10.90 place, $6.20 show; Ticket, $3.70 place, $2.80 show; Midway, $5.10 show.

Winner—Ch.c. by Marco—Lisma, by Persimmon; trained by C. T. Patterson; bred in England by Sir John Robinson.

Went to Post—4:53. Off at 4:57 New York Time.

Start good and slow. Won easily; second and third driving. **Omar Khayyam** began slowly, gained steadily and, saving much ground when turning into the stretch, outstayed **Ticket.** The latter, well up from the start, raced into the lead in the stretch, but tired. **Midway** began slowly, was far back for the first half, but closed an immense gap into a game third. **Rickety** tired after taking the lead while rounding into the stretch. **War Star** raced fairly well. **Star Gazer** tired badly in the last quarter. **Berlin** quit in the stretch. **Manister Toi** ran a good race. **Star Master** failed to stay.

Scratched—Penrod, 114; Sol Gilsey, 117; Diamond, 112.

The Winner's Pedigree

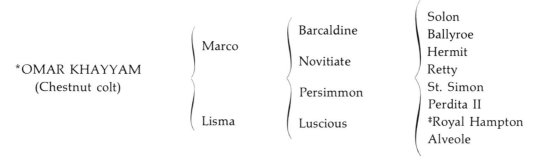

```
                                          ⎧ Solon
                          ⎧ Barcaldine     ⎨ Ballyroe
              ⎧ Marco     ⎨                ⎧ Hermit
              ⎨           ⎩ Novitiate       ⎨ Retty
*OMAR KHAYYAM ⎨                            ⎧ St. Simon
(Chestnut colt) ⎨         ⎧ Persimmon       ⎨ Perdita II
              ⎩ Lisma    ⎨                 ⎧ ‡Royal Hampton
                          ⎩ Luscious         ⎨ Alveole
```

42nd Kentucky Derby, May 13, 1916

$10,000 added. Net value to winner $9,750; second $2,000; third $1,000; fourth $225. 56 nominations.

Horses	Eq't Wt	PP	St	½	¾	1	Str	Fin	Jockeys	Owners	Odds $1 Str't
George Smith......	w 117	8	6	3^2	3^h	1^1	1^2	1^{nk}	Loftus	J Sanford	4.15
Star Hawk.........	w 117	3	9	9	$7^{1/2}$	5^4	3^2	2^3	Lilley	A. K Macomber	†4.45
Franklin	wb 117	1	2	2^2	2^{1}½	2^1	2^h	$3^{1/2}$	Rice	Weber & Ward	‡6.45
Dodge............	w 117	4	1	5^1	4^{1}½	$4^{1/2}$	4^2	4^6	Murphy	Weber & Ward	‡6.45
Thunderer.........	w 117	5	7	7^1	$5^{1/2}$	6^1	6^1	5^1	T McTag't	H P Whitney	§1.05
The Cock.........	wb 110	7	8	8^3	6^h	7^2	7^2	6^5	Garner	A K Macomber	†4.45
Dominant..........	w 117	2	3	1^3	$1^{1/2}$	$3^{1/2}$	5^1	7^5	Notter	H P Whitney	§1.05
Kinney	wb 117	9	5	$6^{1/2}$	8^6	8^6	8^{10}	8^{12}	Gentry	T P Hayes	32.55
Lena Misha........	w 117	6	4	4^h	9	9	9	9	Dugan	Beverwyck Stable	35.30

Time, :22 2/5, :46 2/5, 1:12 1/5, 1:38 4/5, 2:04. Track fast.

Star Hawk and The Cock coupled in betting as Macomber entry; Franklin and Dodge coupled in betting as Weber and Ward entry; Thunderer and Dominant coupled in betting at H. P. Whitney entry.

$2 Mutuels Paid—George Smith, $10.30 straight, $4.80 place, $2.90 show; Star Hawk, $6.00 place, $4.40 show; Franklin, $3.50 show.

Winner— Blk. c. by *Out of Reach—*Consuelo II, by Bradwardine; trained by H. Hughes; bred by Chinn & Forsythe.

Went to Post—5:15. Off at 5:16.

Start good and slow. Won driving; second and third same. **George Smith** was well ridden and, after being saved for the first three-quarters, rushed into the lead, but had to be urged at the end to outstay **Star Hawk**. The latter, away slowly and trailing for a half-mile, came with a rush through the stretch and almost got up to win. **Franklin** showed good speed, but tired after racing in close pursuit. **Dodge** raced well up throughout. **Thunderer** had no mishap. **Dominant** set a fast early pace, but quit badly. **Lena Misha** pulled up lame.

Scratched—St. Isidore, 114; Bulse, 117; Huffaker, 117.

The Winner's Pedigree

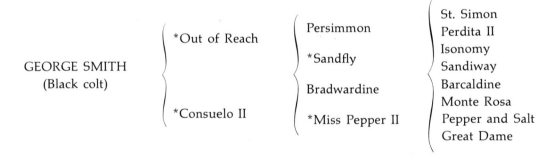

GEORGE SMITH (Black colt)
- *Out of Reach
  - Persimmon
    - St. Simon
    - Perdita II
  - *Sandfly
    - Isonomy
    - Sandiway
- *Consuelo II
  - Bradwardine
    - Barcaldine
    - Monte Rosa
  - *Miss Pepper II
    - Pepper and Salt
    - Great Dame

41st Kentucky Derby, May 8, 1915

$10,000 added. Net value to winner $11,450; second $2,000; third $1,000; fourth $225. 68 nominations.

Horses	Eq't Wt	PP	St	½	¾	1	Str	Fin	Jockeys	Owners	Odds $1 Str't
Regret	w 112	2	1	1¹½	1½	1½	1¹½	1²	Notter	H P Whitney	2.65
Peebles	wb 117	3	3	2¹	2¹½	2¹½	2²	2²	Borel	J Butler	6.35
Sharpsh'ter	wb 114	8	7	3½	3½	3ʰ	3¹	3¹	Butwell	S L Parsons	9.60
Royal II	wb 117	10	16	12²	9¹	6ⁿᵏ	5ʰ	4³	Neylon	J Livingston	15.10
E'n Cochran	w 117	5	2	6½	4¹	7½	4½	5½	Taylor	R L Baker	16.15
Leo Ray	w 117	11	13	10ʰ	8¹½	8ʰ	7ʰ	6¹½	T McTag't	J T Looney	17.90
D'ble Eagle	wsb 117	13	12	9ʰ	7¹½	9½	6²	7⁴	Burl'game	J F Johnson	17.20
Dortch	w 110	1	11	7¹	6½	5¹½	8½	8⁵	Mott	W W Darden	‡5.40
For Fair	wb 117	4	15	16	15	10½	9½	9½	Warton	G M Miller	‡5.40
Ed Crump	wb 117	7	4	4¹½	5½	4½	10½	10ʰ	Goose	J W Schorr	‡5.90
L'tle Strings	w 117	12	10	11¹½	12²	11¹	11¹	11¹½	Pool	M B Gruber	‡5.40
Goldcrest	w 114	6	8	8½	10½	13¹	12¹	12²	Kederis	J W Schorr	‡5.90
Uncle Bryn	wsb 117	16	14	14¹	14¹	12½	13¹	13²	J McTag't	R W Walden	‡5.40
Tetan	w 117	15	6	13²	13²	14⁶	14⁶	14²	Smyth	Johnson-Crosthwaite	x‡5.40
Norse King	wb 117	9	9	5½	11¹	15¹	15	15⁴	O'Brien	F B Le Maire	36.90
Booker Bill	wb 117	14	5	15¹	16	16	16	16	Andress	M C Moore	x‡5.40

Time, :23 3/5, :48 3/5, 1:13 3/5, 1:39 2/5, 2:05 2/5. Track fast.

Ed Crump and Goldcrest Boy coupled in betting as J. W. Schorr entry; Tetan and Booker Bill coupled as Johnson and Crosthwaite-Moore entry; Dortch, For Fair, Little Strings, Uncle Bryn, Tetan and Booker Bill coupled in betting as field horses.

$2 Mutuels Paid—Regret, $7.30 straight, $4.00 place; $3.60 show; Pebbles, $7.60 place, $4.80 show; Sharpshooter, $7.10 show.

Winner—Ch.f. by Broomstick—Jersey Lightning, by Hamburg; trained by James Rowe, bred by H. P. Whitney.

Went to Post—5:18. Off at 5:22.

Start good and slow. Won easily; second and third driving. **Regret**, from a fast start and well ridden, took the lead at once and was rated in front until the last eighth, where she drew away, to win easing up. **Pebbles** raced in nearest pursuit and held on gamely in the final drive. **Sharpshooter** also ran a good race and stood a hard drive resolutely. **Royal II.** closed a big gap. **Emerson Cochran** and **Leo Ray** ran good races. **Ed Crump** showed speed, but failed to stay.

Scratched—Kilkenny Boy, 117; Phosphor, 117; Commonada, 117.

The Winner's Pedigree

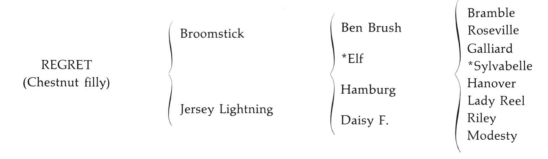

REGRET
(Chestnut filly)

Broomstick
— Ben Brush — Bramble, Roseville
— *Elf — Galliard, *Sylvabelle

Jersey Lightning
— Hamburg — Hanover, Lady Reel
— Daisy F. — Riley, Modesty

40th Kentucky Derby, May 9, 1914

$10,000 added. Net value to winner $9,125; second $2,000; third $1,000. 47 nominations.

Horses	Eq't Wt	PP	St	½	¾	1	Str	Fin	Jockeys	Owners	Odds $1 Str't
Old Rosebud	w 114	6	1	1²	1¹½	1²	1⁶	1⁸	McCabe	H C Applegate	.85
Hodge	w 114	7	2	2²	2½	2⁴	2⁴	2¹½	Taylor	K Spence	5.40
Bronzew'ng	wb 117	4	7	7	7	6½	3²	3⁴	Hanover	A P Humphrey Jr	13.50
John Gund	wb 117	3	6	3½	3½	3½	4²	4⁶	Byrne	A Baker	10.00
Old Ben	wb 114	1	3	6⁵	6³	5¹½	5¹	5²	Turner	W G Yanke	12.50
Surprising	w 117	5	4	5¹	4¹	4ʰ	6⁵	6³	Peak	R F Carman	14.00
Watermelon	wb 112	2	5	4¹½	5¹	7	7	7	French	J E Madden	15.00

Time, :23 3/5, :47 4/5, 1:13, 1:38 4/5, 2:03 2/5 (new track record). Track fast.

$2 Mutuels Paid—Old Rosebud, $3.70 straight, $3.00 place, $2.80 show; Hodge, $3.60 place, $3.60 show; Bronzewing, $4.00 show.

Winner—B.g. by Uncle—Ivory Bells, by Himyar; trained by F. D. Weir; bred by J. E. Madden.

Went to Post—5:03. Off at 5:05.

Start good and slow. Won easily; second and third driving. **Old Rosebud** set the pace under restraint, although going fast to the stretch turn, where, when called upon, he moved away from the others to win hard held as his rider pleased. **Hodge** raced in closest pursuit until the last eighth, where he tired, but stood the drive gamely. **Bronzewing** closed and came with a rush through the last quarter. **John Gund** tired racing well up to the stretch. **Old Ben** and **Surprising** ran fairly well. **Watermelon** quit after three-quarters.

Scratched—Ivan Gardner, 114; Buckley, 110; Belloc, 117; Constant, 117.

The Winner's Pedigree

OLD ROSEBUD
(Bay gelding)

Uncle
   *Star Shoot
     Isinglass
     Astrology
   The Niece
     Alarm
     Jaconet

Ivory Bells
   Himyar
     Alarm
     Hira
   Ida Pickwick
     *Mr. Pickwick
     Ida K.

39th Kentucky Derby, May 10, 1913

$5,000 added. Net value to winner $5,475; second $700; third $300. 32 nominations.

Horses	Eq't Wt	PP	St	½	¾	1	Str	Fin	Jockeys	Owners	Odds $1 Str't
Donerail	w 117	5	6	6^1	6^{1½}	5^1	5^2	1½	Goose	T P Hayes	91.45
Ten Point	w 117	4	1	1^2	1^3	1^2	1½	2^{1½}	Buxton	A L Aste	1.20
Gowell	w 112	3	5	5^2	4^h	4^{1½}	4^1	3^h	McCabe	J T Weaver	87.00
Foundation	w 117	8	2	2^1	2½	2^h	3^h	4^{nk}	Loftus	C W McKenna	2.30
Y. Notions	wb 117	6	3	3½	3^h	3½	2½	5^5	Glass	H K Knapp	4.90
L'd Marsh'll	wb 117	1	7	7^1	7^1	6^2	6^1	6^8	Steele	J O & G H Keene	183.00
Jimmie Gill	wb 110	2	8	8	8	8	7^{10}	7^{15}	Borel	Doerhoefer & West	36.00
Leochares	w 114	7	4	4^h	5½	7^h	8	8	Peak	J W Schorr	14.00

Time, :23 4/5, :45 4/5, 1:12 3/5, 1:39 3/5, 2:04 4/5 (new track record). Track fast.

$2 Mutuels Paid—Donerail, $184.90 straight, $41.20 place, $13.20 show; Ten Point, $3.50 place, $3.30 show, Gowell, $14.10 show.

Winner—B.c. by *McGee—Algie M., by Hanover; trained by T. P. Hayes; bred by T. P. Hayes.

Went to Post—4:51. Off at 4:52.

Start good and slow. Won driving; second and third same. **Donerail,** showing startling improvement over his Lexington form, was restrained to the stretch turn, where he moved up with a rush, and, under punishment, drew away in the last sixteenth. **Ten Point** showed superior speed for the first mile, tired in the last eighth and was distressed at the finish. **Gowell** made a fast and game stretch effort. **Foundation** raced with **Ten Point** to the stretch, then tired. **Yankee Notions** ran prominently to the homestretch and tired in the final drive. **Leochares** was hopelessly beaten.

Scratched—Prince Hermis, 117; Sam Hirsch, 114; Floral Park, 112; Flying Tom, 114.

The Winner's Pedigree

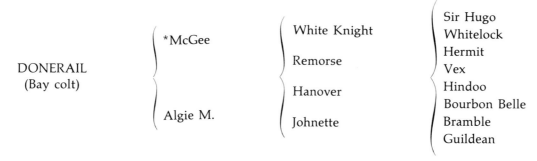

DONERAIL
(Bay colt)

*McGee
- White Knight
  - Sir Hugo
  - Whitelock
- Remorse
  - Hermit
  - Vex

Algie M.
- Hanover
  - Hindoo
  - Bourbon Belle
- Johnette
  - Bramble
  - Guildean

38th Kentucky Derby, May 11, 1912

Value $6,000. Net to winner $4,850; second $700; third $300. 131 nominations.

Horses	Eq't Wt	PP	St	½	¾	1	Str	Fin	Jockeys	Owners	Odds $1 Str't
Worth	w 117	5	1	$1^{1½}$	$1^{1½}$	1^1	1^1	1^{nk}	Shilling	H C Hallenbeck	.80
Duval	wb 117	7	4	4^3	$4^½$	2^1	2^2	2^5	Fain	Gallaher Bros	20.00
Flamma	wb 112	1	7	7	5^1	$3^{1½}$	3^1	3^4	Loftus	G F Condran	17.00
Free Lance	wb 117	4	6	$2^½$	$2^½$	$5^½$	$4^{1½}$	4^1	Peak	G J Long	7.00
Guaranola	wb 117	3	3	6^2	3^n	4^2	5^4	5^6	Molesw'h	Henderson & Hogan	80.00
Sonada	wb 117	6	5	3^h	7	6^8	6^{10}	6^{20}	Koerner	C Woolford	12.50
Wheelwright	w 117	2	2	$5^½$	$6^½$	7	7	7	Byrne	J N Camden	4.20

Time, :24 3/5, :49 2/5, 1:16 1/5, 1:42 3/5, 2:09 2/5. Track muddy.

$2 Mutuels Paid—Worth, $3.60 straight, $3.90 place, $3.30 show; Duval, $14.00 place, $5.70 show; Flamma, $4.50 show.

Winner—Br. c. by *Knight of the Thistle—Miss Hanover, by Hanover; trained by F. M. Taylor; bred by R. H. Mac. Potter.

Went to Post—4:39. Off at 4:41.

Start bad and slow. Won driving; second and third same. **Worth** was hustled into the lead and, maintaining an easy advantage under restraint, appeared to be an easy winner to the stretch turn, but tired and had to be hand ridden near the end to shake off **Duval**. The latter was going gamest at the end. **Flamma** acted badly at the post and was away poorly, but closed a big gap into a good third. **Free Lance** tired in the stretch. **Wheelwright** and **Sonada** ran disappointingly.

Scratched—The Manager, 117; Patrouche, 110.

The Winner's Pedigree

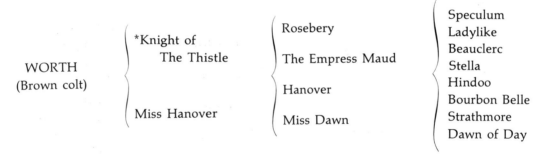

WORTH
(Brown colt)

*Knight of The Thistle
— Rosebery — Speculum / Ladylike
— The Empress Maud — Beauclerc / Stella

Miss Hanover
— Hanover — Hindoo / Bourbon Belle
— Miss Dawn — Strathmore / Dawn of Day

37th Kentucky Derby, May 13, 1911

Value $6,000. Net to winner $4,850; second $700; third $300. 117 nominations.

Horses	Eq't Wt	PP	St	½	¾	1	Str	Fin	Jockeys	Owners	Odds $1 Str't
Meridian	w 117	5	1	1⁴	1³	1²	1²	1¾	Archib'ld	R F Carmen	2.90
Gov'n'r Gray	w 119	7	3	6¹	4¹	3¹	2ʰ	2¹⁵	Troxler	R N Smith	1.00
Colston	w 110	1	7	3⁴	3½	4²	4⁴	3²	Conley	R Colston	19.00
Mud Sill	w 107	2	6	4½	6	6	6	4ʰ	Koerner	Woodf'd-Buckn'r	17.00
Jack Denm'n	w 117	3	5	5¹	5²	5¹	5¹	5¹	Wilson	F J Pons	21.00
R-the-World	w 117	6	2	2²	2³	2ʰ	3²	6¹⁵	McGee	W G Yanke	6.50
Col Hogan	w 110	4	4	7	7	7	7	7	McIntyre	Henderson-Hogan	6.00

$2.00 mutuels sold for first time this year.

Time, :23 3/5, :47 4/5, 1:39 1/5, 2:05 (equals track record). Track fast.

$2.00 mutuels paid—Meridian, $7.80 straight, $2.70 place, $2.70 show; Governor Gray, $2.70 place, $2.60 show; Colston, $3.80 show.

Winner—B.c. by Broomstick—Sue Smith, by *Masetto; trained by A. Ewing; bred by C. L. Harrison.

Went to Post—5:00. Off at 5:02.

Start good. Won driving; second and third same. **Meridian** was rushed into a long lead from the start, and after having disposed of **Round-the-World** and other serious contenders in the first three-quarters, had enough speed in reserve at the end to outstay the fast coming **Governor Gray**. The latter was allowed to drop too far back in the first half, and, coming with a great rush in the last quarter, was going fastest at the end. **Colston** outstayed **Mud Sill** for third place. **Round-the-World** tired in the last quarter. **Mud Sill** finished fast.

Scratched—Ramazan, 110; Jabot, 117; Captain Carmody, 117.

The Winner's Pedigree

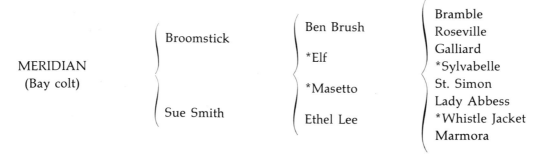

MERIDIAN
(Bay colt)

Broomstick

Sue Smith

Ben Brush

*Elf

*Masetto

Ethel Lee

Bramble
Roseville
Galliard
*Sylvabelle
St. Simon
Lady Abbess
*Whistle Jacket
Marmora

36th Kentucky Derby, May 10, 1910

Value $6,000. Net to winner $4,850; second $700; third $300. 117 nominations.

Horses	Eq't Wt	PP	St	½	¾	1	Str	Fin	Jockeys	Owners	Odds $1 Str't
Donau............	w 117	7	2	$1^{1½}$	1^3	1^3	$1^{1½}$	$1^{½}$	Herbert	Gerst	1.65
Joe Morris........	wb 117	1	1	2^h	2^2	$2^{1½}$	2^h	2^h	Powers	Ander'n	2.77
Fight'g Bob........	wb 117	4	5	7	5^1	$3^{1½}$	3^4	3^n	Page	Reif	3.49
Boola Boola	w 117	3	3	6^h	6^{nk}	5^2	4^6	4^{15}	Rice	Camden	17.95
Topland	w 114	5	7	3^h	4^2	4^h	5^1	5^2	Austin	V'n Meter	25.10
John Furlong	w 107	2	6	$5^½$	3^h	6^4	6^4	6^8	Scoville	Rogers	14.07
Gal't Pirate	wb 117	6	4	4^1	7	7	7	7	Kennedy	W'wright	37.59

Time, :24, :48 4/5, 1:14, 1:39 4/5, 2:06 2/5. Track fast.

$5 Mutuels Paid—Donau, $13.25 straight, $7.50 place, $7.50 show; Joe Morris, $7.50 place, $7.50 show; Fighting Bob, $8.50 show.

Winner—B.c. by Woolsthorpe—Al Lone, by *Albert; trained by G. Ham; bred by Milton Young.

Went to Post—4:50. Off at 4:51.

Start good. Won driving; second and third same. **Donau** went into the lead soon after the start, was restrained in front for a mile and when called on, drew away but tired, and just lasted. **Joe Morris** tried to run out on the first turn, moved up with a rush on the stretch turn, tired, only to come again near the end. **Fighting Bob** stood the final drive gamely. **Boola Boola** closed a big gap and was going fastest at the end. The others never were serious contenders.

Scratched—Eye White, 114.

The Winner's Pedigree

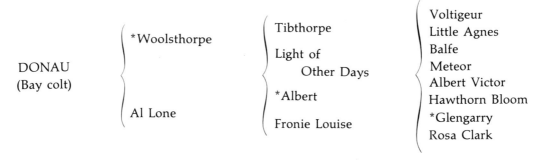

DONAU
(Bay colt)

*Woolsthorpe
- Tibthorpe
  - Voltigeur
  - Little Agnes
- Light of Other Days
  - Balfe
  - Meteor

Al Lone
- *Albert
  - Albert Victor
  - Hawthorn Bloom
- Fronie Louise
  - *Glengarry
  - Rosa Clark

35th Kentucky Derby, May 3, 1909

Value $6,000. Net to winner $4,850; second $700; third $300. 117 nominations.

Horses	Eq't Wt	PP	St	½	¾	1	Str	Fin	Jockeys	Owners	Odds $1 Str't
Wintergreen	wb 117	6	1	$1^{1½}$	1^2	$1^{1½}$	1^1	1^4	Powers	Respess	1.96
Miami	w 117	1	8	$2^{1½}$	2^2	$2^{½}$	2^h	2^3	Shilling	Camden	2.90
Dr Barkley	w 117	3	2	4^2	$4^{½}$	5^3	5^2	3^h	Page	Smitha	41.34
Sir Catesby	w 110	9	9	$6^{1½}$	5^2	4^2	$3^{½}$	4^4	Heidel	Hayes	33.58
Fr'nd Harry	wb 117	7	7	3^h	3^h	3^h	4^2	5^3	Musgrave	Alvey	5.61
Direct	wsb 117	5	3	7^2	7^6	7^3	6^2	6^3	Walsh	Mack'e	†10.01
Mich'l Angelo	w 117	8	4	9^3	8^3	8^{10}	7^2	7^3	Taplin	Hendrie	6.97
Warfield	w 117	10	6	$5^{½}$	$6^{½}$	7^4	8^2	8^8	Austin	Lesh	†10.01
Campeon	w 110	2	5	8^2	$9^{1½}$	9^h	9^1	9^2	McGee	Long	51.25
Match Me	wsb 107	4	10	10	10	10	10	10	Lee	Gorey	56.11

†Direct and Warfield coupled as Mackenzie and Lesh entry.

Time, :25, :49 3/5, 1:15 4/5, 2:08 1/5. Track slow.

$5 Mutuels Paid—Wintergreen, $14.80 straight, $8.75 place, $8.60 show; Miami, $9.15 place, $9.25 show; Dr. Barkley, $20.70 show.

Winner—B.c. by Dick Welles—Winter, by Exile; trained by C. Mack; bred by J. B. Respess.

Went to Post—4:41. Off at 4:44.

Start good. Won easily; second and third driving. **Wintergreen** was bumped into soon after the start by **Dr. Barkley,** but recovered quickly and, taking a good lead, held sway throughout and won in a canter. **Miami,** free of interference, followed **Wintergreen** in closest pursuit and finished fast, but was not good enough. **Dr. Barkley** ran a cracking good race and outgamed **Sir Catesby** in the last few strides. **Sir Catesby** closed a gap and finished resolutely. **Friend Harry** tired badly after three-quarters. **Direct** dropped out after three-quarters. **Michael Angelo** began slowly; closed a good gap in the last quarter. The others were never close contenders.

Scratched—T. M. Green, 114; Ada Meade, 112; Woolwinder, 117.

The Winner's Pedigree

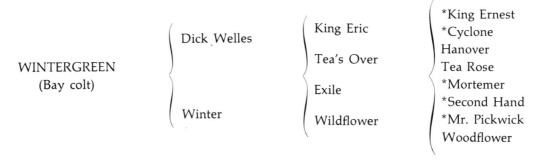

WINTERGREEN
(Bay colt)

Dick Welles

Winter

King Eric

Tea's Over

Exile

Wildflower

*King Ernest
*Cyclone
Hanover
Tea Rose
*Mortemer
*Second Hand
*Mr. Pickwick
Woodflower

34th Kentucky Derby, May 5, 1908

Value $6,000. Net to winner $4,850; second $700; third $300. 114 nominations.

Horses	Eq't Wt	PP	St	½	¾	1	Str	Fin	Jockeys	Owners	Odds $1 Str't
Stone Street	wb 117	4	6	2^{1}½	2^h	1^{nk}	1^1	1^3	Pickens	Hamilton	23.72
Sir Cleges	w 117	2	7	4^1	3^{1}½	2½	3½	2^h	Koerner	Long	1.74
Dunvegan	wb 114	1	5	3^h	4^2	4^4	2^1	3^h	Warren	Camden Jr	†7.37
Synchr'zed	wsb 112	8	2	5^2	5^3	5^5	4^1	4^h	Burton	Armstrong	68.92
Banbridge	wsb 110	5	3	1^{1}½	1^2	3^1	5^5	5^6	Powers	Schreiber	3.24
Milford	wb 117	3	1	6^1	6^4	6^6	6^1	6^h	Minder	Fizer	3.64
Bill Heron	wb 114	6	4	7^{10}	7^{20}	7^{15}	7^{20}	7^{20}	Lee	Young	†7.37
Frank Bird	wb 110	7	8	8	8	8	8	8	Williams	Hughes	22.43

†Dunvegan and Bill Heron coupled as Camden, Jr., and Young entry.

Time, :25, :50 1/5, 1:17 2/5, 1:46, 2:15 1/5. Track heavy.

$5 Mutuels Paid—Stone Street, $123.60 straight, $37.90 place, $14.50 show; Sir Cleges, $11.10 place, $8.50 show; Dunvegan, $11.10 show.

Winner—B.c. by Longstreet—Stone Nellie, by *Stonehenge; trained by J. W. Hall; bred by J. B. Haggin.

Went to Post—4:20. Off at 4:21.

Start good. Won easily; second and third driving. **Stone Street**, favored by the going and in prime condition, ran the best race of his career. He followed Banbridge close up to the three-quarters post, where he went into the lead and easily held the others safe for the rest of the trip. **Sir Cleges** disliked the going and sprawled repeatedly, but made a game effort. **Dunvegan** ran fairly well. **Synchronized** closed a big gap in the last half-mile. **Banbridge** showed the most early speed, but tired after three-quarters. **Milford** was never a factor. The others were always badly outpaced.

Scratched—Balbus, 117; Gilvedear, 117; Dr. Mathews, 117.

Synchronized and Frank Bird, added starters.

The Winner's Pedigree

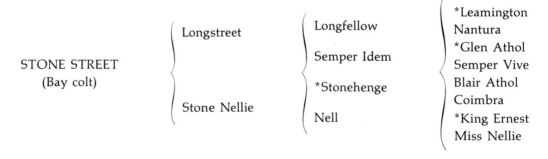

STONE STREET
(Bay colt)

Longstreet
Stone Nellie

Longfellow
Semper Idem
*Stonehenge
Nell

*Leamington
Nantura
*Glen Athol
Semper Vive
Blair Athol
Coimbra
*King Ernest
Miss Nellie

33rd Kentucky Derby, May 6, 1907

Value $6,000. Net to winner $4,850; second $700; third, $300. 128 nominations.

Horses	Eq't Wt	PP	St	½	¾	1	Str	Fin	Jockeys	Owners	Odds $1 Str't
Pink Star	wb 117	6	6	6	6	4^h	3^4	1^2	Minder	Woodford	15.00
Zal	w 117	3	1	1½	1^h	1^{1}½	1^{1}½	2^{1}½	Boland	Gerst	8.00
Ovelando	w 117	1	2	3^h	2^3	2^1	2^h	3^2	Nicol	Doyle	3.00
Red Gauntlet	w 117	5	5	5^5	4^1	5^4	4^1	4^5	Austin	Hayes	1.50
Wool Sandals	w 117	4	4	2^{1}½	3^h	3^1	5^5	5^6	Koerner	Applegate	3.00
Orlandwick	w 110	2	3	4^{1}½	5^2	6	6	6	Lee	Steele	10.00

Time, :24, :36 3/5, :50, 1:17, 1:45, 2:12 3/5. Track heavy.

Winner—B.c. by Pink Coat—Mary Malloy, by Pat Malloy; trained by W. H. Fizer; bred by J. Hal Woodford.

Went to Post—4:08. Off at 4:09.

Start good. Won easily, second driving, third same. **Pink Star,** restrained in the early stages, trailed far back for the first three-quarters, moved up gradually until straightened out for the stretch run, where he came with a rush, wore the leaders down and won going away. **Zal** showed the most early speed and hung on well for the first mile. **Ovelando** was a forward and game contender for a mile. **Red Gauntlet** was under a hard drive, but was not good enough. **Wool Sandals** retired after a mile. **Orlandwick** had no mishap.

Scratched—Arcite, 117; Boxara, 117.

The Winner's Pedigree

PINK STAR
(Bay colt)

- Pink Coat
  - Leonatus
    - Longfellow
    - Semper Felix
  - Alice Brand
    - Hindoo
    - Lady of the Lake
- Mary Malloy
  - Pat Malloy
    - Lexington
    - Gloriana
  - Favorite
    - *King Ernest
    - Jersey Belle

32nd Kentucky Derby, May 2, 1906

Value $6,000. Net to winner $4,850; second $700; third $300. 110 nominations.

Horses	Eq't Wt	PP	St	½	¾	1	Str	Fin	Jockeys	Owners	Odds $1 Str't
Sir Huon	w 117	4	2	2^2	2^2	1^{nk}	1^2	1^2	Troxler	Long	1.10
Lady Nav'rre......	w 117	3	4	4^h	3^{nk}	4^6	2^{nk}	2^3	Burns	Ellison	†1.80
J's Redd'k........	wsb 117	5	5	5^2	4^3	3^h	3^1	3^5	Domin'k	Ellison	†1.80
Hyper'n'll........	wsb 114	2	1	1^3	1^2	$2^{1}\!\frac{1}{2}$	4^h	4^{10}	Austin	Hawk's Co	8.00
De Bar	w 117	1	6	6	$5^{1}\!\frac{1}{2}$	5^6	5^{10}	5^3	Nicol	Shann'n Co	3.50
Velours..........	wsb 117	6	3	3^{nk}	6	6	6	6	Walsh	Franklin	40.00

†Coupled in betting as C. R. Ellison entry.

Time, :24 3/5, :49 4/5, 1:15, 1:41 2/5, 2:08 4/5. Track fast.

Winner—B.c. by Falsetto—Ignite, by *Woodlands; trained by P. Coyne; bred by George J. Long.

Went to Post—4:00. Off at 4:02.

Start good; won driving; second same. **Jockey Troxler** rode a well judged race on **Sir Huon,** saved him from the pace set by **Hyperion II,** and never made a move until well around the far turn, where the colt came fast, and taking command entering the homestretch, held the race safe all through the last quarter. **Lady Navarre** was interfered with while rounding the turn into the backstretch and made a determined effort on the turn for home, but could never get to the winner. **James Reddick** was sore in his warm-up, but ran to his best race. **Hyperion II,** forced a fast pace, but could not stay the route. **De Bar** was always outrun. **Velours** cut no figure.

Scratched—Creel, 117.

The Winner's Pedigree

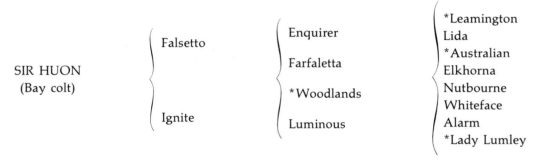

SIR HUON (Bay colt)

Falsetto
— Enquirer
— — *Leamington
— — Lida
— Farfaletta
— — *Australian
— — Elkhorna

Ignite
— *Woodlands
— — Nutbourne
— — Whiteface
— Luminous
— — Alarm
— — *Lady Lumley

31st Kentucky Derby, May 10, 1905

Value $6,000. Net to winner $4,850; second $700; third $300. 145 nominations.

Horses	Eq't Wt	PP	St	½	¾	1	Str	Fin	Jockeys	Owners	Odds $1 Str't
Agile	w 122	1	1	1¹½	1¹½	1¹½	1²	1³	Martin	Brown	.33
Ram's Horn	ws 117	2	2	2⁵	2¹⁰	2¹⁵	2²⁰	2²⁰	Lyne	Will'ms Co	2.50
Layson	w 117	3	3	3	3	3	3	3	Austin	Hayes	16.00

Time, :25½, :50, 1:16, 1:42¾, 2:10¾. Track heavy.

Winner—B.c. by Sir Dixon—Alpena, by King Alfonso; trained by R. Tucker; bred by E. F. Clay.

Went to Post—4:20. Off at 4:21.

Won easily; second the same. **Agile** was full of speed all the way and **Martin** never let him down at any part of the trip. He drew away under restraint in the last furlong, and was only galloping at the end. **Lyne** made his move with **Ram's Horn** while rounding the turn into the homestretch, but could not get to the winner.

Scratched—Dr. Leggo, 122; McClellan, 110.

The Winner's Pedigree

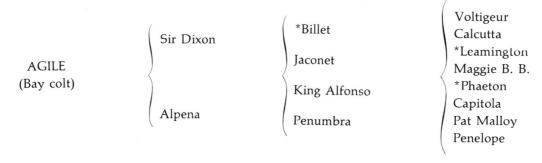

AGILE
(Bay colt)

Sir Dixon
- *Billet
  - Voltigeur
  - Calcutta
- Jaconet
  - *Leamington
  - Maggie B. B.

Alpena
- King Alfonso
  - *Phaeton
  - Capitola
- Penumbra
  - Pat Malloy
  - Penelope

30th Kentucky Derby, May 2, 1904

Value $6,000. Net to winner $4,850; second $700; third $300. 140 nominations.

Horses	Eq't Wt	PP	St	½	¾	1	Str	Fin	Jockeys	Owners	Odds $1 Str't
Elwood..........wb 117		3	4	4¹	4ʰ	4½	5½	1½	Prior	Mrs Dur'l	15.00
Ed Tierney.........w 117		5	3	3¹	3¹½	3¹	3²	2³	Domin'k	Fay & We'f	1.10
Brancas..........w 117		4	5	5	5	5	2½	3²½	Lyne	Gerst	2.50
P Silverw'gs.......w 117		1	2	2²	1¹	1¹	1ʰ	4¹	D Austin	Talb't Bros	7.00
Proceeds.........wb 122		2	1	1¹½	2½	2ʰ	4½	5	Helges'n	Brown	1.00

Time, :13, :25, :49½, 1:51¼, 1:28½, 1:42, 1:54, 2:08½. Track fast.

Winner—B.c. by Free Knight—Petticoat, by Alarm, trained by C. E. Durnell; bred by Mrs. J. B. Prather.

Went to Post—4:15. Off at 4:19.

Start good. Won driving; second easily. **Elwood** was well ridden. Prior rated him along for the first seven furlongs and never made a move until rounding the turn into the homestretch, where he moved up on the outside and fought it out in turn with **Brancas, Prince Silverwings** and **Ed Tierney** in the last quarter, and outstayed the latter in the final drive. Dominick nursed **Ed Tierney** along for the first half and made a determined effort in the stretch run, tiring in the last fifty yards. **Brancas** stumbled at the start and Lyne kept taking him back in the first half-mile, moved him up fast at the home turn and was in front for a few strides, but tired. **Price Silverwings** showed much early speed, but tired after a mile. **Proceeds** stumbled at the start but this cut no figure in the result.

Scratched—Batts, 117.

The Winner's Pedigree

ELWOOD
(Bay colt)

Free Knight
Petticoat

Ten Broeck
Belle Knight
Alarm
Lady Scarborough

*Phaeton
Fanny Holton
Knighthood
Kentucky Belle
*Eclipse
*Maud
*Leamington
*Lady Lumley

29th Kentucky Derby, May 2, 1903

Value $6,000. Net to winner $4,850; second $700; third $300. 140 Nominations.

Horses	Eq't Wt	PP	St	½	¾	1	Str	Fin	Jockeys	Owners	Odds $1 Str't
Judge Himes	w 117	4	3	$3\frac{1}{2}$	$3\frac{1}{2}$	4^3	2^2	$1\frac{3}{4}$	Booker	Ellison	10.00
Early..............	w 117	2	4	4^6	4^6	$1\frac{1}{2}$	$1\frac{1}{2}$	2^6	Winkf'd	Tich'r & Co	.60
Bourbon..........	w 110	5	5	5^2	$5^{1\frac{1}{2}}$	$5\frac{1}{2}$	4^3	$3\frac{1}{2}$	Cowh'st	McDowell	†4.00
Bad News	w 114	1	2	$2\frac{1}{2}$	2^{nk}	3^1	$3\frac{1}{2}$	4^3	Davis	Wo'd-Buc'r	5.00
Woodlake	wb 117	3	1	1^1	1^1	2^{nk}	5^1	5^5	Helg'sen	McDowell	†4.00
Treacy	w 110	6	6	6	6	6	6	6	Landry	Stevens	15.00

†Coupled in betting as T. C. McDowell entry.

Time—25½, :51, 1:16½, 1:42, 2:09. Track fast.

Winner—Ch.c. by *Esher—Lullaby, by Longfellow: trained by J. P. Mayberry; bred by Johnson N. Camden.

Start poor. Won driving; second easily. Jockey Booker waited with **Judge Himes** until well in the last quarter before making a move, came through on the inside at the turn into the homestretch, caught **Early** tiring and, after a sharp struggle, was going away at the finish. Winkfield made his run too soon with **Early**, made up a lot of ground while rounding the far turn, but had nothing left when **Judge Himes** challenged. **Bourbon** finished well and outgamed **Bad News**. **Woodlake** quit badly after going a good half-mile. **Treacy** was never a contender.

Scratched—Dan McKenna, 117; The Picket, 110.

The Winner's Pedigree

JUDGE HIMES
(Chestnut colt)

*Esher
- Claremont
  - Blair Athol
  - Coimbra
- Una
  - ‡Dusk
  - Conjecture

Lullaby
- Longfellow
  - *Leamington
  - Nanura
- Lady Richards
  - War Dance
  - Lucretia

‡by Ellington or Dusk.

28th Kentucky Derby, May 3, 1902

Value $6,000. Net to winner $4,850; second $700; third $300. 112 nominations.

Horses	Wt	Fin	Jockeys	Owners
Alan-a-Dale 117		1	J Winkfield	T C McDowell
Inventor 117		2	R Williams	T W Moore
The Rival 117		3	N Turner	T C McDowell
Abe Frank 122		4	Coburn	G C Bennett & Co

Time, 2:08¾. Weather clear.

Winner—Ch.c. by Halma—Sudie McNairy, by Enquirer; trained by T. C. McDowell; bred by T. C. McDowell.

Bookmaking Odds: Alan-a-Dale (Coupled with The Rival), 3 to 2; Inventor, 11 to 1; Abe Frank, 3 to 5.

The Rival was first to show, but **Alan-a-Dale** caught him in the first eighth, opened a four-length lead going into homestretch, went lame in the final eighth, carried on with flawless courage, and won by a nose.

The Winner's Pedigree

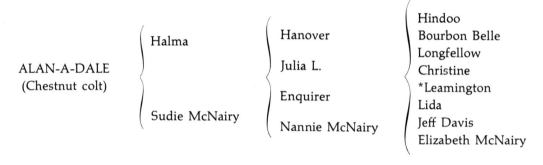

ALAN-A-DALE
(Chestnut colt)

Halma
— Hanover — Hindoo / Bourbon Belle
— Julia L. — Longfellow / Christine

Sudie McNairy
— Enquirer — *Leamington / Lida
— Nannie McNairy — Jeff Davis / Elizabeth McNairy

27th Kentucky Derby, April 29, 1901

Value $6,000. Net to winner $4,850; second $700; third $300. 113 nominations.

Horses	Wt	Fin	Jockeys	Owners
His Eminence........... 117		1	J Winkfield	F B Van Meter
Sannazarro............. 117		2	O'Connor	William Hayes
Driscoll................ 110		3	J Boland	Woodford Clay
Amur................... 110		4	Dupree	George J Long
Alard Scheck 117		5	J Woods	J W Schorr

Time, 2:07¾. Weather clear.

Winner—B.c. by Falsetto—Patroness, by Pat Malloy; trained by F B VanMeter; bred by A J Alexander.

Bookmaking Odds: His Eminence, 3 to 1; Sannazarro, 4 to 1; Driscoll, 20 to 1; Amur, 25 to 1; Alard Scheck, 7 to 10.

His Eminence broke out in front and stayed there, winning easily by two lengths.

The Winner's Pedigree

HIS EMINENCE
(Bay colt)

Falsetto
- Enquirer
  - *Leamington
  - Lida
- Farfaletta
  - *Australian
  - Elkhorna

Patroness
- Pay Malloy
  - Lexington
  - Gloriana
- *Inverness
  - Macaroni
  - Elfrida

26th Kentucky Derby, May 3, 1900

Value $6,000. Net value to winner $4,850; second $700; third $300. 131 nominations.

Horses	Wt	Fin	Jockeys	Owners
Lieut. Gibson	117	1	J Boland	Charles H Smith
Florizar.................	122	2	Van Dusen	H J Scoggan
Thrive..................	122	3	J Winkfield	J C Cahn
Highland Lad	—	4	Crowhurst	H J Scoggan
His Excellency	—	5	Gilmore	T C McDowell
Kentucky Farmer..........	—	6	Overton	Woodford & Buckner
Hindus	—	7	Vititoe	George J. Long

Time, 2:06¼ (new Derby record). Weather clear.

Winner—B.c. by G. W. Johnson—Sophia Hardy, by *Glengarry; trained by Charles H. Hughes; bred by Baker & Gentry.

Bookmaking Odds: Lieut. Gibson, 7 to 10; Florizar, 5 to 1; Thrive, 7 to 1.

Hindus broke first; **Kentucky Farmer,** second; **Lieut. Gibson** third. Going around the first turn, **Lieut. Gibson** moved into leadership and merely breezed the rest of the way, to win by four lengths, never extended.

The Winner's Pedigree

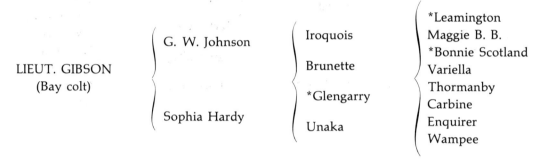

		Iroquois	*Leamington
	G. W. Johnson		Maggie B. B.
LIEUT. GIBSON		Brunette	*Bonnie Scotland
(Bay colt)			Variella
		*Glengarry	Thormanby
	Sophia Hardy		Carbine
		Unaka	Enquirer
			Wampee

25th Kentucky Derby, May 4, 1899

Value $6,000. Net to winner $4,850; second $700; third $300. 151 nominations.

Horses	Wt	Fin	Jockeys	Owners
Manuel................. 117		1	F Taral	A H & D H Morris
Corsini................. 122		2	T Burns	E Corrigan
Mazo................... 117		3	J Conley	J E Madden
His Lordship............ 110		4	Turner	J D Smith
Fontainebleu............ 117		5	Overton	J M Forsythe

Time, 2:12. Weather clear.

Winner—B.c. by Bob Miles—Espanita, by Alarm; trained by Robert J. Walden; bred by George J. Long.

Bookmaking Odds: Manuel 11 to 20; Corsini, 3 to 1; Mazo, 8 to 1.

Manuel broke in front, was taken back, and **His Lordship** led to the half-mile. Then the wraps were taken off **Manuel,** he was permitted to open, won by two lengths, and never was extended.

The Winner's Pedigree

MANUEL (Bay colt)	Bob Miles	Pat Malloy	Lexington
			Gloriana
		Dolly Morgan	Revenue
			Sally Morgan
	Espanita	Alarm	*Eclipse
			*Maud
		Outstep	Blue Eyes
			Etna

24th Kentucky Derby, May 4, 1898

Value $6,000. Net to winner $4,850; second $700; third $300. 179 nominations.

Horses	Wt	Fin	Jockeys	Owners
Plaudit 117		1	W Simms	J E Madden
Lieber Karl 122		2	T Burns	J W Schorr
Isabey. 117		3	A Knapp	Stanton & Tucker
Han d'Or 117		4	J Conley	G A Singerly

Time, 2:09. Weather clear.

Winner—Br.c. by Himyar—*Cinderella, by Tomahawk or Blue Ruin; trained by John E. Madden; bred by Dr. J. D. Neet.

Bookmaking Odds: Plaudit, 3 to 1; Lieber Karl, 1 to 3; Isabey, 12 to 1; Han d'Or, 25 to 1.

Lieber Karl, the favorite, broke in front and made a runaway race of it until nearing the turn for home, when **Plaudit** came with a terrific rush, and won by a neck.

The Winner's Pedigree

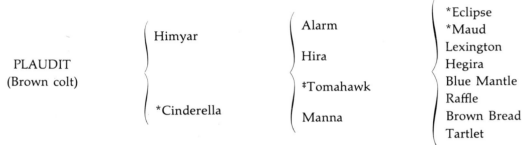

PLAUDIT
(Brown colt)

Himyar
*Cinderella

Alarm
Hira
‡Tomahawk
Manna

*Eclipse
*Maud
Lexington
Hegira
Blue Mantle
Raffle
Brown Bread
Tartlet

‡by Blue Ruin or Tomahawk.

23rd Kentucky Derby, May 12, 1897

Value $6,000. Net to winner $4,850; second $700; third $300. 159 nominations.

Horses	Wt	Fin	Jockeys	Owners
Typhoon II............... 117		1	F Garner	J C Cahn
Ornament 117		2	A Clayton	C T Patterson & Co
Dr Callett............... 117		3	R Williams	Turney Bros
Dr Shepard............. 117		4	J Hill	Foster Bros
Goshen 117		5	Willhite	J Rodegap
Ben Brown 117		6	Ballard	C Fleischmann

Time, 2:12½. Track heavy.

Winner—Ch.c. by *Top Gallant—Dolly Varden, by *Glenelg; trained by J. C. Cahn; bred by John B. Ewing.

Bookmaking Odds: Typhoon II, 3 to 1; Ornament, even; Dr. Catlett, 4 to 1.

Typhoon II led from the start to finish, to win by a head. **Ornament,** the favorite, was off poorly, and in deep going all the way.

The Winner's Pedigree

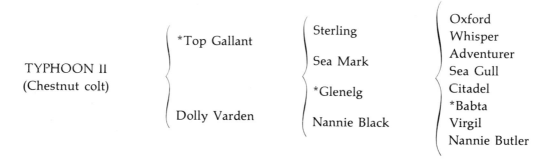

TYPHOON II
(Chestnut colt)

*Top Gallant
- Sterling
  - Oxford
  - Whisper
- Sea Mark
  - Adventurer
  - Sea Gull

Dolly Varden
- *Glenelg
  - Citadel
  - *Babta
- Nannie Black
  - Virgil
  - Nannie Butler

22nd Kentucky Derby, May 6, 1896

Value $6,000. Net to winner $4,850; second $700; third $300. 171 nominations.

Horses	Wt	Fin	Jockeys	Owners
Ben Brush............ 117		1	W Simms	M F Dwyer
Ben Eder............. 117		2	Tabor	Hot Springs Stable
Semper Ego.......... 117		3	Perkins	L B Ringgold
First Mate........... 117		4	Thorpe	Eastin & Larabie
The Dragon.......... 117		5	Overton	James E Pepper
Parson.............. 117		6	Britton	Himyar Stable
The Winner.......... 117		7	Walker	William Wallace
Ulysses............. 117		8	R Williams	Ed Brown

Time, 2:07¾. Weather clear, track good.

Winner—B.c. by Bramble—Roseville, by Reform; trained by Hardy Campbell; bred by Clay & Woodford.

Bookmaking Odds: Ben Brush, 1 to 2; Ben Eder, 2 to 1; Semper Ego, 9 to 1.

At post, 20 minutes, **Semper Ego** took an immediate lead, followed by **The Winner** and **First Mate.** On the first turn, **First Mate** was in command, and led to the three-quarter pole. **Ben Brush,** who had stumbled at the start, nearly unseated his rider, and seemed hopelessly out of it, began to move on the backstretch, together with **Ben Eder.** This pair caught the tired pacemakers going into the stretch, fought it out for almost a quarter of a mile, and **Ben Brush** won by a nose.

The Winner's Pedigree

BEN BRUSH
(Bay colt)

Bramble
- *Bonnie Scotland
  - Iago
  - Queen Mary
- Ivy Leaf
  - *Australian
  - Bay Flower

Roseville
- Reform
  - *Leamington
  - *Stolen Kisses
- Albia
  - Alarm
  - Elastic

262

21st Kentucky Derby, May 6, 1895

$2,500 added. Net to winner $2,970; second $300; third $150; fourth $100. 57 nominations.

Horses	Wt	Fin	Jockeys	Owners
Halma.................. 122		1	J Perkins	B McClelland
Basso.................. 122		2	W Martin	C H Smith
Laureate 122		3	A Clayton	Pastime Stable
Curator................. 122		4	Overton	Bashford Manor

Time, 2:37½. Weather clear.

Winner—Blk.c. by Hanover—Julia L., by Longfellow; trained by B. McClelland; bred by Eastin & Larrabie.

Bookmaking Odds: Halma, 1 to 3; Basso, 9 to 2; Laureate, 5 to 1; Curator, 20 to 1.

Halma led from start to finish, only galloping through the stretch, to win by three lengths.

The Winner's Pedigree

HALMA
(Black colt)

- Hanover
  - Hindoo
    - Virgil
    - Florence
  - Bourbon Belle
    - *Bonnie Scotland
    - Ella D.
- Julia L.
  - Longfellow
    - *Leamington
    - Nantura
  - Christine
    - *Australian
    - La Grande Duchesse

20th Kentucky Derby, May 15, 1894

$2,500 added. Net to winner $4,020; second $300; third $150; fourth $100. 55 nominations.

Horses	Wt	Fin	Jockeys	Owners
Chant 122		1	F Goodale	Leigh & Rose
Pearl Song 122		2	R Williams	C H Smith
Sigurd. 122		3	Overton	Bashford Manor
Al Boyer. 122		4	Ray	Anderson & Gooding
Tom Elmore 122		5	Irving	S K Hughes & Co

Time, 2:41. Weather clear.

Winner—B.c. by Falsetto—Addie C., by Voltigeur; trained by Eugene Leigh; bred by A. J. Alexander.

Bookmaking Odds: Chant, 1 to 2; Pearl Song, 3 to 1; Sigurd, 12 to 1.

Sigurd broke first, followed by **Chant,** which took the lead at the half and won by two lengths.

The Winner's Pedigree

CHANT
(Bay colt)

Falsetto
- Enquirer
  - *Leamington
  - Lida
- Farfaletta
  - *Australian
  - Elkhorna

Addie C.
- Voltigeur
  - Vandal
  - Duet
- Aerolite
  - Lexington
  - Florine

19th Kentucky Derby, May 10, 1893

$3,000 added. Net to winner $3,840; second $400; third $150; fourth $100. 60 nominations.

Horses	Wt	Fin	Jockeys	Owners
Lookout 122		1	E Kunze	Cushing & Orth
Plutus 122		2	A Clayton	Bashford Manor
Boundless 122		3	R Williams	Cushing & Orth
Also ran — Buck McCann 122		—	Thorpe	Scoggan Bros
Mirage 122		—	I Murphy	James E Pepper
Linger 122		—	Flynn	C E Railey

Time, 2:39¼. Weather clear.

Winner—Ch.c. by Troubadour—Christina, by King Alfonso; trained by William McDaniel; bred by Scoggan Brothers.

Bookmaking Odds: 7 to 10 (Cushing & Orth's entry), Lookout, Boundless; 3 to 1, Plutus.

Within the first eighth, **Lookout**, coupled with **Boundless**, took the lead, held it throughout, and won by five lengths.

The Winner's Pedigree

LOOKOUT
(Chestnut colt)

- Troubadour
  - Lisbon
    - *Phaeton
    - *Lady Love
  - Glenluine
    - *Glenelg
    - Lute
- Christina
  - King Alfonso
    - *Phaeton
    - Capitola
  - Luileme
    - Lexington
    - Rosette

18th Kentucky Derby, May 11, 1892

$2,500 added. Net to winner $4,230; second $300; third $150. 68 nominations.

Horses	Wt	Fin	Jockeys	Owners
Azra 122		1	A Clayton	Bashford Manor
Huron................... 122		2	Britton	Ed Corrigan
Phil Dwyer.............. 122		3	Overton	Ed Corrigan

Time, 2:41½. Track heavy.

Winner—B.c. by Reform—Albia, by Alarm; trained by John H. Morris; bred by George J. Long.

Bookmaking Odds: Azra, 3 to 2; Huron and Phil Dwyer (coupled as Corrigan entry), 11 to 20.

Huron broke in front and had a six-length lead well along the backstretch. Then Clayton, aboard **Azra,** made his move, caught **Huron** near the wire, and won by a nose.

The Winner's Pedigree

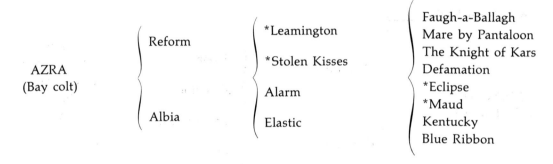

AZRA
(Bay colt)

Reform

Albia

*Leamington

*Stolen Kisses

Alarm

Elastic

Faugh-a-Ballagh
Mare by Pantaloon
The Knight of Kars
Defamation
*Eclipse
*Maud
Kentucky
Blue Ribbon

17th Kentucky Derby, May 13, 1891

$2,500 added. Net to winner $4,550; second $300; third $150. 83 nominations.

Horses	Wt	Fin	Jockeys	Owners
Kingman	122	1	I Murphy	Jacobin Stable
Balgowan.	122	2	Overton	T J Clay
High Tariff.	122	3	R Williams	Easton & Larabie
Hart Wallace.	122	4	Kiley	Bashford Manor

Time, 1:05½ (half), 1:35¾ (six furlongs), 2:01 (mile), 2:52¼. Track slow.

Winner—B.c. by *Glengarry—Patricia, by Vauxhall; trained by Dud Allen; bred by A. C. Franklin.

Bookmaking Odds: Kingman, 1 to 2; Balgowan, 3 to 1; High Tariff, 10 to 1; Hart Wallace, 6 to 1.

This was the slowest of all Derbies. **Hart Wallace** broke on top; **High Tariff,** second; **Balgowan,** third; **Kingman,** fourth. Within a quarter of a mile they were all traveling like a cavalry, side by side, nose and nose, each jockey waiting for the other to set the pace, and none doing it. Each rider had orders to stay back for about a mile and whenever one horse moved a little to the front, his rider restrained him, and the others restrained theirs, too. The mile was covered in 2:01, and the mile and a quarter in 2:26¾. At that point, Murphy started his move with **Kingsman,** and Overton let **Balgowan** have his head, but **Kingman** won the race by a length.

The Winner's Pedigree

KINGMAN (Bay colt)	*Glengarry	Thormanby	‡Windhound
			Alice Hawthorn
		Carbine	Rifleman
			Troica
	Patricia	Vauxhall	Lexington
			Verona
		Minnie Mc	Planet
			Edina

16th Kentucky Derby, May 14, 1890

$2,500 added. Net to winner $5,460; second $300; third $150. 115 nominations.

Horses	Wt	Fin	Jockeys	Owners
Riley 118		1	I Murphy	E Corrigan
Bill Letcher 118		2	Allen	W R Letcher
Robespierre 118		3	Francis	G V Hankins
Palisade 118		4	Britton	S Williams
Outlook 118		5	Breckinridge	B J Treacy
Prince Fonso 118		6	Overton	J C Twymann & Co

Time, 2:45. Track heavy.

Winner—B.c. by Longfellow—Geneva, by War Dance; trained by Edward Corrigan; bred by C. H. Durkee.

Bookmaking Odds: Robespierre, even money; Riley, 4 to 1; Bill Letcher, 5 to 1; Prince Fonso, 5 to 1; Palisade, 8 to 1; Outlook, 10 to 1.

No auction pools or mutuels sold at track after 1889 until 1908. However, auction pools sold in 1890, 1891 and for years thereafter in downtown Louisville, on night before, and morning of Derby.

Bill Letcher was away first, and **Palisade**, second. **Robespierre**, the favorite, took the lead nearing the first turn; **Outlook**, second. **Riley** came from last place, going into the backstretch, and took command, winning easily by two lengths.

The Winner's Pedigree

		*Leamington	Faugh-a-Ballagh
	Longfellow		Mare by Pantaloon
		Nantura	Brawner's Eclipse
†RILEY			Queen Mary
(Bay colt)		War Dance	Lexington
	Geneva		Reel
		La Gitana	Uncle Vic
			Georgia Wood

†Riley was originally named Shortfellow.

Year	Age	Sts	1st	2nd	3rd	Won
1889	2	12	6	3	0	$ 4,505
1890	3	21	11	6	2	21,065
1891	4	15	8	3	1	14,360
1892	5	3	2	1	0	1,050
1893	6	10	2	4	1	2,150
1894	7	3	1	0	0	300
		64	30	17	4	$43,430

15th Kentucky Derby, May 9, 1889

$2,500 added. Net to winner $4,880; second $300; third $150. 94 nominations.

Horses	Wt	Fin	Jockeys	Owners
Spokane	118	1	T Kiley	N Armstrong
Proctor Knott...........	115	2	S Barnes	Scoggan & Bryant
Once Again.............	118	3	I Murphy	M Young
Hindoocraft.............	118	4	Armstrong	Scoggan Bros
Cassius	118	5	Taral	Beverwyck Stable
Sportsman.............	118	6	I Lewis	J K Megibben & Co
Outbound	118	7	Hollis	Fleetwood Stable
Bootmaker.............	118	8	Warwick	Wilson & Young

Time, :24, :48½, 1:14½, 1:41½, 2:09½, 2:34½ (new Derby record).

Weather clear, track fast.

Winner—Ch.c. by Hyder Ali—Interpose, by *Intruder; trained by John Rodegap; bred by Noah Armstrong.

Auction Pools: Prices not available.

Bookmaking Odds: Proctor Knott, 1 to 2; Spokane, 10 to 1; Once Again and Bootmaker (Young entry), 3 to 1; Hindoocraft, 10 to 1; Cassius, 15 to 1; Outbound, 15 to 1; Sportsman, 15 to 1.

Mutuels: ($2 tickets sold for first time this year.) $2 tickets on Spokane paid $34.80 win, $6.30 place; Proctor Knott, $2.90 place. No show tickets sold.

This was last year when auction pools were sold at track, until the method was revived in 1908 by Colonel Matt J. Winn and associates. The auction pools were ruled out after the 1899 Derby by Colonel Clark, following a protest by bookmakers that their business was being handicapped by opposition from auction pool sellers.

Proctor Knott, a wild horse at the barrier, broke away twice, to gallop more than an eighth of a mile, and almost unseated his rider, "Pike" Barnes, during several spectacular lunges. But he broke along with his field. **Hindoocraft** was the early leader, with **Bootmaker,** second, **Spokane,** third. Near the first turn, **Proctor Knott** was rushed to the front, and led by three lengths entering the backstretch, with **Sportsman,** second; **Hindoocraft,** third; and **Spokane,** fifth, under a careful ride. All through the backstretch, **Proctor Knott** was fighting for his head. Leaving the backstretch, **Proctor Knott** was five lengths in front, with **Hindoocraft,** second; **Spokane** had moved into third place, and gradually was increasing speed. Taking the turn for home, Barnes was unable to control **Proctor Knott,** and the colt lost many lengths by racing to the outer rail, where Barnes succeeded in getting him straightened. Barnes chose to ride the outer rail, rather than lose ground by steering his horse back toward the inside fence. **Spokane** skimmed the inner rail, and ran through the stretch on the inside rail, with **Proctor Knott** on the outside rail. **Proctor Knott** had about a half-length advantage an eighth from the wire, but it was obvious that he was a tired horse, while **Spokane** seemed fresh and strong. As the finish wire was crossed, opinion of spectators was divided as to the outcome of the race. One faction was certain that **Spokane,** on the inside, had nosed out **Proctor Knott** on the outer rail; another took the opposite viewpoint. The judges—Colonel Clark, General Robinson and J. K. Megibben—deliberated quite a while then awarded to **Spokane** by a nose.

The Winner's Pedigree

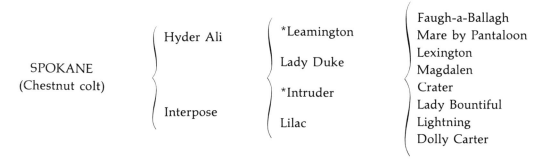

	Hyder Ali	*Leamington	Faugh-a-Ballagh
			Mare by Pantaloon
SPOKANE		Lady Duke	Lexington
(Chestnut colt)			Magdalen
	Interpose	*Intruder	Crater
			Lady Bountiful
		Lilac	Lightning
			Dolly Carter

14th Kentucky Derby, May 14, 1888

$2,500 added. Net to winner $4,740; second $500; third $200. 95 nominations.

Horses	Wt	Fin	Jockeys	Owners
Macbeth II	115	1	G Covington	Chicago Stable
Gallifet	118	2	A McCarthy	Melbourne Stable
White	118	3	Withers	W O Scully
Alexandria	118	4	Jones	Melbourne Stable
The Chevalier	118	5	Lewis	T J Clay
Autocrat	118	6	Hamilton	D Gibson
Col Zeb Ward	118	7	Blaylock	G M Rye

Time, 2:38¼. Weather clear, track fast.

Winner—Br.g. by Macduff—Agnes, by Gilroy; trained by John Campbell; bred by Rufus Lisle.

Auction Pools: Prices not available.

Bookmaking Odds: Gallifet and Alexandria (Melbourne Stable entry), even money; The Chevalier, 3½ to 1; White, 4 to 1; Macbeth II, 6 to 1; Col. Zeb Ward, 12 to 1; Autocrat, 12 to 1.

Mutuels: Pay-off prices not available.

The Chevalier took lead, closely followed by **Autocrat** and **Col. Zeb Ward. Gallifet** raced to the front around the first turn, and remained there until an eighth of a mile from the wire, when **Macbeth II** came with a rush, and won by a length.

The Winner's Pedigree

MACBETH II
(Brown gelding)

- Macduff
  - *Macaroon
    - Macaroni
    - Songstress
  - Jersey Lass
    - *King Ernest
    - Jersey Belle
- Agnes
  - Gilroy
    - Lexington
    - Magnolia
  - Laura Bruce
    - Star Davis
    - Alida

13th Kentucky Derby, May 11, 1887

$1,500 added. Net to winner $4,200; second $300; third $150. 119 nominations.

Horses	Wt	Fin	Jockeys	Owners
Montrose	118	1	I Lewis	Labold Bros
Jim Gore	118	2	W Fitzpatrick	A G McCampbell
Jacobin	118	3	J Stoval	R Lisle
Banburg	115	4	Blaylock	J D Morrisey
Clarion	118	5	Arnold	Fleetwood Stable
Ban Yan	118	6	Godfrey	W O Scully
Pendennis	118	7	Murphy	Santa Anita Stable

Time, 2:39¼. Track fast.

Winner—B.c. by Duke of Montrose—Patti, by *Billet; trained by John McGinty; bred by Milton Young.

Auction Pools: 8 to 5 against Banburg; 2 to 1, Jim Gore; 4 to 1, Pendennis, 5 to 1, Jacobin; 6 to 1, Ban Yan; 10 to 1 each, Montrose and Clarion.

Bookmaking Odds: Montrose, 10 to 1; Jim Gore, 3 to 1; Jacobin, 6 to 1; Banburg, 7 to 5; Clarion, 10 to 1; Ban Yan, 5 to 1; Pendennis, 4 to 1.

Mutuels: Pay-off figures not available.

The Winner's Pedigree

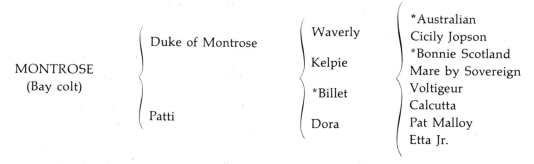

MONTROSE
(Bay colt)

Duke of Montrose

Patti

Waverly

Kelpie

*Billet

Dora

*Australian

Cicily Jopson

*Bonnie Scotland

Mare by Sovereign

Voltigeur

Calcutta

Pat Malloy

Etta Jr.

12th Kentucky Derby, May 14, 1886

$1,500 added. Net to winner $4,890; second $300; third $150. 107 nominations.

Horses	Wt	Fin	Jockeys	Owners
Ben Ali................. 118		1	P Duffy	J B Haggin
Blue Wing.............. 118		2	Garrison	Melbourne Stable
Free Knight............ 118		3	W Fitzpatrick	P Corrigan
Lijero 118		4	I Murphy	E J Baldwin
Jim Gray 118		5	Withers	Gray & Co
Grimaldi................ 118		6	I Lewis	J & J Swigert
Sir Joseph............. 118		7	Conkling	R A Swigert
Harrodsburg 118		8	J Riley	Chinn & Morgan
Lafitte................. 118		9	Stovall	J G Greener & Co
Masterpiece 118		10	West	S S Brown

Time, 2:36½ (new Derby record). Weather clear, track fast.

Winner—Br.c. by Virgil—Ulrica, by Lexington; trained by Jim Murphy; bred by Daniel Swigert.

Auction Pools: Ben Ali, $500; Free Knight, $385; Blue Wing, $150; Jim Gray, $65; Lijero, $50; Field, $70.

Bookmaking Odds: Bookmakers did not operate because of failure to reach license agreement with management.

Mutuels: $5 win tickets on Ben Ali paid $13.60; $5 place paid $12; $5 place tickets on Blue Wing, $10.

Masterpiece broke in front, and was followed to the first turn by **Harrodsburg** and **Sir Joseph.** At the three quarters, **Free Knight** took command, followed by **Blue Wing** and **Ben Ali.** Down through the stretch it was a furious, whipping finish between **Ben Ali** and **Blue Wing,** with **Ben Ali** the winner by half a length.

The Winner's Pedigree

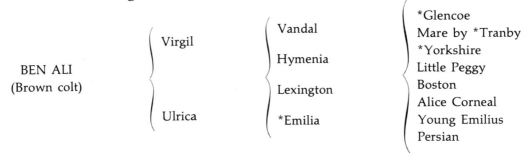

BEN ALI (Brown colt)

Virgil — Vandal — *Glencoe / Mare by *Tranby; Hymenia — *Yorkshire / Little Peggy

Ulrica — Lexington — Boston / Alice Corneal; *Emilia — Young Emilius / Persian

11th Kentucky Derby, May 14, 1885

$1,500 added. Net to winner $4,630; second $200. 69 nominations.

Horses	Wt	Fin	Jockeys	Owners
Joe Cotton 110		1	E Henderson	J T Williams
Berson 110		2	West	Morris & Patton
Ten Booker 110		3	Stoval	M Young
Favor 110		4	Thompkins	Morris & Patton
Irish Pat 110		5	Murphy	E Corrigan
Keokuk 110		6	Fishbourne	W P Hunt
Clay Pete 110		7	Withers	R C Pate
Thistle 110		8	Blaylock	P G Speth
Playfair 107		9	Conkling	G W Darden & Co
Lord Coleridge 107		10	Hughes	W Cottrill

Time, 2:37¼. Weather clear, track good.

Winner—Ch.c. by King Alphonso—*Inverness, by Macaroni; trained by Alex Perry; bred by A. J. Alexander.

Auction Pools: Joe Cotton, $500; Berson and Favor $215 (coupled as Morris & Patton entry); Ten Booker, $75; Irish Pat, $40; Playfair and Thistle, $35 each; Lord Coleridge, $25; Field $30.

Bookmaking Odds: Joe Cotton, even money; Berson, 2 to 1; Ten Booker, 10 to 1.

Mutuels: ($5 win and place betting only): Joe Cotton, $9.30 straight, $8.80 place; Berson, $7.40 place.

Within the first eighth, **Favor** took the lead, **Keokuk,** second, the others strung out. They ran that way into the backstretch, where **Joe Cotton,** in seventh position, started to move. **Joe Cotton** worked his way to the front, going into the stretch, but had to be ridden to his ultimate effort to stave off the rush of **Berson** and **Ten Booker,** who came like whirlwinds in the final eighth.

The Winner's Pedigree

JOE COTTON
(Chestnut colt)

- King Alfonso
  - *Phaeton
    - King Tom
    - Merry Sunshine
  - Capitola
    - Vandal
    - Mare by *Margrave
- *Inverness
  - Macaroni
    - Sweetmeat
    - Jocose
  - Elfrida
    - Faugh-a-Ballagh
    - Espoir

10th Kentucky Derby, May 16, 1884

$1,500 added. Net to winner $3,990; second $200. 51 nominations.

Horses	Wt	Fin	Jockeys	Owners
Buchanan 110		1	I Murphy	W Cottrill
Loftin 110		2	Sayres	A Johnson & Co
Audrain 110		3	Fishburn	T J Megibben
Bob Miles 110		—	McLaughlin	J T Williams
Admiral............ 110		—	C Taylor	Clay & Woodford
Also Powhattan III 110		—	D Williams	R A Johnson & Co
ran Exploit 110		—	Conkling	Wooding & Puryear
Boreas 110		—	O'Brien	R M McClelland
Bob Cook 110		—	Gorham	R M McClelland

Time, 2:40¼. Weather clear, track good.

Winner—Ch.c. by *Buckden—Mrs. Grigsby, by Wagner; trained by William Bird; bred by Cottrill & Guest.

Auction Pools: Audrain, $700; Bob Miles, $600; Buchanan, $530; Loftin (coupled with Powhattan III as R. A. Johnson & Co.'s entry), $270; Admiral, $125; Field $90.

Bookmaking Odds: Bookmakers did not operate on opening day.

Mutuels: $5 win tickets on Buchanan paid $20.60.

Bob Miles beat the flag, and jumped into a two-length lead, followed by **Powhattan III, Audrain,** the favorite, and **Admiral. Buchanan** fractious at the post, was away poorly, but Isaac Murphy, his Negro jockey, saved ground for three-quarters of a mile, and then Murphy called upon him for his best effort. **Buchanan** moved to the front quickly, with gigantic strides, was eased up through the final eighth, and won by two lengths.

The Winner's Pedigree

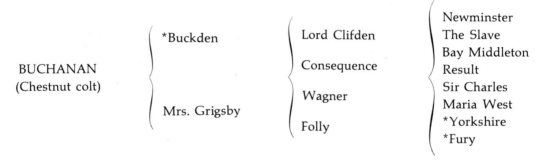

	*Buckden	Lord Clifden	Newminster
BUCHANAN			The Slave
(Chestnut colt)		Consequence	Bay Middleton
			Result
	Mrs. Grigsby	Wagner	Sir Charles
			Maria West
		Folly	*Yorkshire
			*Fury

9th Kentucky Derby, May 23, 1883

$1,500 added. Net to winner $3,760; second $200. 50 nominations.

Horses	Wt	Fin	Jockeys	Owners
Leonatus 105		1	W Donohue	Chinn & Morgan
Drake Carter 102		2	Spellman	Morris & Patton
Lord Ragland 105		3	Quantrell	N Armstrong
Ascender 102		—	Stoval	R C Pate
Also Pike's Pride 102		—	Evans	George Evans
ran Chatter 105		—	Henderson	W C McCurdy
Standiford Keller 105		—	Blaylock	J R Watts

Time, 2:43. Weather drizzling, track heavy.

Winner—B.c. by Longfellow—Semper Felix, by *Phaeton; trained by R. Colston; bred by John Henry Miller.

Auction Pools: Leonatus, $800; Ascender, $500; Drake Carter, $450; Field $500.

Bookmaking Odds: Bookmakers operated, but prices not available.

Mutuels: $5 win ticket on Leonatus paid $14.80—odds of 1.96 to 1.

Drake Carter was away first, but **Leonatus** caught him during the first quarter, and never was headed, winning by three lengths.

The Winner's Pedigree

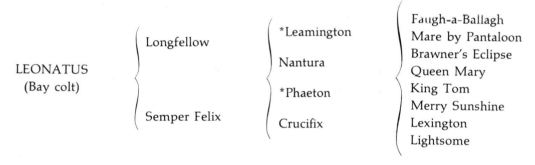

LEONATUS (Bay colt)

- Longfellow
  - *Leamington
    - Faugh-a-Ballagh
    - Mare by Pantaloon
  - Nantura
    - Brawner's Eclipse
    - Queen Mary
- Semper Felix
  - *Phaeton
    - King Tom
    - Merry Sunshine
  - Crucifix
    - Lexington
    - Lightsome

8th Kentucky Derby, May 16, 1882

$1,500 added. Net to winner $4,560; second $200. 64 nominations.

Horses	Wt	Fin	Jockeys	Owners
Apollo	102	1	B Hurd	Morris & Patton
Runnymede	105	2	J McLaughlin	Dwyer Bros
Bengal	105	3	S Fisher	Bowen & Co
Wendover	105	—	Hovey	J B Sellers & Co
Harry Gilmore	105	—	Gibbs	W Cottrill
Ch.c. by Pat Malloy	105	—	Henderson	P C Fox
Robt Bruce	105	—	L Jones	A Jackson
Babcock	102	—	Kelso	W Lakeland
Newsboy	105	—	Quantrell	T J Megibben
Wallensee	107	—	Parker	Rodes & Carr
Mistral	105	—	Stoval	L P Tarlton
Lost Cause	102	—	Taylor	M Young
Highflyer	105	—	Brown	G Kuhns & Co

Also ran — Wendover, Harry Gilmore, Ch.c. by Pat Malloy, Robt Bruce, Babcock, Newsboy, Wallensee, Mistral, Lost Cause, Highflyer.

Time, 2:40¼. Weather clear, track good.

Winner—Ch.g. by *Ashstead or Lever—Rebecca T. Price, by The Colonel; trained by Green B. Morris; bred by Daniel Swigert.

(Three forms of betting in operation, bookmaking, odds being quoted for first time.)

Auction Pools: Runnymede, $250; Mistral, $50; Lost Cause, $40; Robert Bruce, $30; Bengal, $75; Field (with Apollo included), $75.

Bookmaking odds: Runnymede, 4 to 5, favorite; Apollo, 10 to 1.

Mutuels: $5 win tickets on Apollo paid $169. No place tickets sold.

Harry Gilmore broke in front, followed by **Babcock,** the **Pat Malloy** colt and **Robert Bruce.** At the mile, **Harry Gilmore** was still on top, with **Runnymede** moving on the outside to take third place. As they were well into the stretch, **Runnymede** took command, and looked like the winner until **Apollo** started a cyclonic rush an eighth of a mile from home. **Apollo** caught **Runnymede** a few jumps from the wire, and won by half a length.

The Winner's Pedigree

APOLLO
(Chestnut gelding)

‡Lever
- Lexington
  - Boston
  - Alice Carneal
- Levity
  - *Trustee
  - Mare by *Tranby

Rebecca T. Price
- The Colonel
  - Albion
  - Lalla Rookh
- Mare by *Margrave
  - *Margrave
  - Rosalie Somers

7th Kentucky Derby, May 17, 1881

$1,500 added. Net to winner $4,410; second $200. 62 nominations.

Horses	Wt	Fin	Jockeys	Owners
Hindoo 105		1	J McLaughlin	Dwyer Bros
Lelex. 105		2	A Allen	B G Thomas
Alfambra 105		3	G Evans	G W Bowen & Co
Also Sligo 105		—	Donohue	H P McGrath
ran Getaway. 105		—	Fisher	M Young
Calycanthus 105		—	G Smith	H P McGrath

Time, 2:40. Weather clear, track fast.

Winner—B.c. by Virgil—Florence, by Lexington; trained by James Rowe, Sr.; bred by Daniel Swigert.

Auction Pools: Hindoo, $600; Lelex, $75; McGrath entry (Sligo and Calycanthus), $70; Alfambra, $40; Getaway, $25.

Mutuel tickets sold, but no pay-off prices available.

Hindoo went to the front with the break. At one time or another, every horse came up to challenge him, but **Hindoo** shook them off, almost without effort, merely galloped through the stretch, and won by four lengths, eased up.

The Winner's Pedigree

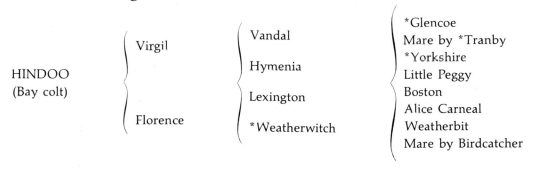

HINDOO
(Bay colt)

Virgil
- Vandal
  - *Glencoe
  - Mare by *Tranby
- Hymenia
  - *Yorkshire
  - Little Peggy

Florence
- Lexington
  - Boston
  - Alice Carneal
- *Weatherwitch
  - Weatherbit
  - Mare by Birdcatcher

6th Kentucky Derby, May 18, 1880

$1,500 added. Net to winner $3,800; second $200. 47 nominations.

Horses	Wt	Fin	Jockeys	Owners
Fonso 105		1	G Lewis	J S Shawhan
Kimball 105		2	Lakeland	W Cottrill
Bancroft 105		3	I Murphy	M Young
Also Boulevard 105		—	Allen	W C McGavock & Co.
ran Quito 105		—	McLaughlin	Dwyer Bros

Time, 2:37½. Weather clear, track fast.

Winner—Ch.c. by King Alfonso—*Weatherwitch, by Weatherbit; trained by Tice Hutsell; bred by A. J. Alexander.

Auction Pools: Kimball, $700; Quito, $362; Fonso, $222; Bancroft, $50; Boulevard was not sold because he was not announced as a starter until after the weighing-in bell was rung.

Mutuel tickets sold, but no pay-off prices available.

This Derby was run in dust many inches deep, and dust kicked up by leading horse practically obscured the nearest pursuers. **Fonso** broke in front and stayed there, winning by a length; **Kimball** was always second, and **Bancroft** always third. Foul claimed lodged by **Kimball's** jockey against **Fonso,** not allowed.

The Winner's Pedigree

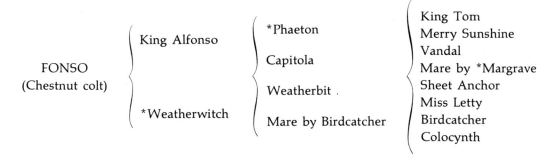

FONSO
(Chestnut colt)

King Alfonso
*Weatherwitch

*Phaeton
Capitola
Weatherbit
Mare by Birdcatcher

King Tom
Merry Sunshine
Vandal
Mare by *Margrave
Sheet Anchor
Miss Letty
Birdcatcher
Colocynth

5th Kentucky Derby, May 20, 1879

$1,500 added. Net to winner $3,550; second $200. 46 nominations.

Horses	Wt	Fin	Jockeys	Owners
Lord Murphy............. 100		1	Shauer	G W Darden & Co
Falsetto 100		2	I Murphy	J W H Reynolds
Strathmore 100		3	Hightower	George Cadwillader
Trinidad 100		—	Allen	D Swigert
One Dime 100		—	Jones	G W Bowen & Co
Also General Pike....... 100		—	Stoval	Gen Abe Buford
ran Buckner........... 100		—	Edwards	H W Farris
Wissahicken 97		—	Hawkins	H P McGrath
Ada Glen........... 97		—	Ramie	G D Wilson

Time, 2:37 (new Derby record). Weather clear, track fast.

Winner—B.c. by Pat Malloy—Wenonah, by Capt. Elgee; trained by George Rice; bred by J. T. Carter.

Auction Pools: Lord Murphy, $175; Strathmore and Falsetto, $60 each; Trinidad, $45; Ada Glen, $25; Field, $30.

Mutuel tickets sold, but no pay-off prices available.

General Pike and **Trinidad** broke together, and ran head and head to the first turn, with **Strathmore,** third; **Falsetto,** fourth; **Buckner,** fifth. Trying to move up at the turn, **Lord Murphy** was bumped by a swerving horse, almost knocked to his knees, recovered, and then, from far back, charged at the field, gained the lead on the back stretch, and won by a length, under a hard drive.

The Winner's Pedigree

		Lexington	Boston
	Pat Malloy		Alice Carneal
		Gloriana	American Eclipse
†LORD MURPHY			Trifle
(Bay colt)		Capt. Elgee	Leviathan
	Wenonah		Reel
		Mare by *Albion	*Albion
			Mare by Pacific

†Lord Murphy originally named Patmus.

4th Kentucky Derby, May 21, 1878

$1,500 added. Net to winner $4,050; second $200. 56 nominations.

Horses	Wt	Fin	Jockeys	Owners
Day Star 100		1	J Carter	T J Nichols
Himyar 100		2	Robinson	B G Thomas
Leveler................. 100		3	Swim	R H Owens
Solicitor 100		—	Edward	L P Tarlton
McHenry 100		—	James	Gen Abe Buford
Also Respond 100		—	Ramey	Rodes & Carr
ran Burgundy........... 100		—	L Jones	J M Wooding
Earl of Beaconfield.. 100		—	Mahoney	A Straus & Co
Charlie Bush........ 100		—	Miller	Jennings & Hunt

Time, 2:37¼ (new Derby record). Weather clear, track good.

Winner—Ch.c. by Star Davis—Squeeze-'Em, by Lexington; trained by Lee Paul; bred by J. M. Clay.

Auction Pools: Himyar, $305; Field, $110. With Himyar out, Day Star, Burgundy and Leveler sold about even.

Mutuel wagering introduced in 1878, with four machines operating, but no prices available.

Day Star led from start to finish, winning by two lengths.

The Winner's Pedigree

DAY STAR (Chestnut Colt)	Star Davis	*Glencoe	Sultan
			Trampoline
		Margaret Wood	Priam
			Maria West
	Squeeze-'Em	Lexington	Boston
			Alice Carneal
		Skedaddle	*Yorkshire
			Magnolia

3rd Kentucky Derby, May 22, 1877

$1,500 added. Net to winner $3,300; second $200. 41 nominations.

Horses	Wt	Fin	Jockeys	Owners
Baden-Baden 100		1	W Walker	D Swigert
Leonard 100		2	Swim	H P McGrath
King William 100		3	Bailey	Smallwood & Co
Vera Cruz 97		—	Murphy	J T Williams
Odd Fellow 100		—	Williams	J J Merrill
McWhirter 100		—	H Moore	Gen Abe Buford
Also Malvern 100		—	S Jones	George H Rice
ran Early Light 97		—	W James	F B Harper
Dan K 97		—	McGrath	Johnson & Mills
Lisbon 100		—	Douglass	D Swigert
Headlight 100		—	Shelton	L B Fields

Time, 2:38. Weather clear, track fast.

Winner—Ch.c. by *Australian—Lavender, by Wagner; trained by Ed Brown; bred by A. J. Alexander.

Auction Pools: Leonard, $150; Vera Cruz, $100; McWhirter, $50; Swigert, $50; Field, (with Baden-Baden included) $45.

Leonard, the favorite, broke in front. **Baden-Baden** moved steadily from fifth place, to take second position going into the stretch, with **King William,** third, and **Vera Cruz,** fourth. Under slight pressure, **Baden-Baden,** ridden by Billy Walker, Negro jockey, passed **Leonard,** and won by two lengths.

The Winner's Pedigree

BADEN-BADEN (Chestnut Colt)	*Australian	West Australian	Melbourne
			Mowerina
		*Emilia	Young Emilius
			Persian
	Lavender	Wagner	Sir Charles
			Maria West
		Alice Carneal	*Sarpedon
			Rowena

2nd Kentucky Derby, May 15, 1876

$1,500 added. Net to winner $2,950; second $200. 34 nominations.

Horses	Wt	Fin	Jockeys	Owners
Vagrant 97		1	R Swim	William Astor
Creedmore 100		2	W Williams	Williams & Owings
Harry Hill 100		3	J Miller	John Funk
Parole. 97		—	Sparling	P Lorillard
Germantown 100		—	Graham	F B Harper
Black colt by Enquirer 97		—	James	F B Harper
Marie Michon 97		—	Stratford	J A Grinstead
Leamingtonian 100		—	Colston	H F Vissman
Bombay 100		—	Walker	D Swigert
Red Coat. 100		—	Hughes	Green Clay
Bullion 100		—	Kelso	A Keene Richards

Also ran — Parole, Germantown, Black colt by Enquirer, Marie Michon, Leamingtonian, Bombay, Red Coat, Bullion.

Time, 2:38¼. Weather clear, track fast.

Winner—Br.g. by Virgil—Lazy, by *Scythian; trained by James Williams; bred by M. H. Sanford.

Auction Pools: Vagrant, $525; Parole, $400; Creedmore, $275; Red Coat, $150; Field $135.

Parole went to front immediately after the break, but **Vagrant** came up on the outside, took the lead at the mile, and increased it through the stretch, to win by two lengths.

The Winner's Pedigree

VAGRANT
(Brown Gelding)

- Virgil
  - Vandal
    - *Glencoe
    - Mare by *Tranby
  - Hymenia
    - *Yorkshire
    - Little Peggy
- Lazy
  - *Scythian
    - Orlando
    - Scythia
  - Lindora
    - Lexington
    - Picayune

1st Kentucky Derby, May 17, 1875

$1,000 added. Net to winner $2,850; second $200. 42 nominations.

Horses	Wt	Fin	Jockeys	Owners
Aristides.	100	1	O Lewis	H P McGrath
Volcano	100	2	Chambers	George H Rice
Verdigris	100	3	Williams	C A Lewis
Ten Broeck.	—	—	Kelso	F P Harper
Searcher	—	—	Colston	J B Rodes
Enlister.	—	—	Halloway	Springfield & Clay
Warsaw	—	—	Masterson	Springfield & Clay
McCreery.	—	—	D Jones	Gen Abe Buford
Bill Bruce.	—	—	Jones	S J Salyer
Gold Mine	—	—	Stradford	J A Grinstead
Grenoble	—	—	Carter	Gen Abe Buford
Bob Wooley	—	—	Walker	Robinson, Morgan & Co
Vagabond	—	—	Houston	A B Lewis & Co
Ascension	—	—	W Lakeland	W C Hull
Chesapeake	—	—	Henry	H P McGrath

Note: "Also ran" bracket covers Ten Broeck through Chesapeake.

Time, 2:37¾. Track fast.

Winner—Ch.c. by *Leamington—Sarong, by Lexington; trained by A. Anderson; bred by H. P. McGrath.

Auction pools: McGrath entry (Aristides and Chesapeake) $105; Searcher $65; Ascension $55, field $270.

The field was away on the first attempt. **Volcano** went to the front, followed closely by **Verdigris, Aristides,** and **McCreery. Chesapeake** was away poorly. On the backside, **Aristides** moved into second place, was lapped on **Volcano** at the end of the mile, went to the front shortly thereafter. The field was strung out for a hundred yards in his wake. **Aristides** continued to increase his lead as **Volcano** was steadied for the final drive. At the head of the stretch, Owner McGrath, who had expected to win with **Chesapeake,** waved Jockey Lewis on. Immediately, **Aristides** moved out to win by a length. **Volcano** came strongly through the stretch, but could not reach the winner.

The Winner's Pedigree

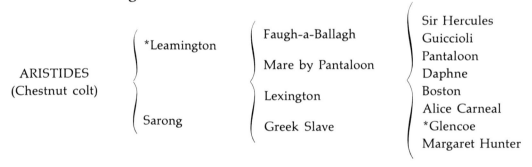

ARISTIDES (Chestnut colt)	*Leamington	Faugh-a-Ballagh	Sir Hercules
			Guiccioli
		Mare by Pantaloon	Pantaloon
			Daphne
	Sarong	Lexington	Boston
			Alice Carneal
		Greek Slave	*Glencoe
			Margaret Hunter

Notes

CHAPTER 1
THE MOST IMPORTANT RACE OF ALL

1. 1936 Kentucky Derby program, Churchill Downs, p. 52.
2. Robert Kelley, *Racing in America 1937–59* (New York: The Jockey Club, 1960), p. 73.
3. Joe H. Palmer, *This Was Racing*, edited by Red Smith (New York: A. S. Barnes, 1953), p. 75.
4. Roger Longrigg, *The History of Horse Racing* (New York: Stein & Day, 1972), pp. 92–93.
5. Longrigg, p. 94.
6. Peter Willett, *The Thoroughbred* (New York: G. P. Putnam's, 1970), p. 152.
7. Keeneland Race Course souvenir program October 1936, p. 24.
8. Keeneland program, 1936, p. 52.
9. Joe Estes, unpublished essay on Kentucky Derby's effect upon thoroughbred breeding, property of *The Blood-Horse*.

CHAPTER 2
THE PRESIDING JUDGE

1. Bradley Smith, *The Horse and the Blue Grass Country* (New York: Doubleday, Inc., 1955), p. 136.
2. Smith, p. 146.
3. Dan M. Bowmar III, *Giants of the Turf* (Kentucky: The Blood-Horse, 1960), p. 20.
4. Bowmar, p. 16.
5. John Hervey, *Racing in America 1665–1865* (New York: The Jockey Club, 1944), p. 3.
6. Hervey, p. 3.
7. Bowmar, *Giants of the Turf*, p. 97.
8. *Turf, Field, and Farm*, November 19, 1897, p. 647.
9. *Turf, Field, and Farm*, November 19, 1897, p. 647.
10. *Turf, Field, and Farm*, November 19, 1897, p. 211.
11. *Daily Louisville Commercial*, May 7, 1875.
12. Frank G. Menke, *The Story of Churchill Downs and the Kentucky Derby* (Kentucky: privately printed, 1940), pp. 12–13.
13. Colonel Matt J. Winn as told to Frank G. Menke, *Down the Stretch* (New York: Smith & Durrell, 1945), p. 27.
14. Winn to Menke, *Down the Stretch*, p. 33.
15. *Turf, Field, and Farm*, November 19, 1897, p. 647.
16. *Turf, Field, and Farm*, November 19, 1897, p. 647.
17. *Turf, Field, and Farm*, November 19, 1897, p. 647.
18. *Turf, Field, and Farm*, November 12, 1897, p. 615.

CHAPTER 3
THE LITTLE RED HORSE

1. *Turf, Field, and Farm*, September 20, 1872, p. 177.
2. *Turf, Field, and Farm*, September 30, 1870, p. 201.
3. Kent Hollingsworth, *The Great Ones* (Kentucky: The Blood-Horse, 1970), p. 273.
4. Henry Chefetz, *Play the Devil* (New York: Clarkson N. Potter, 1960), p. 264.
5. Edward L. Bowen, "1875 and All That," *The Blood-Horse* (April 24, 1972), p. 1408.
6. Bowen, p. 1409.
7. Bowen, p. 1409.
8. Hollingsworth, p. 274.
9. Frank G. Menke, *The Story of Churchill Downs and the Kentucky Derby* (Kentucky: privately printed, 1940), p. 15.

CHAPTER 4
"Who did Haggin think he was"

1. *The Thoroughbred Record* (V. 49, 1899), p. 197.
2. Frank G. Menke, *The Story of Churchill Downs and the Kentucky Derby* (Kentucky: privately printed, 1940), p. 22.
3. Colonel Matt J. Winn as told to Frank G. Menke in *Down the Stretch* (New York: Smith & Durrell, 1945), p. 10.
4. *Daily Louisville Commercial*, May 16, 1894, p. 1.

5. Joe Jordan, Lexington *Leader* (no date).
6. Jordan.
7. Kent Hollingsworth, *The Wizard of the Turf* (Kentucky: privately printed, 1965), p. 50.

CHAPTER 5
IKE AND WINK

1. Len Tracy, "Memoirs of the Kentucky Derby," *The Thoroughbred Record* (February 21, 1959), p. 19.
2. Roy Terrell, "Around the World in 80 Years," *Sports Illustrated* (May 8, 1961), p. 73.
3. Terrell, p. 75.
4. Helen Drusine, "Jimmy Winkfield, a Winner at 92," *International Herald Tribune*, Paris, May 20, 1972.
5. Billy Joe Purdom, "The 'Walking Derby,'" *Turf and Sport Digest* (May 1968), p. 22.
6. Keeneland Race Course souvenir program, October 1936, p. 65.
7. Keeneland program, October 1936, p. 65.
8. L. P. Tarlton, "Isaac Murphy: A Memorial," *The Thoroughbred Record* (March 21, 1896), p. 136.
9. Peggy Keilus, "The Great Isaac Murphy," *Turf and Sport Digest* (March 1964), p. 31.
10. *The Thoroughbred Record*, March 21, 1896, p. 136.
11. *TTR*, March 21, 1896, p. 136.

CHAPTER 6
BLACK GOLD

1. John Hervey, *Racing in America 1922–1936* (New York: The Jockey Club, privately printed, 1937), p. 50.
2. New Orleans *Tribune*, January 19, 1928.

CHAPTER 7
"for money, marbles, or chalk"

1. New York *World* (no date).
2. John Ney, *Palm Beach* (Boston: Little, Brown, 1966), p. 169.
3. *The Blood-Horse*, August 31, 1946, p. 567.
4. Edward Riley Bradley with John I. Day, "My Four Kentucky Derby Winners," *Saturday Evening Post* (May 8, 1937), p. 18.
5. Day, p. 19.
6. Day, p. 40.
7. Day, p. 42.
8. Len Tracy, "Memoirs of the Kentucky Derby," *The Thoroughbred Record* (March 12, 1960), p. 38.
9. *New York Times*, May 19, 1929.
10. *New York Times*, May 19, 1929.
11. *The Blood-Horse*, May 13, 1933, p. 559.
12. *Cincinnati Enquirer*, May 7, 1933.
13. G. F. T. Ryall, "Derby and Preakness," *Polo Magazine* (June 1933), p. 24.
14. Louisville *Courier-Journal*, May 9, 1933.
15. John Hervey, *American Race Horses 1940* (New York: The Sagamore Press, 1940), p. 93.
16. Hervey, p. 93.
17. *The Blood-Horse*, August 24, 1946, p. 535.

CHAPTER 8
"Devil's red, blue collar, blue hoops on sleeves"

1. Red Smith, *New York Times*, September 15, 1971.
2. Hambla Bauer, "Boss of Calumet Farm," *Saturday Evening Post* (September 11, 1948), p. 116.
3. Eddie Arcaro as told to John O'Hara, *I Ride to Win* (New York: Greenberg, 1951), p. 41.
4. O'Hara, p. 61.
5. Leon Rasmussen, "Joneses' Faith in Bull Lea Pays Off," *Daily Racing Form*, September 1, 1959.
6. Lexington *Leader*, May 3, 1962.
7. *Leader*, May 3, 1962.
8. *Leader*, May 3, 1962.
9. *Leader*, May 3, 1962.
10. *The Blood-Horse*, June 13, 1961, p. 1170.
11. Alex Bower, "Calumet Takes Up Its Option," *The Blood-Horse* (May 10, 1952), p. 880.
12. Bob Considine, "The Kentucky Derby's Bill Corum," *Colliers* (May 6, 1950), p. 64.
13. William H. P. Robertson, *The History of Thoroughbred Racing in America* (New Jersey: Prentice-Hall, 1964), p. 404.
14. *Daily Racing Form*, September 1, 1959.
15. *Time*, May 30, 1949, p. 45.
16. *Daily Racing Form*, June 14, 1961.
17. *DRF*, June 14, 1961.
18. *DRF*, June 14, 1961.
19. *DRF*, June 14, 1961.
20. M. A. Stoneridge, *Great Horses of Our Time* (New York: Doubleday, 1972), p. 39.
21. John Hervey, *American Race Horses 1941* (New York: The Sagamore Press, 1941), p. 138.
22. Bill Corum, New York *Journal American*, May 6, 1941.
23. Eddie Arcaro, *I Ride to Win*, p. 105.
24. Arcaro, p. 107.
25. Arcaro, p. 107.
26. Lexington *Leader*, May 3, 1962.
27. Arcaro, p. 108.
28. Arcaro, p. 109.
29. Hervey, p. 140.
30. Arcaro, p. 113.
31. Dan Parker, New York *Daily Mirror*, May 9, 1941.

CHAPTER 9
"He ran so fast he scared me"

1. *The Blood-Horse*, August 15, 1970, p. 2624.
2. *The Blood-Horse*, p. 2622.
3. Eddie Arcaro, *I Ride to Win* (New York: Greenberg, 1951).
4. Kent Hollingsworth, *The Great Ones* (Kentucky: *The Blood-Horse*, 1970), p. 60.
5. Len Tracy, "Memoirs of the Kentucky Derby," *The Thoroughbred Record* (March 17, 1962), p. 47.

CHAPTER 10
"McCreary has lost his nerve"

1. Herb Goldstein, "Jack Amiel's Big Day," *Turf & Sport Digest* (August 1967), p. 4.

2. Goldstein, p. 4.
3. *Turf & Sport Digest* (no date).
4. *Turf & Sport Digest* (August 1967), p. 5.
5. Clinton B. Alves, "The Third Count," *Turf & Sport Digest* (July 1951), p. 19.
6. Len Tracy, "Memoirs of the Kentucky Derby," *The Thoroughbred Record* (April 7, 1962), p. 44.
7. Tracy, p. 44.
8. *Turf & Sport Digest* (August 1967), pp. 28–29.
9. *T&SD*, 1967, p. 29.
10. *T&SD*, 1967, p. 29.
11. *The Thoroughbred Record*, April 7, 1962, p. 45.
12. *TTR*, 1967, p. 45.

CHAPTER 11
THE LONGEST DERBY

1. Boston *Herald* (no date).
2. Boston *Herald Traveler*, April 25, 1968.
3. *Traveler*, 1968.
4. *Traveler*, 1968.
5. Red Smith, *New York Times*, May 1968.
6. Gene Ward, "Ward to the Wise" column, New York *Daily News*, May 4, 1968.
7. Ward.
8. *The Blood-Horse*, May 11, 1968, p. 1341.
9. Whitney Tower, "It Was a Bitter Pill," *Sports Illustrated*, May 20, 1968, p. 21.
10. Tower, p. 21.
11. Billy Reed, Louisville *Courier-Journal*, July 9, 1972.
12. Reed.
13. Associated Press, May 7, 1968.

CHAPTER 12
A DIVINE VICTORY

1. Louisville *Courier-Journal*, May 2, 1970.

CHAPTER 13
DR. JENNY'S MASTERPIECE

1. *The Morning Telegraph*, April 1, 1971.

CHAPTER 14
CANONERO SEGUNDO

1. William F. Reed, "What a Fiesta We Will Have!" *Sports Illustrated* (May 31, 1971), p. 27.
2. Frank T. Phelps, "Leanin' on the Rail" column, Lexington *Leader*, May 4, 1971.
3. *Sports Illustrated* (May 31, 1971), p. 27.
4. Joe H. Kelley, "At the Races" column, Washington *Evening Star*, May 3, 1971.
5. Kelley.
6. *Sports Illustrated* (May 31, 1971), p. 28.
7. Louisville *Courier-Journal*, May 2, 1971.
8. *LC-J*, 1971.
9. *Sports Illustrated* (May 31, 1971), p. 28.
10. Lexington *Leader* (May 7, 1971).
11. Whitney Tower, "Missing Data Unavailable," *Sports Illustrated* (May 10, 1971), p. 21.

12. Whitney Tower, "Arriba! Canonero Does It Again!" *Sports Illustrated* (May 24, 1971).
13. Baltimore *Sun*, May 11, 1971.
14. *Sports Illustrated* (May 31, 1971), p. 31.
15. Gerald Strine, "Around the Track" column, Washington *Post*, June 7, 1971.
16. Washington *Post*, June 7, 1971.

CHAPTER 15
THE MISTRESS OF THE MEADOW

1. Gerald Strine, Washington *Post*, March 22, 1972.
2. Robert W. Collins, "Word Portrait," *The Thoroughbred Record* (July 8, 1972), p. 94.
3. Tom Buckley, *New York Times*, June 9, 1973.
4. Buckley.
5. Washington *Post*, May 1972.
6. Edward L. Bowen, *The Blood-Horse* (March 20, 1972), p. 988.
7. Bowen.
8. *The Blood-Horse* (June 19, 1972), p. 2009.
9. *Daily Racing Form* (no date).
10. Joe H. Palmer, *This Was Racing* (New York: A. S. Barnes, 1953), p. 4.
11. *Fort Lauderdale News*, March 9, 1972.
12. *The Thoroughbred Record*, July 8, 1972, p. 92.
13. *The Blood-Horse*, April 3, 1972, p. 1161.
14. Joe Hirsch, *Daily Racing Form*, April 8, 1972.
15. Washington *Post*, April 28, 1972.
16. Red Smith, *New York Times*, May 3, 1972.
17. Dean Eagle, Louisville *Courier-Journal*, May 3, 1972.
18. Washington *Post*, April 30, 1972.
19. Washington *Post*, April 26, 1972.
20. Washington *Post*, April 30, 1972.
21. *Post*, April 30, 1972.
22. Whitney Tower, "Just To Be in the Derby Picture" *Sports Illustrated* (May 8, 1972), p. 30.

CHAPTER 16
THE HORSE WITH THE NIELSEN RATING

1. Arnold Kirkpatrick, "Doubts Dispelled," *The Thoroughbred Record*, May 12, 1973, p. 1160.
2. *The Blood-Horse*, July 30, 1973, p. 2818.
3. Peter Chew, "The 'Mostest Hoss,'" *American Heritage* (April 1971), p. 27.
4. Louisville *Courier-Journal*, May 1973.
5. Andrew Beyer, Washington *Star-News*, May 3, 1973.
6. Beyer.
7. Lexington *Leader*, April 29, 1973.
8. *The Thoroughbred Record*, May 12, 1973, p. 1162.
9. Edward L. Bowen, "Resumption of a Legend," *The Blood-Horse*, May 14, 1973, p. 1666.

Index

(The numbers in italics refer to pictures.)

Haggin, James Ben Ali, 29–31
Hagyard, Dr. Ed, 60
Halma, 30, 35, 180, 181
Ham, Elizabeth, 139, *140*, 144, 151
Hamburg Place, *3, 4, 5,* 148, 180
Hancock, Arthur Boyd, Jr., 74, 139, 153, 162
Hancock, Seth, 139, *140*, 153
Hanford, Ira, 180
Harbut, Will, *9*
Hard Work, 118
Harper, Frank B., 22, 23
Harriet Sue, 78
Harris, Lewis, 112
Harris, Russ, *106*
Hart, James J., *2, 30*
Hartack, William, 37, 67, *105–7,* 110, *114,* 142, 179
Harthill, Dr. Alex, 2, *93–96,* 106, 107–10, 112–14, 115
Harthill, Henry, 94
Harum, David, 4
Harvey, John, 14
Hassi's Image, 148, 150
Hastily, *63*
Hastings, 24
Hastings, Chappie, 56
Hasty Matelda, 140
Hatton, Charlie, *4, 72,* 155, *159*
Hayes, Casey, 140, 142
Hayes, H. J., 139
Hayes, T. P., 27
Head, C. Bruce, 44, 63
Head of the River, 147, 150
Head Play, 60–62
Heffering, Jim, 43
Helene de Troie, 55
Heliopolis, 141
Henderson, Erskine, 33, 180
Henry, William, 24
Hermitage Farm, 93–94, 112
Hertz, John D., 32, 72–73, 87, 88
Hervey, John, 41
Herz, Emil, 52
Hibiscus, 147
High Echelon, 121
Hildene, 54–55, 139
Hildreth, Sam, 44
Hill Gail, *67,* 68, 145, 179, 180
Hill Prince, 55, *136, 137,* 139
Hill Rise, 107
Himyar, 12–13, 180
Hindoo, 26, *27,* 180, 181
Hines, Mike, 149
Hira, 12
Hirsch, Joe, 108, 150, 171
Hirsch, Maximillian Justice, 90, *137,* 179
His Eminence, 14, *34,* 111, 179, 180
Hobeau Farm, 136
Hogg, Elijah, 63
Hoist the Flag, *122–27, 123, 124, 125,* 131
Hold Your Peace, 144, 147, 148, 150

Hollingsworth, Kent, 14, 85, 145
Holy Land, *120*
Hooper, F. W., 66
Hoop Jr., 66, 145, 179, 180
Hoots, Al, 41–42
Hoots, Rosa, 44, *46*
Hopeful Stakes, 34
Horace N. Davis Farm, 42
Howard, C. S., 79
Howard, Jack, 47
Howard, Colonel Maxwell, 74
Huntley, Gordon, 143
Hurd, Babe, 33, 180
Hurley, Bill, 63–64
Husing, Ted, 3
Hydrologist, *141*
Hyperion, *101*

Iberia, 135, 139, 140–*41*
Idle Hour Stock Farm, 42, 48, *50–51, 52–56,* 59, 180
Imperatrice, 139
Impetuosity, 131, 133
Insco, 78, 180
Intent, 89
Introductivo, 150
Inventor, 36
Iron Gail, 68
Iron Liege, *67, 71,* 82, *106,* 145, 179, 180
Iron Rule, 104
Iroquois, 22
Isaiah, 61
Isolde, 93
Ivan the Terrible, 42

Jack Atkin, 42
Jackson, Laban, *113*
Jacobs, John, 120
Jane Gail, *67*
Jenny, Eleanor, 124, 126
Jenny, Dr. Jacques, *124–26,* 127
Jerkens, Allen, 136, 137
Jerome Park, 15
Jersey Derby, 14
Jet Pilot, 145, 180
Jimenez, Marcos Perez, 128
Jim French, 131, 133, 134
jockeys, black, 33–35
Joe Cotton, 14, 180
Johnson, Albert, 43, 54, 179
Johnson, Chief, 42, 44, 45
Johnson, Harrison, 34
Johnson, Colonel W. H., 24
Johnstown, 74, 179
Jones, Ben, *67,* 90, *105;* and Useeit, 41; early career of, 51, 76–78; and Bimelech, 64; and Calumet Farm, 72–76, *75,* 78; and Bull Lea, 74, 78; and Lawrin, 74–75; and Kentucky Derby, 74–75, *76,* 79–82, 84–85, 104, 144, 145, 179; and Whirlaway, *75,* 78–80; and Seth, 77–78; and Woolford Farm, 78; and Citation, 84–*85*